THE POLITICS of TV VIOLENCE

PEOPLE AND COMMUNICATION

Series Editor: F. GERALD KLINE *University of Minnesota*

Volumes in this series:

Volume 1: How Children Learn To Buy: The Development of Consumer Information-Processing Skills
SCOTT WARD, DANIEL B. WACKMAN, ELLEN WARTELLA

Volume 2: Big Media, Little Media: Tools and Technologies for Instruction
WILBUR SCHRAMM

Volume 3: The Costs of Educational Media: Guidelines for Planning and Evaluation
DEAN T. JAMISON, STEVEN J. KLEES, STUART J. WELLS

Volume 4: Radio for Education and Development
DEAN T. JAMISON and EMILE G. McANANY

Volume 5: The Television Experience: What Children See
MARIANN PEZZELLA WINICK and CHARLES WINICK

Volume 6: Social Theories of the Press: Early German and American Perspectives
HANNO HARDT

Volume 7: Videotape on Trial: A View from the Jury Box
GERALD R. MILLER and NORMAN E. FONTES

Volume 8: Community Conflict & The Press
PHILLIP J. TICHENOR, GEORGE A. DONOHUE, and CLARICE N. OLIEN

Volume 9: The Public's Use of Television: Who Watches and Why
RONALD E. FRANK and MARSHALL G. GREENBERG

Volume 10: Media Imperialism Reconsidered: The Homogenizing of Television Culture
CHIN-CHUAN LEE

Volume 11: Almost Midnight: Reforming the Late-Night News
ITZHAK ROEH, ELIHU KATZ, AKIBA A. COHEN, and BARBIE ZELIZER

Volume 12: More than News: Media Power in Public Affairs
MICHAEL BRUCE MACKUEN and STEVEN LANE COOMBS

Volume 13: Communication and Education: Social and Psychological Interactions
GAVRIEL SALOMON

Volume 14: Positive Images: Breaking Stereotypes with Children's Television
JEROME JOHNSTON and JAMES S. ETTEMA

Volume 15: Turned-On TV/Turned-Off Voters: Policy Options for Election Projections
PERCY H. TANNENBAUM and LESLIE J. KOSTRICH

Volume 16: The Politics of TV Violence: Policy Uses of Communication Research
WILLARD D. ROWLAND, Jr.

THE POLITICS of TV VIOLENCE

Policy Uses of Communication Research

by

Willard D. Rowland, Jr.

foreword by

Horace Newcomb

SAGE PUBLICATIONS
Beverly Hills / London / New Delhi

For information address:

SAGE Publications, Inc.
275 South Beverly Drive
Beverly Hills, California 90212

SAGE Publications India Pvt. Ltd.
C-236 Defence Colony
New Delhi 110 024, India

SAGE Publications Ltd
28 Banner Street
London EC1Y 8QE, England

Printed in the United States of America

Library of Congress Cataloging in Publication Data

Rowland, Willard D.
The politics of TV violence.

(People and communication ; v. 16)
Bibliography: p.
1. Television broadcasting—Social aspects—United States. 2. Violence in television. I. Title.
II. Title: The politics of TV violence.
III. Title: The politics of television violence.
IV. Series.
PN1992.6.R68 1983 302.2'435'0973 82-23009
ISBN 0-8039-1952-2
ISBN 0-8039-1953-0 (pbk.)

FIRST PRINTING

CONTENTS

FOREWORD

This book is a critical study in the best sense. It is not critical because it questions received notions or calls to task prominent figures or comes, on occasion, to negative conclusions. Rather, it is critical because it examines, and asks readers to examine, fundamental questions regarding its subject. Indeed, it goes beyond the questions themselves to the assumptions on which they are based, assumptions that probe our conceptions of how knowledge is gained, how it is to be used, and by whom it is to be applied. This book deals with "interests" in the profound sense of that term as developed by Habermas.

In contrast to so many works that attempt to clarify the role of interests, however, this one is not primarily theoretical and abstract. The exploration of vested concerns that is presented here is truly a case study. Choices were made, alliances formed, money was requested and paid, hearings were held, radio and television did develop, broadcast, and take profits — real events in which interests were played out. Additionally, this "case" happens to be one that has spanned more than half a century, and calls for historical analysis as well as critical. Willard Rowland, then, has assumed the formidable task of critical historian, of guide, explicitor, and evaluator. It is a mark of his skills as researcher and writer that a clear picture of complex social interactions emerges in these pages. It is a mark of his own intellectual purpose that the reader is called upon, finally, not to put down a book with the satisfaction of having gained knowledge, but to examine his or her own scholarship, methods, and motives. Because the "case" on which this study is based continues, the questions are still open. Thus the writing of recent history drives toward reform and renewal, and the sloppily inflated phrase "contribution to the field" regains its significance. This book has the quality of conscience about it.

The thesis here is clear and straightforward. In the decades following World War I mass communication industries developed rapidly, altering the industrial and cultural terrain of America. Public concern about potential effects of this development resulted in calls for attention to the new industries by Congress and related government agencies. A new academic field, "communication studies," appeared and proceeded to interact with industry and government in complex patterns.

This set of events cannot, however, be adequately described in such neutral terms. A pattern developed that continues today. The communication industries, like other industries in American capitalism, desire to regulate themselves in their own interests. The government does not wish to regulate in any manner that would challenge received notions of "free" enterprise. The research community, casting its lot with social science, contributes to the goals of both parties. Because some of the research is conducted at the expense of the industries, it can be used or shaped to argue many sides of complex questions, or used, as proprietary research, to counter "academic" research. But because the findings of "pure" research are bound with appropriate scientific care, there is insufficient evidence here for more stringent, system-altering control. Both government and industry, then, turn to the research community for aid, assistance, support, comfort, and care. For its part, "communication studies" establishes itself as a legitimate field of study, acceptable in universities throughout the nation.

These theses and the arguments supporting them will undoubtedly be questioned and rebutted. The interpretations of events, the construction of sequences, the biographical patterns will be quarreled with, responded to. The facts remain. Communications industries have not engaged in serious self-regulation in response to strongly suggestive research findings. Government agencies have not posed basic systemic alterations in policies surrounding those industries. And schools or departments or institutes of communication research flourish. Money may not be so available as it once was, but undergraduates flock to the courses and jobs are available for well-trained graduate students who wish to pursue academic or industrial careers.

These conclusions, of course, do not prove the theses. For proof there must be analysis, the establishment of links, the careful outlining of historical sequences, and the clear interpretation of sources. Those proofs form the heart of this book. Repeatedly, Rowland clarifies the connections and brings forward evidence to support his interpretations. The sheer bulk of the material, bulk that repeatedly reflects the *same* assumptions, the *same* choices, stands to convince us of the accuracy of the conclusions.

Rowland takes us through this very large account with grace and clarity. In part this is because he frames his study as a "drama," with the four principal groups as "actors" playing out their parts over and over. There is great danger here. Rowland is well aware that the world of experience is not a play, not something to be attended to and put away after diversion. To assert that the world is a stage is to confront the power of metaphor, risk dismissal, flirt with cynicism.

Rowland avoids these traps. He carefully unmasks interests by showing that many of the things we take as natural are constructions, born in real choices. He finds in the dry interchanges of congressional hearings a text that is to be searched for motive and avoidance. He chronicles directions not followed, questions not asked, a bargain struck here, a rise to power there. In it all, human agency is at work. This, we see, is no fiction.

If that were not enough, another reality factor is at work. The relative newness of the field of communication studies means that many of those involved in Rowland's history are still active. And most readers of this book, even new students, will be able to trace a direct line of influence on their own work, their own interests, that reaches to the founders of the field. The "play" is not yet done. Acts remain to be written in actions that we will take. Whether we are more self-conscious of our choices, more critically aware of our interests in the sense that Rowland calls for, remains to be seen. The sure thing is that this book should make it impossible for us to step onto the stage without truly knowing our parts.

– *Horace Newcomb*
Austin, Texas

ACKNOWLEDGMENTS

One does not complete a project of this sort without considerable help from a number of people. I am grateful to have had the opportunity to have worked at several of the institutions and with a number of the people who figure in this book. Their influence and encouragement, whether for this project or in other more general matters, must not go unacknowledged. Even where there have been implicit differences of view, the spirit of good-natured collegiality has always prevailed.

It is particularly pleasurable to note the strong support of my many colleagues and friends in the Institute of Communications Research and College of Communications at the University of Illinois. It has been my good fortune to be a part of an institution that has continued to foster a distinguished, pathfinding set of approaches to scholarship in communication studies.

Among those at Illinois and elsewhere deserving special recognition in this book are: Jim Carey, for his steady, wise counsel throughout; Ann Lowry Weir, for her excellent advice on the major necessary revisions to the initial manuscript; Jerry Kline, for his unflagging enthusiasm for the project and his thoughtful editing; Al Kreiling, Ellen Wartella, Kim Rotzoll, and Chuck Whitney, for careful critiques of the manuscript or other guidance; Kevin Cain, Denis Gosselin, Don Hurwitz, Bill May, Bish Sen, and Greg Wuliger, for, variously, research, proofing, or other forms of direct or indirect assistance; and Marvene Blackmore and Anita Specht, for good-humored patience and consistent support in preparing the manuscript. To all of these go the credit for many insights and improvements; to none of them responsibility for any remaining errors or other deficiencies.

To my wife, Laura, and my children, Alyssa, Andrea, and Daniel, I extend my deepest gratitude for a continuingly delightful domestic environment and a warm, affectionate tolerance for all the vagaries and sacrifices of the academic life.

PREFACE

Even without the reminders by historians such as Daniel Boorstin and David Noble, it is all too apparent that the experience of twentieth-century American life is increasingly ambiguous and that fundamental paradoxes persist (Boorstin, 1974; Noble, 1958). The strengths and meanings of many of our principal institutions and values have been widely called into question, we seem never able to break cleanly with the mistakes of the past, and expressions of the attendant uncertainties may be found in various cultural and political forums.

Public policy concerns about the role of mass communication in American life and related questions about human social behavior represent two such expressions. This book examines a major aspect of those concerns — the issue of research into the effects of violence on television and how it has been used in the policymaking process for broadcasting. The history and institutional interactions related here constitute an examination of the public attempts through the vehicle of legislative oversight and the language of social science to comprehend and interpret the significance of mass communication and its content.

This approach rises out of the developing tradition of critical cultural studies with its emphasis on history and symbolic analysis. To paraphrase the political scientist Murray Edelman, this is a study of the symbolic uses of communication effects research. Edelman strives to call "attention to wide gulfs between our solemnly taught, common sense assumptions about what political institutions do and what they actually do" (Edelman, 1964: 2). He asks us "to look searchingly at every unquestioned or widely taught assumption about how government works, for it is a key characteristic of myth that is generally unquestioned, widely taught and believed, and that the myth has consequences, though not the ones it literally proclaims" (1964: 4).

The general subject matter here is the interaction among the federal, political process of communication policymaking, the broadcasting industry, the public or citizens' interest groups, and the communication research community. The specific focus is on the terms of this interaction as it bears on the question of the effects of violence on television, and in keeping with Edelman's charge, I will examine the beliefs implicit in these relationships and the consequences that derive from them. Thus, the book treats the concerns with violence and with television as essentially symbolic issues, as problems bespeaking the uncertainties of the modern era. The separate American traditions of anxiety about violence in the society and about the impact of new forms of communication have combined in the concern about the effects of violence on television, and together they represent a major aspect of contemporary public discourse. Their unification as a prime subject of popular debate serves as an important barometer of broader sociocultural and political anxieties.

The major institutions and figures in this book are the members of Congress, commissions, staffs, and bureaucracies that have provided the forum for debate of the television effects issue, the prominent spokespersons for communication research who have striven to become principal actors on that stage, the reformers who have also tried to carve out a larger role in the policy drama, and the management and research figures in the broadcasting industry who have sought to influence the form and substance of the play. In focusing on these leading actors, this book is consciously selective, giving lesser weight to events, ideas, and individuals who in other approaches might figure more prominently. It is informed by that approach to intellectual history that Hugh Duncan, building on Kenneth Burke's notion of historiography as parable, calls a "dramatic reconstruction" (Duncan, 1970: 50; Burke, 1965: 274). It responds to, and tries to capture, the flavor of the emerging linkages among the institutions and patterns of thought in twentieth-century industry, politics, reform, communications, and the academy.

In an important sense the perspective is that of the cultural anthropologist attempting to write the ethnography of four tribes meeting on the common ground of a shared ritual. As they dance around the fire of contemporary tensions and uncertainties, as they marvel at the powers and dangers of modern communication technology, and as they invoke the deity of science in an effort to allay those fears and control that technology, the tribes — politicians, broadcast industry executives, reformers, and academic researchers — create a certain definition of reality and in the process reveal much about the structure of their society and its political, economic, and cultural values.

The book is organized in three parts. Part I traces the early history of mass communication research in the context of the rise of American social science research, giving particular emphasis to the association of science with industrial and political needs in public policymaking. Part II presents the first three or four phases of the history of violence effects research and its interaction with the almost continuous political inquiry into the impact of television, examining the relationships among the principal interested institutional parties and the research role in shaping popular imagery and public policy toward television. Part III recounts the most recent phases of that history, tracing its development in light of the increasingly complex environment of technological change and telecommunications policymaking, and summarizing some of the academic and political implications of the persistent violence inquiry process.

The history related in this book relies heavily on the hearings records and reports of the various congressional committees and national commisions involved in federal attempts to grapple with television and the question of its content. These records are examined for the patterns of argument advanced by the leading research spokesmen, industry representatives, public interest group leaders, and political figures. As a body of symbolic material, these texts are significant in two ways. First, they provide a set of public speeches about effects, and from them may be recovered a record of the structure of social relations that has guided the effects research debate. These speeches reveal much about the external conditions in the society — its systems of reward and punishment and the interactions among its major institutions — that influence the histories of effects research and of our concepts about television's impact. Second, while the primary focus of these documents is on the issues of violence, television, and effects research, the symbolic significance of the texts extends far beyond the content of their immediate subject matters. That is, these documents and the hearings they record turn out to be important elements in American cultural expression. They are part of our ritual of social self-examination, and as such, they serve as a rich record of the dimensions of the public debate about the nature of contemporary American life.

The book examines representative samples of the research debated. But the focus is not so much on the design, methodology, and consequent validity of the subsequent findings — the sort of analysis most typically provided — as it is on the character of the interaction of the figures involved, their approach to the use of research, and the consequent conditions of their further interaction. The argument does not conclude that the terms of the communication research and political review accommodations were explicit and mutually agreed on from the outset. Rather, it suggests that these accommodations have emerged from a gradually developing process, one that in many ways remains more implicit than explicit and little understood by most of the principal parties.

Chapter 1

INTRODUCTION

Effects Research as a Mediator of Television

A comprehensive social history of mass communication effects research remains unwritten. Summaries of the literature abound, and popular textbooks now present standard descriptive chronologies (see, for example, Klapper, 1960; Weiss, 1969; DeFleur and Ball-Rokeach, 1975; Katz, 1977; Comstock et al., 1978). But most such accounts mainly attempt to legitimate mainstream empirical trends in mass communication theory and research methodology. Occasionally this effort fosters some attention to intellectual roots and the processes by which the several theories and approaches have emerged, competed, and variously failed or prevailed. But, as part of a longstanding American tradition of pragmatism in the social and behavioral sciences, effects research reviews tend to cast themselves in light of the applied research needs or trends of the moment.

There is little inclination in these accounts to perceive developments in communications and in communication research as part of the broader American social and political history or to see the research developments as expressions of a social science that has also emerged in interaction with that complex web of changing events and ideas. That is, the standard chronologies of mass communication effects research have a relatively shallow historical consciousness. They are published and faithfully regurgitated in communications curricula with virtually no recognition of the impact of general ideological and sociopolitical developments on such research or of the cultural significance of the emergence of effects research in association with the rise of science as a preeminent institution in American life.

THE RECEIVED HISTORY

The standard accounts of effects research appear in several sources, but may be summarized as follows: During the two decades following World War I, widespread concern about the power of the developing forms of mass communication emerged. There was disturbing evidence of the effective deceptions visited on public opinion through the press and motion pictures by wartime propaganda. Public attendance at motion pictures increased during the 1920s and then leaped ahead again with the arrival of sound, pausing only slightly at the outset of the Depression. Meanwhile, the rapid development of a commercial radio industry added further impetus to the redeployment of leisure time and to the emergence of a national entertainment and information culture. Responding to widespread anxiety about the moral and social implications of these developments, the sciences of psychology and sociology, newly emergent themselves, sought to measure the impact of these startling, somewhat awesome, media. Special studies of matters such as the effects on children of violence depicted on film, the consequences of the radio broadcast of a science fiction play, the causes of changes in voting decisions, and the effects of official campaigns of persuasion during World War II began with the assumption that the mass media have widespread, direct, and powerful effects on attitude and behavior. Heavily influenced by general learning theory and conditioning models in behavioristic psychology, these studies grew out of a "hypodermic needle" concept of communication effects.

The received history goes on to argue that, in light of unexpected discoveries in these studies and of ever more sophisticated models, methods, and findings in sociology and social psychology, researchers became increasingly suspicious of the earlier assumptions about direct effects. They claimed to have found mounting evidence of important intervening variables and defenses — factors such as the demographic background of the audience, group dynamics, selective perception, and other social and mental states that could be taken as mitigating the direct impact of the media or as accounting for considerable portions of the changes occurring during political and commercial campaigns. The consequent "limited effects" models tended to exonerate the media, suggesting that their impact could largely be explained as a function of the social environment in which they operate, that at most their effect is to activate and reinforce preexisting dispositions, and that their impact is diffused through the interpretative agencies of "opinion leaders" and a "two-step flow" of communications.

Such histories contend that because of these findings the effects research program turned away from an examination of "what the media do to people" toward the study of "what people do with the media." In one direction, guided increasingly by diffusion models from rural sociology, communication researchers attempted to trace patterns of innovation and information dissemination and the media's role in these processes. In another direction, due to the failure of causal models, with their unfulfilled promises of empirical generalization and predictability, and due to the rise in social and organizational sciences of gestalt, systems, and other holistic theories, communication researchers adopted functional models from general sociology, hoping to find an explanatory framework of "uses and gratifications" through which audience preferences and reactions are presumably shaped. Later elaborations included attempts to determine the "agenda-setting" functions and, under the influence of symmetry and balance theories, the "coorientation" uses of communication media. Here the communication research models respond even more fully to the modern social science concepts of the individual and the communication process as being well seated in a nexus of social contexts and structures. Down yet another, somewhat parallel path, responding to the rise of cognitive development perspectives in psychology, there has been increased emphasis on "information processing" and applied formative and critical skills research.

While the emphasis varies from version to version, the essential elements of the standard history are here. They represent the received view of an increasingly self-confident, legitimized effects research enterprise. Such an account does not, however, represent the only way of relating the story. To set the stage for an understanding of the specific history of the violence effects research tradition, it is necessary to recast somewhat the general effects developments.

AN ALTERNATIVE VIEW

As the received version suggests, communication inquiries during the past two generations have been informed for the most part by the predominant perspectives of the social and behavioral sciences. In many instances developments in communication research have lagged a decade or so behind the "parent" sciences, but even in those cases in which the association has been closer in time, the trend has been one of imitation and following. A fundamental, yet seldom asked, question in this regard is, why should communication studies be captured so thoroughly and so early in the United States by the empirical sciences?

After World War I, with the rapid spread of film and radio, the economic and social impact of mass communication became a more serious public issue. Building on earlier important changes in popular culture, these more universally visible, national, economically significant media became closely associated in the public mind with cultural and political dislocations that defied easy analysis or acceptance. The growing complexities and ambiguities of modern life, and the role in them of new communications technologies and cultural forms, cried out for explanation.

A normal channel for such interpretation rested in the process of political debate over proper legislative options. But the rise of radio placed the political leadership in a particularly uncomfortable position. The physical properties of broadcast transmission and fears of monopoly control led to an unprecedented degree of communications regulation by government. Limited access to the spectrum dictated a general public interest mandate that offered licenses under a fiduciary principle. Beyond requiring an acceptable standard of technical service, that mandate provided that broadcasters be evaluated on the basis of their programming service. Having set such criteria, Congress and its agents (first the Federal Radio Commission [FRC], and later the Federal Communications Commission [FCC]) were faced with establishing and reviewing them. However, in view of constitutional protections for freedoms of speech and press, closely associated with a libertarian mythology that accepted the dangers of governmental censorship, but that could not recognize its existence in the private, corporate imperatives of competitive commercial communications, regulatory power over broadcasting was severely constrained. Moreover, the Radio Act of 1927 and the Communications Act of 1934 had been written largely to the specifications of the principal industry forces, so as to preserve the fundamental system of commercial private enterprise control and network programming dominance that had been developing prior to their passage. The terms of public interest broadcasting implied as a major element the preservation of conditions for a stable, profit-making broadcasting business, and no subsequent congressional review could ignore the general political-economic environment dictating that that basic system be allowed to proceed unhampered.

All of these conditions were established before the rise of television, which of all the ambiguities of modern life was among the most troubling. As Boorstin (1974: 390-397) observes, television conquered America with dizzying speed, extending, segregating, and democratizing experience so as to make everyday life yet more vague and befogged. It reenergized the debate about the impact of modern communications and ever-changing technology.

In simple structural terms, television's growth during the 1950s greatly changed patterns of leisure time use and commercial and political practices. At the outset, major consequences included the decline of attendance at movie theaters, the relegation of radio to background music and news, and the perceived waning of the authority of newspapers. The consumer goods industries discovered in television a powerful new marketing tool, and political figures quickly found it necessary to adjust the style and substance of their campaigns and performances in office in order to attract and exploit the particular projective characteristics of the new medium. These developments combined with other changes in the economy and the political process to enhance the position of national forms of marketing and distribution and to undermine the power of local forms of party organization.

In more general terms, the conflicting reactions generated by television included the extreme poles of evaluation, taking it as both messianic and demonic. As the newest, most spectacular piece of communications technology, television was cast by the American progressive tradition as the repository of hope for a revived democratic process, a stronger set of social bonds, a richer cultural life, and a vastly improved educational system. On the other hand, it was perceived by established institutions and brokers of morality and values as the latest and most dangerous in a series of technological and social inroads on their authority and status. It represented yet another assault on the family, interpersonal relationships and small-scale, local forms of community by large, bureaucratic, impersonal, and nationally oriented forms of organization. From this perspective, the political, social, and cultural orders were in serious jeopardy.

Several examples of this mixture of love and fear have been expressed by observers and critics in various forums over the decades. While it would eventually focus on television, the conflicting critique emerged as part of the more general attempt to grapple with the entire developing universe of popular culture. Perhaps one of the most vivid examples was reflected in the major swings of opinion during the career of Gilbert Seldes, with first his praise of popular entertainment, then his ominous warnings about the uses and effects of those popular arts, and finally his struggle for a middle ground (see Seldes, 1951, 1952, 1956).

This conflict forced on television the role of lightning rod in the storms of public controversy about the nature of contemporary life, and it became of increasing importance to find better ways to interpret the significance of this latest development in communications. The public debate required means and terms to mediate the medium, but the customary interpretative institutions no longer seemed suited for the task. As epitomized by the attacks on "masscult" by Dwight Macdonald (1962) and others, traditional criticism approached the problem as a matter or aesthetics, reducing the debate about this pervasive new experience to the class-struggle terms of high and low culture, more appropriate in European than in American contexts of social and political commentary. Religious and educational institutions could only fulminate moralistically against television's content values and its presumed impact on family and social structures. Such an attack seemed to become increasingly moot as it became apparent that it was at least in part motivated by the discoveries of the intellectual, sacred, and instructional domains that once again their authority was in the process of being bypassed by yet another form of popular communication.[1] Political, educational, and religious institutions were all paralyzed by the conflict between their apprehensions about television and their various interests in harnessing and exploiting it for themselves and their definitions of the public interest.

Some have observed that toward the end of television's first quarter century the number of active parties at interest in broadcast policymaking increased. For instance, several sources show how during the late 1960s and early 1970s the original triumvirate of major policy setters — the Congress, the FCC, and the broadcast industry — were joined in new and significant ways by the White House, the courts, and the various groups in the public interest or citizens' action movement (see, for example, Krasnow, Longley, and Terry, 1982; Branscomb and Savage, 1978: 25-34; Guimary, 1975; Grundfest, 1976; Cole and Oettinger, 1978).[2] Yet the growing role of the research community goes generally unacknowledged. Standard textbook histories take note of the research issues, but such accounts are largely attempts to relate the trends in the theories of effects (for example, see Head, 1976; DeFleur and Ball-Rokeach, 1975). In virtually no cases have the principal broadcasting sources or public policy-makers recognized the institution of research — or more importantly, the ideas associated with its particular language, assumptions, and methods — as at least equally important as the other institutions in the changing terms of reference for debate at all levels about the significance of, and the necessary response to, television.

Since the normal channels of interpretation had proved unequal to the mediating task, and since it was accustomed to doing so in other areas of public policy, the political and popular imagination seized on the investigative promise of science to an increasingly significant degree for the television policy debate. For over a century science had steadily grown to undergird a widening range of advances in industrial and commercial enterprise. For nearly as long certain aspects of science had also been finding their way into prominence in governmental policymaking.[3] Beginning with engineering and the natural sciences in matters of defense, agriculture, and public works, and then with statistics and economics in matters of social planning, the political process and its attendant bureauracies later became adept at employing the increasingly self-confident forms of applied sociology and psychology. During the second quarter of the twentieth century, particularly with the crisis of the Depression and the enhanced role for government reflected in the New Deal, the social and behavioral sciences began to make themselves indispensible elements in public planning for a variety of programs in social reform and welfare. With the ground well prepared by this experience in the applied use of social science, the dilemmas encountered in the rise of electronic mass communication could be seen as perhaps equally susceptible to social scientific investigation and analysis.

That the record of social science in public policymaking was far from clearly successful and appropriate was irrelevant. American corporate and government affairs were seen as a series of problems to be solved. Public policy involved less debate over ends and more over means; the issues were those of technique and engineering, not values and morals. The comfortable association of industrial and political objectives dictated a science that was long on technical sophistication and short on epistemological reflection. With goals unspecified, only implicit in the overall structure of commercial and political enterprise, the primary criteria for evaluation were validity, reliablility, efficiency, and objectivity. From more removed perspectives, particularly those of the philosophies of science and hermeneutics, the existence of such attributes in social science has come to be highly debatable.[4] Nevertheless, the image of their certainty and irrefutability was well entrenched. Their acceptance meshed neatly into the interaction of industrial, political, communications, and academic interests.

Earlier in the century, simultaneously with the advancement of film and radio, there emerged in the academy and in commerce a powerful science of behavior that seemed to offer the analytic framework necessary to explain the nature and significance of mass communications. Whether concerned with the effectiveness of propaganda in film or of advertisements in radio, behavioral psychology associated itself easily with the few-to-many, neutral-channel transmission model of modern communications. The fears about the health of democracy, cultural values, and social bonds embedded in the debate over mass society and the nature of the new industrial and communications orders found a ready translator in the thoroughly modern science of behaviorism. Its quantitative and experimental methodologies, its efficient empiricism, its positivistic faith in data, and its claims of objectivity fit well in the age of corporate and bureaucratic planning, of massive commercial and governmental enterprise.

Meanwhile, the tradition of applied research in American science began to develop an institutional form in the social and behavioral sciences that had considerable significance for the focus of the emerging studies of communication. That is, as reflected in the creation of centers or bureaus for applied social research at major universities, there emerged a structure for the pursuit of audience research in the United States that was rooted firmly in a combination of fascination with empirical social science methodology, practical marketing research experience, and broadcast industry commercial and political needs. The legacy of the initial research bureau movement was at least twofold:

(1) Developing on the margins of the academy during the 1930s and World War II, it served as a vehicle for administrative contract research underwritten by both industry and government, often jointly, and as such it became a model for the development during the postwar arrival of television for a host of centers, institutes, and schools of communication research that also depended heavily on commercial and governmental grant funding.
(2) The work of one of the earliest bureaus (at Columbia University) helped set the agenda for much of a whole generation of American mass communication scholarship growing up in those new applied research centers.

Another thread that contributed to the genesis of American communication research during the war years was the interaction (vis-à-vis the Office of War Information, the Army's Information and Education Division, and other aspects of the Allied propaganda and behavioral research efforts) of communications industry and government officials with a substantial body of behavioral and social scientists who were turning their attention increasingly to communications problems. This nexus of contacts and projects led to continued support for the new university-based research institutes, the development of major lines of administrative research and related social-psychological studies of media effects, and a broader set of personal and professional relationships that were to be reflected in the postwar development of communication research in universities around the country and in various other series of basic readers and texts on effects.

As television became an increasingly significant factor in postwar society and culture, the pressure to explain it became more intense. An important aspect of the response to that pressure is revealed in the history of political inquiry into the effects of media violence. The central story here is the experience of interaction among the mass communication research community, the broadcasting industry, its reform critics, and the political process overseeing the introduction and advancement of television in American society. Part of this history can be traced back to the motivations and findings of the Payne Fund studies of the effects of violence in film (1928-1933). It subsequently moves through the successive phases of congressional and national-level commission investigations of television violence represented by the Harris hearings (1952), the juvenile delinquency investigations (Hendrickson-Kefauver, 1954-1955; Dodd, 1961-1964), the inquiries of the National Commission on the Causes and Prevention of Violence (1968-1969), and the research of the Surgeon General's Scientific Advisory Committee on Television and Social Behavior, engendered and reviewed by the Pastore hearings (1969-1972).

A rereading of this history reveals how in the violence effects issue and political concern about television's social impact the mass communication research community found the vehicle necessary for it to begin to obtain identity and ultimately to achieve legitimacy in the academy. The struggles therein for supremacy among competing social sciences carried over into the effort to interpret the new medium. A liberal, optimistic, and newly retooled American social psychology proved to be a highly attractive competitor for research funds and public recognition. During and shortly after the war, studies of interpersonal behavior and communication began to propose more complicated theoretical models and methodological approaches. In light of such work, the original behavioral models of communication appeared to be breaking down. Attention turned increasingly from the outcome of communication to the networks of interpersonal relationships and the demographic characteristics that were perceived to intervene in and guide the process of mass communication. This newer approach, more comfortable with the technology and complexities of contemporary life, and more secure in its perceptions of emerging social and political stability, was less pessimistic and fearful. It was also closely associated with a long tradition of liberal, progressive reform, which in spite of anxieties about large corporate enterprise, has always remained hopeful for the long-promised ameliorative, educative social and political impact of each new technology of communication. In reviewing the previous research, the new approach seemed to conclude that the proof of deleterious effects claimed under the original models could no longer be sustained. Emerging by the end of television's first decade, and on the heels of a host of seemingly confirming research, these "limited effects" models tended to exonerate television, arguing that it did not have demonstrable negative effects (as in Klapper, 1960).

In view of such findings, a number of social scientists, for many of whom communication research had never been the primary interest, felt that the field had exhausted the possibilities and that the time had come to move on to matters of more pressing concern to social and public welfare. Indeed, a communication research equivalent of the "God is Dead" debate took place during the late 1950s (see Berelsen, 1959, and Schramm et al., 1959). However, the critics retained the view that communication issues remained serious and substantial, and many of them therefore resisted the pressure to turn away entirely from the study of effects. But the new generation, trained during the postwar period with primary emphasis on methodology and technique, was not encouraged to reflect from a critical, self-conscious perspective on the assumptions and consequent implications of the contending scientific models. As a result there was among many proponents of the expanding study of mass communication a rush to embrace the new approaches and to redefine communication research in terms of the new sociology and social psychology. That this remodeling had been fostered by and tended to serve the interests of the television industry, now increasingly on the defensive before congressional committees, and that the shift of emphasis was not in the end any real departure from behavioristic views, went largely ignored, or at least little acknowledged. In academic forums the critique of the media turned toward the rationalizations of functionalism and uses and gratifications; in popular debate it turned toward the McLuhanesque embrace of technology and the celebration of an electronic nirvana. The role of the effects research community had ascended from the prophetic to the priestly.

However, the complaints about television content never completely abated. Common sense argued that television was having an obvious major impact on attitudes and behavior, and the evidence of daily observation during the 1960s was unsettling. On the street, violence appeared to be increasing. At one level it became the focus of concern over the rapidity of change and the threat to traditional, mainstream values represented by urban and racial conflict. At another level it stunned the popular psyche by injecting itself into domestic and foreign politics. Assassinations and war, and their attendant dislocations, were no longer problems of only previous, presumably less settled eras. Intertwined with these developments were the inroads of television into the national consciousness. In whatever forms of fiction — news or drama — it served at least as a messenger of the behavior of force and its related confusions. High levels of television violence persisted, becoming an inescapable part of the evening viewing diet. To many the association of medium content and the social experience of violence was no longer coincidental, nor was it explicable any longer merely as a mirroring phenomenon. The issue of effects still could not be ignored.

In particular, the legislative review machinery, that element of the political process responsible for overseeing and representing the public interest in broadcasting, found itself increasingly embroiled in the controversy over the impact of television. As separate issues, violence and television both became matters of greater symbolic import in the general social commentary. Soon they became inextricably intertwined as a single issue at the heart of the debate over the character and directions of an increasingly complex, ambiguous society.

In playing on the scientism of their approaches, communication researchers found themselves tapping popular anxieties about the newest medium of mass communication and associating their work with the highly technical, quantitative social and behavioral research methodologies of other disciplines that had already achieved considerable popular and political acceptance in public policy debate. Throughout this process of development, the broadcasting industry alternately supported and opposed the research enterprise, carefully cultivating — and thereby shaping — certain aspects and allowing others to wither. Whether or not the product of a conscious choice, the communication research leaders managed to ignore the industrial and political terms of their origins and the closely related problematic issues of epistemology that were wrapped up in their approaches. As a result, the public controversy over television's effects was allowed to proceed in virtual ignorance of the particular institutional accommodations and sociocultural conceptualizations on which it was based. To the extent debate was permitted, it centered on issues of methodology and narrow aspects of theory. In the process of legitimation there was little willingness or ability to transcend discussions of research technique to consider the linkages of the entire research enterprise to the general pattern of commercial and political expectations for social science research.

For their part the politicians may be depicted as having found in the effects research efforts the vehicle necessary for them to project an image of concerned inquiry, while ensuring that that inquiry would force them into little, if any, legislative action. Investing in the rise of mass communication research, the federal communications policymaking process associated itself with the popularly acceptable terms of scientific research. All the while, however, the officials involved in this process were discovering that, due to a combination of fundamental constitutional and political economic commitments and the actual inconclusiveness of the research efforts, the research approach not only failed to address accurately the underlying problem of control and purpose of communications, but also served to mask and divert attention from such issues.

In all this, for similarly diversionary purposes, the broadcasting industry carefully avoided outright opposition to the trend toward greater governmental attention to the research tool, choosing instead to infiltrate the process of decision making about appropriate and inappropriate lines of inquiry. Building on the prior relationships with university-based research centers and joint governmental funding, the industry continued to support and promote selected research efforts while overlooking or avoiding others.

As for the reform groups, the research agenda was well structured by the time they became a more organized part of the policy debate; there was little opportunity to affect its basic assumptions and terms of implementation. Further, as has been the case throughout the history of American progressivism, the goals of the newer groups were susceptible to severe compromise due to a continuing pattern of paradox between the ideals of reform and the changing practical conditions under which it has always had to work. As with many of the liberal research community critics with whom they were often affiliated, the media reformers had little ability to recognize the symbolic nature of the debate and the ways in which it might actually be working against the changes they hoped it would foster.

In the period since the surgeon general's report, many of the earlier policy difficulties have persisted. The problems are apparent in such matters as the House appropriations committee hearings (1970-

1974), the related pressures on the FCC, the arrival and fate of the "family viewing hour," the 1974 Senate violence hearings, the industry response, the research interests reflected in the Reston, NSF/RANN (Research Applied to National Needs Office of the National Science Foundation), and "prosocial" effects projects, the debate over the validity of the "cultivation analysis" extension of the violence profile, the partial shift of the reform and research focus away from violence toward advertising and its effects on children, the associated backlash against the Federal Trade Commission (FTC), the continuing research community campaign to update and ratify the surgeon general's findings, the new round of House hearings (1976-1977), the spread of cable and other new technologies, the increased pressures for deregulation of the broadcasting and telecommunication industries, and the emergence of the effort to "rewrite" the Communications Act. These developments reveal much about the enduring problems for communication research of the political and reform demands for applicability, industrial participation in setting the research agenda, and the research community's presumptions about its value-freeness and independence.

A persistent, principal difficulty for this specific strain of research, indeed of most effects research, is to develop the capacity to reexamine its origins and therefore to think more carefully about the assumptions guiding its definition of important problems in the relationships between television and society. Under the current frame of reference, the basic images of television, of communications in general, and of their social import remain those of the peculiar, and particularly American, tradition of positivistic science that, as it is reflected in the mass communication research community, continues to be largely unaware of the significance of the industrial and political influences on it.

Thus there remains for communication scholarship the prodigious task of critically reviewing in considerable detail the intellectual assumptions of the theoretical and methodological forms of that tradition. The discussion in the following two chapters seeks to support that effort. But it does so by accepting the more modest burden of attempting to recast the general and violence effects research history, particularly its early and middle phases, in a broader context than is customarily the case — to see it in light of changes in the social, political, and economic status of science in general and of mass communication research in particular. The specific objective is to elucidate the relationships — the intellectual and institutional accommodations — established during the 1930s and 1940s among representatives of the broadcasting industry, government, and social science community and to suggest how these relationships determined much of the character of communication effects research for the next generation or more.

NOTES

1. The origins of this "movement" in the United States can be traced at least back to the formation of groups protesting the content of the nascent and then later more fully developed film industry (see Jowett, 1976).

2. Much of the focus and origins of concern of the television reform movement are closely related to the terms of the film reform effort traced by Jowett.

3. A useful history of the relationship between science and government is Lyons (1969). One observes, however, that this account is at heart a celebration of the relationship and must be critically read for its argument that closer cooperation between science and government is desirable.

4. Among the leading discussions of such attacks, and their own shortcomings, is Habermas (1971).

Part I

THE EARLY HISTORY OF COMMUNICATION EFFECTS RESEARCH

Chapter 2

THE RISE OF AMERICAN SOCIAL SCIENCE

THE PRAGMATIC TRADITION

The histories of American science can hardly fail to note the pragmatic, utilitarian spirit informing its origins. Gene Lyons begins his examination of the federal government's use and support of social and behavioral research by recalling the approach to science at the birth of the republic:

> The scientific spirit of the Founding Fathers had its roots in the Enlightenment with its emphasis on reason, progress, and earthly salvation. But this spirit was also shaped by a pragmatism and utilitarianism that grew out of the practical demands of settling new land that have characterized American society and American science from the beginning. For men like Franklin and Jefferson, science was not an abstraction. Both were eminently practical, little given to theorizing. Their inclination was to put science to work to make the lives of people more productive and to further the development of their country. It might be said that they possessed the technological, rather than the scientific, spirit — no less empirical, but highly utilitarian in emphasis.
>
> The empirical attitude found its way into the Constitution through provision for a census of population once every ten years in order that "Representatives . . . be apportioned among the several States . . . according to their respective numbers." The census, as Price has put it, "thus . . . became the ultimate basis of sovereign power in the United States" [Lyons, 1969: 2-3].

In addition to the official endorsement of a quantitative methodology to underlie the very structure of the American democratic process, one might also note the determination of the Constitutional Convention "To promote the Progress of Science and useful Arts, by securing for limited Times to Authors and Inventors the exclusive Right to their respective Writings and Discoveries" (U.S. Constitution, Art. I, Sec. 8). A practical, applied science implied progress through invention and more sophisticated technology. Moreover, rising in the service of a free enterprise, commercial order, that science and its products were imbued with aspects of private property requiring both protection and promotion. Identified with a new style of intellectual inquiry, American science became as well a commodity and a form of industrial and political organization.

The demand for increasingly inventive, applied natural and engineering sciences intensified throughout the industrial and economic expansion of the nineteenth century. No less than in any other area of commercial endeavor, discoveries in the sciences were quickly applied to develop new industrial enterprises in communications. New principles in steam and electrical power, chemistry, and electromagnetic energy served as the basis for the emerging technologies that were to engender and drive industrial processes in the print media, photography, motion pictures, telecommunications, and broadcasting. Across the range of developments in basic industries, construction and architecture, production of consumer goods, utility services, transportation, and communication, theoretical science was constantly brought before the bar of technological — and commercial — applicability.

As an integral element of the middle-class, commercial, democratic spirit, American science rejected its roots in European traditions of natural and social philosophy, disdaining what were seen as the irrelevant abstractions of metaphysical inquiry and, in social commentary, lines of argument that were associated with either conservative or radical positions in debates about morality, authority, and order.

One cannot speak of American social science as thoroughly divorced from its European origins, but to understand the setting in which mass communication research arises, one must note how those origins are denied or redefined in light of the assumptions and needs of the American experience. For instance, much of American ideology and constitutional and economic organization centered around concerns for individual rights and freedom. This heritage was reflected in the first generation of American social psychology and its setting of pragmatic social philosophy. Among representatives of the Harvard and Chicago school, in scholars such as William James, Charles Cooley, George Mead, and John Dewey, there was a determined emphasis on the development of the individual mind and spirit. The context of concern was, like that of much early European social theory, the preservation or return to the perceived values of small, local, *gemeinschaft* community. Rather than focusing on the large social whole or the complex of institutions defining it, and in reaction to the more typically European concern with the preservation of hierarchical social authority, the abiding American interest was to understand and foster the process of individual growth. The method was the study of the individual unit of personality and primary group social interaction.

The practical needs of an expanding American society and the related fascination with facts and figures were reflected in the emergence of the dominant forms of American sociology. Again there were vestiges of European influence, for instance, in the agreement with Durkheim and others about the need to study society sui generis and to pursue social study through analysis of the new forms of social, economic, and population data. But there was a tendency to reject the concerns about the loss of the particular forms of social authority that had led the Europeans to examine the history and roles in social organization of major institutions such as religion and law. Further, Americans had little patience for painstakingly deep analysis of symbolic material (e.g., public statements, codes, or observed rituals). American sociology might turn to Weber for general theoretical inspiration, but it rejected his method of building the case "ideal typically," of filling in the details of the social portrait historically and dramatically in light of traditional, understood structures and values. Instead, much of American social thought began, particularly through the Parsonian general theory of action, to reinterpret the significance of the European aspects of its origins, recasting them in light of American social and economic problems — and the search for solutions.

In view of his own European training, Parsons is aware of the different traditions:

> Karl Mannheim once stated that one of the principal differences between European and American sociology lay in the concern of the Europeans, especially on the Continent, with the diagnosis of the larger social-political problems of their time, a trait of sociology which connected it with the philosophy of history, while American sociology had been much more concerned with specific and limited empirical studies of phases of our own contemporary society [1964: 12].

But the Parsonian agenda is clearly pointed toward restructuring the balance between the two traditions. He speaks of "convergence," but his primary purpose appears to be "in acquiring for sociology the status of an empirical science with rigorous operational procedures and standards of validation [and to show] that the theory of action, including its sociological branch, is applicable over a microscopic-macroscopic range" (1964: 13).

In the American context the study of social phenomena as facts was, like the republic itself, actively seeking new structures of organization. It sought explanation and prediction in service of the political and social experiment. Endeavoring to be free of traditional forms of authority and organization, or to avoid radical prescriptions for them, and seeking the crisp, confident style of the new industrial and technological order, it adopted the mantle of empiricism and positivism. Its credo was objectivity, and its tools were statistical.

These values and approaches were seen in the census requirement and the response to it. Not only did the population count stimulate development of survey methods; it also promoted statistical conceptualizations of publics and democratic processes. Expressions of the public will became identified with political polling, and demographic and numerical communities replaced those of language, religion, and occupation.

As Daniel Boorstin suggests, in turning away from the Old World, Americans embraced numbers and the creation of statistical communities because they were taken as neutral, they avoided the invidious distinctions of traditional categories of social class, and in keeping with the promise of the New World, they were infinitely expandable (1974: 165). That the "neutral language of numbers" and facts also failed to provide a "moral guide" and therefore had subtle, but important, valuation implications was a problem that went unrecognized during the economically expansive age of industrialization and applied science and technology.

Indeed, in Robert Wiebe's eyes, statistical conceptualization became an ethic in itself. It became a means to celebrate American nationhood while avoiding the conflicts in values lurking beneath the political rhetoric of a distended society:

> Americans emphasized the obvious. What they saw about them were more tracks and more factories and more people, bigger farms and bigger corporations and bigger buildings; and in a time of confusion they responded with a quantitative ethic that became the hallmark of their crisis in values. It seemed that the age could be comprehended in bulk. Men defined issues by how much, how many, how far. Greatness was determined by amount, with statistics invariably the triumphant proof that the United States stood first among nations.

> Quantitative values received a good measure of support from religion, architecture, and literature [Wiebe, 1967: 40-41].

The primary value was "quantity of results, not quality of belief."

> As the network of relations affecting men's lives each year became more tangled and more distended, Americans in a basic sense no longer knew who or where they were. The setting had altered beyond their power to understand it, and within an alien context they had lost themselves. In a democratic society who was master and who was servant? In a land of opportunity what was success? In a Christian nation what were the rules and who kept them? The apparent leaders were as much adrift as their followers. For lack of anything that made better sense of the world, people everywhere weighed, counted, and measured it [Wiebe, 1967: 42].

The realities of late nineteenth-century American social and industrial experience further channeled the development of a particularly practical, predictive social science. Stimulated by the changing industrial and economic order, immigration, and the increasing flow of rural populations to the cities in turn prompted novel social and political tensions. These conditions directly contradicted the assumptions about the nature of the democratic experience built into the Jeffersonian mythology of an agrarian, decentralized, small-community republic. The attendant strains and ambiguities set up a demand for convincing analysis and explanation. Part of the response, particularly in some of those universities benefiting from the Morrill Land Grant College Act of 1862 and other subsequent federal legislation for higher education, was the development, largely in the midwest, of a wide-ranging rural sociology. Encouraged in part by a desire to help develop the conditions and imagery of a less onerous and more satisfactory rural life, that sociology, in conjunction with increasingly sophisticated agricultural sciences and extension services, promoted considerable study of such phenomena as the processes of adoption and diffusion of new farming techniques and implements. Federal policy concerns had come to help shape the structure of the academy and the substance of its inquiries.

With roots stretching back to the political economics developed by the physiocrats during prerevolutionary, Enlightenment France, the discipline of agricultural economics also provided an early American forum for linkages between government and social science. As John Kenneth Galbraith points out, the physiocratic tradition, with its emphasis on the importance of land as the basis of national wealth, served as a major contributor to the emergence of a modern science of economics. This heritage is of interest here, because, although Quesnay and Turgot were associated with aspects of the then young doctrine of laissez faire, their concern for the development of a state economic policy through land management and their interest in making economic study a key element in government policy foreshadowed the growth of more formal modern relationships between economic research and government action. They also demonstrated the irony that, at least in part of its continental origins, free enterprise economic theory was never as thoroughly free of identity with state policy and action as much economic history would suggest, at least as it is based on certain English and American rarified interpretations of Smithian doctrine (Galbraith, 1977: 16-22).

One of the first offices of the federal government to attend to formal theories and methods in the social sciences was the Department of Agriculture, which "almost from its establishment in 1862, [had] created an important place for scientific research in its structure" (Lyons, 1969: 31). Its efforts, also conceived of as helpful in stemming the tide of the move toward urbanization, the loss of small rural communities, and later, the trend toward increasingly large and complex farming enterprise, provided an unprecedented amount of statistical data and studies of population flow, production control, and marketing problems. It too depended greatly on the research and extension expertise of the land-grant universities, several of which were also to become leaders in the development of the communication effects research enterprise.

As mass production and industrial capacity expanded during the decades following the Civil War, investment and marketing decisions began to assume greater significance. As the potential for profit — and failure — became ever more spectacular, the fiscal decision-making process required more information and better evaluative tools. Boorstin notes that scientific attention came to focus increasingly on the consumer to study, and thereby to help predict and guide, his "needs" and market decisions. After the turn of the century, together with newer, bolder forms of advertising, a science of marketing research emerged. This effort began with the simple enough concern of advertisers and publishers to verify assumptions about the size of readerships. The objectives — and consequences — soon became much more complex:

> Publishers now tried in earnest to discover what they were really selling. Circulation figures, they began to see, were not enough. They asked who bought their paper, where they lived, what they did for a living, and what they wanted to buy. This knowledge, destined to affect not only American advertising but even the products themselves and the development of new products, made the relationship between seller and buyer more self-conscious. The seller set up his own "intelligence agency," and planned his strategy to conquer the

> market. The buyer meanwhile began to see himself as a significant unit in the mass of "consumers" who had a power to affect the flow of goods.
>
> The efforts of craftsmen to please monarchs were crude beside those of modern American market researchers to anticipate the tastes, habits, and desires of their majesties The Public [Boorstin, 1974: 151-152, 153].

Marketing and advertising research had arisen as a response to specific questions emerging from the new forms of production, distribution, and sales capacity. They soon came to play a key role in managing the overall cycles of investment, production, advertising, and consumption. The studies of demographics, social patterns, and individual behavior had found an attentive and wealthy client. Social and behavioral research profited in their response to fundamental American virtues, particularly that of applicability in support of commercial enterprise. Simultaneously through the advertising tool, the various media of mass communication came to be increasingly important elements in that enterprise and its management.

Meanwhile, the emerging forms of social science research had begun to secure themselves in other quarters as well. During the last quarter of the nineteenth century, the increasing concentration of private capital and the extension of industrial monopolies began to evoke political reactions. As part of the progressivist antitrust movement, the federal and state governments began to establish a variety of official and quasi-official monitoring and control institutions such as regulatory agencies and industrial and economic advisory commissions ("brain trusts"). From the standpoint of social science these agencies proved to be outstanding opportunities for public display of its practical applicability. Social scientists began to play ever more important staff and leadership roles in these institutions. More important, the forms and values informing their ideas became absorbed in and in turn adapted to the political process of setting government policy toward business. Out of the struggles — and accommodations — among government, business, and reformers, social science emerged as an acceptable, seemingly neutral, medium of resolution.

The received histories of social science, and particularly those such as Lyons's, which emphasize the interaction of social science and government, tend to celebrate the positive value of the emergence of these sciences and their authority. They write in the liberal tradition of John Dewey, for whom the "means to a responsible solution lay through the scientific method" (Schlesinger, 1957: 132). Such promotion fails to account for the particular sociocultural and political economic context out of which that method rises. Little if any thought is given to the observation that the significance of the emerging social sciences lies not so much in the capability of their statistical methodology and ostensible objectivity as in the discovery that those very characteristics, while helping plow important new ground in public policy, also tended to reinforce and advance certain common assumptions among business interests, government, and reformers about appropriate measures of success and progress.

REFORM AND THE PROGRESSIVE TRADITION

As with the pragmatic scientific spirit, the origins of political reform in the United States rest in the Constitution and in the experience of the American rebellion itself. The rights to freedom of speech and to petition for redress of grievances imply more than the ability of individuals simply to express their discontents. Within the framework of powers and obligations established by the Constitution there exists a fundamental recognition of the potential need for change as time and circumstance dictate, and a political process is provided that presumably can accommodate it. Yet this commitment to flexibility is a conservative doctrine. For while the pragmatic, scientific spirit of the Constitution contemplates improvements in the applied democratic process, its expectations are for neither radical nor necessarily frequent change. There is an assumption that progress will occur with the increasing practical enlightenment of the citizenry and its improving material condition. The doctrine of individualism informing the emergence of the republic further assumes that such progress is possible through the Constitution's guarantees of order and private libertarian action supported by a structure of law.

Of course, the concept of reform is much older than the American state, and it is even a precursor to libertarian ideology. "Reform" is at root a term of religious politics and a model for change through return to a former, simpler state of grace. The Reformation grew out of attempts initially to restructure the Roman Catholic Church, not necessarily by creating new doctrines as in Protestantism, but by recapturing a certain direct relationship between the individual and God, a condition that was presumed to have been better facilitated by the earlier Church and through direct individual experience of the scriptures (see, for example, Bainton, 1959: 4-5; Beard, 1907: 112-146). The contemporary popular discussions of reform tend to emphasize its characteristics of improvement and correction. The restoration heritage of the concept and its religious overtones tend to be overlooked. Yet they have considerable significance in light of the secular political and social experience with reform during the past century, particularly in its association with questions of social science and public policy.

For any discussion of American reform movements it is useful to start with Richard Hofstadter (1954) and David W. Noble (1958). Hofstadter's sharpest focus is on the progressivism of the 1900-1914 period, but his study deals with clashes of social philosophies, interest groups, and economic pressures that stretch from Jeffersonian agrarian idealism to the pragmatism of Roosevelt's New Deal. Noble discusses progressive thought during the period roughly from 1880 to 1920, but he too, perhaps ever more determinedly, seeks to root progressive thinking and its inherent dilemmas in the much older traditions of American and Western liberalism. Together, these studies encourage us to see that the reform narrative stretches back at least to the eighteenth-century European strains of Enlightenment faith in progress and forward into the current generation of persistent civil libertarian and consumer movement beliefs in the power and perfectability of the individual.

Dealing with the earlier period of American history one notes the initial expressions of reform concerns and their legacy throughout the nineteenth century in the terms of rural views and needs. Thus the populist movement, coming at the end of that stage, was essentially agrarian, combining the mythology of the yeoman farmer with the practical demands of an emerging commercial agricultural industry. However, by the turn of the century populism's hold on the reform movement was greatly weakening. The social and political conditions of the ever-growing, increasingly complicated urban environment engendered a somewhat different approach. Yet it is important to keep in mind that the populist dream of a return to the small, independent, self-sufficient, freeholding worker of the land has never been entirely repudiated. Aspects of it have remained in older, less rural reform movements, and its appeal informs much of the contemporary belief in the salutory effects of the flight from the city — from the crime, the violence, the pervasive intrusions of mass media, the information glut, the relentless inflation, and the energy shortages that mark much of the urban condition.

During the last decade of the nineteenth century the center of reform activity shifted to efforts of progressivism, an essentially urban, middle-class, nationwide movement. In time progressivism absorbed many of the populist themes, and in practical political terms it depended greatly on widespread, multipartisan support from members of Congress representing all sections of the country, rural and urban. Progressivism expressed itself in the form of concerns about "labor and social welfare, municipal reform, the interest of the consumer," but its legislative program also dealt with tariff, financial, railroad, and antitrust matters that were national in scope, of interest both to those concerned about kickbacks in grain transportation rates and those worried about the quality of life and politics in the cities (Hofstadter, 1954: 133).

The progressive impulse was, of course, much more than an applied political program. It was a sentiment felt widely among the populace; in many ways its actual goals were vague, and it was infused with the spirit of recovery:

> It was not nearly so much the movement of any social class, or coalition of classes, against a particular class or group as it was a rather widespread and remarkably good-natured effort of the greater part of society to achieve some not very clearly specified self-reformation. Its general theme was the effort to restore a type of economic individualism and political democracy that was widely believed to have existed earlier in America and to have been destroyed by the great corporation and the corrupt political machine; and with that restoration to bring back a kind of morality and civic purity that was also believed to have been lost [Hofstadter, 1954: 5].

Put more succinctly, "Progressivism, at its heart, was an effort to realize familiar and traditional ideals under novel circumstances (Hofstadter, 1954: 213). The difficulty was that many of those ideals were based on myths about both the former character of American society and the changes that had overtaken it. There was a tendency to believe too fully in the image of the noble rural citizen, the enlightened small community, "town meeting" democratic process, and the prior, general existence of free enterprise economic conditions, civic virtue, and personal morality.

There certainly were among the progressivists those with sufficient insight to recognize some of the realities. They were able to note the mean aspects of rural life, to recognize the essential differences of political heritage and cultural values accompanying the large influx of immigrants into the cities, to see in machine politics an often necessary and useful process for responding to what frequently was a closed, impersonal, legalistic American social and political order, to recognize the role of new industrial and financial organization in substantially improving general economic conditions, and to realize that many of the social and economic changes underway were largely irreversible. Yet the myths persisted, and as a result there was a tremendous ambivalence in the outlook of progressivism. There was a tendency to be of two minds about all the major issues — the great corporations, immigrants, labor, bosses, and city life, the identity between freedoms of speech and enterprise and the values of science and technology (Hofstadter, 1954: 133-134).

As Noble suggests, there was underlying the progressive movement a tradition of paradox in all generations of liberal thought, chief among which were the hope for the simultaneous triumphs of "civilization and savagery" and the untroubled notion that "total liberty [might be] accompanied by total uniformity" (1958: v-viii). Liberalism has always tended to believe in both the Garden and Manifest Destiny and in the doctrines of both individual freedom and absolute equality. Periodically, as during the years immediately following World War I, it becomes aware of and disillusioned by the contradictions inherent in its beliefs, but typically it comes to accept, though never to resolve, those paradoxes and to move on without significant reconceptualization to the next phase of its continuing struggle with conservatism.

In the end, then, there was substantial failure in progressive aspirations. The movement managed to encourage certain improvements in the political process, including changes in electoral proceedings and the passage of female suffrage, and to help place certain limits on the growth of the major trusts. But it can hardly have been said to have effected massive, substantial reform in American social and political affairs. Antitrust legislation never quite fully dealt with the growing concentration of corporate power, indeed it may have legitimized certain aspects of that growth, and changes in the character of cultural values responded more to developments in social organization and communications than to progressive sermons. The clock could not be turned back, the pace of change had gathered too much momentum, and the impossible moral and political standards of the reformers could not be legislated.

Perhaps most important, the structure of all forms of organization, private and public, had grown beyond the ability of the reformers to control. As Hofstadter argues, progressive reform failed because it ignored or could not come to grips with the extent to which developments in large, complex corporate and governmental enterprise had changed the fundamental rules of economics and politics. Leading spokesmen and institutions in the reform movement, while critical of the emerging forms of organization, were at the same time unwitting parts of them. "One of the ironic problems confronting reformers . . . was that the very activities they pursued in attempting to defend or restore the individualistic values they admired brought them closer to the techniques of organization they feared" (Hofstadter, 1954: 7).

Further, as Wiebe notes, there was in the Progressive movement an "illusion of fulfillment."

> What the reformers failed to comprehend was that they had built no more than a loose framework, one malleable enough to serve many purposes, and that only its gradual completion would give meaning to an otherwise blank outline. They had carried an approach rather than a solution to their labors, and in the end they constructed just an approach to reform, mistaking it for a finished product [1967: 222-223].

Given the professional, social, and financial stature of many of the progressive leaders, this conclusion may be somewhat surprising. But in his study of the backgrounds of the leading reformers, Alfred Chandler (1954: 1465) finds that, in large part due to their individualistic spirit, there was a political independence that also reflected inexperience in national politics, a weakness that was to undermine their aspirations for achieving lasting, institutionalized reform.

This legacy of clouded vision and ambivalence may also be seen in the rise of social science and eventually of mass communication research. Influenced by optimistic tenets in evolutionary theory, though rejecting social darwinism, the progressive movement held out hope for amelioration of individual and group life within the framework of established order. Committed to reform within the context of constitutional law and privately controlled economic structures, progressivism sought to discern and attach to the process of reform those aspects of modernity seen as capable of reinvigorating community. Modern man was perceived as a rational, essentially perfectible being who possessed the analytic capability and who sought the information necessary to deal with the complexities of contemporary life, in order that he might master those difficulties and return political and economic decisions to the individual and to identifiable communities. To appeal to this individual, progressivists seized on education, communications, and technology as primary instruments of reform. Science and research were taken as integral elements in the process of providing that requisite information and the capability for its dissemination. Therefore, social science research and optimistic analysis of educational and communications technology potentials were implicitly joined well before any specific field of communication effects research emerged.

However, in hoping to reconnect the individual to the political process through the new forms of information dissemination, the progressivists failed to note the significance of the somewhat different purposes implied in the emerging private systems of ownership and funding of those media and the public systems for their monitoring and control. As a part of the new pattern of bureaucratic corporate and governmental management, social science was a contributing factor in the advancement of its technique and authority. As part of the reform movement it was, to a large extent, no less perspicacious about the ideological commitments and historical failures of its own assumptions.

SOCIAL SCIENCE AND PUBLIC POLICY

The arrival of social science to a position of status and authority is closely related to the rise of a large government regulatory apparatus during the first half of the century. This development tends to be seen as a function of the New Deal and to be argued within the framework of the tired liberal-conservative dichotomy. It is, however, a phenomenon that substantially antedates the administration of Franklin Roosevelt. The proliferation of federal administrative agencies derives from the series of regulatory and antitrust laws beginning with the Interstate Commerce Act of 1887 and the Sherman Antitrust Act of 1890, and it is a reflection of the general shift of social concerns from civic morality to administrative technique (Schwartz, 1973; Salomon, 1959). To be sure, its final major stage of growth began during Roosevelt's first term, but its essential logic and forms and its politically legitimate status were all instituted well before the advent of the Depression and the popular plea for relief from Washington. Increases in the power and authority of the federal government proceeded all through the first two decades of the twentieth century, as the range of federal legislation and executive branch initiatives extended further into those economic and social affairs that could be increasingly seen as coming under the realms of interstate commerce.

Mobilization demands during World War I substantially enhanced the power of the national government and thus the social and behavioral sciences' public policy role. Operations of the War Industries Board depended on and in turn stimulated developments in economic planning and measurement techniques. Such efforts, however, implied more than just a tie between government and social science. Economic planning required the active cooperation of business, and social science methods employed in one sector would spill over into and be influenced by the assumptions and needs of the other. For instance, to facilitate the rapid screening necessary for the military's massive induction effort, the intelligence testing techniques that had been emerging out of experimental psychology were quickly put into service by the government. The effectiveness of such an approach did not go unnoticed in other areas, and this application of psychology became widespread in education and business during the next two decades.

Centralized economic planning did not last beyond the Armistice. Renewed faith in the American industrial and commercial system, seen as largely responsible for the allied victory and the emergence of the United States as a leading world power, silenced much of the prewar reform movement and encouraged the demand for return to the application of a purer, if somewhat mythological, vision of free enterprise. Rather than raising doubts about such visions, the depression of 1919-1921 was laid at the feet of wartime dislocations and antilibertarian social and political movements. The emergence of a state-controlled economy in Russia in the wake of the Bolshevik revolution and the continuing nervousness about the power and intentions of domestic labor movements contributed to support for the procommercial Harding, Coolidge, and Hoover administrations.

Nonetheless, the federal apparatus remained intact and actually grew. For, while the number and scope of federal regulatory agencies were still limited, such offices, particularly the Department of Commerce, were turned unabashedly from supervision of big business to its promotion (Schlesinger, 1957: 84). The power of the government grew in partnership with that of the commercial economy.

During the height of the laissez-faire euphoria of the mid-1920s, none of the Republican administrations could afford to appear to be too deeply involved in extensive government economic planning, except as it might be seen as fostering conditions for expansion of private enterprise. Structurally, the discussion of economic planning was banished from visible governmental offices, and the use of scientific methods in governmental economic administration went "underground" to privately financed, ostensibly independent institutions such as the National Bureau of Economic Research, the Social Science Research Council, the Institute for Government Research, the Institute of Economics, and the Brookings Graduate School of Economics and Government (the latter three of which merged in 1928 to become the Brookings Institution).[1] Nonetheless, these agencies served as forums for regular consultation by government officials with social scientists, and the appearance of separation was always greater than the practical reality. The one major exception to the image of separation appears to have been in the Department of Agriculture, which in 1921 created the Bureau of Agricultural Economics to provide a better coordinated research capacity in the department and to maintain its direct ties to academically based research in rural sociology and agricultural economics, particularly to use their regular accumulations of statistical data.

The general growth of social science to quasi-official status was also promoted in other ways. The role of Herbert Hoover is revealing. Hoover was the great proponent of "progressive individualism," based on his belief in the possibilities of cooperation between "the principles of equality of opportunity and of service" (Schlesinger, 1957: 82-85). His method was to encourage the development of trade associations, codes of good practice and other demonstrations of "social responsibility" and then with proper financial incentives to draw business into cooperation with government programs, all designed to protect and promote private enterprise. First as secretary of commerce under the Harding and Coolidge administrations, and then later as president, Hoover formed, chaired, or otherwise promoted the establishment of a variety of governmental advisory commissions. In many cases these bodies were controlled or heavily influenced by leaders from the industries involved, and in several instances they came to depend on social scientists for staff and consulting research.

> Both as Secretary of Commerce and as President, he chaired general conferences on economic and social issues which brought together business, labor, and agricultural leaders and which were often either preceded or followed by major research projects. . . . He also sought to persuade industry and the philanthropic foundations to support basic scientific research in the universities as an essential underpinning for continued economic development. In all of these ventures he made wide use of groups of experts drawn from among the leading physical and social scientists of the period. His intention was to develop broad channels for cooperative action among influential segments of the society, to support these efforts with scientific and economic advice, and, in the process, to avoid the necessity for action by the central government [Lyons, 1969: 34-35].

A significant manifestation of this method appeared early in broadcasting history, during the effort in the mid-1920s to establish a framework for control of the infant, but unruly, radio industry. As secretary of commerce, Hoover convened a series of four National Radio Conferences in Washington between 1922 and 1925. In view of the signal chaos beginning to envelop broadcasting, and in conjunction with a series of judicial decisions undermining the Department of Commerce's regulatory policies as developed under the terms of previous, pre-broadcast radio legislation, the secretary sought in these conferences advice about how to apply what powers remained to him and help in developing recommendations to Congress for remedial legislation (Senate, Comm. on Interstate Commerce, 1926). That these conferences were dominated by radio manufacturing and commercial broadcasting industry representatives and that this approach did much to shape and ratify a certain set of attitudes about the appropriate purposes and forms of organizations for broadcasting apparently went unquestioned. The Radio Act of 1927 and its successor, the Communications Act of 1934, substantially reflected the concerns of the major elements in the industry and their views of the appropriate extent of government authority in broadcasting as articulated during these conferences.

Hoover's method may be seen at work in another forum also of interest here. During the first year of his presidency, and in the wake of the economic failures that brought on the Depression, Hoover created the President's Research Committee on Social Trends. This committee consisted of several of the then major figures in American social science, individuals closely involved in the work of a variety of governmental agencies, in several of the leading professional associations, and in the new Social Science Research Council (SSRC). A number of these, including the SSRC chairman, Wesley Mitchell of Columbia, had served on previous Hoover commissions or in conference-related research projects. The work commissioned by the committee involved over 400 social scientists in dozens of universities. It spanned nearly the entirety of Hoover's term, and it ran almost coextensively with the Payne Fund study of film violence and its effects on young people (see Chapter 4). The committee completed its work and published its report in 1933 under the title, *Recent Social Trends,* with a preface by the president written shortly before he left office. This "summary" volume, consisting of 29 chapters in more than 1500 pages, was backed by thirteen volumes of special studies, and altogether the material dealt with a vast array of issues bearing on the nature of American life in the pre-Depression era. Among its many topics, the committee's report analyzed trends in such areas as natural resources, communications, education, ethnic groups, youth, occupations, leisure, religion, health, law, and government. It represented an attempt to take advantage of social science, but to do so at arm's length. The Hoover administration had to acknowledge the expanding economic crisis and attendant social disruptions that marked his administration. But his political philosophy resisted direct government involvement, and university-based research efforts served as a useful way of examining the crisis, of evidencing concern — or at least the appearance of concern — without implying subsequent governmental action.

It is unclear how the research of the President's Committee actually influenced governmental programs, particularly as its publication coincided with the departure of its sponsor and the inauguration of Roosevelt, with his own programs for action. Nonetheless, the symbolic import of the report is evident. It marked the arrival at the upper echelons of public policy deliberations by the social sciences generally. The report

> advocated nothing less than the fullest application of knowledge and intelligence to the whole decision-making process in the society. It proposed to apply the very methods that social scientists had employed in writing *Recent Social Trends* to the formulation of public policy: combining qualitative interpretation of trends with quantitative statistical measurements and putting them to work in making major political decisions [Lyons, 1969: 48-49].

Even though there might be reservations about the reliability of these instruments, and even though the proponents of their use were careful not to recommend a mechanical application of social science to the problem of public policy, the social and economic crises of the moment made it easy to turn to the presumably objective, rational techniques of experimentation and empiricism for help in understanding the turmoil and in seeking a path out of the disorder.

The New Deal offered the political structure for placing social scientists in high advisory posts, and the continuing rapid growth of those sciences in the academy offered an increasingly large, self-confident pool of talent from which to draw. But the practical politics of government administration greatly limited the extent to which social science research was effectively applied. In agriculture, Indian affairs, and elsewhere there were vivid instances of "the vulnerability of research when it becomes a threat to political and bureaucratic interests" (Lyons, 1969: 59). Under the specific fiscal policies of the Roosevelt administration economic research came to play an increasingly important role in federal government planning efforts. While there was no full-scale, centralized planning to the degree emerging in a number of European governments, offices such as the National Resources Planning Board came to wield considerable influence in federal executive and legislative economic decisions. However, while affording some ground for the implementation of aspects of Keynesian doctrine, this application was again more influenced by practical political problems than by grand economic theory, and in comparison to the more fully integrated role of the natural sciences in government (e.g., in agriculture, public health, and defense) the social science role as a whole remained relatively less important at least for the time being.

As Robert Nisbet makes clear, the situation for the social sciences, and then even the humanities, would soon change. With the widespread emergence during and shortly after World War II of new research institutes, centers, and bureaus, and with the associated expansion of the federal, industrial, and foundation funding system, there would rise a process of large-scale project research, a spirit of academic entrepreneurship, a "higher capitalism," and an "academic bourgeoisie" whose influence would redefine the structure of authority and the very nature of teaching and research in the academy (for an in-depth examination of these issues, see Nisbet, 1968, 1971, 1975).

At the outset there emerged some serious disagreement among social scientists about the appropriate extent of their role. Lyons cites Robert Lynd's call for scientists to recognize the reality of the political world, not to pursue a policy of empiricism for its own sake and without other purposes, and to recognize that decisions would be made without them if they stood on the sidelines waiting for all the data to accumulate. This position carried much further the call for active involvement of social science in policymaking than that of the earlier generation of spokesmen for social science.

> Mitchell, and even Merriam, had insisted that the politician — or the manager or the judge — had to make the decision. The social scientist did not and could not. The task of the social scientist was to accumulate and give order to the knowledge on which the decision was based. They recognized that the social scientist might be appointed to a position in which he made policy. But then he was not acting as a scientist, however much he applied the skills and outlook of a scientist to his work. . . . The next step was to relate research to policy without compromising the integrity of the research itself. This was a dilemma for them, and one that they never solved in the years that preceded the outbreak of World War II [Lyons, 1969: 78].

However, as Nisbet's discussion of general problems such as the subtleties of academic politicization and of specific events such as Project Camelot would suggest, this dilemma has never been resolved for the social sciences during the decades since the war (see Nisbet, 1968, 1971, 1975). The following chapters would suggest that it has not been resolved for mass communication effects research either.

NOTE

1. Lyons (1969: 31-46). Brookings, of course, continues to serve as one of the major, "independent" sources of economic research and consultancy for the federal government.

Chapter 3

THE RISE OF MASS COMMUNICATION RESEARCH

The previous chapter suggests that the rise of mass communication research must be seen in two lights. In one respect its appearance was an aspect of the arrival of the social and behavioral sciences, which themselves were emerging in response to the develoment of a particular commercial and political structure. Infused at the outset with a certain element of the theoretical concerns of European social philosophy, they rapidly abandoned that framework, redefining their theoretical and methodological commitments in view of a generally practical American approach to the role of science in the affairs of business, government, and reform.

As industry at large continued to develop certain informational needs relevant to its control of production and consumption cycles, advertising and marketing research took on increasing importance. In this form the methods of social science became indispensible to the new large commercial enterprise. As the media of communications waxed in importance as vehicles for facilitating that control, questions about their reach and effectiveness became more crucial, and the new marketing and advertising research capacity developing under the social science umbrella became a central weapon in their own industrial arsenals. Thus, from the outset an important root of mass communication research was greatly nurtured in the needs and purposes of a commercial communications industry.

In another respect, however, those same social and behavioral sciences were also part of the liberal, reform responses to the excesses and other implications of the very forms of organization that had fostered them in the first place. This response is readily seen as economic and political. But it is also social and cultural. That is, the reform movement reflects much of the class and status conflicts occasioned during the significant nineteenth-century shifts in population and in economic and political organization. As social science research found a place in the reform camp, it took on aspects of the moral commitments and sociocultural identities of the reformers themselves. Social science thus rose as part of the effort by those progressivists, interested in preserving certain values and relationships of an older tradition, to respond to the uncertainties of a rapidly changing world by providing a means not only for analysis, but also for guidance and redirection. As pragmatists their search for new approaches was not opposed to — indeed, they often embraced — compromises that would employ modern practices and techniques. Aspects of the nascent mass communication effects research enterprise reflected much of that critical, represcriptive flavor.

In general the social sciences were responding to the anxiety and conflicts engendered by a broad range of major social and economic upheaval. Changes in the form and content of mass communication added fuel to the fire of anxiety, and effects research is that part of the liberal social scientific tradition focused on the particular issue of the presumed deleterious impact of these new cultural experiences. In this light one notes that the roots of the critical effects enterprise stretch back beyond the first empirical work of the interwar years. As disturbing as were the revelations about the manipulation of public opinion through the press during World War I and the implications of the rapid growth of film and radio during the following decades, the sorts of fears they incited had already been raised in response to the changes a generation before in the forms and symbolic experience of the several print media. The emergence during the late nineteenth century of sensationalistic journalism, popular periodicals, and cheap novels all provoked concern about the nature of the new community and the role of the media in it. Some critics, such as Anthony Comstock (1967), who saw children being subverted on all sides, even became professional suppressors of vice. The context of social and cultural conflict in which the social sciences were already emerging must then be seen as also substantially shaping the eventual range of theoretical inquiry and public policy implications of mass communication effects research.

MASS COMMUNICATION RESEARCH AND INDUSTRY

The study of the mass media and their impact was not a major federally supported enterprise prior to World War II. At the request of President Roosevelt, Congress passed the Communications Act in 1934. But, other than combining the prior, separate terms of regulation for broadcasting and common carrier communications, and making more permanent the regulatory capacity, the 1934 law did little that was new. Its broadcasting provisions were drawn almost verbatim from the Coolidge/Hoover Radio Act of 1927, and its principal significance therefore tends to lie in how it ratified the legitimation of industry interests reflected in the earlier law.

Among the few changes in the new Act was the addition to the list of duties for the new Federal Communications Commission (FCC) of the requirement that it: "Study new uses for radio, provide for experimental uses of frequencies, and generally encourage the larger and more effective use of radio in the public interest (P. L. 416: Sec. 303(g)). Potentially the basis for far-reaching investigation of the nature of the electronic media and their impact, the FCC apparently has never felt that the legislative history supports such a broad interpretation of this provision, and even in purely technical matters of engineering research, it has been relatively reluctant to take a leadership role, prefering to defer to industry initiative.[1] The only serious examinations of broadcasting structures and practices by the FCC in its early years came with its first network study (1938-1941) and the "Blue Book" investigation of public service practices, published in 1946.[2] The former did lead to one significant structural change in broadcasting — the divestiture by NBC of one of its two radio networks and that chain's subsequent emergence as a competing, third network. But the Blue Book, largely the work of a few staff members and consultants, did not command enthusiastic response among the majority of the FCC and though published by it, was never adopted as a formal FCC policy statement.

By far the greatest amount of money and effort going into social research on broadcasting before World War II was that expended in the development of a reliable, efficient audience measurement capability. Defined increasingly as a commercial enterprise linking audiences and advertisers, the radio industry, like the press a generation earlier, found it increasingly necessary to be able to rationalize its rates for the advertising client on some basis of circulation. Ironically, that need developed to a great degree as part of the radio industry's challenge to the print media for national and local advertising. To demonstrate its value as a commercial medium, radio had to adopt, and if possible redefine in terms of its own interest, the research techniques and rhetoric of its older competitors.

While the technical problems were in many ways far different in broadcasting audience research (unlike estimating circulation for the press, there were no tangible copies to count), the sampling techniques of sociology and, especially, marketing research were quickly adopted. By the late 1930s audience ratings had become a formal, central part of broadcast industry operations. The "public interest" criterion of the Communications Act became increasingly identified with those programs earning the largest audiences (and thereby the highest ratings). Explications of broadcasting's purpose, public need, and communication value all came to be associated with the statistical tools of an applied social science.

It is hardly surprising, therefore, that the two most prominent figures in early broadcasting research, Frank Stanton and Paul Lazarsfeld, were social scientists closely associated with the effort to apply marketing research techniques to broadcast audience measurement. Stanton recalls that he had been a premedical student during the Depression, without sufficient funds to go on to medical school (Bartos, 1977: 26-29). Instead, he says, he took an opportunity to study and teach industrial psychology at Ohio State University. As a graduate student who became interested in radio research, he wrote a dissertation entitled, "A Critique of Present Methods and a New Plan for Studying Radio Listening Behavior." Concerned about the errors he discerned in then current marketing research methods as applied to radio audience analysis, "I . . . did some work on checking the various techniques — the telephone coincidental, the hear recall, and the personal interview" (Bartos, 1977: 26). As part of his research he "developed an automatic recorder, a poor man's version of today's Nielsen device" (Bartos, 1977: 26). During this period he also apparently served as a research assistant on one of the Payne Fund studies (Briand, 1969: 321). This work, in conjunction with his general studies, presumably provided him with an inside view of the methods, motives — and vulnerabilities — of media violence effects research efforts.

The Columbia Broadcasting System, during its mid-Depression commercial battles with the print media, the then dominant, two-network NBC, and the new Mutual network, had already begun to see the advantage of using statistical audience response tabulations in attracting advertisers. Stanton's interests and academic polish fit neatly into the corporate effort to employ research in the promotion of its commercial service capability. He "was a find — a man who could provide quality grist for the propaganda mill. If he only would" (Metz, 1975: 58). Through interviews with Stanton's superiors and earliest colleagues (at the time, CBS's chief promotion and sales personnel), Robert Metz describes what happened when the young academic became a commercial broadcasting executive:

> Frank was flabbergasted to learn that his new associates — who seemed like nice people — weren't the slightest bit interested in the truth with a capital T.
>
> [Victor] Ratner explained what happened:
>
> Like any advocate, we weren't looking for the facts as such, but for the facts that would make the best case for CBS. We were perfectly willing to tell a whopping lie if we could get away with it.
>
> In time, an interesting thing happened to Frank psychologically. He began looking for data that could be used by salesmen. It was quite a different thing from looking for data showing the facts as they really were.
>
> Frank said a year or two later that he could never go back to honest research again. He had been corrupted like us. He had been an academic, he said, and we had turned him into a salesman [1975: 58-59].

On the strength of his prior academic work and his new appreciation of the sales needs of the industry, Stanton was able to work with the marketing research community to develop a more reliable audience measurement process. As a result he was increasingly able to demonstrate to the advertisers the value of their expenditures on radio and, particularly, on the junior network.

The demand for an audience research tool led to the emergence of a number of competing companies, among them Crossley, Hooper, and Nielsen, which together came to constitute yet another division in the increasingly large, complex industrial enterprise of radio. Borne on the tide of their own marketing research heritage, which was respected for its seemingly sophisticated, applied science in commercial management, these firms helped introduce new values into broadcasting. The broadcasters sought speedy, clear, convincing data and were willing to pay. The marketing research firms had the experience, methods, and rhetoric, and were seeking new markets of their own. To manage this interaction the broadcasters turned to those, of whom Stanton became the archetype, who were not of program planning and production, neither of news or public affairs, nor even of showmanship, but primarily of social and administrative science. The mutual needs of broadcasting as an industry and of its marketing allies introduced into the electronic media the language and perceptions of probability theory, behavioral measurement, and opinion polling. Competing for network and station contracts, often valued more for their prestige and promotional value than for their direct financial reward, the several ratings companies sought increasingly efficient, rapid, and reliable sampling techniques. Telephone coincidental formats, listener diaries, and automated recording devices became the standard tools in the ratings enterprise. The need for technical proficiency placed a premium on technological innovation and on those who, like Stanton, could demonstrate competence in such realms.

The technological competition even led to patent battles not unlike those experienced throughout other aspects of the history of broadcasting and telecommunications. Because of its successful patent purchase and protection program and its engineering capabilities for adaptation, the A. C. Nielsen marketing firm was able to develop a series of "audimeter" devices that allowed it a competitive edge in national audience sampling, thereby leading it to dominance in the broadcasting research industry.

While content to delegate responsibility to the marketing firms for the bulk of the technical development and operations of the audience measurement process, the networks did not abrogate overall control of developments in the field. To retain some elements of guidance for the contract research industry and to develop the capacity for internal interpretation and use of the findings, the networks created their own audience research departments. Reflecting similar developments in the advertising industry, where research capacities had also become key elements in the sales effort, the networks carefully crafted their research offices as servants of the larger sales and public relations needs. Attending to the value of such a relationship, Stanton helped establish the CBS research office as a division of the promotion department. Having demonstrated awareness of the necessary priorities, he rose first to the post of research director, and then by 1946 to the corporation's presidency, a position he was to hold for 25 years.

Nor were all technical matters delegated to the ratings firms. Stanton, whose work as a graduate student had anticipated the Nielsen meter system, had also early in his career at CBS created yet another piece of hardware and the related analytic system that were to remain symbols, however methodologically dubious, of CBS and network commitment to the use of research techniques in gauging audience responses to broadcast programming. With the help of Paul Lazarsfeld, Stanton developed the "program analyzer," which allows continuous registration of favorable and unfavorable reactions to program pilots by members of audience panels. The panels are usually drawn from the tourist centers in Los Angeles and New York, where CBS "flatters them by asking if they would like to help pick the shows the nation's viewers will watch on CBS" (Metz, 1975: 61-62). Each member pushes a pair of red and green buttons to register responses that are tabulated and graphed in a control room adjacent to the screening area. Panel members are later probed for details of their likes and dislikes. One former CBS staff member explains that in spite of its manifest weaknesses, the analyzer has continuing utility. Dubbed "Little Annie," the system, "defies a hundred marketing rules. . . . It's lousy research. The sample stinks, it's not representative of any group. It's not large enough. People view in an unnatural situation. The way they register their opinions is unnatural. You can go on and on and show why it shouldn't work, but it works — our batting average is 85 percent."[3] It and systems like it remain a basic part of CBS and other network program planning.

Perhaps in recognition of his ability to mix technical innovation with his training in research methodology and then to blend both with sophisticated salesmanship, the Nielsen company apparently attempted to lure Stanton away from CBS in 1940 with an offer of a threefold salary increase (Metz, 1975: 67). Stanton himself recalls that at one point "I almost left CBS to become a partner with Elmo [Roper]" in his opinion polling firm (Bartos, 1977: 27). In any case, in response to a question about what he considers to be his most unique contribution to the field of research, Stanton replies: "I think the marriage of research to management in broadcasting is something that I would point to with considerable pride" (Bartos, 1977: 28).

Had the business of measuring audience size and reactions remained solely an internal matter in network operations, it would still have been of interest as an application of social research in the communications industry. Its very existence says much about broadcaster perceptions of audiences and general industry purposes. But almost from the outset it was clear that such research would have important political implications — that it would become associated with broader debates about the impact of broadcasting and appropriate policy responses. While ratings themselves have usually been thought of as an internal evaluative tool, and although they are widely criticized on both methodological and ideological grounds, the association of marketing research techniques, institutions and personnel with the realms of public, academic, and political debate over broadcasting has always been greater, and therefore more significant, than is commonly acknowledged.

In this respect it is clear that the career of Frank Stanton represents a major aspect of the interaction among social science, the broadcasting industry, the academy, the public, and the general political process. As will be seen, his efforts in hiring Joseph Klapper for the Office of Social Research at CBS, in funding certain kinds of attitudinal and impact research, but not others, and in speaking for the industry against the deleterious effects findings emerging from other sources constitute an important and widely unperceived element in the political use of social science research. Yet there are other aspects of the relationships among the broadcast industry, social science education, and public policymaking that may be revealed in the parallel career of Paul Lazarsfeld.[4]

Lazarsfeld is most widely known in communication research for his work with Stanton on the radio audience studies during the 1938-1948 period and for his simultaneous and later collaboration with Merton, Katz, and others on the political and personal influence "campaign studies." The influence research has been widely revered and typically cited as baseline material against which subsequent effects research must be compared. From a variety of critical perspectives it has become apparent that the standard interpretation of the value of this research in the normal history of effects theory is increasingly suspect and requires wider examination in public forums. I will allude to this criticism below, but for my primary purpose here it is most useful first to review Lazarsfeld's background and affiliations to see something of how the organizational context of his research tended to help guide the effects research tradition into certain industrially and politically acceptable channels.

While Stanton represents the social scientist who, totally employed by industry, becomes the consummate organization man and whose science is dedicated to corporate service, Lazarsfeld represents a more complex facet of the relationships among the academy, private enterprise, and public policymaking for communications. For Lazarfeld tended to work in the middle ground, in that twentieth-century academic creation known as the research bureau or institute that, while based in the university of the formal pedagogic process, nonetheless also exists largely for service to clients outside the academy. It is fair to say that Lazarsfeld unabashedly saw himself as a, if not *the*, foremost sculptor and promoter of such dual-purpose social science research institutions in the modern American university.

Not long after finishing his graduate studies in economics, political theory, and applied mathematics at the University of Vienna in the mid-1920s Lazarsfeld helped establish there a research center affiliated with the department of psychology that permitted the application of psychological research to contract studies of social and economic problems (this account is drawn largely from Lazarsfeld's own published recollections; see Lazarsfeld, 1969; Morrison 1976, 1977). An earlier involvement in the German youth movement and an interest in finding ways to improve socialist propaganda led to studies of labor education and of social stratification and its relationship to employment opportunities. Trained in statistics and traditional case study methods, Lazarsfeld had learned how to gather large amounts of data. But their analysis remained problematic until exposure to developing forms of American marketing research — for determining motivations for consumer purchases — provided a handier technique.

> If I wanted to combine statistical analysis with descriptions of entire choice processes, I had better, for the time being, concentrate on more manageable material. For the methodological goal I had in mind, consumer choices would be much more suitable.
>
> Such is the origin of my Vienna market research studies: the result of the methodological equivalence of socialist voting and the buying of soap [Lazarsfeld, 1969: 279].

In a pattern that was to become typical of much emerging American social science, the efficacy of a methodology and the industrial need for an operational research capacity led to a shift in the definition of a subject matter. As Lazarsfeld later flatly stated, "Look, you have to understand that I had no interest whatsoever in mass communications" (Morrison, 1977: 4).

Lazarsfeld's applied research in Vienna brought him to the attention of the Rockefeller Foundation, which in 1933 offered him a traveling fellowship in the United States. During this period Lazarsfeld visited a number of those universities teaching social research, and he participated in several related studies.[5] Meanwhile, the Austrian political situation had deteriorated and the tides of anti-Semitism were rising; return to Vienna was undesirable. With the help of Robert Lynd, who had become executive secretary of the Social Science Research Council, Lazarsfeld found employment at the short-lived University of Newark, where in 1936 he became director of a new research center built on the Vienna model. Shortly thereafter, in 1937, under the joint guidance of John Marshall, Hadley Cantril, and Stanton, the Rockefeller Foundation established at Princeton a research project ostensibly to study the effects of radio on American society. The project was given the formal title of Office of Radio Research, and initially Stanton was sought as director. Failing that, Marshall and Cantril, following advice from Lynd, arranged to have the post go to Lazarsfeld, with Cantril and Stanton as codirectors. In view of the advisability of exile from Austria, yet still also having a somewhat uncertain position in the American academy, Lazarsfeld was anxious to retain his identity in the Neward center, to have it "stand for him" in much the same way "any German professor of distinction would expect to have *his* own 'Institut' " (Morrison,

1977: 4). Thus, against some resistence from Cantril, Lazarsfeld managed to have the project jointly affiliated for a time with Newark and Princeton.

The purpose of the office appears to have been deliberately vague. It had a mandate "to try to determine eventually the role of radio in the lives of different types of listeners, the value of radio to people psychologically, and the various reasons why they like it" (Lazarsfeld, 1969: 305). But Theodor Adorno, one of the many other recent immigrant scholars who were briefly associated with the office, recalls that there were strict limitations:

> There appeared to be little room for . . . critical social research in the framework of the Princeton Project. Its charter, which came from the Rockefeller Foundation, expressly stipulated that the investigations must be performed within the limits of the commercial radio system prevailing in the United States. It was thereby implied that the system itself, its cultural and sociological consequences and its social and economic presuppositions were not to be analyzed [Adorno, 1969: 343].

The Adorno account is a most valuable counterweight to the "normal science" recollections of Lazarsfeld. It provides an important insight into the clash of traditions that was occurring in American social science during the second quarter of the twentieth century, and it suggests much about the intellectual losses stemming from the victory of empiricism. In this light the effects-oriented rhetorical packaging of those studies eventually emerging from the office ought not to be allowed to obscure the implications of the Rockefeller support, CBS's involvement, and Lazarsfeld's background in the development of this first, major, organized broadcasting research enterprise. In the eyes of Stanton and Cantril the project was "designed to investigate certain problems in radio research."[6] That is, the project had an immediate, practical methodological purpose; it was to be pragmatic, administrative research. As Stanton himself recollects, "[Cantril] and I thought that there ought to be some work done on methodologies in radio research, work removed from the pressure of developing reports on a time schedule, and so forth. We went to the foundation for a grant" (Bartos, 1977: 28). They anticipated that the project "would require two years of preliminary work on methods — that is, methods which we hoped to work out that would eventually enable us or others to get the final answers to the sort of questions that interested us." (Lazarsfeld, 1969: 306). Indeed, after the first two years, as the project began to amass considerable amounts of data without, however, demonstrating any clear sense of practical direction, Marshall and others arranged a series of seminars at the office (1939-1940) precisely to give a more applied focus to Lazarsfeld's efforts, to clarify his "sailing orders," and to carry through on the Rockefeller mandate to the office "for bettering broadcasting" (Morrison, 1977: 10-13).

From the start, then, the needs of the broadcasting industry were not to be ignored, and with this understanding Rockefeller continued to provide the necessary funding, supplemented eventually by CBS and others. As it happened those needs fit well with Lazarsfeld's original interests. In his "Memoir," Lazarsfeld quotes a letter he wrote to Cantril about his purposes in establishing his initial Newark office:

> I invented the Newark Research Center for two reasons. I wanted to direct a rather great variety of studies, so that I was sure that from year to year my methodological experience could increase — and that is, as you know, my main interest in research. And I tried to build up groups of younger students to be educated just in this kind of research procedures [sic] I tried to develop. Now as to the first point I think that your project would do splendidly. Radio is a topic around which actually any kind of research methods can be tried out and applied satisfactorily [1969: 306].

One might argue that throughout the development of communication effects research the primary concerns have remained those with methodology and flexing the muscle of scientific technique. Further one might note that the definition of the subject matter as a series of problems in the nature of human social and cultural behavior has suffered concomitantly. To an extent even Lazarsfeld is aware of this divergence, but he is apparantly untroubled by it. For instance, he admits that *The People's Choice* began as an attempt to study the impact of radio programs produced by the Department of Agriculture yet turned out to be an analysis of influences in voting choices (1969: 330). He accepts this shift as unimportant and appropriate.

Elsewhere in the "Memoir," though again apparently without awareness of the significance, Lazarsfeld reveals another aspect of the intellectual adjustment occuring in the office. He discusses Theodor Adorno's brief association with the project and his attempt to "induce Adorno to try to link his ['critical theory'] ideas to empirical research" (1969: 322). The thought had been to use Adorno's approach in the project's attempt to analyze the role of music in society and the impact of radio on that role. However, as Lazarsfeld notes, "The direction he [Adorno] gave could hardly be translated into empirical terms" (1969: 324). Moreover, Lazarsfeld admits elsewhere a certain annoyance with Adorno's aggressive behavior and lack of tact with industry people (Morrison, 1977: 7-8). Therefore, in 1939 Rockefeller dropped that part of the project's budget for the music analysis. Lazarsfeld reflects, "I have an uneasy feeling that my duties in the various divisions of the Princeton project may have prevented me from devoting the necessary time and attention to achieve the purpose for which I engaged Adorno originally" (Lazarsfeld, 1969: 325).

However, Lazarsfeld's concern seems less related to the intellectual loss implied in Adorno's departure than to his chagrin that it was the Berkeley group, and not Lazarsfeld's, that during the work on *The Authoritarian Personality* converted Adorno's "idea into the famous F-scale" form of analysis. In any case, the office was established with the understanding that its primary concerns would be with improved empirical methodology and administrative needs, and not with critical or philosophic reflection about communications. One must then consider how that orientation influenced the eventual work of the office and therefore how the office in turn influenced the structure of the effects research tradition and its role in the communications policymaking process of serving the mutual interests of the industry, government, and academy.

After a year of two, during which the project's research contacts came increasingly to center on New York and during which continuing policy differences between Lazarsfeld on the one hand and Cantril and/or the Princeton administration on the other became too serious, the office was moved to Columbia University.[7] There Lazarsfeld became a tenured faculty member in the Department of Sociology, and by 1945 the radio research office had been retitled the Bureau of Applied Social Research — therein reflecting Lazarsfeld's original and primary purposes for it — and it had been formally incorporated into the university structure.

The origins of the bureau are important because of the impact they had on the program of research developed by it and because of the influence that program then had on the interpretations of media effects during the subsequent generation of communication education. That is, Lazarsfeld's studies of communication in political and consumer decisions and the literature reviews and associated theoretical reformulations of his colleagues and students in the bureau have served as major elements in the received history of communication effects research summarized above. For instance, among those participants in the 1939-1940 research office seminars were Charles Siepmann, Lyman Bryson, and Harold Lasswell, and it was during those discussions that Lasswell first proferred his famous "who says what to whom in what channel with what effect" model (Morrison, 1967: 13). That image of the communication process had, of course, grown out of the behavioral science paradigms then prevalent in the American schools of psychology and social psychology, and it would turn out to have considerable impact on the research thinking in communication for years thereafter. Additionally, and not surprising in light of the prodigious amount of work by Lazarsfeld and his colleagues, nearly all the basic texts on effects during the postwar rise of mass communication studies were products of research and/or training conducted at the bureau. These included Lazarsfeld's work with Berelson and Gaudet on *The People's Choice* (1944, 1948, 1968), and with Katz on *Personal Influence* (1955), Klapper's *The Effects of Mass Communication* (1949, 1960), Wright's *Mass Communication* (1959, 1975), Berelson's *Content Analysis in Communication Research* (1952), and De Fleur's *Theories of Mass Communication* (1966, 1972, 1975).

There were a number of major texts in the introductory mass communications syllabi during the early years that were not direct products of the bureau. These included such efforts as Hovland's work with Janis and Kelly on *Communication and Persuasion* (1953), Schramm's series of anthologies, *Communications in Modern Society* (1948), *The Process and Effects of Mass Communication* (1954, 1971), and *Mass Communications* (1949, 1960), and the Berelson and Janowitz *Reader in Public Opinion and Communication* (1950, 1953, 1963). Yet even here there were important indirect links. As is explained in more detail below, under governmental aegis during World War II such research principals as Lazarsfeld, Schramm, and Hovland and a number of industry leaders established a series of important and lasting professional relationships. For instance, Lazarsfeld and other bureau staff members participated in the Army's research planning that led to the Hovland work, and Schramm was at the Office of War Information (OWI), where Lazarsfeld served as a consultant and where much of the strategy for adapting psychological and sociological research methods to wartime communication problems was developed. Further, when they began to put together the first of their anthologies shortly after the war, editors such as Schramm, Bryson, Berelson, and Janowitz relied heavily for material on bureau-produced research, including several of the reports cited above.

The industrial concerns represented by the Stanton-Lazarsfeld collaboration were reflected in the focus and findings of the radio research reports that emerged from the office/bureau during its first decade. For the most part presented and taken as providing a set of objective, scientific evaluations of radio's impact, these studies demonstrated the ability of client-inspired research to guide academic social inquiry into lines of argument that in this case have the effect of promoting favorable impressions of the broadcast industry and of blunting or turning aside criticism of its structures and practices. The significance of this finding becomes apparent when one realizes that the program of radio research overlapped with the campaign studies and limited effects reformulations emerging simultaneously in the bureau. Close attention to the credits and footnotes in the several research reports reveals that Lazarsfeld, Merton, Berelson, Klapper, and a host of others, whether as leaders and teachers or as assistants and students, were involved across the range of the interlocking aspects of the bureau's work. Consequently, the individual or team efforts, the forms of their support, and the purposes of their research as reflected in any one part of the program must be seen as closely related to those in all others.

There were at least six volumes in the radio series. Lazarsfeld is credited as the author of one, *Radio and the Printed Page* (1940), and Lazarsfeld and Stanton as editors of three: *Radio Research, 1941* (1941), *Radio Research, 1942-1943* (1944), and *Communications Research, 1948-1949* (1949).[8] The contents of all four consisted largely of reports on research conducted by the bureau, or cooperating opinion polling and marketing research firms, often with direct broadcast industry support. The other two volumes were reports on public opinion surveys commissioned by the National Association of Broadcasters (NAB) and conducted by the National Opinion Research Center (NORC): *The People Look at Radio* (Lazarsfeld and Field, 1946) and *Radio Listening in America: The People Look at Radio – Again* (Lazarsfeld and Kendall, 1948).

On the surface these reports are reasonable, worthwhile efforts to investigate the nature of radio's impact, a field that had otherwise been ignored by social science. However, several points about their timing and contents may cast their significance in a somewhat different light. For instance, the decision in the late 1930s to undertake the radio research project coincided with official reevaluations of certain conditions obtaining in the broadcast industry and generally ratified by the passage of the Communications Act of 1934. On the basis of its promises to fulfill a variety of expectations under the public interest standard of the legislation, the industry had been spared any serious restructuring when the previous Radio Act was reincorporated into the 1934 law. Emerging problems in programming range, in network-affiliate relationships, and the decline of a noncommercial service had not gone unnoticed before 1934. But remedial provisions, such as the

Wagner-Hatfield amendment, had been defeated in part as a result of promises by industry leaders to sustain program diversity and a strong local flavor (see Blakely, 1979: 64-79). By the late 1930s the vacuity of such promises had become increasingly apparent, providing sufficient pressure in Congress for at least some limited support for regulatory inquiry and action. This pressure led to perhaps the most actively reformist and critical of all FCC administrations under Chairman James Fly, with the particularly strong support of Commissioner Clifford Durr. FCC activity during this period took the form in 1938 of experimental channel reservations for noncommercial radio licensees in the new higher frequency bands, the initiation of the FCC's network inquiry (1938-1941) and its investigation of monopoly conditions in newspaper ownership of broadcast stations, and the Blue Book study of licensee programming practices.[9] While none of these activities ever seriously threatened the basic structure, purpose, and profitability of the commercial broadcasting industry, they came at a time of impending war and a good deal of uncertainty about the fate of Western democracy in general and about associated forms of free enterprise and communications in particular. Political and economic developments in eastern, central, and western Europe even before the outbreak of war must have been seen as inauspicious omens by leaders in privately held American communications industries. Any stirrings of public dissatisfaction with such enterprises had to be met with carefully marshaled publicity, declarations of social responsibility, and evidence of public support. The promotional departments and lobbying organizations for most media industries were becoming adept at providing the first, film and broadcast industry codes of conduct and the Hutchins Commission report were examples of the second, and the radio and communication research reports from within the broadcasting industry, and especially from the bureau, provided the third.[10]

Lazarsfeld's recollection, somewhat inaccurate on at least one point, provides one view of the bureau's role in the policymaking process:

> In all of the work of the Princeton Office I tried to relate the research to public controversies, but usually thought of our office as serving a mediating function. Thus, for example, we served as a channel for a project of the progressive chairman of the Federal Communications Commission, Clifford Durr [sic]. He had commissioned Charles Siepmann to develop ideas on how the FCC could better work for higher broadcasting standards. This assignment resulted in two documents, the FCC's "blue book" promulgating stricter licensing standards, and Siepmann's *Radio: A Second Chance*. To both pub-

> lications the industry reacted with violent antagonism, and I prevailed upon John Marshall of the Rockefeller Foundation to provide a special budget so that I could organize a two-day conference among the industry, the FCC, and prominent scholars in the research field to discuss the issues. Nothing much came of it, but I think this was partly because the beginning of the Second World War and the approaching involvement of the United States eclipsed interest in this kind of topic [Lazarsfeld, 1969: 316].[11]

No doubt Lazarsfeld was sincere in his liberal, reformist hopes for the role of radio in society and for the ability of the bureau's research to help achieve radio's presumed potential in educational and political progress. Yet, from this remove, it is increasingly apparent that the bureau served a somewhat different purpose. For one thing, as Lazarsfeld himself admits in his discussion of the FCC investigations, the bureau was commissioned by a group of stations owned by newspapers to provide a study of the way they handled news (Lazarsfeld, 1969: 316-317). The purpose of that study could be nothing other than an effort by the newspaper-station combinations involved to develop evidence in opposition to the FCC findings and thereby fend off the threat of divestiture. Such research demonstrates that the terms of the bureau's support, that is, the necessity for outside, industry-sponsored contracts, determined much about the areas of inquiry permitted — and denied — the scientists on its staff.

Further, as made clear in the conduct of the studies for the first volume, a report that had as its primary purpose the renewal of the original Rockefeller grant to the office, the research was to be designed and conducted under the terms of close cooperation among the office's academic staff, the commercial research firms, and the broadcasting industry. In addition to Stanton and Cantril, participants in that first project included Samuel Stouffer, George Gallup, and Harold Lasswell. In acknowledging Stanton's help, Lazarsfeld reveals how thoroughly involved the industry was: "Many an invaluable source of material was tapped, and many a research idea initiated through Dr. Stantion's advice. There is scarcely a conclusion in this volume which has not profited somehow from Dr. Stanton's cooperation" (Lazarsfeld, 1940: viii).

As a result, the 1940, 1941, and 1942-1943 reports present a variety of studies and analyses that had a subtle, but persistently disarming effect. For example, among the list of sins laid at radio's feet by the advocates of the direct effects position were the concerns about the alleged diversion of audience attention from serious matters and the provision of frivolous or unwanted material. Relying on a survey conducted by Gallup, Lazarsfeld (1940: 255) concludes that

> radio is the medium by which the large, lower income groups of the population prefer to get their news, just as they prefer it as a source of information on how to run their homes and how to improve themselves. News having recently become a topic of immediate interest for large parts of the population, radio is supplying the new consumer with just the kind of elementary news diet he wants. In meeting the needs of people not adequately served by other media, radio undoubtedly is performing an impressive social service.

Elsewhere he finds that

> there are no signs that news broadcasting have reduced newspaper reading. Quite to the contrary, it seems likely that owing to the rising interest in news transmitted by radio, there is now by and large more newspaper reading than ever before [1940: 276].

As for reading in general:

> The few data collected by now seem to show that radio has not impaired the reading habits of the population and that if properly used radio offers a rich opportunity for the promotion of reading [1940: 329-330].

This argument appears again in the second volume, where Lazarsfeld and Stanton point out that one of the studies (Meine) "definitely shows that as they grow up, young people add printed media to their news diet. . . . In all age groups those who both read *and* listen to the news are the best informed. Thus the future of reading does not appear too dark" (1941: xi).

In the first volume Lazarsfeld presents radio as having little deleterious impact. He candidly acknowledges its purposes and portrays the consequences as acceptable:

> So far as radio is concerned all signs point to the unlikelihood of its having, in its own right, profound social consequences in the near future. Broadcasting is done in America today to sell merchandise; and most of the other possible effects of radio become submerged in a strange kind of social mechanism which brings the commercial effect to its strongest expression. There are no sinister tendencies operative in radio; it works all by itself. . . . You have the picture of radio as a stupendous technical advance with a strongly conservative tendency in all social matters [Lazarsfeld, 1940: 332].

Another of the criticisms of developing commercial radio was that, the promissory testimony of the Sarnoffs and Paleys notwithstanding, "educational" and high cultural forms of broadcasting were being squeezed off the air by other, less expensive and more popular serial and musical formats. Therefore one of the 1941 studies (Adorno) is an analysis of those characteristics of radio favoring or disfavoring symphonic transmission. The study attempts to demonstrate how the experience of a live symphony is transformed by the broadcast experience, and thus the argument becomes, perhaps unwittingly on the part of the author (see above), an element in the rationalization by the editors for changes in programming:

> It was established, for instance, that if a person's love for music is due mainly to his experience as a radio listener, he is likely to prefer composers different from those who, in pre-radio times, had been considered "classical." There seems reason to believe that composers who place greater stress on melodic elements and who have a less rigid musical style, are more suitable to presentation over the radio [Lazarsfeld and Stanton, 1941: x].

Criticism of radio's impact on public taste is diverted by another study (Mac Dougald) of "the way in which the popularity of hit songs is determined by the agencies controlling the popular music business." The study tries to develop "the theme that the making of the majority of 'hits' is largely predetermined by and within the [music] industry" (Lazarsfeld and Stanton, 1941: 65). Oversimplified in any case, this conclusion is unleavened by any discussion of the impact on music industry practices of the economic imperatives implicit in a commercial broadcasting business.

The third volume (1942-1943) devotes an entire section to "daytime serials" (soap operas). One of these studies (Arnheim) is a content analysis that gives vent, albeit mildly, to the widespread criticism of serials as presenting inadequate pictures of "private and social life," approving improper "attitudes," and generally "lowering the cultural level (Lazarsfeld and Stanton, 1944: 34). On the other hand this critique is bracketed by analyses of listener composition (Herzog) and program appeal (Kaufman) that tend to explain the role of these programs functionally, emphasizing their value as vehicles of entertainment and information. The notion of "gratifications" that Lazarsfeld introduced in the first volume reappears in Herzog's paper in the third. It is, of course, a progenitor of a major element of the limited effects model, and as expressed here, rationalizes the effects of radio content for its ability to provide "emotional release," compensatory diversion, and advice (Lazarsfeld and Stanton, 1944: 24-25).

Another focus of this volume is particularly reflective of Lazarsfeld and Stanton's interests in developing improved, industrially applicable methodology. For instance, one study (Hollonquist and Suchman) explains the workings of the program analyzer and, in the process of justifying its operational use, has the effect of demonstrating how research is presumably making the broadcaster more responsive and therefore more responsible. Another report (Sturmthal and Curtis) even promotes the use of the analyzer in studying other media — in this case educational, nontheatrical films. An entire section of five studies is devoted to analysis of methodological problems and related issues such as audience flow, panel surveying, interview bias, and commercial effectiveness.

The next section of this chapter discusses the third major area of interest in the 1942-1943 bureau volume — the relationship between radio research and government during the war. For the moment, however, it will be useful to note the remaining aspects of the research-industry relationship as reflected in the other volumes in the series.

By the time they published their final collection of research reports (1948-1949), Lazarsfeld and Stanton were able to draw on a range of empirical studies sufficiently wide ranging for them to title the volume *Communications Research*. Hardly comprehensive, the book carried reports on neither the film industry nor its impact. Nonetheless it did present papers on such varied topics as comic book reading (Wolf and Fiske), newspaper gratifications (Berelson), "cultural value" relationships among magazines (Kass), interpersonal influence in communications behavior (Merton), and broadcasting in the Soviet Union (Inkeles).

This collection suggests that the bureau had come to see itself as part of an emerging mass communication research discipline, one in which the principal parties were well known to one another, of similar intellectual persuasions, and mutually interdependent: "It is no longer necessary today either to justify communications research as a special discipline or to outline its general scope. Because the field has developed so rapidly and because its pioneers have been a rather closely knit group, it has been taught in a surprisingly similar way at many universities (Lazarsfeld and Stanton, 1949: xiii).

Lazarsfeld and Stanton go on to take note of such work in the field as that of the Payne Fund studies, Lasswell's propaganda analysis, and the then recent anthologies edited by Schramm and Bryson (see Chapter 4; see also Laswell, 1927; Schramm, 1948; Bryson, 1948). The purpose here is to claim legitimacy for communication research as a science grounded in respectable experimental and survey methodologies and as "an important element in the formulation of policy and social philosophy" (Lazarsfeld and Stanton, 1949: xiv).

Again, however, the theoretical and methodological emphases are pragmatic. Several of the studies parade the bureau's effort at improved techniques of surveying and analysis (e.g., representative sampling, snowball interviewing, and statistics). These and other studies also provide elaboration of the bureau's theoretical model of the communication process and the acceptability in that light of the basic structure and practices of American mass media. The increased, loose use of functional language, especially the notion of gratifications, reflects the degree to which the neolibertarian outlook of social science and industry leaders alike had become a joint, dominant ideology. More so than in the previous volumes, the Introduction and the reports here take cognizance of the societal and cultural dilemmas implicit in modern communications:

> Impressive technological development and coincident advances in general education have led to a rapid increase of literacy. But what people can now read, see, and hear is provided in the main by a number of large-scale, fairly centralized communications industries. What, then, are the effects of this general development on the spiritual and social life of our times? Since these central agencies have means of collecting and presenting facts to which no single individual could have access, this development in communications may provide a greatly broadened range of interesting information. But on the other hand, if the communications industry were not continually aware of its social responsibility, the same development might lead toward uniformity and bias in social thinking. Perhaps the most involved of all implications is the question of what relationships should exist between the wants of the audience and the cultural function of the industry. In order to keep financially alive, the industry must serve the whole community, the industry should be the voice of its intellectually and morally most advanced sector [Lazarsfeld and Stanton, 1949: xiii-xiv].

The research assumes that the forms of control for the communications media are ultimately acceptable — the exhortation to social responsibility is as much a descriptive declaration as a warning — and the practical psychological and sociological sciences informing it are built on a systemic, optimistically organic notion of social organization and communication functions within it. The use of Merton's paper is particularly revealing. The "patterns of influence" research was but one of those several industry-supported "campaign studies" being conducted by the bureau that came to emphasize the complex social nexus through which the content of mass media has to pass. In his discussion of the Rovere study, Merton drew his useful and apt distinction between "cosmopolitans" and "locals," but for the development of communication research the more lasting, and in retrospect the more troubling, legacy was the study's contribution to the limited effects model emerging in the bureau's series of political and medical information diffusion studies.

Here again the relationship between commercial needs of the media industries and the findings and theoretical formulations of academically based communication research must be underscored. Tunstall relates that *The People's Choice* was partly funded by *Life* magazine, that *Time* financed Merton's work, and that MacFadden underwrote *Personal Influence*. Further, it appears that the entire Merton scheme was developed as part of the magazine industry's competitive battle for advertisers with the newspaper industry. The notion of "locals" was generated as a characterization of newspaper readers, whereas "cosmopolitans" were said to be magazine readers. The value of the distinction for the magazine industry is readily apparent (Tunstall, 1977: 206).

In this context one notes that the research associate helping coordinate this volume for the bureau was a doctoral candidate named Joseph Klapper. At the time, Klapper was completing his dissertation, "Mass Media Effects," which was published by the bureau in 1949. It reemerged in updated form in *The Effects of Mass Communication* and served as the consummate statement of the limited effects position (Klapper, 1960). In reviewing the effects literature, Klapper argues that the media serve as agents of reinforcement and that audiences are active seekers of gratifications who use media content for preexisting needs — in short, that fears of direct, deleterious societal effects are for the most part groundless.

As is freely acknowledged by Klapper, but generally ignored or given little consideration in the academic recitation of his conclusions, his work was directly underwritten by CBS. His findings, so useful to an industry increasingly sophisticated in its political use of research, and his obviously close ties to the professional and academic social research community through the bureau and the American Association for Public Opinion Research, of which he was an officer, earned Klapper a position with CBS, where Stanton made him director of a new Office of Social Research. As is explained in Chapter 5, that office has never had any direct, operational role in the daily affairs of the network. Instead it was designed to act out a more subtle part of political diversion. As such, Klapper's office fit a pattern of industrial manipulation of communication research that began with Stanton's cosponsorship of the Lazarsfeld Office of Radio Research, continued with his support of the bureau throughout the 1940s and 1950s, and, as we will see, culminated in industry involvement in government-sponsored investigations during the 1960s and early 1970s.

The value to the industry of the efforts in the early radio research project is further revealed in the opinion survey reports with which Lazarsfeld was also associated. Although conducted by the National Opinion Research Center, the support for these studies and the initial questionnaire designs came from the National Association of Broadcasters. The first survey was conducted in 1945 while the NORC was still at the University of Denver. It was directed by Harry Field, but the data were analyzed for publication (1946) by Lazarsfeld. The second survey was conducted in 1947, after the NORC had moved to the University of Chicago, under the direction of Clyde Hart. Again the data were analyzed for publication (1948) by Lazarsfeld, though this time with coauthorship by another bureau staff member, Patricia Kendall.[12]

The promotional purpose of this research is readily apparent. Though delayed by wartime exigencies, the first survey had been planned by the NAB as early as 1943 in the wake of the Supreme Court's affirmation of the FCC's network regulations and during the height of Chairman Fly's critical appraisal of industry practices. Publication of the first survey coincided with issuance of the Blue Book, and the second report appeared just at the moment the FCC was preparing to impose its "freeze" on television expansion and possibly reevaluate its overall set of policies toward the new medium.

The surveys ask seemingly dangerous questions about broadcasting performance, audience sources of information, and preferences as to advertising and among programming types. But in view of radio's continuing popular appeal, the unique services it provided during the war, the hints of better things yet to come with television, and a still waxing enthusiasm for developments in electronics and technology generally, it was unlikely radio would come under any widespread, sustained criticism, especially through a survey the industry designed.

Both surveys are replete with questions whose subjects, phrasings, and response options could hardly have led to damaging conclusions. At the outset of the interview the questionnaires appear to give away their interest in radio. Whenever various ratings are called for, when radio is compared to other institutions or when current programming emphases or advertising levels are questioned, the model responses invariably are "good," "about right," or other expressions of satisfaction with the status quo — the only experience most respondents are likely to have had.

Responding to his methodological interests, Lazarsfeld does raise questions about some of the weaknesses in these surveys, for example, the vagueness of rating terms used in comparative performance questions and the difficulties of drawing out criticisms of anything from respondents. But what is most significant here is to observe how such problems are not taken by Lazarsfeld as serious enough to call into question the overall results. That is, throughout the analyses in both reports Lazarsfeld provides good technical criticism, yet the findings are allowed to stand, and the general impression is given that, although there may be some difficulties, they are to be dismissed as minor, and the surveys as a whole are to be taken as reliable and valid.

One might note as well the sorts of questions and information to support the questions that the surveys do not ask or provide. For example, while there are questions about the interruptions, taste, and claims of commercials, there are no questions seeking evaluations of their impact on programming. Although there are questions about relative sources of news (newspapers versus radio), there are none dealing with a broader notion of information and learning, nor are there any proposing other sources of information. While there are questions about whether the government or the industry ought to control profits, there is no background information about the financial status of the industry, and although there are questions about preferences for government or private ownership, there are none about public corporation or other forms of control.

To an industry whose very structure and profitability required maintenance of the balance between the concept of fiduciary licensing (implying both social responsibility and self-regulation) and minimal federal regulation, Lazarsfeld's conclusions must have been gratifying.

> The results add up to an approval of exactly the type of system we have in this country. People do not want the government to run radio. They want it left in the hands of private industry, where indeed it is. But they are also aware of the power which such a system puts in the hands of commercial companies; and as good Americans, when they see power somewhere, they look at once for checks and balances. They feel that business institutions should be complemented by a government, which watches to see that the public gets a square deal. Should the industry to which they have entrusted their airways not keep faith with them, the government should see to their interests [Lazarsfeld and Field, 1946: 89-90].

The industry, however, will reserve the right to initiate and design that process of evaluation which will determine if a "square deal" is given and whether faith is kept.

Having discovered the value to it of periodic surveys such as these, the industry has continued to place confidence in them. Throughout the television era, the NAB and the networks have funded a considerable volume of research on public attitudes toward the new medium. Through Klapper's office CBS has underwritten two major surveys (Steiner, 1963; Bower, 1973) that borrow "The People Look at . . ." rhetoric from the earlier bureau versions and for one of which (Steiner) the bureau gathered the data. Through the Television Information Office, its publicity arm, the NAB has sponsored a long series of briefer, biannual polls on public preferences among news sources and general perceptions of commercial television (Steiner, 1963; Bower, 1973; Roper Organization, 1979). Conducted by the Roper organization these surveys and the CBS studies have many of the methodological characteristics — and weaknesses — of the original bureau versions. The reports generated by them serve essentially the same promotional and protective purpose. The Steiner, Bowers, and Roper analyses are widely disseminated by the industry and then faithfully and uncritically cited in press, political, and academic discussions of television's significance, thus guaranteeing a high return on the industry's investment and making these surveys a major element in the industry's program for the use of social science.

At the end of the second NORC report, and after having drawn conclusions similar to those in the first report, Lazarsfeld reveals something of the degree to which the industry and the research interests had by the late 1940s become increasingly intertwined.

> It is fortunate indeed that broadcasters themselves want to be kept on their toes. Radio is still the only industry which periodically surveys people's attitudes and then frankly publishes the findings. It can only be hoped that this triple alliance of research, vigilant criticism and creative leadership will continue; and that it will be taken as an example by other communications industries [Lazarsfeld and Kendall, 1948: 113].

The research tool could now be touted as a key part of the self-regulation package. Critics and federal regulators could be answered. The broadcast industry was calling on a wide-ranging program of science to help define its responsibilities and in so doing was invoking a prime symbol of progressive modernity. That the origins and terms of application of that science of communication also tended a priori to coincide with basic industry assumptions and needs went unacknowledged.

Although the understanding was probably more implicit than explicit, it was clear that for financial support and other manifestations of legitimacy in public, governmental, and academic eyes, the new communication research enterprise would continue to provide that variety of ostensibly objective, even slightly critical, scientific research that would, however, ultimately support the imagery of a responsible, trustworthy broadcasting industry.

Ever the salesman, Lazarsfeld did not pass up this opportunity to suggest that comparable rewards might accrue to the other communication industries if they were to join the bureau's program. He was never that successful in attracting those additional potential clients. Nonetheless, Lazarsfeld had to feel that the ties with the broadcasting industry had been highly profitable. His program of research was being enthusiastically received in academic, industrial, and political circles; his colleagues and students were in great demand; the bureau had become a permanent fixture at Columbia; and it had emerged as a model for new structures in the academy generally.

For their part, Frank Stanton and his colleagues must have begun to feel that their cultivation of the social science community and their faith in the bureau had been handsomely repaid. The research tool had done much to help stem the tide of severe regulatory scrutiny, and with those waters now receding and with the public rushing to embrace television, the critique of past transgressions could be ignored, at least temporarily.

MASS COMMUNICATION RESEARCH AND GOVERNMENT

Returning to the third Lazarsfeld-Stanton volume (1944), one finds another focus, appearing in the section, "Radio in Wartime," that illuminates a second dimension of the legitimation of communication effects research. The reports here reveal the origins of a specific series of relationships among the academy, broadcasting, and government. Although the bureau emerged as a product of the mutual needs of university-based social research and the broadcasting industry, its work, like that of so many institutions in the academy, became closely allied with research and policy needs of the federal government. Though forged in the exigencies of wartime, this relationship became an important part of the later peacetime advance of communication research generally and violence effects research particularly.

The candid analysis of the role of the Radio Bureau of the Office of War Information (OWI) by Charles Siepmann reveals the terms of accommodation worked out between the government and the industry, and it indirectly suggests something about the related role of the communication research community.[13] The Executive Order establishing the OWI provided that among other things it

> formulate and carry out through the use of the press, radio, motion pictures, and other facilities, information programs designed to

> facilitate the development of an informed and intelligent understanding at home and abroad of the status and progress of the war effort and of the war policies, activities, and aims of the Government [Lazarsfeld and Stanton, 1944: 115].

Siepmann argues that, because of suspicions about governmental manipulation of the press during the previous war, the combined weights of press, film, and broadcasting industry opposition to governmental control, and the substantial technical and fiscal difficulties of direct takeover, "it was decided to pursue what we call the democratic way, to continue the peacetime management and operation of radio stations and to harness their services as closely and effectively as possible to Government without jeopardizing private enterprise or forfeiting the confidence of listeners" (Lazarsfeld and Stanton, 1944: 114). For this, the broadcasting and advertising industries cooperated in providing time for government programs and ads, in building government messages into normal dramatic programming, in providing industry leaders to serve on advisory councils, and in conforming to guidelines for censorship and news dissemination. Most such programs, advertisements, messages, and guidelines were produced by OWI.

While Siepmann does not discuss it directly, it is clear from other sources that the broadcast industry provided personnel for leadership in OWI and other governmental and military information activities of the war effort. For instance, the director of OWI was former CBS newsman Elmer Davis, and his associate director was Ed Klauber, who had been with CBS from its earliest days, serving as its first news director, as executive vice-president, and as William Paley's principal advisor (Metz, 1975: 37-47, 89). Paley himself served in the Psychological Warfare Division (PWD) on the Eisenhower staff (SHAEF) in London. Much of the research, propaganda, and dissemination work of this division was closely related to similar work in OWI, and many OWI personnel were regularly seconded to PWD posts (Office of War Information, 1945: 4).

RCA, of course, had been born of joint U.S. Navy and electrical manufacturing industry concerns for maintaining American control over the development of radio technology after World War I. Its first president as an independent corporation was Major General James G. Harbord, formerly chief of staff to General Pershing and a Marine brigade and division commander in World War I (Dreher, 1977: 61-62). RCA's emergence as the leading American electronics manufacturer was in large part stimulated by larger and regular government contracts. Such work placed it in close association with national security and military policy developments. When World War II broke out,

David Sarnoff, by then RCA's president, helped establish conditions for even closer cooperation with the government (Dreher, 1977: 148-157). Sarnoff himself served first as a Signal Corps consultant in Washington and then during the last year of the war as coordinator of military and press communications facilities under Eisenhower. A host of other broadcasting personnel served in a variety of wartime communications posts.

The broad informational responsibilities assigned OWI implied more than program production and dissemination. The office concluded that effective decision making required attention to matters of impact and effectiveness:

> We have advanced little in our knowledge of techniques; we have comparatively little evidence of success and failure — of what programs succeed and fail and why. Radio research, apart from the still crude and by no means infallible or accurate measurement of gross audiences for program, is still in its infancy. The psychology of radio is still largely an unwritten work. We count heads, but reckon little what registers *in* the head [Lazarsfeld and Stanton, 1944: 147-148].

Such concerns were shared by the military services and implied turning to social and behavioral science for organized programs of research. To help develop and administer such programs, those responsible for research in the War Department and OWI approached many of the social scientists who had become associated with communication research, men such as Stanton, Lazarsfeld, Cantril, Bryson, Gallup, Roper, Samuel Stouffer, George Stoddard, and Wilbur Schramm.

Stouffer, from the University of Chicago, was one of those academics with whom Lazarsfeld had established ties during his early years in this country. During the mid-1930s the Social Science Research Council had sponsored a series of monographs reviewing the research on the effects of the Depression. Stouffer was the series' director and, at the suggestion of Robert Lynd, he asked Lazarsfeld to prepare the review on the family. That association initiated a period of continuous consultation between the two, and Lazarsfeld eventually asked Stouffer to come to New York to help analyze the data and assemble the original (1940) bureau report, *Radio and the Printed Page* (Lazarsfeld, 1969: 329). Indeed, in the Foreword to that book Lazarsfeld acknowledges that Stouffer's work on it was so substantial that he ought to have been listed as coauthor (Lazarsfeld, 1940: viii).

Within a year of that particular collaboration, the United States had entered the war and Lazarsfeld explains something of the impact on communication research:

> Stouffer had become research director for the United States Army and used the Bureau and its personnel for a variety of services. The fees provided by these assignments were turned over to the Bureau and were an important financial help. (We had a similar arrangement with the Office of War Information.) Robert Merton worked for a short while with Stouffer in Washington but returned to New York and channeled his work through the Bureau. He has remained an associate director and has played a crucial role in its subsequent development. In our wartime work we concentrated on the testing of films and radio programs devised to maintain the morale of various sectors of the civilian and military populations. The main record of this effort is reported in the third volume of *The American Soldier,* which records, among a great many other things, the contribution to the war effort of the program analyzer, thinly disguised, on the advice of the editor of the volume, Carl Hovland, as the polygraph [Lazarsfeld, 1969: 331].[14]

The civilian and military leadership needed information on public attitudes and on ways of guiding opinions on such issues as price controls, rationing, war bonds, consumer needs versus war production priorities, workers' attitudes and habits, civilian morale, reactions to war news, and the government's handling of it. As well, OWI and the Army required evaluations of the effectiveness of their respective programs of information, education, and morale building.

Consequently, in addition to its support for the Army research supervised by Stouffer, Congress authorized a continuous, extensive research program in OWI. The Polling Division of the Bureau of Intelligence and the Survey Division of the Bureau of Special Services, both parts of OWI, collaborated with other governmental agencies and a number of academic and commercial polling firms to establish an elaborate series of surveys that were conducted throughout the war. "In addition to its own field staff, the Bureau of Intelligence regularly employs the interviewing facilities of the Denver University National Opinion Research Center. Much of the material presented and interpreted in this volume comes from this source (Office of War Information, 1942: 63).

The NORC was, of course, the same institution providing the National Association of Broadcasters and Lazarsfeld's bureau with the data for their reports on public attitudes toward radio. Lazarsfeld's consultancy with OWI seems to have involved him in a capacity analogous to his role with the NAB. While the NORC actually gathered the data, Lazarsfeld or others from the bureau appear to have worked closely with the OWI staff in designing the instruments and writing the analyses. Stanton, too, seems to have been involved, at least to the extent of monitoring the research reports as they appeared.[15]

In addition to noting the role of NORC, the OWI documents acknowledge receiving data and assistance from the Program Survey Division in the Department of Agriculture, the Princeton University Office of Public Opinion Research (directed by Cantril), the American Institute of Public Opinion (owned by Gallup), and Elmo Roper's firm. In short, the social science research community, particularly that aspect of it touching on communication issues, quickly came to play an important part in the government's wartime propaganda and information dissemination activities.

The consequences of this association for the content of communication research are fairly clear. As indicated above, one of the disturbing observations about the early communication research, particularly the campaign studies in the bureau, is how it starts by asking questions about the impact of mass communication in society, yet usually ends up sliding off into analyses of personal influence and the process of decision making in political and consumer choices. It is evident from the literature reviews in the received history that some of those major bureau efforts — Merton's study of the Kate Smith war bond drive, his "Patterns of Influence" paper, and Lazarsfeld's analyses with others in *The People's Choice* and *Personal Influence* — became "classic" studies in the postwar generation of mass communication curricula and anthologies, serving as pivotal documents in the shift to a limited effects model. Yet as indicated by their origins in, or at least their intimate associations with, the governmental and military research needs during the war, the questions for the early communication research efforts in government policymaking had to do with applied problems in influence and information flow, in the mechanics and enhancement of persuasive messages. Matters of societal and cultural impact were not the motivating concerns.

As we have seen, the broadcasting industry's cooperation with the government in the official programs of censorship and information dissemination substantially helped it fend off other governmental pressures for investigation, more severe regulation, and even possible, if only temporary, expropriation. For its cooperation with government the emerging communication research community was no less rewarded. Again the experience of the Bureau of Applied Social Research is instructive. Although Lazarsfeld had been carefully cultivating industry support and had garnered therein considerable financial assistance and related academic influence, there always existed the danger of becoming overly identified with industrial needs and motives. Thus its wartime service offered an important counterbalancing focus for the bureau, while also enhancing its image by demonstrating its role in matters of substantial public policy import. Its contracts with OWI and the Army helped ensure the bureau's solvency during a period when its financial status was still somewhat shaky. The combination of that support and the prestige associated with it can be seen as playing an important part in the decision by a special committee at Columbia to recommend in 1945 acceptance of the formal "status which the Bureau has today, 'a research unit of the Graduate Faculty of Political Science of Columbia University' " (Lazarsfeld, 1969: 333).

In this light the efficacy of including the Inkeles study in the bureau's 1948-1949 report is perhaps more readily apparent. It served both the industrial and government clients while further consolidating the legitimacy of the communication research enterprise. The report was prepared during the early, most inflammatory phase of the Cold War, and of all the reviews of foreign broadcasting systems that might have been presented in the volume only this one on the Soviet Union was included. In juxtaposition to a description of such a state- and party-controlled system, but without reference to any of the other, less thoroughly government-identified systems in Europe, any criticism of American media structures and content could be dismissed as relatively unimportant. Government officials deliberating the future conditions of control for television would be reminded of the traditional democratic values presumably embodied in the private American broadcasting structure. Further, in providing such a timely study the communication research community could itself be seen as responsible and patriotic, characteristics that at the time were increasingly important not only for continued federal funding, but also for continued general support in a nervous academy.

The role of the Army's program in establishing the Stouffer-Hovland line of inquiry is obvious. But the broader significance may lie in the set of personal and institutional relationships it fostered. Congress and the Army had decided to fund this and other work on the strenth of recommendations by Frederick H. Osborn, director of the Army's Information and Education Division (IED). Osborn's background combined all the ingredients for establishing successful accommodations among science, industry, and government. He had written two books on social science and he was a member of the Social Science Research Council. Yet he was also a businessman, a trustee of the Carnegie Corporation (foundation), and a Major General in the Army (Lyons, 1969: 105).

Osborn had served as chairman of a Joint Army and Navy Committee on Welfare and Recreation, set up in 1941 with a Carnegie grant, and that committee helped form the research branch in the Army's IED. It was that branch that ultimately had responsibility for the initial research in the *The American Soldier* project. After the war the project was continued with further support from Carnegie and under the guidance of a special committee of the Social Science Research Council. That committee was chaired by Osborn and had among its members Hovland and Stouffer.

Among the initial participants in the project during the IED period were Lazarsfeld, Stanton, Cantril, Merton, and Hovland, plus Irving Janis, and Nathan Maccoby. As we have already seen for some of these, all were to become leaders in the postwar effort to establish formal programs of communication studies in major American universities. Stouffer had already been involved in the bureau's first radio project. After the war he moved to Harvard, where he established the Laboratory in Social Relations. Maccoby eventually went to Stanford, where, after Wilbur Schramm's retirement, he became director of its Institute for Communications Research. Hovland and Janis continued at Yale the attitude change research begun in the *Soldier* series.

Schramm was one of the many academics drawn to wartime service in OWI. His graduate work had been in American civilization (M.A., Harvard; Ph.D., Iowa), and with experience as the cofounder and editor of a literary journal and as an accomplished short story writer, he was well grounded in the humanities (Chaffee, 1974). He had, however, undertaken a two-year postdoctoral course in communication theory, psychology, and sociology at Iowa, signaling a shift of attention from matters of symbolic creativity to scientific inquiries of processes and effects. Schramm went to OWI (1942-1943) with one of his Iowa social science mentors, George Stoddard, an educational psychologist who had been a participant in both the Payne Fund and the President's Research Committee studies (see Chapter 4). At OWI Schramm came even more directly into contact with the world of social science research and its application in communication. His services as educational director appear to have exposed him to the regular flow of NORC attitude and evaluation research, and one of his superiors, Lyman Bryson, who had already been associated with Lazarsfeld and the bureau, was also to become, like Schramm, an editor of one of the early communication anthologies.[16] Offered the directorship of the School of Journalism at Iowa, Schramm returned to Iowa City in 1943.

After the war Stoddard became president of the University of Illinois. The university had had a long and distinguished record of academic accomplishment and public service. It was the land grant institution in Illinois, and it had a reputation as the leader among the public universities in the state in a wide variety of fields. However, shortly after the war the general pressure throughout the country for expanded opportunities for higher education and the specific political pressures in Illinois for construction of new or expanded colleges and universities elsewhere began to challenge the sanctity of the senior university. To help improve the information dissemination capability of his administration, Stoddard lured Schramm from Iowa in 1947, made him his assistant and then helped him establish and made him director of a new unit in the university, the country's first Institute of Communications Research. Designed to provide social and behavioral science research support for studies in communication, the institute also gave Schramm an academic base from which to operate in helping Stoddard with his administrative problems. Schramm and Stoddard then worked out a plan for consolidation of all academic, professional, and administrative units in the university concerned with communication media. In 1950, the university's Board of Trustees approved their proposal for creation of a Division of Communications with Schramm as its Dean (Champaign-Urbana Courier, Feb. 16, 1950: 3). This post gave him administrative control over such professional/academic units as the journalism and communications departments, the library school and aspects of the extension program, and over such nonacademic activities as the university press, broadcasting and film services, and the information activities of the athletic and alumni associations.

Schramm's legacy in communication research is threefold. First, in creating the institute at Illinois, he adopted the Lazarsfeld model for developing a locus, supported largely by contract research, for application of social and behavioral science methods to practical communication problems and for facilitating formal graduate training in what is seen as the *science* of communication. In so doing he associated the establishment of that unit and that science with the administration of publicity and information control. In this case the first client was the host institution itself, but the pattern was similar to that of the service by Lazarsfeld's bureau to the industry and government. In time at Illinois, too, the government became a prime contractor for research conducted by the institute. The Air Force, the Army, the U.S. Public Health Service, the National Science Foundation, the Department of Defense, and even (though unwittingly on the part of the principal investigator) the Central Intelligence Agency supported research, and thereby the pedagogic role, of the institute.[17] Schramm was to create another such institute when he moved to Stanford in 1955, and since then like institutions under similar terms of purpose and support have been established at many American universities.

Second, Schramm began publication of that series of mass communication research anthologies noted above. Those collections were, of course, largely made up of reprints of the research papers published by Lazarsfeld's bureau. The first of Schramm's compendia was published by the University of Illinois Press while he was serving as its director. That anthology, its successors, and a number of other closely related texts have retained a firm grip on the introductory mass communication curricula throughout American higher education. Little noticed in the early enthusiastic reception of these lines of inquiry were the series of industrial and political accommodations reflected in them. Further, they benefited only marginally from the less positivistic, more critical, and interpretive traditions of communication research that had been generally withering in the American academy.

Third, and closely related to the second, Schramm effected a marriage of general learning theory models with those of the emerging information sciences. Associating the stimulus-response conceptualizations and methods of behavioristic psychology with the sender-receiver, feedback, and noise imagery of cybernetics and information theory, Schramm created a popular, easily recognized pictorial diagram of the earlier verbal models articulated by Lasswell and Lazarsfeld. Like the anthologies, and in spite of serious intellectual opposition rising out of other disciplines, this model has captured much academic and popular thinking about communication. It has done so by responding almost unconsciously to certain basic American idealogical and institutional conditions and committing communication research to a number of lines of inquiry that tend to reveal more about the powerful appeal of social science in communication than about the purported issues of study.

It is difficult to understate Schramm's role in the postwar development of communication research. But it is important as well to keep in mind that the combination of interests and talents represented in this one man was shared in various ways by many others discussed in this chapter. Moreover, there lay behind all of them a whole series of institutional interrelationships and intellectual values that infused the emerging field with its particular set of heuristic models and applied, pragmatic purposes. As we shall see, these purposes and the associated accommodations made among industry leaders, political figures, and communication scientists during the early years have had far-reaching impact on the effects research agenda and on public debate about the significance of television in American society. Yet the implications of the origins of the general communication research tradition and the pressures shaping the effects research enterprise have gone largely unacknowledged. The following three chapters will trace the further progress of these accommodations and their consequences as they manifested themselves in the debate over the effects of violence on television and the attempt to apply research to its resolution.

NOTES

1. Which is not to say that there is a clear distinction between engineering problems and social and cultural questions. Lawrence Lessings' biography of Edwin Armstrong reveals that there is not. Further, the Lessing account demonstrates the manner in which competitive commercial considerations have dominated policymaking in the development of new broadcast services (see Lessing, 1956).

2. FCC (1941), amended October 11, 1941, and upheld in National Broadcasting Co., Inc., et al. v. United States et al. (319 U.S. 190), May 10, 1943; and "Public Service Responsibility of Broadcast Licensees," March 7, 1946 (Kahn, 1973: 151).

3. Although this quote appears in Metz (1975: 62), one should note that it was used first by Mayer (1972: 92). In fact, virtually all of Metz's material on the program analyzer (1975: 61-62) appears to have been lifted, without attribution, from Mayer (1972: 90-92).

4. For more on the significance of such relationships, see Tunstall (1977: chap. 12). Although his focus is on the international impact of American effects research, Tunstall also emphasizes the professional interrelationships among those in industry, government, and the academy fostering the development of communication research.

5. One of these visits was to the University of Pittsburgh, where there was a Retail Research Institute that had been established by another individual associated with educational and communication effects research, W. W. Charters, who had earlier directed the Payne Fund studies of film violence and its impact on children (Lazarsfeld, 1969: 298).

6. Hadley Cantril letter to Lazarsfeld in 1937 (Lazarsfeld, 1969: 305).

7. This event, like many of the details of this history, is recalled differently by the several principals. Stanton sees the problem as resting in the failure of the then Princeton administration to appreciate Lazarsfeld and the importance of studying radio. Lazarsfeld himself suggests the importance of the New York connection, but notes policy differences with Cantril from the outset.

8. Several of the individual studies from these volumes are cited by name(s) of the author(s) in the text below. The volumes and the cited contents are:

- Lazarsfeld (1940).
- Lazarsfeld and Stanton (1941): T.W. Adorno, "The Radio Symphony: An Experiment in Theory"; Frederick J. Meine, "Radio and the Press among Young People"; Duncan MacDougald, Jr., "The Popular Music Industry."
- Lazarsfeld and Stanton (1944): Rudolf Arnheim, "The World of the Daytime Serial"; Herta Herzog, "What Do We Really Know about Daytime Serial

Listeners?" Tore Hollonquist and Edward A. Suchman, "Listening to the Listener: Experience with the Lazarsfeld-Stanton Program Analyzer"; Helen J. Kaufman, "The Appeal of Specific Daytime Serials"; Charles A. Siepmann, "American Radio in Wartime: An Interim Survey of the OWI's Radio Bureau"; Adolf Sturmthal and Alberta Curtis, "Program Analyzer Tests of Two Educational Films."

- Lazarsfeld and Stanton (1949): Bernard Berelson, "What 'Missing the Newspaper' Means"; Alex Inkeles, "Domestic Broadcasting in the U.S.S.R."; Babette Kass, "Overlapping Magazine Reading"; Robert K. Merton, "Patterns of Influence: A Study of Interpersonal Influence and of Communications Behavior in a Local Community"; Katherine M. Wolf and Marjorie Fisk, "The Children Talk About Comics."

9. Much of this material and a discussion of the personalities involved may be found in an appendix, "FCC Chronology and Leadership from 1934 to 1970," in Emery (1971: 455-499); see also note 2.

10. The codes: "Thirteen Points," first written in 1921, "Don'ts and Be Carefuls," in 1927, and "The Motion Picture Production Code," in 1930 (see Jowett, 1976: 157, 238-242); the NAB "Code of Ethics," first written in 1929 (see White, 1947: 70-71); the Hutchins report (Leigh, 1947), including as a staff study White (1947).

11. Durr was never actually chairman though he did have a major role in hiring Siepmann, and the use of the term "promulgate" implies far more about the commission's use of the Blue Book than was, in fact, the case.

12. Kendall also became Lazarsfeld's third wife. His first two had been, respectively, Marie Jahoda and Herta Herzog, both of whom were psychologists trained, like Lazarsfeld, in Vienna. Herzog was with the original Radio Research Office from 1938 to 1941, and with the bureau until 1943; Jahoda was with the bureau from 1948 to 1949. This information is drawn from vitae material in "300 Notable Emigres," an appendix in Fleming and Bailyn (1969: 675-718).

13. As noted above, Siepmann was simultaneously serving as a consultant to the FCC, where he was helping to prepare the Blue Book, the highly critical, but largely ineffectual, report on public service practices of broadcasting licensees.

14. *The American Soldier* series consists of four volumes collected under the heading, *Studies in Social Psychology in World War II,* edited by a special committee of the SSRC chaired by Frederick Osborn (1949). The third volume is *Experiments on Mass Communication,* edited by Carl I. Hovland, Arthur A. Lumsdaine, and Fred D. Sheffield.

15. Among the series of the Office of War Information Bureau of Intelligence (Report Nos. 3-14, 1941-1942) held in the library of the University of Illinois, the cover of one, No. 3, is stamped "January 26, 1942, File of Frank Stanton."

16. The OWI materials in the University of Illinois library suggest that Schramm, too, received copies of the OWI research reports. Copy No. 255 of OWI's *Report from the Nation* (1942) is signed for by Schramm, presumably during that period in which he was at OWI and long before the report was declassified.

17. Much of this information is drawn from the files of the Institute of Communications Research, University of Illinois.

Part II

THE HISTORY OF VIOLENCE EFFECTS RESEARCH

Chapter 4

THE EARLY EFFORTS AND THE POLITICAL PROCESS (1928-1964)

In part due to general First Amendment considerations and to the specific statutory provisions that have constrained the degree of governmental interference in broadcasting, Congress has generally been cautious in establishing any criteria, scientific or otherwise, that would permit it or its agencies much direct influence in broadcast programming. Nonetheless, over the years Congress has argued that the physical properties limiting access to use of the broadcast spectrum require governmental licensing and, as well, a certain degree of technical and content regulation. The courts have repeatedly sustained this argument.[1] Moreover, beyond establishing a regulatory mechanism, Congress has assumed for itself a right to investigate, regularly and in great depth, broadcast programming standards and performance.

Yet that willingness to investigate has been accompanied by a marked unwillingness to legislate. Since passage of the Communications Act of 1934, the various committees and subcommittees of Congress have held dozens of hearings into matters pertaining to the broadcasting portions of the 1934 Act, but out of those hearings there have emerged only a few, relatively minor changes in the Act. With the possible exception of the Public Broadcasting Act of 1967, virtually none of those amendments has effected significant changes in the fundamental terms of ownership, control, or policy in American broadcasting. In spite of major changes in the technology and the potential social uses of electronic communication, modern television remains organized, supported, and utilized primarily along the lines of a model already well established for commercial radio by 1927. Thus, Congress has succeeded in maintaining the appearance of frequent, close scrutiny of radio and television, while yet carefully avoiding any radical, or even substantial, changes in them.

Increasingly during the late 1960s and throughout the 1970s, pressures mounted for a review of the communications legislation. The rapid pace of change in electronic technology, the associated breakdown of distinctions among systems and forms of communication, the attendant industrial competition and realignments, the various industrial and reform attacks on the regulatory process, and the continuing general anxieties about the societal impact of the electronic media have all combined to encourage reassessments of federal policy toward broadcasting and telecommunications. The review effort has proceeded on a number of fronts inside and outside of government and in both the executive and legislative branches, leading to attempts during the 95th, 96th, and 97th Congresses to "rewrite" the Communications Act. To what extent such legislation may ever prove to be as comprehensive as some interests would have it remains a matter of considerable debate. What is less doubtful however is the observation derived from most initial analyses of this effort that the general pattern of political and economic constraints that have discouraged significant change in public policy for broadcasting are still at work (see, for instance, Haight, 1979; Rowland, 1982b).

Over the years science has played an important yet subtle, little understood, and often unconscious role in the process of political avoidance. This chapter and the next two attempt to outline how one form of the effects research tradition has been a party to that process. In presenting the history of congressional approaches to the issue of violence in television programming and its putative effects on children, we will see how, on the one hand, social science has been admitted to the legislative forum to press forward its world view and to improve its material well-being without also being asked to examine and explain its underlying conceptualizations of communication. On the other hand, the history demonstrates how politicians and industry interests have been able to use the trappings of scientific inquiry to avoid making changes in public communications policy.

BACKGROUND

As Gene Lyon's (1969) history suggests, throughout the early decades of the twentieth century the social sciences, particularly such studies as statistics, economics, and psychology, came to play increasingly prominent roles in a wide variety of federal activities. Moreover, this impact was felt throughout American society. Beginning long before the arrival of television, the patterns of logic and debate associated with the most quantifiable and empirical aspects of the social and behavioral sciences had become attached to many American social, cultural, political, and economic institutions. In the academy, in industry, in governmental administration, in politics, indeed, in the public consciousness at large, great faith came to be invested in the self-proclaimed reliability and validity of the several social sciences. So pervasive did this outlook become that eventually it emerged as a major factor in shaping the frames of reference for congressional inquiry into all manner of social and cultural problems.

The prospects for social science were particularly enhanced during and after World War II when the pursuit and support of science in all its forms advanced at an unprecedented rate. As we have already suggested, a variety of events prior to the war signaled the increasing role of the social and behavioral sciences in many aspects of public policymaking. During the war perhaps the clearest statement of the increasing significance of this relationship came when, with congressional blessing, the War Department, the Army, and the Social Science Research Council cooperated in *The American Soldier* series of studies in social psychology, portions of which dealt largely with issues of media effects (see Chapter 3; see also Osborn et al., 1949: Vol. 3).

It is significant, then, that the advent of television, seen as rapidly ubiquitous, immensely powerful, but otherwise difficult to explain, coincided with the postwar acceleration of science. Almost without hesitation a major element of social science research, already partially mapped out by Hovland's wartime experiments with film messages, came to orient itself around questions bearing on the impact of this promising, but troubling, new medium. As we have seen, the study of mass communication in the United States quickly became closely identified with the predominant social and behavioral research paradigms. It was, therefore, not surprising that the federal legislative process for reviewing and evaluating television also became increasingly the captive of these approaches to defining the issues bearing on the nature and significance of the medium.

Yet it was not as if the political process was innocently seduced. For, as much as social scientists became increasingly capable of dictating the terms of reference for congressional investigations of television programming, those legislators wishing to generate the appearance of undertaking major reassessments of public policy toward broadcasting found their efforts made easier by their ability to adopt the rhetoric and the caveats of social science. Granting social scientists the status and recognition implied by their testimony as expert witnesses before congressional committees investigating matters of great public concern, and holding out the promise of increased access to federal funds, politicians were in turn granted license to traffic in the theories and jargon of communication research. Disputes about methods and findings might regularly erupt, but such debates only lent further weight to the aura of serious political and scientific concern, and neither party felt it necessary to examine their motives or the consequences of their interaction.

Precursor: The Payne Fund Studies (1928-1933)

In a sense, the research directions to be taken, the scientific and empirical framework, and the rhetoric of findings and conclusions to be employed were all determined long before television made its appearance. The advent of motion pictures had already created substantial popular controversy about the effects of modern communications media. During the years immediately following World War I, a period in which American social, cultural, and economic affairs were marked by a series of rapid, often contradictory, changes, the modern American, liberal social sciences began to assert themselves and to take shape. Behavioral theory finally displaced introspective psychology, and a formal systemic American social psychology and sociology began to emerge, shifting attention away from the more characteristically European study of ideas, experience, and meaning in society and toward the more organizational American concern with laws, mechanisms, and models. Public opinion polling became an integral part of the political process, decisions within national consumer industries came to rest increasingly on marketing research methods, and in support of all these "sciences" ever more value came to be ascribed to experimental and statistical methods.

Within this environment of general sociocultural flux and specific changes in social and behavioral science, the questions of the social and psychological effects of film became a subject of increasing research interest. In 1928, at the peak of the postwar economic frenzy and just prior to the plunge into the Depression, this new research focus coalesced. The National Committee for the Study of Social Values in Motion Pictures (later the Motion Picture Research Council) secured $200,000 from the Payne Fund to create a special Committee on Educational Research to study the effects of film on children.

The committee consisted of eighteen well-known psychologists, sociologists, and educators, and it developed a program of research to be funded by Payne that by 1933 produced twelve studies and a general summary. Its work was necessary, according to its chairman, W. W. Charters, because "no one in this country up to the present time has known in any general and impersonal manner just what effect motion pictures have upon children. . . . [Therefore] it's obvious that a comprehensive study of the influence of motion pictures upon children and youth is appropriate" (1933: v). Heralding the arrival of an era in which social science research was beginning to be harnessed to the public dialogue about all manner of social and economic problems, the role of the Payne research was "to find the facts and publish them to stimulate discussion from which programs of action will eventually crystallize" (1933: 63).

And from the start there was little doubt that the "facts" could be found. As with the later television violence effects research, the Payne investigators bravely set out to answer questions bearing on content, attendance, perception, retention, and emotional and behavioral response. There is in the Payne monographs almost no uncertainty as to the efficacy of the science to be employed and the value of the results to be achieved.

The only partial exceptions are found in the studies by Blumer (1933) and by Blumer and Hauser (1933). Trained in the Chicago school of sociology, a student of and the successor to George Herbert Mead, Blumer did recognize part of the problem in applying social science to the study of motion picture effects:

> The customary methods of study used in social and psychological science have not seemed to be of much promise. In this investigation the writer has dispensed with sophisticated techniques. He has simply asked people to relate or write as carefully as possible their experience with motion pictures [Blumer, 1933: xi].

Blumer's approach here is a manifestation of the theory and method that he later came to term "symbolic interactionism." Indeed, in subsequent work Blumer became a strong critic of mass media effects research, arguing a quarter century later that the standard "variable analysis" approach "does not faithfully reflect the operations of mass media in the real world, that it gives rise to the setting of fictitious problems, and that it favors false generalizations" (Blumer 1969: 184).

Yet at the time of the Payne studies, Blumer's critical posture was apparently still emerging, and, although he offers a method unique in this research project, he does not reflect the validity of searching for evidence of media effects in conventional S-R, experimental terms. In complaining that much previous research on film effects was little more than opinion, he states that now there are studies "of a more scientific and penetrating character. These investigations [the Payne studies] seek to ascertain the influence of motion pictures under experimental and control situations" (Blumer, 1933: 2). And even his own more open-ended work assumes a direct media-stimulus to audience-response process, asking such leading questions as: "Have such pictures or scenes made you more receptive to love-making?" or, "Did you ever have the inclination or temptation to engage in crime as a result of the movies?" (1933: 203-207).

Overall, then, the studies were confident in their discovery of effects, e.g., "The evidence is massive and irrefutable." Yet in the end they also demonstrated the dilemma of uncertainty that, in fact, plagued interpretation of their findings and that of every subsequent round of effects research:

> The motion picture situation is very complicated. It is one among many influences which mold the experience of children. How powerful this is in relation to the influences of the ideals taught in the home, in the school, and in the church, by street life and companions or by community customs, these studies have not canvassed [Charters, 1933: 61].

The pattern of inconsistency among the results of May and Shuttleworth versus those of Stoddard, Thurstone, and others "complicates the question of total influence."

Published during the depth of the Depression, the Payne Fund studies appear to have had little public policy impact. In his social history of film, Garth Jowett (1976: 226-229) notes that these studies, and a number of popular accounts of them, created a bit of a public stir and that the motion picture industry itself was somewhat disturbed by the attacks they stimulated. But other than perhaps serving a catalytic function in promoting "stricter enforcement of self-regulation," the research had little clear-cut effect on public or film industry policy.

A review of congressional hearings on motion picture issues during the years immediately following publication of the studies also suggests that they played only a minor role in the political debate over film during the pre-World War II period. The research surfaced most explicitly during hearings in 1934 before the House Committee on Interstate and Foreign Commerce. These hearings were held to consider legislation that would have created a Federal Motion Picture Commission to inspect, classify, and license films. The bill would have made it unlawful to distribute any film that

> in the judgment of the Commission harmfully portrays the life, manners, or customs of this or any other nation or which holds up to ridicule or contempt or disparagement any race, nationality, or religion, or which fosters ill will among or toward the people of this or any other nation, or tends to debase or corrupt morals or to incite to crime or to disrespect for law or religion or which promotes or encourages war against the peace of the world, or which is harmful to the public or any part thereof in any respect [House, Comm. on Interstate and Foreign Commerce, 1934: 3].

Obviously of questionable constitutionality, this bill appears to have had little currency in Congress. The committee chairman, Sam Rayburn, seems to have been little interested in the bill, apparently holding the hearings only as a courtesy to his fellow Democratic congressman from Texas, Wright Patman. Rayburn permitted the hearing to consume only two hours of the committee's time, and he took almost no role in it himself, turning it over to Patman and his witnesses. Several of those witnesses supporting the bill were either religious or educational leaders and two of them were officers of the privately supported "Federal Motion Picture Council in America." Most of them cited the Payne Fund studies as demonstrating the deleterious social and moral impact of film. However, it is important to note that in these hearings, none of the researchers themselves testified, nor did any of the congressmen either refer to or raise questions about the research. The witnesses were allowed to introduce their scientific "evidence," but the citations were effectively ignored.

Also it appears that by the time of this hearing, and certainly by the time of hearings on motion picture legislation in both the House and Senate two years later, the issue of a federal film commission was rapidly losing whatever political popularity it might have had (Senate, Subcomm. of the Comm. on Interstate Commerce, 1936; House, Subcomm. of the Comm. on Interstate and Foreign Commerce, 1936). Instead, members of Congress were increasingly intent on issues of monopoly in the film industry. They were clearly much more comfortable with scrutiny of the film industry in the context of antitrust legislation and economic regulation. This approach had been proved constitutional in other fields, it had great popular appeal and, in fact, it tended not to be a serious economic threat to industries subject to it. Indeed, regulation in interstate commerce had often proved of considerable benefit to utility and transportation industries. In any case, by the time of the 1934 hearings, although largely devoted to the film commission proposal, Representative Patman had already introduced anti-restraint-of-trade legislation. By 1936 the concern with block booking and blind buying had displaced film censorship as the primary focus of congressional interest.

To a certain extent, the lack of impact of the Payne Fund investigation may be due to the remarkable disassociation of the studies from their temporal and political context. One searches in vain through the reports for any reflections of the economic agony and social disruption gripping the nation during the period of the Payne research. Indeed, a suggestion to analyze several important financial, legal, economic and administrative aspects of the nature and impact of motion pictures as an industry was rejected as being inappropriate for "our group of investigators [who] were psychologists, sociologists and educators" (Charters, 1933: 1-2). No explanation is given as to why the investigators could be only these. Additionally, the studies take no cognizance of two other research efforts — substantial studies of contemporary American social, cultural, and economic life that, if considered, would have offered a rich backdrop against which to interpret the attitudes and behavior elicited by the Payne investigations.

First there was the extensive, unprecedented collection of studies conducted under the direction of the President's Research Committee on Social Trends (1933). As noted in Chapter 2, the committee was appointed by President Hoover in 1929, the research under its auspices spanned nearly the entirety of the Hoover administration, and it ran almost coextensively with the Payne Fund effort.

While the near-simultaneous publication of the Payne and Social Trends reports may explain something of the lack of cross-reference between the two, it is curious that the larger project, involving so many social scientists and institutions and dealing with such a range of issues, did not have any impact on the work of the Payne group. In part the explanation may lie in the observation that the Payne research represented a lingering element of certain extremes in the early twentieth-century reform movement that had already either become discredited in the experiences of World War I and Prohibition or that, as Hofstadter (1954) argues, were to become coopted by New Deal legislative and regulatory developments. Jowett points to certain indirect evidence to suggest that from the start, William Short, the executive director of the Motion Picture Research Council, had fully intended to use the Payne-sponsored efforts "to form the bulwark of an attack upon the industry that would result in some form of organized control" (Jowett, 1976: 231, fn. 48). He argues that both the MPRC and the study director, Dr. Charters, cooperated fully in the publication of a popularized version of the results before the Payne studies were themselves released. This report, prepared by a journalist, Henry James Forman, "was a blatant attack on the industry, and its thrust was in the direction of outside control of the motion picture industry" (Jowett, 1976: 225). Many of the new disciplines providing for the scholarly study of society had themselves grown out of the Progressive movement, but in the process their leaders had found that if these fields were to achieve legitimacy as sciences in the academy they were first going to have to disassociate themselves a bit more clearly from the most directly applied and reformist aspects of their origins. Many of those serving on or working closely with the President's Research Committee were key figures in that legitimization effort, and they may therefore have been unwilling to deal with or consider the work of a group suspected of having a prior, not entirely scientific purpose.

For whatever reasons, the Payne group and the President's Committee seem to have had little relationship with one another. Only two of the eighteen Payne investigators (Stoddard of Iowa and Freeman of the University of Chicago) appear to have been involved in any of the social trends projects, and in the committee report the chapter on communications barely takes notice of motion pictures (Wiley and Rice, 1933: 167-218). Of its 51 pages, 24 deal with transportation and another 12 with postal and telecommunications matters. Altogether the mass media are dismissed in only 12 pages, and, of those, motion pictures occupy only 3. Apparently unaware of the Payne work, the authors of the communications chapter and its subsection on film provide little more than descriptive data about the industry and attendance, concluding that "the need for thoroughgoing study of the social effects of the motion picture seems clear" (Wiley and Rice, 1933: 210).

The other research effort curiously unacknowledged by the Payne studies was the first *Middletown* book (1929), by Robert and Helen Lynd, reporting on their extensive study of life in a midwestern city (Muncie, Indiana). As described by Clark Wissler, the study is "a pioneer attempt to deal with a sample American community after the manner of social anthropology" (Lynd and Lynd, 1929: vi). It was an instantaneous popular success and was widely acclaimed by leading social scientists (Madge, 1962: 128).

Among the many other influences they examine, the Lynds deal persuasively with the changing experience of reading and the impact of radio and motion pictures:

> It seems not unlikely that, while furnishing a new means of diversified enjoyment, [radio] will at the same time operate, with national advertising, syndicated newspapers, and other means of large-scale diffusion, as yet another means of standardizing many of Middletown's habits. Indeed, at no point is one brought up more sharply against the impossibility of studying Middletown as a self-contained, self-starting community than when one watches these space-binding leisure-time inventions imported from without — automobile, motion picture and radio — reshaping the city [1929: 271].

In summarizing their observation about film the Lynds write, "Like the automobile, the motion picture is more to Middletown than simply a new way of doing an old thing; it has added new dimensions to the city's leisure" (1929: 263). The Lynds perceived and recorded much about the intrusive, controversy-creating nature of the medium's effect on the social fabric. In view of the book's popularity and the Lynd's concern with the social power of motion pictures, it is startling that the Payne studies make no reference to this research, at least on the level of analysis of the medium's effects. Given the rich, detailed picture of sociocultural issues painted by the Lynds, material that went far beyond questions of communication, it is all the more significant that the Payne research not only eschewed mention of this work, but also steered carefully clear of adopting that part of its methodology that was clearly influenced by the ethnographic approaches of cultural anthropology. While the Lynds, in fact, integrated a variety of formal methodologies into their work, the flavor of their report is often impressionistic and openly subjective. Perhaps the Payne group's heavy emphasis on new, "objective" methodologies could not tolerate association with such presumably less scientific approaches.[2]

Several factors, then, seem to have contributed much to the inability of the Payne studies to achieve more substantial impact. There was that underlying hesitancy detectable in the studies themselves and engendered by the conflict between the findings of laboratory and field research. There was the association of the research with a certain political heritage from which many social science leaders had long been trying to extricate themselves. And there was the unwillingness of the MPRC to examine the economics and structures of film and the broad sociocultural context of the medium's significance in a time of extreme national crisis. Furthermore, since the research emerged at a time when the public was experiencing the full impact of the immediate material problems posed by that crisis, the somewhat fuzzy and highly moral concerns reflected in the Payne reports must have been widely seen as relatively superfluous.

Further, like the print media, film was not subject to direct governmental regulation. Though the structures of the industry could become the subject of congressional or federal agency antitrust investigation (as they had from the early 1900s on), there was far less legal legitimacy for political attention to film content than was to be the case for television. In 1934 Congress was hardly enthusiastic about the film commission legislation, evidencing little willingness to establish an agency and a set of federal legal standards that would raise serious censorship questions. It much preferred to dabble in the realm of antitrust investigation, and in light of improving economic conditions, it could afford to do so. In the end, though the film industry had seen its attendance levels and revenues drop off dramatically during the early 1930s, by mid-decade those figures were reapproaching their pre-1929 levels (U.S. Census statistics reported in Jowett, 1976: 475; DeFleur and Ball-Rokeach, 1975: 59). If there was any temporary inhibiting impact on the success of the film industry, it was clearly due to the Depression, and not to the fledgling efforts of communication effects research.

Finally, there was simply the failure of social science research to have yet achieved status as a primary vehicle of public policy imagination among federal legislators. While, as is suggested in Chapter 2, social science was gaining currency in a number of public and private administrative capacities, it had not yet become central and indispensible in political debate. It may have begun to offer practical advantages in dealing with problems in executive branch departments of the federal government and in private corporate enterprise at large, but its efficacy in the process of legislation and the management of political debate had not yet been recognized. That discovery is in part the story of the rise of communication effects research in the context of congressional inquiry about violence on television.

THE CONGRESSIONAL INQUIRIES (1952-1964)

The Harris Subcommittee (1952)

Television was not immediately haled before the court of science. Nonetheless, Congress wasted little time in subjecting it to scrutiny. In May 1952, barely a month after the FCC had issued its Sixth Report and Order (lifting the "freeze" on television station construction that had been in effect since 1948), the House of Representatives passed a resolution authorizing its Federal Communications Commission Subcommittee:

> (1) To conduct a full and complete investigation and study to determine the extent to which radio and television programs currently available to the people of the United States contain immoral and otherwise offensive matter, or place improper emphasis on crime, violence and corruption; and
> (2) On the basis of such investigation and study, to make such recommendations (including recommendations for legislative action to eliminate offensive and undesirable radio and television programs and to promote higher radio and television standards) as it deems advisable [House Interstate and Foreign Commerce Comm., FCC Subcomm., 1952: 1].

During the course of intermittent hearings that summer and fall, the subcommittee, under chairman Oren Harris (D-Ark.), took testimony from a variety of broadcast critics and spokesmen. Unlike later hearings, when the issue of specific effects and the question of research evidence would become increasingly important and, finally, central factors, these hearings dealt with research only briefly. As an example of the periphery position of research, one network official made a passing reference to the Payne studies, emphasizing their inconclusiveness. He also argued that television was still so new and in such a rapid state of change that there had not yet been time for "an overall definitive sociological survey."[3] That position was not seriously challenged by the subcommittee.

Clearly the interest of the subcommittee, like that of other elements of the Congress at the time, lay elsewhere. The old concern about immorality in film was carried forward, complete with its temperance linkages. But that concern was now animated and even being replaced by another, more pervasive fear:

> You have complained in Congress about what Communists have been doing about carefully infiltrating all media of public communication. . . . They could very, very, easily . . . break down everything in American life we hold sacred, and certainly if they break down the respect for home and the high standard for womanhood, they will have succeeded.[4]

But, in spite of this climate of fear, the hearings were on the whole remarkably congenial. The subcommittee members and staff handled the network representatives most gingerly, commending them for their claims of concern and their assurances of adequate self-regulation. There was none of the sharper tone that was to mark later hearings.

In part it would appear that many members of Congress had important reasons of self-interest for avoiding a vigorous investigation of broadcast practices. Never subject to divestiture as a condition of office, members of Congress had found investment in broadcast properties to be profitable and politically useful undertakings. With the rise of television the attraction was even greater. Subsequent investigation revealed that at just about the time that Chairman Harris was to begin leading his subcommittee's study, he had become the owner of 25 percent of a Little Rock television station. Apparently he paid little or nothing for his share, but almost immediately the station did receive FCC approval for a substantial increase in power — a request that the commission had previously denied.[5]

Another part of the subcommittee's reticence can perhaps be explained more charitably by the uncertainties about the proper congressional role that permeated this first legislative investigation of television. There was much explicit concern about the essential dilemma presented by governmental regulation of broadcasting. In the words of one witness, the subcommittee endeavored "to escape the

Scylla of dictatorial censorship on the one hand and the Charybdis of unbridled license on the other hand."[6]

The Hendrickson-Kefauver Subcommittee (1954-1955)

By 1954 it was not clear whether Congress wished to avoid such perils entirely. But it was more certain that Congress was perfectly willing to embark on voyages that would confront them. And by now it had fully determined that for help in charting its course it would take on science as a navigator.

The scene of the inquiry also changed. The House had initiated the 1952 investigation, but by 1954, the Senate assumed primary responsibility for scrutiny of television content. Although that responsibility would shift among different committees, Senate dominance was to remain, at least through the mid-1970s. But, while the later investigations would become the prerogative of the commerce committee's Subcommittee on Communications, the initial Senate action was taken by the judicary committee. The aegis for examination of television's presumably deleterious effects was the decade-long Senate study of juvenile delinquency. In an enabling resolution in 1954, the Senate directed that special attention "be given to . . . determining the extent and character of juvenile delinquency in the United States and its causes and contributing factors"[7]

Creating a special Subcommittee to Investigate Juvenile Delinquency, the judiciary committee authorized it, among many more things, to study the relationship of comic books, motion pictures, and television to this perceived problem. As part of its work, the subcommittee held a series of hearings on the role of these several media. The initial hearings on television were held in June and October 1954 under the chairmanship of Senator Robert C. Hendrickson (R-N.J.). These hearings were devoted largely to presentations by staff investigators and industry professionals and executives, their primary purpose apparently being to state the political concerns about television and to allow the industry to describe its patterns of operations and its view about the question of effects.

The initial industry representative, Ralph Hardy, vice-president for government relations of the National Association of Radio and Television Broadcasters (NARTB, later NAB), presented what was to become the classic industry gambit. Clearly associating the conditions of the new television enterprise with those of radio thirty years before, he notes that although in its early days "there were loud and insistent voices raised to lay at radio's doorstep many of the social ills and malfunctions of the day," there have been "no research findings to establish any reliable relationship between the various manifestations of juvenile delinquency and radio broadcasting." As for television, the industry continues to resist all charges of undesirable effects, arguing that "expert and informed opinion now tends to be extremely cautious and reserved in assigning any clearly definable relationship between television fare and influences tending to accelerate the incidence of juvenile delinquency" (Senate, Judiciary Comm., Juvenile Delinquency Subcomm., 1954: 42-43). Not to appear unreasonable and socially irresponsible, Hardy is nonetheless careful to reiterate the industry's voluntary adherence to self-enforcement standards, and he explains the content and operations of the Television Code, first adopted in 1952 (a similar radio code had been in effect since 1929; see White, 1947: 70-71).

While these hearings do not rely on social science findings to the extent of later investigations, the intention to turn to science is clearly indicated. The executive director of the subcommittee staff, Richard Clendenen, notes that this investigation had begun by reviewing "what survey studies, research, has revealed in relation to this question, in an effort to really determine whether or not there would seem to be some kind of a sound basis for the concern which has been expressed so widely by parents in this country." Having reviewed "a very large number of surveys and studies," he summarizes what they say in three forms: the "extent to which youngsters are exposed to television programs . . . the content of the programs to which these youngsters were exposed . . . [and] the effects of such exposure" (1954: 2-3).

In a pattern to be picked up and elaborated by social scientist witnesses in later hearings, Clendenen offers baseline data on the amount of juvenile viewing and the incidence of violent content. His summary of the effects reveals the controversy among proponents of the catharsis, fantasy-release, and direct detrimental effects theories, and he extablishes the subcommittee's interest in seeing substantial effects research efforts undertaken. Throughout the hearings Senator Hendrickson and his staff regularly turned their duscussions with witnesses toward the need for credible long-term effects research. The effort to encourage research activity culminated during the presentation by the final witness, NARTB president Harold Fellows. In reviewing the association's plans for attending to the question of the relationship between television and juvenile delinquency, Fellows indicated that in an effort to prepare the groundwork for a large-scale, long-range research effort the NARTB would be undertaking "a pilot study of attitudes toward television" (1954: 261).

In opening the second round of hearings on the issue of television programs, Senator Kefauver interpreted part of the subcommittee's mandate as being one of determining "what the long-range effects of television may be on the Nation's youth." To him this meant taking testimony from "the social scientists who have done much work in the field of television upon the effects of its audiences" (1955b: 1). Thus the commitment to entertain and even to promote the development of scientific evidence was firmly made:

> We are objectively going into these hearings to look into the research projects that have been done to determine how much we can generalize from them, determine why there has been very little done in this area, and also to find out how we on the subcommittee can aid in bringing about planning for research and possibly lay out the framework of necessary funds and personnel [1955b: 3].

As with the initial round, these hearings immediately established the primary structure of the debate, and its inconsistencies. Descriptive data about the extraordinary amount of time children seemed to be investing in television viewing were quickly offered and accepted. But uncertainties about the accuracy of competing effects theories surfaced just as quickly, and the hearings, though eliciting explanations of such notions as chatharsis, arousal, aggression, learning, and differential functions, soon revealed the inability of the scientists to be definitive in their conclusions. Behavioral psychologists found themselves resisting arguments of direct causality, noting that heavy viewing and antisocial behavior were only correlated.[8]

Some researchers were explicit in their warnings about the limitations involved in using social science as the basis for policymaking in broadcasting. As Paul Lazarsfeld put it "one should not look to research as a kind of panacea which will now solve all your problems." He gave two reasons:

> First, in this whole matter of the mass media, there are questions of convictions and taste which can never be settled by research.
>
> Secondly, there is a great danger that research is being used as an alibi. Let us just wait until we have enough research and then we will do something [1955b: 91-92].

There was clear evidence to support the latter assertation. Industry spokesmen, taking a stand that was to sustain them for at least three more decades, fell back on the scientists' own doubts. Harold Fellows, in another appearance before the subcommittee, citing a trade journal account of interviews with members of the American Psychiatric Association, argued that "there is no scientific body of facts in existence that could in any way prove that television is one of the causes of juvenile delinquency" (1955b: 48).

The subcommitte report acknowledged that it did not have the "conclusive research" evidence it sought. Yet it did seem to lean toward the argument, disputed though it obviously was, that certain effects were evident or probable: that "violence materials are anxiety and tension producing," that acts of crime and violence may "teach techniques of crime," lead the "hostile child . . . to imitate these acts in expression of his aggression," and "blunt and callous sensitivity to . . . human suffering and distress" (1955c: 33-34).

In the end, then, the subcommittee, unable to demonstrate the proof it needed, inverted the argument:

> It [the subcommittee] has been unable to gather proof of a direct causal relationship between the viewing of acts of crime and violence and the actual performing of criminal deeds. It has not, however, found irrefutable evidence that young people may not be negatively influenced in their present-day behavior by the saturated exposure they now receive to pictures and drama based on an underlying theme of lawlessness and crime which depict human violence [1955c: 50].

But this argument was sufficient to make only those kinds of recommendations that fell far short of substantial change in legislative policy toward broadcasting. The industry was urged to modify its program code and otherwise recognize its obligations. Citizens were urged to create and maintain "listening councils," and the FCC was called upon to improve its fact finding about programming content and to take such results into account in license renewals (1955c: 50-51). But these recommendations were never backed by any firm proposals for legislation.

In effect, a standoff was achieved between the politicians and the broadcasters. Congress managed to demonstrate its putative concern, but on the basis of the evidence it avoided taking substantial action. The industry allowed its knuckles to be rapped, but otherwise suffered no significant, formal strictures nor any changes in the legal and regulatory conditions of its operation.

The prospects for some actors did change, however. Throughout these hearings and in the subsequent report there were regular reiterations of the difficulties presumably posed by the lack of adequate research. Lazarsfeld, for instance, noted the problem of intermittent foundation funding, and he used an extraordinary analogy with applied physics research to suggest that central planning was necessary:

> I do not want to make an invidious comparison, but we certainly would not have an atomic bomb today if the development had been merely left to Ph. D. dissertations. I don't think we exactly need a Los Alamos Laboratory to study the effects of television, but we need, if it is an urgent social problem, then some central planning

and central organization, and some pressure; some priority has to be put on it [1955b: 88].

He went on to urge the subcommittee to press the National Science Foundation to extend its support to the nonphysical sciences and to encourage substantially funded, centrally coordinated, long-range research efforts in the area of television effects (1955b: 92). The subcommittee staff was apparently heavily influenced by Lazarsfeld's testimony, and it adopted these recommendations as part of its interim report (1955c: 53-57).

In the end, then, there were no substantive changes effected in the respective roles and prerogatives of the government or the television industry, but the cause of social and behavioral research, cast here in the form of the need for better mass communication effects findings, was considerably advanced. There was virtually no attention given to the apparent contradiction between this call for more and better organized research and the earlier assertion, particularly by Lazarsfeld himself, that there are here important "questions of convictions and taste which can never be settled by research."

The Dodd Subcommittee (1961-1964)

By the turn of the decade the Senate had renewed its authorization for the Committee on the Judiciary to continue its study of the causes and extent of juvenile delinquency.[9] The Subcommittee to Investigate Juvenile Delinquency remained the agent of this examination, though now it was under the chairmanship of Thomas Dodd (D-Conn.).

As before, the terms of this renewed investigation implied considerable concern about the mass media, particularly television. By the early 1960s television had revealed itself as a pervasive and controversial social force. On the one hand, by the end of fiscal year 1961, fully 90 percent of American households had one or more television sets, and on the average those sets were in use some five to six hours a day. Commercial television revenues had reached $1.3 billion a year by 1960, and they were growing at a rate of about 10.4 percent annually between 1958 and 1960.[10]

On the other hand, problems and criticism were also mounting. For all its touted promise as an educational and information medium, television was increasingly dominated by commercial entertainment. News and public affairs programming amounted to only a small percentage of the commercial network schedule, and the country's noncommercial service remained an underfinanced collection of stations that, while growing at a rate of nine or ten a year, numbered only just over fifty in 1960. There was as yet no federal policy of support for these stations, which were licensed to local school systems, state school boards, institutions of higher learning, and nonprofit community groups, and whose funding, while diverse, remained small and always uncertain. Due to the differing goals reflected in various licensee types, stations remained severely torn about the range and emphasis of programming appropriate for themselves especially through their national service (NET), which in any case was then providing only five hours or less of programming a week (and that only through a postal exchange system; see Blakely, 1979: 115-119, 123-124).

As a result of increasing competition, the content of commercial network programming had begun to change, but not in ways that satisfied the critics. In searching for popular new vehicles during the late 1950s, the networks seized on the action/adventure concept, an adaptation of certain film and network radio formats. As Barnouw (1975: 213) relates, the production efforts of the Hollywood film studios soon submerged the network schedules in "waves of action films," sweeping over American television with surges of crime-mystery, international-intrigue, and, above all, western formats. These series featured quick action and simple solutions. "Their business was victory over evil people," and as such they lent themselves to formula violence.

Barnouw catches the coincidence of then current public anxieties and the particularly acute sensitivity of television's response.

> The American people, exasperated with their multiplying, unsolved problems, were looking for scapegoats, and . . . telefilms provided these in quantity.
>
> Telefilms rarely invited the viewer to look for problems within himself. Problems came from the evil of other people, and were solved — the telefilms seemed to imply — by confining or killing them.

The violent final scene became a stock feature of television drama: "There seemed to be an unspoken premise that evil men must always in the end, be forcefully subdued by a hero; that the normal processes of justice were inadequate, needing supplementary individual heroism." By 1960 the series considered "probably the most violent show on television," *The Untouchables,* was also the most highly rated, and success in television had become closely associated with the portrayal of violent conflict and solutions (Barnouw, 1975: 214, 215, 260-261).

Meanwhile, between 1957 and 1960, investigations by the New York District Attorney and Congress had confirmed charges of organized cheating in the conduct of the highly popular commercial network quiz programs. Also the result of intense audience competition, these program practices in turn led to questions about the methods, accuracy, and use of the commercial audience measurement ("ratings") process:

> A Federal Trade Commission investigation in 1962 resulted in Cease and Desist Orders alleging misrepresentation by three major rating companies. A full-dress Congressional investigation in 1963-1964 revealed not only carelessness and ineptitude by research companies, but even extensive doctoring of data and outright deception [Head, 1972: 306].

Thus, the renewed Senate investigation of television effects on youth proceeded simultaneously with two separate House Committee on Interstate and Foreign Commerce inquiries into the quiz show and ratings scandals, and they can be seen as part of a growing general climate of criticism of television. Yet, where a certain aspect of that criticism had to do with the methods and abuse of marketing research as it was applied to program decision making, the critiques never penetrated to the broader, underlying questions about the implications of adopting the emerging science of communication effects in evaluating the medium. Not surprisingly, then, there proceeded without check at the political level a growing interest in applying social and behavioral science methods to the study of television's role and impact.

Under Senator Dodd, the subcommittee came to justify its efforts largely on scientific grounds, and in the process it fully legitimized the role of science in public communications policymaking. In outlining the reasons for its continuing inquiry the subcommittee closely linked the "mounting concern . . . [about] crime, brutality, violence and suggestive sex portrayed on many television programs" with "the development of new findings by qualified media research scholars which supported the thesis that televised crime and violence had adverse effects on the attitude and behavior of many young viewers" (1964: 2). There was little hesitancy in concluding that, as in other spheres of social life, if there existed a problem of public concern, scientific evidence could by adduced to analyze and guide solutions to it. Some of the subcommittee questions were similar to the original Payne concerns. There was an interest in the incidence of crime and violence in television content and uncertainty about the nature and adequacy of the existing research findings about effects. Yet there was also an explicit interest in matters of programming structure and policymaking and an implicit goal of bringing research findings to the attention of key forces in the broadcast industry (Senate, Judiciary Comm., Juvenile Delinquency Subcomm., 1961-1962: 1639-1640).

To pursue its questions the subcommittee undertook a three-part investigation. It held formal, public hearings in 1961 and 1962, during 1961 and 1964 its staff continued the television monitoring project begun in 1954, and it arranged to have reviewed the available effects research literature. However, for all the public concern with scientific evidence, the monitoring and research review activities were little documented. With virtually no explanation of its research design or methodology, the subcommittee staff reported that the number of programs containing crime or violence amounted to 50.6 percent of all prime time programming in 1961, compared with 16.16 percent in 1954. Apart from data from four cities, all the staff could report for 1964 was that there were "comparable figures" (to the 1961 data; Senate, Judiciary Comm., Juvenile Delinquency Subcomm., 1964: 7-10).

The research review appears not to have been published in any comprehensive form. This may have been part of a general weakening of resolve on the part of subcommittee chairman Dodd. As Erik Barnouw reveals, "No report on his violence probe was ever published. An interim report was mimeographed in a watered-down version for subcommittee members, but never released to the public (1975: 306). The issue of a possible "sell out" ought not to be ignored (see below), but for the moment it is useful to attend to the research conceptualizations wrapped up in that interim report. It contains a series of seven concrete conclusions about the power of televised violence to reinforce, teach and stimulate aggressive attitudes and behavior. These "findings" are summarized in a general statement:

> The prevailing view among qualified independent researchers concerned with the mass media and with the juvenile delinquency problem in particular is acceptance of the thesis that excessive televised crime, violence, and brutality has an adverse effect upon many child viewers. Generally speaking, the research people are somewhat more cautious than are the professionals who must cope with the delinquency problem directly, but there is growing agreement that television represents a contributing factor in inciting delinquent behavior in many cases [Senate, Judiciary Comm., Juvenile Deliquency Subcomm., 1964: 16].

One sees here the conflict between the wish to affirm the direct causality between medium content and antisocial behavior and the grudging awareness that the issue cannot be so easily characterized. The politicians need a simple explanation, yet, while many of the scientists might wish to oblige, for moral and ideological reasons of their own, the research will not fully cooperate. Neither the politicians nor the scientists are dealing with the underlying questions about the implications of their quest. The necessary intellectual self-awareness and independence is still lacking. Instead, the issue is beginning to emerge in the political forum solely in terms of a simple theoretical debate about competing effects models.

Although the mid- and late 1950s had witnessed the popularization of the multistep, opinion leader concepts, as represented in the several campaign and diffusion studies, the discomfort of many theorists with the S-R models underlying even these more complex configurations had led them in search of more optimistic views of human communication behavior and media impact. The result had been the functionalist attention to viewer needs and motivation and to the importance of demographic environments and intervening variables, reflected in Klapper's 1960 summary. The shifting focus manifested itself in part in the Dodd subcommittee hearings and its interim report. The subcommittee's staff research consultant, Dr. Ralph Garry, argues that

> for some time we had the mistaken notion that children were the passive recipients of the culture, not only as far as television is concerned, but also in other aspects of their development. We have learned that children are active participants in the growth process, and this point has been forcefully made by Dr. Schramm when he suggests that we have to look at how children use television [Senate, Judiciary Comm., Juvenile Delinquency Subcomm., 1961-1962: 1668].

This elementary lesson in social psychology and the reference to Schramm was stimulated in part by the latter's publication (1961), with Lyle and Parker, of their study of children and television. Yet even here there was evidence of the inconsistency of the revisionist (uses and gratifications) model, with its persistent underlying assumption of direct causality. In his own testimony before the subcommittee Schramm notes that "it would be unfair and unscientific to think of television as the only cause, as a sole and sufficient case for delinquency." Yet he went on to argue that "children will learn a great deal from television . . . [and] the fact of so much violence on television makes it, at least statistically, more probable that there be some violence, violent behavior apart from television" (1961-1962: 1770).

The subcommittee staff could thus have it both ways. It could call on the behavioral models of clinical and experimental psychology, e.g., the Berkowitz testimony that "in the absence of any strong inhibition against aggression, people who have recently been angered and have then seen filmed aggression will be more likely to act aggressively than people who have not had those experiences" (Senate, Judiciary Comm., Juvenile Delinquency Subcomm., 1964: 61).

Ignoring the extraordinarily rare, dual-factor circumstances required by such a theory (absence of inhibition and incidence of prior arousal), the subcommittee report offered the conclusion that "on the basis of expert testimony and impressive research evidence . . . a relationship has been conclusively established between televised crime and violence and antisocial attitudes and behavior among juvenile viewers." Immediately, however, it remembers the caveats in both the behavioral and functional models and states that "the subcommittee does not believe that television is either the sole or most significant cause of the juvenile delinquency" (1964: 36).

Again the networks come in for strongly worded criticism: "The subcommittee is satisfied that primary responsibility for the prevailing policy, which features excessive crime and violence, rests with the three major networks." Quoting from a House Committee on Commerce report, the Senate subcommittee observes that "it is entirely clear that the notion that actual responsibility for network programming is exercised at the station level is unreal" (1964: 37-38).

The situation of redelegated authority through advertisers, independent producers, and others "may involve a diffusion of control which verges on irresponsibility." Furthermore "the dollar is not the only end of broadcasting . . . [and] no broadcaster has the legal right to make that dollar at the expense of good taste and best interest of the community" (1964: 38-39).

Nonetheless, the subcommittee carefully restrained its analysis of the relationship between the medium's economic foundation and programming content, stopping far short of any conclusions that might imply the need for substantive changes in commercial broadcasting structure and systems of control. The subcommittee deferred to the free enterprise purpose of broadcasting, arguing first that networks and broadcasters "do have their economic problems, their internal stress, and their need to realize a profit on their investment" (1964: 39). In its final comment the subcommittee fell back on the constitutional guarantees of freedom of speech and press:

> We are not introducing legislation at this time. This is an interim report and our investigation is continuing. Further, it is our earnest hope that the broadcasting industry will heed our recommendations and will immediately take realistic steps to improve its programming and to substantially reduce the violence and crime which today is fed the Nation's children as an all-too-steady diet. Effective self-policing is the desirable approach to this problem which poses so clear a threat both to our present and our future [1964: 45].

In effect this interim report was the subcommittee's final statement on television, violence, and children. For although the subcommittee appears to have continued in existence until at least 1971, and although network programming practices seem not to have changed substantially during the years immediately after 1964, the subcommittee's investigations into juvenile delinquency followed other channels.

There may be several reasons why the subcommittee eventually did nothing that would have brought it any closer to recommending legislation that would have affected broadcasting. For one thing, despite the protracted sparring with the networks and broadcasters during the first decade of the juvenile delinquency subcommittee's investigation, it was never clear that there was any firm commitment to allowing the investigation to proceed to the point where amendments of the Communications Act would appear to be in order. In part there was a legitimate concern about the real constitutional constraints governing the permissible extent of congressional definition of broadcasting policy, structure, and content. However, there was as well a carefully weighed political judgment that, although perhaps unpalatable in certain respects, commercial broadcasting performance was on the whole not an issue of pervasive public concern, or at least not of sufficient concern to demand, and support, wholesale and wide-ranging legislative reform. Congress seems to have been content to use its investigatory and hearings powers as a threat. What public concern was manifest seemed assuaged by this legislative version of what has come to be known as "regulation by raised eyebrow." Whether or not commercial network programming practice and content in fact changed was almost irrelevant.

Moreover, the cloud of conflict of interest had once again descended into this arena of public debate, and again it involved the chief political figure. Barnouw argues that Senator Dodd had achieved wide popularity and a national reputation during the 1961-1962 rounds of hearings and investigation, but that by the end of 1962 his zeal was waning. Barnouw charges that "as a member of important committees he received many blandishments and gifts, to which he responded warmly." Further, "He was on friendly terms with executives of Metromedia," receiving "campaign contributions and other gifts" from them (1975: 304-306). One result was his veto of his staff's plans for a new set of inquiries into the syndication of violent programs among independent stations. A major target of this investigation was to have been Metromedia's station in Washington. Barnouw also claims that the staff cross-examination of NBC Chairman Robert Sarnoff during the final hearing in 1962 was softened on orders of the senator and that he even "ordered the transcript of the session locked up." Finally, as noted above, the interim report on this investigation was never publicly released, and no final report seems ever to have been published.[11]

How fully responsible such factors were for the ebbing subcommittee interest can only be inferred. In any case, after the interim report was issued in 1964 the subcommittee appears to have conducted no further work in this area. Eventually two of the subcommittee members (Senators Hart and Hruska) were appointed to serve as members of the National Commission on the Causes and Prevention of Violence (1968-1969). By 1969 the Senate's Subcommittee on Communications, chaired by John Pastore, had asserted itself as the new locus of congressional investigation of television violence and its effects.

Whether during the Dodd era the threat of legislative action had been real or merely a ploy, the investigations served a community other than the public or broadcasters. As was the case in the earlier round of investigations, the immediate beneficiaries of the congressional inquiry were members of the mass communication research fraternity. Like Lazarsfeld in the earlier hearings, Schramm used this opportunity to call for a concerted funding effort for long-term effects research. He argued that "it would take about $50,000 per year for about ten years," or that "$100,000 per year for experimental research directed toward specific problems would pay off just tremendously" (Senate, Judiciary Comm., Juvenile Delinquency Subcomm., 1961-1962: 1773). Bandura expressed a similar faith in the power of money: "I would expect $40,000 to $50,000 a year over a period of 5 years would answer most of the important questions we have about the influence of television on the behavior of young children" (1961-1962: 1955).

Senator Dodd was quick to indicate a political interest in aiding the researchers, and in the process he sent a clear signal to the affected government agenicies. Addressing Bandura and referring to the Senate's passage of the Delinquent Children's Act and its provision of $25 million for research, he said:

> I hope that you will be encouraged that we are at least making some progress. It is a field in which we ought to be doing a lot of work, and I hope you will get the funds to carry on your work. Of course, it will be up to the Secretary of Health, Education and Welfare, but I am confident he will be interested in what you are doing and others are doing as well [1961-1962: 1957].

Eight years later, in a different committee, under the leadership of a much more determined senator, that hint would become a direct request and, in effect, an order that HEW become substantially involved in funding research on children and television violence.

For the moment Bandura responded to Dodd with straightforward confidence: "There seems to be a general feeling of the fact that the phenomena are extremely complex and therefore not studied very easily. My own impression is that the problems are subject to solution. It is not a difficult task. It is a matter of having the funds to carry out experimentation" (1961-1962: 1957). Thus, as the final recommendation in its Interim Report the subcommittee urged that "a coordinated, large-scale research attack should be launched to develop more precise information as to the impact of television on juvenile behavior and as to the interaction of television and other forces affecting such behavior" (1964: 42-43).

The subcommittee was careful to avoid asserting sole governmental responsibility for support of such an effort. It called attention to the initial plans of the Joint Committee for Research on Television and Children, a group formed in December 1962, representing industry, foundations, universities, and government and designed to coordinate the funding and direction of research in this area. However, it sensed difficulties ahead, noting that "the subcommittee feels that this research program is off to a promising start but that it is neither moving as rapidly as the problem warrants nor does its current approach and financial support seem adequate to the problem posed" (1964: 44).

THE EMERGING PATTERN

By the end of commercial television's first decade of full national service, politicians, broadcasters, and social scientists had begun to map out the terms of an alliance for approaching the issue of policymaking for the medium. Members of Congress had discovered in communication research a series of models and theories that allowed them in public hearings and reports to imply much more about the presumed direct or indirect links between television programming content and antisocial behavior than was warranted by the content of the available research. For their part, communication researchers, finding in Congress an enthusiastic, authoritative audience for their reports, discovered as well a ready willingness to use that research selectively and to ignore the inconsistencies in their data, theories, and philosophic presuppositions. Working under constitutional and self-imposed constraints, members of Congress could use the rhetoric of science to transmit to broadcasters the opinions, whether real or perceived, that television programming was too often challenging the tolerances of national taste. Yet that same science could be strategically reinterpreted to defend the decisions of politicians to avoid consideration of new terms for broadcasting ownership and control.

The broadcasting industry, having already firmly established its influence in the origins of the communication research enterprise, continued to use the research tool to safeguard its interests. The networks increased their support and institutional capacity for directing internal and external social research projects, particularly in the areas of communication literature reviews and surveys of public attitudes toward television. The proliferating academic programs in communication and their affiliated research institutions provided ambitious faculties who proved to be ready takers of industry or joint industry-government research funds. Industry research executives and research-minded management spokesmen began to appear regularly at congressional hearings, both to monitor and to guide the debate about the impact of television.

Long predisposed to ignoring the implications of the industrial foundations of their work, communication researchers appeared to be little troubled by doubts about the meaning of the increasing political interest in it. They found in their eager congressional audiences the authoritative instrument for further legitimation of their normal science activities. In a process similar to the experience in so many other areas of the social and physical sciences before them, communication researchers developed increasingly strong industrial and political sponsorship by

(1) debating the effects issue in congressional hearings at the surface level, in popular terms and simple models;
(2) not muddying the waters with overly complicated examination of the meaning and terms of the science they employed in their research;
(3) accepting industry contracts for operational and attitudinal research problems and allowing such efforts to become confused with industry and government projects ostensibly designed to investigate serious questions about impact; and
(4) not questioning the motives of the broadcasting industry and the political oversight process in their mutual use of research in the approach to broadcast policymaking.

Like the representatives of a vast array of sciences who had found important roles for themselves in other aspects of governmental policymaking, the communication research community began to find itself elevated to the status of indispensible expert. With the promise of increasing public approbation, funding, and prestige, there was little pressure to consider any questions about the intellectual and policy accommodations implicit in allowing a research field to define itself largely in light of the needs of its industrial and governmental clients.[12] There was even less disposition to examine the prior question of the propriety of applying science to an issue of taste, morals, and conviction.

NOTES

1. For example, see Red Lion Broadcasting Co., Inc. et al. v. FCC et al. (395 U.S. 367), June 9, 1969. One notes, however, that the changing technology, particularly the use of cable, fiber optics, or other "wired" systems to deliver what have previously been largely over-the-air broadcast signals, may eventually remove such services from the open spectrum, thereby making moot the spectrum scarcity rationale for regulation.

2. The status and role of the Lynds are intriguing. *Middletown* was widely acknowledged as a most important piece of social research, and Robert Lynd eventually was appointed professor at Columbia and became executive secretary of the SSRC. Yet *Middletown* and those appointments came before he had earned his doctorate. This was granted to him finally by Columbia, which eventually agreed to accept parts of *Middletown* retroactively as his dissertation. As noted in Chapter 3, Paul Lazarsfeld acknowledges his debt to Lynd in finding his first position in the United States. On the matter of Lynd at Columbia, see Madge (1962: 126-133).

3. Charles R. Denny, Vice President, NBC (formerly Chairman of the FCC) in U.S. House, Committee on Interstate and Foreign Commerce, FCC Subcommittee (1952: 257).

4. Elizabeth A. Smart, Women's Christian Temperance Union, in U.S. House, Committee on Interstate and Foreign Commerce, FCC Subcomittee (1952: 77-78).

5. The later investigative effort was conducted by Bernard Schwartz under the aegis of the Senate Legislative Oversight Subcommittee (see Barnouw, 1975: 200).

6. Bishop Wilbur E. Hammaker, Methodist Church, quoted in U.S. House, Committee on Interstate and Foreign Commerce, FCC Subcommittee (1952: 102).

7. Senate Resolution No. 89 (83.1) quoted in U.S. Senate, Committee on the Judiciary, Subcommitte to Investigate Juvenile Delinquency (1955a: 34).

8. Elenor Maccoby, then Lecturer, Department of Social Relations, Harvard University, cited in U.S. Senate, Committee of the Judiciary (1955b: 7-10).

9. Senate Resolution No. 48 (87.1) quoted in U.S. Senate, Committee on the Judiciary, Subcommittee to Investigate Juvenile Delinquency (1964: 2).

10. Revenue and receiving set data compiled from FCC (1958-1961); sets-in-use figures from Steiner (1963: 17).

11. The document to which Barnouw is referring appears to be the 1964 Interim Report. Where available in libraries it appears to have been photocopied and not acquired as part of the official process of government document distribution.

12. Again, it should be emphasized that communication research was not alone in this susceptibility. As Nisbet all too painfully reminds us, after World War II the universities succumbed "to the view that there was no limit to what they could do in and for society," thereby losing their sense of proportion, of the true roots of knowledge, and of what had up to that point been their "unique authority in culture" (see Nisbet, 1971, 1975: 131-139).

Chapter 5

THE NATIONAL COMMISSION ON THE CAUSES AND PREVENTION OF VIOLENCE (1968-1969)

On the surface it would appear that for an eighteen-month period in 1968 and 1969 the primary arena of federal concern with the effects of violence on television shifted into the hands of a presidential commission. In fact, as we will see below, congressional dominance of the issue was never seriously challenged. Although a commission-based investigation of television began during the summer of 1968, it was from the start a thoroughly political body, and by the spring of 1969, Senator Pastore had undertaken measures that were to allow his subcommittee, like the Subcommittee to Investigate Juvenile Delinquency from 1954 to 1965, to reassert full Senate control and to guide public debate about the issue for at least the next five years. Nonetheless, the brief diversion into the commission forum stimulated further demand for behavioral research into television effects, and it accelerated the process whereby previously established social science perspectives were to achieve almost total hegemony in popular commentary on the medium's significance. Accordingly, it is important to consider several aspects of this brief interlude.

ORIGINS

The immediate origins of the National Commission on the Causes and Prevention of Violence (the NCCPV, or the Eisenhower Commission, after its chairman, Dr. Milton Eisenhower) are fairly clear, and television was only one, if not a minor, factor in the impulse to create it. The proximate cause was the assassination on June 5, 1968, of Senator Robert F. Kennedy, then a leading contender for the Democratic presidential nomination. But for some time other events had been building up, creating pervasive images of America as a violent society and fostering those doubts about its stability and health that perenially become sufficiently powerful to demand a political response.

Whereas the political images of social violence during the 1950s had been largely associated with juvenile delinquency and its nature as a regrettable yet tolerable and probably unavoidable by-product of the affluent society, the violence capturing the public's attention and tapping its fears during the 1960s appeared to have taken a more serious and often uglier turn. The assassination of President Kennedy in 1963, the civil disobedience throughout the South during the "freedom ride" period in the early 1960s, the police reactions to this and other manifestations of the civil rights movement, the escalation of American involvement in the Vietnam War, the related but also more deeply rooted protests and violent demonstrations spreading across college campuses and among major cities during the mid-1960s, three successive summers of ghetto riots that began in several inner cities, including Watts, in 1965, and the murder of Martin Luther King, Jr., only a month before Senator Kennedy's death all contributed to the pressure for further, concentrated examination of the issue of violence in contemporary society.

Nor was the form of the official response to these pressures an isolated phenomenon. In general it was part of a longstanding Anglo-American tradition that provides for high-level, empirical inquiries into events and issues of varying degrees of public or official concern. As such, however, it was also subject to important weaknesses reflected in the very purposes, status, and terms of such bodies. In a principal study of American presidential commissions, Frank Popper contrasts them with what usually are the more authoritative, independent, and uncompromising British Royal Commissions, and he notes that the American versions tend to have no more effect than the president of the moment intends for them (1970: 50-55). Moreover, the use of the commission device during the mid-1960s had become so regular and frequent, and the use of their recommendations so selective, as to raise doubts about the motives for their creation. To see it in perspective, the sheer number of these commissions was reminiscent of the Hoover and Franklin Roosevelt years. The NCCPV was only one of twenty presidential commissions (and many more national-level task forces) that President Johnson either appointed or sanctioned during his five years in office, more than twice the number of the Eisenhower and Kennedy administrations combined (Popper, 1970: 66-67, App. 1).

The NCCPV was part of that pragmatic political instinct that created or encouraged such bodies as the President's Commission on the Assassination of President Kennedy (Warren, 1963-1964), the President's Commission on Law Enforcement and Administration of Justice (Katzenbach, 1965-1967), the Carnegie Commission on Public Broadcasting (Killian, 1966-1968) the President's Commission on Postal Organization (Kappel, 1967-1968), the President's Task Force on Communications Policy (Rostow, 1967-1968), the National Advisory Commission on Civil Disorder (Kerner, 1967-1968), and the Commission on Obscenity and Pornography (Lockhart, 1968-1970). Perhaps not surprisingly, in the climate of the mid-1960s many of these commissions were dominated by one or another or both of two themes that had come to be seen as ever more closely interrelated, namely, the apparent challenges to the basic structure of law and social order and the question of the content and impact of modern systems of communication. In a sense, then, the work of the mass media task force in the NCCPV is a distillation of two of the most crucial political and social issues in twentieth-century American culture.

President Johnson created the NCCPV by executive order on June 10, 1968. With careful attention to political balance, he appointed representatives from the "major parties, liberal-conservative, houses of Congress and even regional Congressional representation . . . a representative of the church . . . two jurists . . . a female . . . two other lawyers . . . a longshoreman, author, philosopher . . . and [a] psychiatrist" (Short, 1975: 64). The commission was originally to serve for only a year, though a subsequent order by President Nixon extended it somewhat, but only for another six months, to December 10, 1969.

The political and hasty, crisis-response nature of the commission's origins had an immediate impact, clearly reflected in the charge given to it:

> The Commission shall investigate and make recommendations with respect to:
>
> (a) The causes and prevention of lawless acts of violence in our society, including assassination, murder and assault;
>
> (b) The causes and prevention of disrespect for law and order, of disrespect for public officials, and of violent disruption of public order by individuals and groups; and
>
> (c) Such other matters as the President may take place before the Commission [Graham and Gurr, 1969: ii].[1]

The explicit concern with research and causality and the implicit interest in the role of the media of communications led to creation of a media task force, one of whose codirectors, Sandra Ball, was a sociologist, and well over half of whose staff consultants were social scientists.

If this context was insufficient to guide the commission toward a relatively standard gloss of the effects research problem, the commission had to operate under an additional constraint:

> Because President Johnson was to go out of office early in 1969, it was requested that the Commission submit a report of progress prior to the inauguration of a new president. The Commission agreed to this request and scheduled and completed the primary staff efforts within six months. But, since most of the first two months were taken up by staff organization and the Academic Conference, the staff effort was even more highly concentrated, roughly from late July until early December, when the Commission met to hammer out the Progress Report. Furthermore, it was during that first six-month period that nineteen full days of hearings and another conference — all requiring enormous expenditures of staff time and energy — were held [Short, 1975: 77-78].

This account by James F. Short, Jr., NCCPV co-director of research, goes on to point out that it was during that first six-month period that "a 'research presence' was most conspicuous and most effective in the Commission's activities. Most of the research of all of the task forces was completed during this period, and in the *Progress Report,* the basic outlines of the Commission's report became clear" (Short, 1975: 79).

Because of the short lifespan of the commission, most of that "research presence," as it bore on television and its effects, was summative. Rather than undertaking or sponsoring new research, the commission turned "to acknowledged leaders of research in the behavioral sciences. They were asked to prepare papers on media effects by critically examining for their discipline what is known, what inferences can fairly be drawn from that knowledge, what needs to be known through further study, and what procedures are required to discover the relevant information" (Baker and Ball, 1969: 240).

The one exception to the pattern of merely reviewing previous research was to sponsor the first in what was to become an annual series of content analyses of commercial television programming. Focused primarily on the incidents and character of violent episodes in prime time and Saturday morning network programming, this research, of all the possible projects and directions contemplated by effects researchers at the time of the commission's formation, has had the single greatest success in capturing policymaker imagination and therefore in also securing continued federal funding. This project was to continue to stretch out for many years (see, for instance, Gerbner et al., 1980).

Not unlike the experience of the congressional investigations of television violence before and after it, a major tension in the operations of the NCCPV arose through the competing perspectives of lawyers and social scientists. Since at least the late nineteenth century, and as Max Weber and Robert Merton (1975: 165) have both observed, lawyers have been widely perceived as particularly well suited to service "in every arm and function of government," including high-level commissions of inquiry, be they British Royal Commissions or American presidential bodies. Unlike academics, the professional work style of lawyers makes them almost always detachable from projects of the moment and therefore available for immediate seconding to special study groups. Furthermore, at least in the United States, the congressional and executive branch officials likely to be involved in creating, advising, or serving on national commissions are often themselves lawyers, perceiving the problem at hand primarily in the context of constitutional and legislative possibilities.

Social scientists naturally object to the prevalence of the legal world view. They contend that this perspective is often insensitive to the known complexities of the social and psychological factors involved, that the various relevant issues and options require long, careful analysis and debate, and that even then, sure, definitive policy recommendations are seldom possible. But the usually brief lifespan and largely political considerations of commissions of inquiry have, at least until relatively recently, militated against the scientific lament, making it comfortable and easy for politicians to turn to those with legal backgrounds for service both as commissioners and as staff.

Save for a few appointments and operational differences, the NCCPV was no exception to the overall pattern. Nine of the thirteen commissioners, most of the key senior staff, fifteen of the twenty-five task force directors and many of the staff assistants were lawyers in practice or by training, and among these the vast majority came from government posts or from prestigious Washington or otherwise nationally prominent law firms.

When the commission began its work there was an attempt to build in checks that would counter the dominance by attorneys. It was hoped that each of the separate task forces would have a pair of codirectors, one a lawyer and the other a social scientist. However, this plan succeeded for only three of the task forces (one of which was the media group), and in the end the legal-scientific dispute went unresolved and, by most parties, insufficiently analyzed.

In dealing with this tension Short would have it that the academic-scientific approach is more reflective and theoretical and therefore, he implies, preferable. As he views it, the problem is that lawyers are "accustomed to the quick gathering and assimilation of concrete facts and their use in advocacy, in contrast to the more deliberative academic style of research and preference for abstract theoretical formulations in the search for knowledge" (1975: 71).

Merton appreciates the practical differences between the legal and social scientific approaches to public issues, but his analysis is more complex and less value-laden, arguing that "It is not the contrast in detachability of lawyers and academic social scientists, but the differences between them in styles of work, intellectual perspectives, and, specifically, conceptions of evidence that must be noted here" (1975: 165). Then, using the rules of evidence as his example, he penetrates close to the hidden significance of the dispute. That is, it is not merely that there exists the

> preference of lawyers for use of sworn eye-witness depositions, and the contrasting preference of sociologists for interviews, social surveys, and other quantitative evidence. These preferences are sustained by a considerable professional apparatus and a not inconsiderable academic apparatus by which the evidence is evaluated. The reward system of science and learning, centered in peer review, reinforces the differential attachment to types of evidence [Merton, 1975: 165].

And, one might add, to visions of truth.

Thus the social-scientific analysis of commissions and the political investigations of social issues present us with a curious anomaly. While the positivistic critique is sensitive to the crucial implications of the predominantly legal approach to such problems, it seldom appreciates the full significance of this lesson from its own sociology of knowledge. That is, it typically ignores the sociopolitical nature of its own origins and fails to comprehend that there is no absolute validity inherent in the perceptions and methods of social science either. Couched in the rhetoric of objectivity, system, quantification, and "the search for knowledge," the social-scientific critique of legal or other disciplines often fails to deal with the presuppositions and biases wrapped up in its own approaches.

HEARINGS AND REPORT

Clearly, the growing confidence in the role of behavioral research and its presumed applicability to communications policy questions that we observed in earlier congressional inquiries was fully adopted by the NCCPV members and staff. In the staff report to the commission of the findings of the media task force, the editors offer a token nod to libertarian concerns about content control, but then rush determinedly into a justification and promotion of research in evaluation of media performance:

> In the context of our concern with the media and violence, however, while continuing to believe fully in the concept of free expression, it is clear that the media — including their educational and professional organizations — have shown an appalling lack of concern about the effects of particular media practices and little interest in research to determine how, under any reasonable standards, they might do better. . . . If the government's statements are to rise above the level of diatribes or platitudes, they must be based on research and reasoned deliberation of the issues [Baker and Ball, 1969: v].

The Hearings

A key similarity between the work of the NCCPV and related congressional investigations lay in the use of hearings. While it appears that this method of eliciting information and structuring the debate was resisted by some of the social scientists on the staff (an example of the differing views about what constitutes necessary and valid data or evidence), for our purposes the hearings record again provides a useful opportunity to observe how the social-scientific perspective colors the issue of effects and guides the public debate about them. Further, the very process of the NCCPV hearings begins to reveal even more clearly the dramatistic purpose for the commission or committee form of investigation. In the words of Jerome Skolnik, who served as a task force director for the commission, the hearings reflect the "ultimate art" of "social science as theater. . . . Conclusions must be presented to evoke an emotional response in both the commissioners and the wider television audience" (1970: 241-242).

For reasons already outlined, the NCCPV hearings present a relatively straightforward account of the standard effects research debate. Of the two dozen witnesses, over a quarter were social scientists, and their testimony dominated the first two days of the five-day media hearings. At the outset Bradley Greenberg provided the almost obligatory statistical overview: amount and patterns of usage, audience attitudes, perceptions and preferences, and a catalogue of presumed functions and gratifications (Briand, 1969: 1-14). Many of these data involved comparisons between two large social groupings, but were otherwise all normative — contrasting the mass communication behavior of "John Smith," a "typical" middle-class American, and that of the average, "less advantaged" urban poor. From the outset, then, the hearings proceeded to define the issues of effects in terms of the behavior, opinion, and functions that are most easily measured and statistically manipulated.

As during the Dodd subcommittee hearings, Leonard Berkowitz served as a proponent of the experimental S-R model. He cast the argument for film and television effects in a manner that descends directly from the Hovland group and their antedecents in general learning theory, Freudian psychology, and small-group psychology:

> Basically, a considerable body of research has all indicated that the sight of some event can produce within the individual, within the observer, matching of closely related sensations, feelings, and ideas. And further, this research or at least some research suggests under some conditions that these internal reactions, sensations, feelings and ideas, can instigate open aggression [Briand, 1969: 37].

Anticipating criticism, Berkowitz acknowledges the obvious vulnerability of his position, but in each case he develops a line of reasoning that ends in a behavioristic effects conclusion:

> Now again the question might come up, can I prove this? I cannot. But I think that it is worth noting that with fairly great consistency across many different studies, carried out in many different laboratories, they all seemed to add up to a probability statement that while not perfect, it is certainly not zero either [Briand, 1969: 37].

And then:

> It could well be that in the real world that these conditions which facilitate the chances of agression are rather slight. But . . . If the conditions are appropriate, then the observer does indeed have a greater chance of acting aggressively himself [p. 39].

Obviously debatable conclusions, they are nonetheless not to be dismissed lightly, for later in the debate over the surgeon general's report they become key elements in forging Senator Pastore's consensus.

Testimony by Percy Tannenbaum, another behavioral scientist and a former Berkowitz colleague, is valuable for additional insight into the intellectual position and policy conclusions of the experimental researcher. At one point early in his remarks, Dr. Tannenbaum notes that

> most of the experiments — in fact I think all of them — that Berkowitz reported and that Dr. Klapper alluded to and so on — were not done for the purpose of investigating the effects of television on aggressive behavior. They were done mainly for the purpose

> of investigating some theoretical speculation about how aggressive behavior is instigated or may be instigated [Briand, 1969: 45].

That is, the focus of this research has typically not been television or film, nor even on the mass media generally. Rather it has been on the general question of aggressive behavior. The studies cited are in almost all cases not primarily studies of communication; instead they are psychological studies that for the most part treat content, and to a great extent even the medium, as largely irrelevant.

Tannenbaum clearly allies himself with the experimental camp, yet he is careful to point out that limitations still exist in the research findings. He appears to be in favor of calling on science as a major foundation on which to justify public policy decision making in areas related to communications and violence; yet the call for action is based, not on scientific certainty, but on the doubts, suspicions, and general trends he sees in the research:

> The verdict, as I said, is not proven. I don't think it will be proved in my lifetime, certainly not in the lifetime of this Commission. And if that is what you are looking for, I think you better stop now.
>
> The question is, when is there a reasonable doubt; when are there grounds so that we can take the chance? There are a lot of things at stake [Briand, 1969: 47].

Again in this subtle, elusive analysis lie the seeds of logic to be used not only in the final NCCPV staff report, but also in the more determined congressional probe yet to come.

The functionalist, minimal-effects position was reflected in the testimony of Joseph Klapper, who with remarkable disingenuousness attempts to disassociate himself from his commercial network employment. Describing himself as "more of an academician than a corporate soul," he argues that he is not an "operating person," making "no program policies or decisions" and only "competent to talk about what is known about the social effects of mass communication" (p. 15). Noting that there has been a long history of concern with the effects of fictional depiction of violence, he suggests that television is only the latest target, thereby implying that the significance of the effects debate is that television is merely serving as the newest and currently most vulnerable scapegoat for popular and political concern over an issue that has complex origins.

Unchanged since his book in 1960, Klapper's fundamental theoretical outlook remains that "the major effect of mass communication appears to be a reinforcement effect and that mass communication reinforces whatever tendencies are brought to it, with fine — and

I should say impersonal — disinterest for whether these predispositions are socially wholesome or socially unwholesome (p. 16) Distinguishing between the two types of effects research, surveys, and laboratory experiments, he dismisses each in turn:

> What the surveys indicate, in short, is that mass media depictions of violence are not prime movers toward crime and delinquency. They — the surveys — suggest that certain personality traits lead to a taste for violent media material, and that this material serves some sort of very ill-understood psychological function — perhaps good, perhaps bad, and perhaps neither — for children with certain maladjustments. The surveys really do not tell us very much about whether such fare will render audiences more likely to behave violently [p. 17].

As for the laboratory experiments, he finds them misinterpreted: "The studies are apparently much more widely discussed than they are read, which, in reference to a topic of this importance, is a great misfortune. Because the articles are discussed by people who do not really know what is in them, the discussion has given rise to extreme misconceptions about what the articles prove (p. 17). He argues that the studies bear hardly at all on the central effects question, and he gives reasons stemming from their methods and setting:

> I propose that there are two characteristics of these studies which prevent them from bearing on this question. The first of these is that the experiments do not deal with violence in the sense in which we are all concerned about violence. The second is that the experiments do not deal with the effects of witnessing mass media as these media are witnessed in real life [p. 17].

That is, of course, the classic issue of validity — are the scientists, in fact, measuring that phenomenon they say they are measuring? Experimental social research in general has difficulty meeting the criterion of validity, and experimental television violence effects research is particularly vulnerable to this criticism. It is typically conducted in laboratories, outside the normal domestic and social environments of viewing, and it supplies subjects with unusual means of aggression (e.g., paper measures of attitude and mechanical scales of willingness to administer electric shock) that are assumed to be adequate substitutes for the full range of physical, oral, and mental violence potentially manifest in the outside environment.

His clever attacks on the validity and significance of violence effects research notwithstanding, Klapper is careful enough to sense the drift of the political current:

> It is not my contention by any means at all that one shouldn't move forward because we don't know if there are harmful effects.
>
> If research has revealed nothing that one can base a policy decision on, it seems to me there are two things you do: one is you try to do more research, and the other is you take common sense steps [p. 35].

Thus, having argued the inconclusiveness of the research and its questionable utility as a foundation for public policymaking (a position essentially identical to that taken by CBS, and the NAB, and other industry spokesmen in the previous hearings), this social scientist nonetheless joins his opponents and makes the plea for yet more research in the area. Additionally, having begun his testimony denying his corporate soul, Dr. Klapper ends his presentation by aligning himself with the new public position of CBS. This position was expressed in the form of a telegram from then CBS President Frank Stanton to NCCPV Chairman Milton Eisenhower when the commission was formed:

> [CBS] shares the President's concern as to the possible effect of the content of television entertainment programs upon the nature of our society. We will, of course, cooperate in every way possible.
>
> We believe, however, it may take a considerable length of time to determine whether there is a causal relationship between the fictional portrayal of violence in the mass media and any increase of actual violence in American life. Nevertheless, we are re-examining our policies and practices in this entire area. As an initial step, although the integrity of the creative process will be fully respected, programming executives of the CBS Television Network will immediately undertake individual conferences with producers and writers to discuss specific measures to de-emphasize violence in programs now in production [Briand, 1969: 35-36].

Designed to demonstrate one network's alleged concern and sense of responsibility, this telegram reveals the broadcaster's strategy of trying to head off criticism, censure, or major recommendations inimical to the continued patterns of commercial broadcaster operation. Where this strategy is obvious in network programming policies that periodically declare intent to reduce violent content, to a large degree a similar objective is implicit in the social research policies of the networks. It is probably true that, as Dr. Klapper claims, his role is not directly related to program decision making. Program-related audience research is handled under different auspices. There are special departments designed to control and use the marketing or ratings research on which program planning and scheduling is based. Offices of social research, such as that of Klapper's at CBS or Dr. Thomas Coffin's at NBC, have a much different role to play. Far from providing a day-to-day operational service, they are designed for a less obvious, but perhaps more crucial, political objective. They serve as key elements in network attempts to provide the image of serious, scientifically committed concern about the impact of television, while yet striving to belittle those efforts of that very science that might support charges that that impact is deleterious. It is not surprising, therefore, that the theoretical perspective developed by Klapper in his earlier work (1960: xi), with its emphasis on media as agents of reinforcement and audiences as active seekers of gratifications for preextant needs, was based on research support by CBS.

The NCCPV hearings proved particularly successful in revealing the political purpose and lack of substance in much of the networks' research efforts. A persistent issue during the Kafauver and Dodd subcommittee hearings had been whether the networks were in fact willing to support basic effects research. Frequently led by Dr. Stanton, the one senior network official trained as a behavioral scientist, industry resistance to congressional investigation and to imputations of television's socially undesirable effects had been rooted in the argument that effects research findings had been unconvincing and that standard methodologies had been suspect. As noted in Chapter 4, Harold Fellows, president of the NARTB (NAB), had promised in 1954 that his organization would sponsor a pilot study that would lead to a long-range program of research into the impact of television programming on children and adults (Senate, Judiciary Comm., Juvenile Delinquency Subcomm., 1954: 261-263). But by 1961 no such research had been commissioned. The NAB claimed that, because CBS had announced plans of its own to undertake a similar, but apparently broader, study, the trade association had deferred to the network. However, it turned out that the CBS effort was to be Gary Steiner's 1963 report on public attitudes about television. While significant in its own right and a major reference source for a decade, the Steiner research could never have been construed as an effects study in the sense that the various subcommittees intended.[2]

In response to further questions by the Dodd committee during the 1961-1962 hearings, the networks and the NAB agreed to form, with representatives from foundations and the federal government, a Joint Committee for Research on Television and Children (JCRTC). Leroy Collins, Fellow's successor at the NAB, even reported on a decision "to proceed with the initial planning of an NAB research and training center in association with one of the leading universities in the nation" (Senate, Judiciary Comm., Juvenile Delinquency Subcomm., 1961-1962: 2244-2245). At the time of the 1963-1964 investigation, inquiries by Senator Dodd or his staff revealed that, while much had reportedly been planned, little JCRTC research had in fact been forthcoming. In 1968 the NCCPV staff determined that after six and a half years only one Joint Committee report had been published, and that proved to be the critical review of the effects literature that served as the basis of Klapper's antieffects testimony before the commission. A second project was assigned to Seymour Feshback, who had long been known as a firm proponent of the catharsis theory, and his research for the JCRTC did not disappoint the networks. A third project, on the effects of repetition, was never completed (Baker and Ball, 1969: 596).

Because in addition to the Steiner survey CBS had sponsored Klapper's 1960 review, which also had received a good deal of academic and press attention, the industry had been able to create the impression that it was supporting substantially more research than in fact was the case. Under probing by NCCPV commissioners and staff during the 1968 hearings, it finally became clear that those projects had had little to do with primary analyses of television violence and its effects on children. Throughout his testimony Dr. Stanton carefully attempted to skirt the issue of the JCRTC research program, but in the end he was forced to admit the lack of activity:

> I am embarrassed — and I referred to it this morning — about the fact that the industry committee, which is not purely broadcasting but involved representation from HEW and other outside organizations, fell apart. We financed our share. Others did their share. Some of the money is still left. It has been a very dormant organization. We tried to stimulate it through Dr. Klapper. We have been unsuccessful in doing so.
>
> I have no doubt that as a result of these hearings this will be given more stimulation. In fact, I promise you that it will [Briand, 1969: 347; slightly misquoted in Barker and Ball, 1969: 597].

In fact, little more at all ever came of the JCRTC program, and although occasional effects-related research projects have since been sponsored by one or more of the networks, the bulk of the work in this area has been carried out under the various NIMH (National Institute of Mental Health) and NSF (National Science Foundation) programs. Nor were there any reported developments in the NAB's putative plan for a research center at a university.

The significance of the JCRTC episode is that it helped give the broadcasting industry nearly a decade and a half of grace in which to present the appearance of being concerned enough to sponsor scientific investigation of television's impact, while it was actually doing very little.[3] Its major efforts in this area appear to have been directed at undermining political confidence in this sort of research. Indeed,

Dr. Stanton proved particularly adept at manipulating the issue of scientific inadequacy. While technically representing only CBS, he served as the spokesman for the entire industry. As is recounted in detail in Chapter 3, Stanton had been trained in psychology during the 1930s at Ohio State University, where as part of his work he assisted with one of the Payne Fund effects studies. He was hired by CBS to turn his scientific training to the commercial and promotional needs of the network, but also, as revealed by his sponsorship of Paul Lazarsfeld's Office of Radio Research and Bureau of Applied Social Research, he carefully cultivated the academic communication research community for its operational and political value to the industry. In time, as a senior broadcasting executive, he was able to trade on his academic background of scientific investigation into television audience effects, while yet always being able to testify authoritatively about the methodological shortcomings of those very research efforts. It was not until the latter stages of the 1968 NCCPV hearings that this tactic was exposed. The waning of the industry's ability to maintain the image of its commitment to basic effects research proved to be a crucial link in the development of an increased national-level political determination to puruse substantially more violence effects research.

The Final Report

Whereas the edited record of the hearings and the long, wide-ranging series of papers that constitute the Media Task Force report to the commission were published with disclaimers as to any interpretation of them as official NCCPV positions, the chapter "Violence in Television Entertainment Programs" in the commission's final report is the formal expression of its view. Prepared by a commission with unmistakable political origins and purposes, this part of its report carefully touches several obligatory bases, neatly marshaling the scientific evidence, but in the end thoroughly avoiding a confrontation with the fundamental policy dilemma. Demonstrating awareness of the complex nature of violence and its roots in American society, the commission notes that it has approached "this question with care," that "it is easy to make television a scapegoat," and that "there is no simple answer to the problem of violence — no single explanation of its causes, and no single prescription for its control" (NCCPV, 1970: 160).

Yet the commission also hastens to reassure the critics, and, though it is less angry in tone than parts of the report by its task force, the commission quickly adopts a posture of stern reprimand for the broadcast industry: "We are deeply troubled by television's constant portrayal of violence, not in any genuine attempt to focus artistic expression on the human condition, but rather in pandering to a public preoccupation with violence that television itself has helped to generate" (1970: 160).

This review of the research projects and summaries commissioned by the task force staff provides a brief documentation of the several dimensions of television viewing behavior among the general public and children, the highlights of the quantitative and contextual findings of the first round of prime time and Saturday morning television content analysis (1967 and 1968), and a review of the evidence for negative effects on children of televised violence. Noting the special vividness of television and its constant availability to the young, the report falls back on standard empirical research findings:

> A large body of research on observational learning by preschool children . . . confirms that children can and do learn aggressive behavior from what they see in a film or on a TV screen, and that they learn it equally from real life and fantasy (cartoon) models. They retain what they learn for several months if they practice the aggressive response at least once, and their re-enactment of such learned behavior is, in large part, determined by the perceived rewards and punishments meted out to the models they have observed [1970: 168-169].

Arguing against the vicarious release or catharsis theories, the report states that "laboratory experiments on the reactions of adults and teenagers to violent film content provide little support for this theory. In fact, the vast majority of experimental studies on this question have found that observed violence stimulates aggressive behavior, rather than the opposite" (1970: 169). The report notes the higher likelihood of such results when the material is presented in justified contexts of situations perceived to be similar to those of the viewers. Other emotional effects such as desensitization are briefly touched on, and the commission summarizes its view:

> We believe it is reasonable to conclude that a constant diet of violent behavior on television has an adverse effect on human character and attitudes. Violence on television encourages violent forms of behavior, and fosters moral and social values about violence in daily life which are unacceptable in a civilized society.
>
> We do not suggest that television is a principal cause of violence in society. We do suggest that it is a contributing factor [1970: 169-170].

The commission takes cognizance of the broadcast industry position that "its standards for the portrayal of violence and its machinery for enforcement of these standards are adequate to protect the public interest" (1970: 171). But the commission disagrees with this view, arguing that the NAB codes, while better than nothing at all, are "an essentially cosmetic approach" that in practice does not address the fundamental concerns of program format and mix.

Without dwelling on the matter, the commission seems to be recognizing the broadcast industry's purpose in creating the radio and television codes. On the one hand, the codes serve as a base-level guide to producers, providing an estimate for the industry of minimal standards that must be more or less followed to avoid the sort of complaints that would generate unfavorable images and thereby tempt stricter legislation and regulatory scrutiny. On the other hand, like the limited research efforts of the industry, the codes serve as a tool with which the industry can craft an impression of having a responsible, adequate self-regulatory mechanism. Subsequent research, while revealing the elaborate procedures involved in program content review at the network level, was to leave little doubt about the extent of the charade and the political purposes of the process.[4] The commission report is significant for refusing to permit the code process to go unchallenged.

As for the industry's attitude toward research, the report refers to the networks' critiques of research inconclusiveness, but, apparently having been alerted by the revelations in the hearings, the commission refuses to accept the industry arguments:

> It is time for them to stop asserting "not proved" to charges of adverse effects from pervasive violence in television programming when they should instead be accepting the burden of proof that such programs are not harmful to the public interest. Much remains to be learned about media violence and its effects, but enough is known to require that constructive action be taken at once to reduce the amount and alter the kind of violent programs which have pervaded television [NCCPV, 1970: 172].

With the NCCPV position cast in a widely critical tone, one might have expected its recommendations to be equally provocative. This was not to be the case. The commission's major recommendations were few, unsurprising, and briefly put:

(1) The broadcasting of children's cartoons containing serious, noncomic violence should be abandoned.
(2) The amount of time devoted to the broadcast of crime, western, and action-adventure programs containing violent episodes should be reduced.
(3) More effective efforts should be made to alter the basic context in which violence is presented in television drama.

(4) The members of the television industry should become more actively and seriously involved in research on the effects of violent television programs, and their future policies, standards, and practices with regard to entertainment programs should be more responsive to the best evidence provided by social scientists, psychologists and communications researchers [1970: 172-173].

Other recommendations included appropriate antitrust clearances for any necessary television industry joint action, provision of adequate and permanent funding for the Corporation for Public Broadcasting, better supervision of children's television viewing by parents, public expression of opinions to the networks and stations about programs, and evaluation of the effectiveness of the then new movie rating system (1970: 174-175).

These recommendations are more remarkable for what they omit than for what they include. The commission carefully avoids offering measures that might raise questions about the basic structure or purpose of American television. At one level the commission is willing to lament the commercial purpose of broadcasting: "Television entertainment based on violence may be effective merchandising, but it is an appalling way to serve a civilization — an appalling way to fulfill the requirements of the law that broadcasting serve the 'public interest, convenience and necessity'" (1970: 176). But in the end the commission proves to be unwilling to confront the fundamental conflict between its implicit interpretation of that legal mandate and the programming imperatives of broadcasting's existence as a profit-making institution.

In this light the significance of the NCCPV investigation may be characterized in two ways. In the first place, the commission's work was emotionally engaging and politically cathartic in much the same manner as the congressional investigations before it. In a pattern that had become ritualistic, the commission arose as a theatrical, political response to a perceived climate of fear and anger about the levels of violence in contemporary American society. The research of its Media Task Force and the apparent causal linkages suggested by that work allowed the commission to don the mantle of science and to adopt the stern demeanor of public authority disappointed in the performance of an industry licensed under a mandate of sacred public trust. Yet, while suggesting that serious problems existed, the commission stopped short of all but the weakest, least controversial recommendations. Its political and dramatistic purpose served, the commission concluded its work, knowing that even if favorably received and promoted by the president (soon to be Nixon), its efforts, at least in the realm of communications, would lead to no significant policy changes.

Second, and also like its congressional predecessors, the NCCPV investigation of television violence led to a greater role and status for communication research in federal policymaking circles. The staff report of the Mass Media Task Force begins with an invocation of the research approach, suggesting that "if the government's statements are to rise above the level of diatribes or platitudes, they must be based on research and reasoned deliberation of the issues" (Baker and Ball, 1969: v). As noted above, the fourth major recommendation near the end of the commission's final report reiterates the need for the television industry to become more involved in, and responsive to, the "evidence" of social science. The commission was quick at that point to reemphasize its "conclusion that enough is known to make inexcusable any delay in taking action along the lines we have recommended." But it did not turn away from endorsing continuing research efforts. Indeed, in light of subsequent research projects, its final comment on this recommendation is significant: "We especially urge the Surgeon General's committee and independent research groups to undertake regular analyses of television program content for the purpose of ascertaining whether a reduction in televised violence is being carried through, both by the networks and by the local stations" (NCCPV, 1970: 173).

The continuing project that provides annual content analyses of television violence has been the direct beneficiary of that recommendation, and this work remains as the prime symbol of the arrival of the methods and interpretative perspectives of communication research to a place of communications policymaking authority. Yet the limited range of data sought by policymakers from the project, and its very existence as the most visible continuing research effort supported by government says much about the way by time of the Eisenhower Commission the communication research and federal policymaking communities had begun to accommodate themselves to one another and how, the findings of the commission staff notwithstanding, the industry was still able to influence the terms of the research.

NOTES

1. "Establishing a National Commission on the Causes and Prevention of Violence," Executive Order No. 11412, June 10, 1968.

2. This history is outlined in an appendix to the NCCPV task force report (see Baker and Ball, 1969: Appendix III-K, 593-599). The attitude survey was the re-

search reported in Steiner (1963). CBS also sponsored an update of that research ten years later (see Bower, 1973).

3. For elaboration on this conclusion, see the first-hand account by Ralph Garry, a former member of the steering committee that established the JCRTC and a former consultant to the Dodd Subcommittee on Juvenile Delinquency, related in a 1971 speech in Pittsburgh and reprinted as part of the record of the Senate Committee on Commerce, Subcommittee on Communications hearings (1972: 13-19) chaired by John Pastore.

4. The author served as field investigator for that later project, one of those in the surgeon general's program (Chapter 6). It was a study of the codes and program review procedures of the industry, and it involved interviews with representatives from all the network programming and program standards and practices departments, as well as the director of the NAB code authority (Gerbner, 1972a).

Chapter 6

THE SURGEON GENERAL'S SCIENTIFIC ADVISORY COMMITTEE

The Origins, the Report, and the Senate Hearings (1969-1971)

Early in 1969, well before the Eisenhower Commission had concluded its work and a full six months before it began issuing the separate statements that were later collected in its final report, the chairman of the Senate Subcommittee on Communications, John O. Pastore, had set in motion machinery that would reestablish at least the nominal primacy of congressional control over approaches to violence effects research. But the broader significance of Senator Pastore's action lay in its implications for the status of communication research in the television policy struggle.

During the 1960s the number and power of active parties at interest in broadcast policymaking expanded. While that expansion is correctly seen to include steps taken by such institutions as the executive branch of the federal government, the courts, and public interest or citizen action groups, little notice has been taken of the strengthening role of the mass communication research institution during this period. It is evident from the history above that closer association between federal policymaking entities and the communication research community had been emerging for some time. The previous two chapters outlined the development of the idea that effects research might offer a powerful, politically effective basis for decisions about the necessary type and extent of television regulation. This chapter and the next deal with the conditions and terms of reference accompanying the climax of that thinking.

THE LITERATURE

The surgeon general's project was formally known as the Television and Social Behavior Program, and it produced seven publications (see References). The first, *Television and Growing Up: The Impact of Televised Violence,* was written jointly by the Scientific Advisory Committee (SAC) staff coordinator and the committee members themselves, providing the official committee summary and analysis of the research reported in the supporting technical volumes. It also contained the advisory committee's formal, though limited, recommendations. The bulk of the material generated for reference in the summary report was collected and published en masse in five large volumes. As organized by the NIMH technical staff, each volume was introduced by a long summary or overview chapter prepared by one of the investigation participants, and a final volume provided an annotated bibliography.

After publication of these reports, and in the wake of the concurrent and subsequent subcommittee hearings (1971 and 1972) and press coverage, the process and findings of the project and much of its research were summarized and evaluated by at least a half-dozen academic papers, one book, and dozens of newspaper and magazine articles. The papers are a diverse collection of published and unpublished materials. They include descriptive analyses, research summaries, critiques and apologia; some dealing solely with the surgeon general's project and research, while others treat the overall, general content of violence effects research. Several of the sources will be discussed in passing below. However, three of them ought to be reviewed briefly here, for in similar ways they offer insight into both the strengths and weaknesses of the literature that has emerged dealing with the advisory committee project. On the one hand, these reports provide a wealth of material of considerable value to the history as related here. On the other hand, they are also closely identified with the normative communication research effort to associate itself with the federal policymaking process and as such must be carefully and critically treated.

For example, growing out of the strengthening interface between the academy and the planning, implementation, and evaluation of federally supported social programs, the account by Matilda Butler Paisley (1972) attempts to refine a research and evaluation formula into which communication problems can be plugged for systematic solution. Paisley is responding to those calls during the late 1960s and early 1970s from within government (by members of Congress, the Office of Management and Budget, and the National Science Foundation) and from without (by the Social Science Research Council, the Brookings Institution, and the Ford, Markle, and Russell Sage Foundations) for more permanent mechanisms for interaction between government and social science. Her analysis is designed to explicate the need for, and workings of, a "steering wheel" of policy research that revolves around a core of methodological and basic research and that provides an ongoing evaluative process for social programs. This is a formal model that is couched unabashedly in the technical language of social engineering: "ideal system-state," "three-factor co-optimization," "micro parameters," and "policy-calibration research." The primary goals here are the expansion of rational social planning and the application of the testing mechanism to any issue that happens to be current and possibly grist for the planner's mill. While the paper provides much useful historical detail, it gives little or no thought to the social, cultural, and political implications of seeing the issues in communication as susceptible to the planning process it advocates.

It appears that this draft of Paisley's paper was never published, but it did circulate sufficiently to have some impact on the thinking of some advisory committee members and other reviewers of the project. Of particular interest was Paisley's account of how the report was written, and that part of her paper is actually quoted in the 1972 hearings, and it figures in the interpretations of the overall process and the "blackballing" issue by Cater and Strickland and by Bogart.

The Cater and Strickland (1975) account operates at a less formal, more practical level and is written for a wider audience. It is a fairly comprehensive history of the formation of the advisory committee, its progress, the contents of the report, and the major events in the aftermath of the report's publication. But as much as it is a record of the "evolution and fate of the Surgeon General's report," it is an attempt to demonstrate the need for new structures for employing social science in communication policymaking: "We need to develop new social institutions for establishing the vital linkages between research and public policy, between policy and action" (Cater and Strickland, 1975: 24). Presumably the then recently formed Aspen Institute Program on Communications and Society, which sought sponsorship from the Russell Sage Foundation for the book and for which Cater served as director, would be considered a worthy locus for establishing such "linkages."[1] The availability of departments of communication in universities and their affiliated research institutes had long before been demonstrated. Again the research debt for the historical data made available in this report must be acknowledged.

But it is important to keep in mind that in arguing for new institutional approaches to the coordination and utilization of social science in communication policymaking, the Cater and Strickland effort reflects that persistent strain of American pragmatism, an overriding interest in how to exploit social science, not in examining prior questions about the implications of resorting to it in the first place.

A paper by Leo Bogart (1972-1973) is significant on a number of accounts. Dr. Bogart held perhaps the highest research post in American publishing, serving as executive vice-president and general manager of the Bureau of Advertising of the American Newspaper Publishers Association, and as a sociologist he had written one of the earliest texts on television and its impact on American life (Bogart, 1972). Hardly overcritical of television, as a sociologist and practicing market researcher Bogart was thoroughly familiar with the strengths and weaknesses of the empirical audience research — and the television industry's role in it. In view of his knowledge and of his employment by a competing industry, he was one of the social scientists whose participation on the advisory committee had been vetoed by the television industry. The expectation that he would generally tend to agree with the negative effects argument and to call for responsive public policy action was borne out in the paper, and it emerged as a part of the post hoc effort by many of the critical social scientists to join Senator Pastore in correcting the public impression that the report undermined the negative effects position.

The importance of the paper becomes ever more apparent when considered in light of its publication in the *Public Opinion Quarterly.* For years a central journal in American communication research, *POQ* has been sponsored by the American Association of Public Opinion Research and Columbia University's Advisory Committee on Communications, both of which have been intimately tied to Paul Lazarsfeld's Bureau of Applied Social Research. *POQ* is thus a direct heir of the traditions of research and industry and government sponsorship established at the bureau and at subsequent institutes and centers of communication research at other universities (see Chapter 3). Indeed, at the time of the paper, Bogart, Klapper, Wright, and Nathan Maccoby served on the *POQ* editorial board, and Lazarsfeld and Merton served on the advisory committee. So the paper carried with it a certain unmistakable authority. It both spoke for and guided much of the normative social science thinking on the content and conclusions of the surgeon general's report.

Yet the paper is also significant because, in addition to presenting a somewhat "official" academic view of the report, it goes into matters and raises questions that are generally overlooked by most other commentators and that would appear to be a bit daring for *POQ*. For instance, in outlining the possible approaches to thinking about the report, Bogart raises an explicit concern of this book: "We may look at the report as the product of a three-way process of interaction between government, powerful business interests, and social science. In this last respect what was studied and why become more interesting than was what was learned" (1972-1973: 492). Toward the end of the paper he returns to aspects of this theme, arguing that "the link between media violence and subsequent antisocial behavior in children was already well indicated before the project was undertaken" and that "the issue should never have been made one of 'proving' a case against TV violence, or failing to prove it" (1972-1973: 515-516). Noting that "this project is still unique in the federal budget in its size, scope, and focus," he asks, "why . . . has the subject of TV violence received such a high research priority" (1972-1973: 521)?

Unfortunately, for the most part Bogart does not address these questions, and the greater portion of the paper is devoted to summarizing and critiquing the studies. While he does manage to question the necessity not only of this project, but also of any other effort mounted on a less "crash" and more continuing basis, his concern seems to rest in the lack of a direct link between the project and social policymaking. In this regard Bogart reflects the interests of most other social science critics of the report — to see the fruits of communication research put to practical use. As such, this attitude directs him, and the *POQ* readership, away from the more intriguing problems associated with his questions about the implications of television violence research being pursued at all.

BACKGROUND AND THE REPORT

During the years immediately preceding the Eisenhower Commission review, the primary locus of congressional interest in violence on television had been in the successive special Senate Subcommittees to Investigate Juvenile Delinquency. The Subcommittee on Communications had not, however, been out of touch with those investigations. Nor had it shrunk from expressing its own concerns about network and broadcaster programming performance. For instance, in his 1969 subcommittee hearings, Senator Pastore takes note of discussions he had had with industry representatives in his office at least as early as 1962: "I told them that this is one of the responsibilities of the industry, to so regulate themselves to bring about a proper restraint of this violence so that no harm or injury would be done to the American people (Senate, Commerce Comm., Communications Subcomm., 1969: 38).

Later, during his opening remarks before the second round of hearings in this series, the chairman elaborates on his interest and the extent of his study of the issue:

> My concern with crime and violence on television has been long and continuous. We have talked about this many times before, publicly and privately. You are aware, I am sure, of my most recent effort leading up to the request I made to the Secretary of Health, Education and Welfare. For many months I have had my committee staff consulting prominent psychiatrists, psychologists, communication experts and doing extensive research on what has been said on the subject of crime and violence [1969: 335].

Confronted with the same public climate of fear, anger, and frustration that led to formation of the Eisenhower Commission, the chairman responded in a similar manner, seeking a means for fixing, or at least appearing to fix, responsibility in aspects of performance by the electronic mass media. That the NCCPV was in part doing just that appears to have been insufficient for the senator's needs. During the first day of the 1969 hearings, he begins to reveal his own plans for pursuing the violence effects issues. He takes note of the commission's work, but he implies that the subcommittee cannot wait further: "Now, I realize that the President appointed a Commission some time back. I was hopeful that many of the Commission task force reports would be available at this time, but unfortunately they are not" (1969: 2).

It was never made clear just what the urgency was. The chairman couched the need for hurry in terms of allegedly dire conditions getting always worse and requiring early attention: "These communications problems are very weighty problems and have to be decided. The more you wait the more confused they become, the more complex becomes the solution of the problems" (1969: 2).

But the logic of this assertion, particularly the efficacy of "solutions," was never demonstrated, and the rush by the subcommittee seems to have been calculated to overlook the facts of the commission's history. The NCCPV had only been created in June 1968, and although the task force reports were not published by the time of the subcommittee hearings in March 1969, they were available before the end of the year. Furthermore, it was apparent that well in advance of publication the chairman and the members of the subcommittee had ready access to preliminary drafts of the reports, or at least to relevant portions of them. In fact, only a week after the hearings had begun and Senator Pastore had displayed his impatience with the NCCPV, other members of the subcommittee had a preliminary report from the commission inserted into the record of the continuing hearings (1969: 361).

The situation is made more curious by an apparent discrepancy between the senator's stated concern about wishing to avoid duplication and his actual activities in setting the study in motion. On the first day of the 1969 hearings (March 4), the senator not only takes note of the NCCPV's work, but he goes on to suggest that in order to resist duplication with the commission "we ought to wait and see [its report]. All I am saying is that we ought not to do the same things twice at the taxpayers' expense" (1969: 79). Yet the very next day the chairman announced that he had just sent a letter to the secretary of HEW requesting that he direct the surgeon general to form a committee to investigate precisely the subject of the effects of television violence that had been a major area of concern to the Mass Media Task Force of the Eisenhower Commission (1969: 83).

Thus the political motives in the development of the surgeon general's project must be seen as varied and complex. To set the Pastore action in perspective it is necessary to recall the broader context of government-media relationships during this period. Books and articles by William Porter, Thomas Whiteside, and others recount the closely related series of events between 1969 and 1974, the years of the Nixon administration, that in various ways served to impose more than the usual degree of constraint on the practice of broadcast and press journalism. As Porter (1976: 3) sees it:

> The administration of Richard Nixon differed [from other presidencies] in the speed with which it moved to attack the media at many levels and in the intensity and scope of its well orchestrated activities. From the Nixon White House there emanated, for the first time, attacks intended to damage the credibility not of a single journalist but of a whole class of them; to intimidate publishers and broadcasting ownerships; and, almost unthinkably, to establish in American jurisprudence the legality of censorship.

FCC Chairman Burch's request for network news transcripts, Vice President Agnew's speeches in Des Moines and Montgomery, the challenges of *Post-Newsweek* television station license renewals in Florida by friends of the president, the prior restraint precedent established during the appeal process in the Pentagon papers cases, the contempt citations in "the selling of the Pentagon" affair, the funding veto and other interference in public broadcasting, the Department of Justice's antitrust suits against the networks and its intervention in cross-ownership license renewal cases, and the efforts by the Office of Telecommunications Policy to tie industry requests for elimination of the fairness doctrine and passage of a five-year license renewal bill to stronger local station review of network news content all amounted to extraordinary amounts of government scrutiny and levels of intimidation and harrassment. Yet, rising during and in the wake of the troubled period of the Vietman War, inner-city riots, and campus protest, but before the revelations of the Watergate investigations, government initiatives against the media generated little public opposition. Indeed, they seem to have tapped a vein of confusion and resentment so wide and deep that the political attack may actually have been emboldened.

Seen in this light the general critical climate of opinion was probably sufficient to encourage the violence inquiry. But part of the explanation for Senator Pastore's interest in proceeding so quickly into the surgeon general's project may also rest in a probable need to counteract the impression created by another aspect of his subcommittee's work. This affair warrants some detailed attention, not only because it directly involved the subcommittee in ways that other events during the period did not, but also because it led to difficulties that laid bare the intricate, sensitive political interactions among the Congress, the White House, the FCC, the broadcasting industry, the courts, and the public, and that were now intimately to involve the communication research community as well.

By way of background it might be helpful to note that some students of Senator Pastore's role as subcommittee chairman find his posture toward the industry to be one of careful vacillation. In her paper, Matilda Butler Paisley (1972: 15-16) explains:

> *Behavior Today* [July 20, 1970] has called him the "watchdog and friend of the T.V. industry." Sandra Ball-Rokeach, who was co-director of the Media and Violence Task Force of the Violence Task Force of the Violence Commission, has said one must realize "that every so many years Senator Pastore brings up the mass media violence issue giving the appearance of a hard line, but his voting record regarding FCC and other legislative matters which involve the interests of the mass media is hardly consistent with a hard line approach" [personal communication with Paisley, Nov. 19, 1971].
>
> Pastore's own words and actions suggest his position vis-à-vis the television industry. During his hearings he often seems favorable to the industry.

As a case in point she refers to the events following the decision by the FCC in January 1969 to deny the license renewal application of WHDH-TV in Boston. Examining this episode as part of a case study in the politics of broadcast regulation, Krasnow, Longley, and Terry (1982: 208-209) explain its significance:

> The decision aroused great anxiety in the broadcast industry. For the first time in its history the FCC had refused to renew the license of a broadcast station that had an "average" record of performance; instead, it awarded the license to an applicant that, reportedly, would be more actively involved in the station's operation and would add to the diversity of control over mass communications media in the area.
>
> The importance of the precedent-shattering WHDH decision lies in the sequence of political events it triggered. It stimulated widespread controversy in the broadcasting industry, the Congress, the White House, and among citizen groups.

Krasnow et al. go on to note that "shortly after the release of the WHDH decision, the National Association of Broadcasters began a lobbying campaign to obtain congressional passage of a bill that would prevent the FCC from considering competing applications when acting on the renewal applications of a licensee" (1982: 210).

Senator Pastore's response was twofold. First, in March, he addressed the annual NAB convention, expressing his concern that broadcasters have "reasonable assurance" that their investments would not be jeopardized by license renewal challenges. Second, in April he introduced legislation (S.2004) that "would amend Section 309 of the Communications Act to provide that the FCC could not consider competing applications for a license at renewal time unless it had first found, based on the licensee's renewal application, 'that a grant of the application of a renewal applicant would not be in the public interest, convenience, and necessity' " (Krasnow et al., 1982: 210; legislative quote from Broadcasting, May 5, 1969: 58). One will note that this initiative on behalf of the broadcasters came from Democrat Pastore's subcommittee well before the new Republican administration had created the OTP and through its director, Clay Whitehead, had proposed its own "two-step," longer-term license renewal measure.

Krasnow et al. relate that during hearings on the Pastore bill later in 1969, the senator was shocked to find his bill savagely attacked as "unnecessary, unfair, and unworthy" and even "racist" in its perceived effect of shutting out minority challenges to renewals of broadcast licenses. He was reduced to exclaiming, "I'm not a patsy for the broadcasting industry. I'm nobody's patsy" (Krasnow et al., 1982: 212). In light of this embarrassment, congressional support for the bill began to erode rapidly. During 1970 the FCC, by sidestepping its normal rule-making procedures, tried to enact the provisions of the bill in a commission policy statement. A court of appeals decision in June 1971 declared the policy illegal and ruled that the commission, particularly in the absence of any new legislation, had to return to its previous license renewal procedures under the Communications Act (FCC, 1970; Citizens Communication Center et al. v. FCC [447 F. 2d 1201], D.C. Cir., 1971).

Up to this point the senator may not have yet come to appreciate the strength of the growing public interest group movement. He certainly did not anticipate the vehemence of its reaction to his bill, and it is important to record that his formal activities on behalf of S.2004 came after his call for the surgeon general's study. Nonetheless, as was the case with the timing of his letter to Secretary Finch, his initial decisions here were probably taken over a period of several weeks, if not months — a period long enough to overlap considerably with his deliberations about the violence study and perhaps sufficient too for him not only to take a reading of the broadcast policy intentions of the new administration, but also to learn enough about the new public interest group temper to realize how well it might mesh with the different executive and legislative branch interests in the project.

Whatever the exact thinking at the time, the broader context of government and public interest group initiatives in broadcast policy cannot be ignored, nor can one dismiss as mere coincidence the neat balance struck by these effectively simultaneous projects of the subcommittee. Overall, then, much of the significance of the surgeon general's project must be seen in its emergence as part of the continuing struggle among politicians, public interest groups, and broadcasters, and among the different subgroups of each, over aspects of American communications policy. That struggle was now to be joined in a fuller and more formal way than ever before by the mass communication research community.

Senator Pastore's letter to Secretary Finch is a crucial document in the development of the relationship between communications research and the political process (Senate, Commerce Comm., Communications Subcomm., 1969: 337-338). To begin with, it summarizes the long-standing political interest in the problem of television violence, and it casts that interest in the compelling context of a concern with "the minds and hearts of our young people." Again the chairman takes note of the current work of the NCCPV, but as before he claims ignorance of when its report and recommendations will be available, always implying that there has been some unnecessary delay and an equally pressing need to begin pursuing the matter in some new forum. Whatever his private reasons for calling for another government-sponsored study at this precise moment, Senator Pastore invokes what he suggests is the widespread protest of scientists, educators, the clergy, writers, and parents. The impression created is one of a large-scale public demand for more certain information and appropriate government action.

While establishing a rationale for his request, the senator demonstrates a keen awareness of the major arguments in the effects debate. He is particularly careful to note the complexity of the effects question and to explain something of the no-effects position. But on the whole the letter appears to be rooted in a conviction that there are negative effects. More crucially for the argument here, the letter is built on the assumption that those negative effects can be scientifically ascertained. Again, the letter is cautious, noting the difficulties in methodology and the complexities of the environmental factors influencing behavior. Further the scientific conclusions are requested "insofar as possible." But overall the sense is one of frustration at the lack of "definitive information" in this area, and there is an implication that, all the problems aside, a concerted research effort ought to be able to provide the conclusive answers.

Of course, it is clear from the letter and from Senator Pastore's earlier testimony that he had in mind a model of scientific investigation and government response that had already achieved a great deal of popular success. At the outset of the 1969 hearings, before revealing that he intends to send the letter — and perhaps as a last-minute check on its political feasibility — the chairman indicates his thoughts on procedure:

> My own idea now parallels the way the Surgeon General of the United States explored the question of the relationship of cigarette smoking and lung cancer. . . . Maybe the Surgeon General ought to make a study so that we can get professional conclusions as to whether there is actual damage to the mind of a youngster who continuously looks at this violence on television, and how it may affect him in his future life [1969: 2].

With no apparent reservations, the decision to pursue the violence effects issue under the aegis of a surgeon general's committee proceeded on the assumption that the problems of causal relationship between smoking and cancer and between televised violence and antisocial behavior were essentially similar and susceptible to similar methods of evaluation and solution. Captured by the putative definitiveness of the earlier surgeon general's report on smoking, political and popular thinking was unable to distinguish between problems of physiology and culture. As a result, from the first day of hearings in

1969 to the last in 1974, and in spite of all the other controversies that surrounded the Scientific Advisory Committee's report, remarkably few questions were publicly raised about the validity of the exercise.

On the basis of the published record it is difficult to determine if there were any unvoiced doubts about the validity of the general strategy of attacking the problem through scientific means. But, as in previous congressional hearings on the matter, this device proved helpful in providing the senators with a means that they could project as neutral and independent for pursuing the matter of broadcaster responsibility. From the outset of the SAC project it was clear that Senator Pastore had finely honed the political use of the scientific tool. During the initial hearings he decries the failure of the broadcasters to exercise adequate responsibility in programming, asserting that "they have not kept the promises they made to me," and he raises the specter of the consequences of this alledged failure: "The industry . . . ought to get on their toes and they ought to begin doing something about this. The American people are disturbed about this violence. . . . And unless they do it, someone is going to take drastic action, and woe be that day, woe be that day" (1969: 38).

Yet, while thus raising his eyebrows and warning that things have "gone too far, absolutely too far," the senator carefully prepares a line of retreat from this implicit threat of legislative action. On the one hand there is the presumed lack of knowledge and the need for the scientific prescription:

> We don't have the expert information that we need. I think that should be developed, that we should have the highest authority just as we had the highest authority with regard to cigarette smoking and what effect it has on cancer of the lungs. We need expert authority. You just can't legislate here, and you can't debate here in an area of darkness. We have to find out first scientifically what effect it does have so that we will have proof positive when we begin to move [1969: 31].

On the other hand there is the earlier reference to the serious constitutional questions involved in just that threat "to move." For "when it comes to the format of a program you get into the area of censorship, and it is hard to legislate, if at all possible. You run into the freedom of speech under the first amendment, and how far you can go" (1969: 31).

Thus, the politicians again come increasingly to refine the image of themselves as caught in a communications policymaking bind. They purport to be trapped among the countervailing pressures represented by public dissatisfaction, industry indifference or intransigence, constitutional restrictions, and scientific inconclusiveness. While avowing awareness of the dangers lurking in the swamp of uncertain research and related communications legislation, they nonetheless keep hinting that some action — never explicitly defined — might be forced on them. For the moment, they claim, they cannot "move," because the authority and the evidence of need to do so are unclear. Indeed, the subcommittee's action in proceeding to hold hearings on S.2004 would suggest a willingness to move more toward a position of protectionism for the industry. But, because the pressure for action is said to be increasing and because the scientific community has proved to be of some political value in a widening variety of public policy deliberations, the legislative leadership finds it increasingly easy to accept the idea of developing a formal process of scientific inquiry into a specific area of television effects.

That the report fails to provide the definitive answers sought is never officially acknowledged. In fact, in the rush to confirm the original mandate, the tentativeness of the report's conclusions is swept aside, and the popular impression is created that, in spite of great pressure brought to bear by the industry and the cautious language of academics, the social and behavioral sciences have answered the vexing problem of causality in the affirmative. How that impression has been engineered and under what terms are the subjects of the rest of this chapter and the next.

THE REPORT

Apparently operating under no illusions about the importance attached by Senator Pastore to his request of Secretary Finch, the then surgeon general, William Stewart, responded quickly and affirmatively. Within a week of the Pastore request Stewart appeared in person before the subcommittee to accept the task and to announce that he was appointing

> an advisory panel of experts in the behavioral sciences, the mental health disciplines and communications to study the effects of televised violence, . . . to review what is presently known, and to design and to recommend the long-range research studies which will help answer the specific questions now under discussion.

The surgeon general also related that

> because of the National Institute of Mental Health's long-term involvement and support in all these areas and because it has been designated as the focal point for behavioral sciences in the Public Health Service, I am asking the Institute to act as the technical staff

> and assume responsibility for the functions of this panel [Senate, Commerce Comm., Communications Subcomm., 1969: 338-339].

Thus, the guiding framework for the research problem was quickly and firmly set. The surgeon general apparently saw the issue of "solution" as unproblematic, and there was no hesitancy in conducting the project within the confines of the behavioral sciences, as represented by the research approaches characteristic of the NIMH. That there was some thought for the need of "long-range research" appears in retrospect to be significant insofar as it ignored the entirely different schedule envisioned by Senator Pastore.

Within three weeks of his initial letter, the chairman received a response from President Nixon endorsing the study and thereby assuring full HEW cooperation (Senate, Commerce Comm., Communications Subcomm., 1971: 2). Within three months Secretary Finch appointed the advisory committee; within five months the NIMH staff director for the project, Eli Rubinstein, appeared before the subcommittee to give a progress report (as previously requested by Senator Pastore); and within nine months Secretary Finch issued a public interim progress report.

In September 1970, the new surgeon general, Jesse L. Steinfeld, released a second progress report, outlining the 23 major research projects then underway. A year later in September 1971, after some of the contract research findings had been publicly reported at an academic convention, the subcommittee held a day of hearings and the surgeon general presented a third interim report. In January 1972, the advisory committee published its final report to the surgeon general, and then in March 1972, in the wake of the widespread and conflicting press accounts of that report, Senator Pastore held a series of hearings to clarify its conclusions and consider relevant "action." In April 1974, the chairman held a subsequent round of hearings to review the progress of one recommendation from the 1972 report and to urge industry cooperation in reducing televised violence.

Two events occurring relatively early in the process of establishing the project reveal, on the one hand, the strength of the political determination to press forward with the project and, on the other, the misdirected concern about the nature of bias built into it. The first event occurred during that second round of hearings in March 1969, when the surgeon general reported his intention to proceed with Senator Pastore's plan. At this point the only overtly discordant note in the initial set of hearings was struck when Senator Hartke raised a series of questions about the expected cost ($1 million) of the study (Senate, Commerce Comm., Communications Subcomm., 1969: 343-344). Couching his questions in the context of concern about extra, unbudgeted public expenditures, Hartke wondered from where the necessary funds would come. Stewart explained that some reprogramming authority existed within HEW and that congressional authority for further reprogramming was "not a very complicated procedure."

Irritated by this minor rebellion on the part of a colleague, the chairman reminded Senator Hartke that he had sent Pastore a letter urging that hearings on violence be held, thereby associating Hartke with the request for the research effort deemed necessary to conduct such hearings. Again invoking the rhetoric of a dire threat to American civilization, the chairman argued that the research would be well worth the cost: "If you break down the morality of this Nation, it will be the end of this Republic." He went on to note that although the surgeon general did not then have all the necessary funds, Senator Pastore and commerce committee chairman Magnuson both served "on the Appropriations Committee and I don't think we will have much problem." Apparently they did not, and NIMH was able to "provide approximately $1 million for new research and another $500,000 for administrative expenses. That money was squeezed out of existing budgets by the simple device of eliminating or postponing construction projects in the Community Mental Health Center Program" (Cater and Strickland, 1975: 21). Another estimate puts the administrative expense figure at $800,000 (Bogart, 1972-1973: 497).

In the wake of this demonstration of political power there were virtually no further public dissents to the chairman's plans by any member of the subcommittee over the subsequent five-year period during which four more rounds of hearings on the surgeon general's report were held. A minor episode in some respects, the funding squabble nonetheless served to notify all concerned that this project had the effective backing of the congressional leadership and the White House, that it would be undertaken quickly, and that it would be given high priority among affected government agencies and programs.

The other event, more widely publicized, occurred early among the many decisions associated with the establishment of the advisory committee. However, while the implications of this decision have been widely discussed, it has remained generally misinterpreted. Operating under Senator Pastore's model of the earlier advisory committee on smoking and cancer, the surgeon general submitted the names of potential appointees to the broadcast industry for review and comment. Cater and Strickland explain:

> The rationale had been that if the Committee subsequently issued an adverse report on cigarette smoking, as in fact it did, no one could

> complain that it had been prejudiced against the industry. The question was whether the television industry, which might be the target of criticism in the new Advisory Committee's report, should be given a similar opportunity to review candidate lists. On the advice of Dr. Rubinstein, Surgeon General Stewart answered "yes" [1975: 22].

From an initial list of 200 candidates, 40 were submitted to the three networks and the NAB. CBS declined to make any suggestions, but in the selection of the final twelve:

> Evidently others felt no such reservations. NBC, ABC, and the NAB did comment on the list, raising objections to seven of the preliminary nominees. Surgeon General Steward deferred to this industry "veto." In addition, the television industry was allowed other prerogatives. Five of the thirty-five persons nominated by the networks and the NAB were selected to serve on the Advisory Committee. Two of them, Joseph Klapper and Thomas Coffin, were network officials as well as social scientists. The other three had been employed as network consultants [1975: 22-23].

Much like the by then regular process in selecting other high level advisory groups, it appears that the final list was further influenced by questions of "race, sex, political acceptability, and heterogeneity of background" (Paisley, 1972: 21).

To critics of the surgeon general's report who feel that the findings fall short of the interpretations warranted in the research, the veto affair is seen as a primary villain. Many included in this group come from among the social scientists who performed much of the research for the advisory committee, and the implication of their complaints is that without the veto and without industry representatives on the committee the data in the several research reports would have been interpreted much more affirmatively as demonstrating the negative effects of televised violence. There is then a cloud of industry bias associated with the final report.

But undiscussed by virtually all commentators was the more fundamental question of the particular scientific biases built into the advisory committee and its staff support from the outset. In keeping with the general scientific mandate established by Senator Pastore and the behavioral science context represented in the government agencies attached to the project, the SAC was weighted heavily toward the disciplines of experimental and clinical psychology and quantitative sociology and political science. Only one or two committee members had any roots in the qualitative social sciences or in the historical, critical, or cultural studies aspects of communications, and none came from the humanities. Under the circumstances of the advisory committee's origins, its subsequent character is hardly surprising. What is significant is that that character should have been seen as being not only obvious and inevitable, but also appropriate.

The remarkable feature of the debate about the constituency of the committee is that, amid all the controversy over industry representation and veto power, no consideration seems to have been given to the general shape of knowledge, to the particular philosophy of science binding the members of the committee. There is little or no awareness of the consequences of turning to those who see the communication process as either part of the study of deviant social behavior or as reducible to statistical data and formal theories of empirically verifiable individual or group action. The critics appear to possess no conceptual framework for recognizing that there exist entirely different perspectives on the nature of communication and the significance of television content and viewing. In the end it might have been observed that the complaints about the vetoes ignore the argument that, regardless of persuasion about the effects issue, those scientists who were industry critics and those who were its apologists all had similar world views and that for the political purposes of the surgeon general's report, their differences were insignificant.

To help establish this argument it is necessary to consider selected aspects of the research in the report. It is impossible here to deal with every element in the massive corpus of the several dozen research papers included in the five volumes of the advisory committee report. For more detailed information about their contents and for summaries of their findings the several sources already cited are sufficiently thorough. However, in order to better grasp the terms in which the report was cast and thereby to understand its political significance, it is helpful to consider aspects of a few of the key studies and the overviews in the technical reports.

Although the amount of research commissioned directly by the committee constituted considerably more centrally coordinated work than ever before undertaken in conjunction with such investigations, much of it was not wholly new. A number of projects were continuations or updates of work previously conducted, others were extensions of such lines of research. Matilda Paisley puts it somewhat less charitably: "Proposals came mainly from an 'invisible college' of researchers — colleagues of the [NIMH] staff who were already working in this area and were delighted to have more money to carry on their work. Other proposals were submitted by researchers who were willing to change the focus of their research somewhat to secure support" (1972: 25).

As a result, the overall pattern of the research and findings, while often providing new data, fell into configurations essentially similar to those developed during the earlier inquiries. There were those groups of studies providing descriptive trend data on broadcast industry operations, or programming processes and content, and on audience viewing patterns and preferences. To gather evidence of direct, short-term effects there were a number of fundamental laboratory-type experimental studies, and detailed reviews of several of those that had been conducted before the SAC projects began. The committee also commissioned field studies to provide not only the viewing behavior data, but also measures of correlation with patterns of aggression. Several such projects, designed as field experiments, attempted to combine the methodological rigor of the laboratory experiments with the more "natural" settings of the field studies.

The formal content analysis work had, of course, begun during the period of the Eisenhower Commission study. As had been the case there, this analysis played a central role in the political efficacy of the advisory committee report. Systematic trend data on the levels of violent content and its role in the dramatic structure of programming was now readily available (Gerbner, 1972b). Not unlike the experience during the debate over the necessity of noncommercial television reservations in 1951-1952, close formal study of commercial television content patterns proved to be a key element in building the critics' case against industry protestations of improved practice and in providing grounds for possible policy decisions.[2] Representing no direct testimony on the question of effects, the content analysis nonetheless helped lay the base for charges of presumed deleterious impact. In part this strategy included an element from the previous investigations. Having established that high levels of violence existed in network programming, with the highest levels found in Saturday morning cartoons, the advisory committee was able to call on research that showed substantial amounts of viewing among children, particularly of the more violent prime time fare. As before, this association served for many as sufficiently damaging circumstantial evidence, leading to the conclusion that if there are such high levels of violence in television programming and if that content is so widely and heavily attended, the social impact, regardless of what other research might find, must be more negative than positive.

In laying its descriptive foundations, however, the surgeon general's project added another line of inquiry. As well as the content analysis reported in its first volume, the committee published studies of the processes by which television programming is chosen and produced, including analyses of producer attitudes, network program standards and review practices, and economic incentives. In what was perhaps some of the clearest and least ambiguous language in the entire series of reports, individual researchers and the senior NIMH staff research coordinator thought these studies conclusive enough to make the following observations:

> The Federal Communications Commission and the NAB Code Review Board have authority but little effective power. Power stems from the chief client relationships between major national advertisers and the managements of the three national networks. That basic structure determines the process of program control and development and shapes symbolic content [Gerbner, 1972a: 412].

> The reality of the marketplace at this time is that if a producer wishes to make television shows to be shown on commercial television, he must please two audiences: first the buyers of the film; eventually the viewers. But the buyer necessarily becomes the most important audience. No program can ever be judged by the general audience unless it first pleases a buyer — in most cases, a network.

> If the networks must function so as to try to capture the largest possible audience (as has been so often suggested), they may be unable to basically change program content without losing a large part of their anticipated viewing audience [Cantor, 1972: 278, 279].

> The most striking impression left by the studies in this volume is the intractability of violence in commercial television entertainment in the United States. The evidence converges on a single point: violence is extraordinarily difficult and perhaps impossible to control within the present context of commercial broadcasting [Comstock, 1972: 25].

Sufficient for some, this was not the sort of research that Senator Pastore has in mind when he established the project. Further, given its political purpose, the implications of these conclusions (see below) were perhaps *too* compelling. Such considerations may explain why issues bearing on economic imperatives and on questions about how the content takes the shape it does were discussed only hastily in the middle of the advisory committee's 210-page summary report:

> Although many among network personnel express interest in reducing violence in their programs, they feel constrained by the economic realities of broadcasting. In order to induce advertisers to finance programming, networks must draw large audiences with demographic characteristics attractive to advertisers. As both network officials and creators of programs see it, "action" is among the best, fastest, and easiest ways of attracting and keeping large audiences, and "action" is considered as almost synonymous with violence. This reality looms large and is a source of contention among both creators of programs and the network officials who oversee and judge the programs [Scientific Advisory Committee, 1972: 79].

As potentially powerful as this discussion might be, it is only three pages long, and it deals as much with the complexity of group decision making in television programming as it does with economic imperatives. Moreover, none of this discussion is presented in the summary chapter of findings and conclusions of this volume — the twenty page section that is probably the most widely read and quoted segment of the entire seven-volume series. It should also be noted that these few, brief studies of institutional processes were as far afield as the SAC project was allowed to go. Dominated by professional researchers and academics trained primarily in the behavioral sciences, neither the committee nor the NIMH staff were predisposed to define the problem of effects broadly enough to include a wider range of studies of structures and operations, nor to permit any basic economic research whatsoever.

The "patterns of use" research reported in Volume IV represents the other, more typical link with the content analysis. Here, among other reports, LoSciuto presents results of a national survey of viewing behavior; Israel and Robinson describe the demographics of viewers of television violence and news programs; Robinson provides cross-national data on leisure time use; Lyle and Hoffman provide survey results on Southern California grade school and adolescent viewing behavior and preferences, updating much of the research from Schramm et al. (1961); and Ward, Wackman, and others present a series of eight studies on the impact of television advertising on children.

While achieving the objective of demonstrating substantial amounts of television viewing among the nation's young, these studies do not provide the easy measures of correlation with evidence of antisocial behavior that had been the assumption of previous discussions. Indeed, some of the most interesting conclusions from this line of research emphasize the complexity of the viewing experience, finding significance in television in matters far removed from questions of violence and its effects.

In his overview to Volume IV, Lyle did report some evidence of modeling behavior on the part of children at various age levels and some "positive relations between preference for violent television programs and actual (self-reported) participation in aggressive delinquent behavior among young men just out of high school" (1972: 11). But more striking were the observations about general usage patterns and attitudes. Found now to be thoroughly ubiquitous (96 percent of American households), television could be said to be "deeply integrated into our lives," filling large amounts of time, providing major topics of conversation, and serving as a point of conflict in parent-child and sibling relationships. Yet in a number of ways television also was found to be less engaging than earlier research had suggested it might be. From both self-report and direct observational measures it became apparent that people tend to view in relatively opportunistic and unplanned patterns, and to be more ready now to characterize their viewing simply and undefensively as relaxation or as a way of killing time. The survey research also suggested that other activities often accompany television, and that few viewers accept uncritically the fare provided.

Perhaps the most imaginative, if technically most cumbersome, audience study of the entire SAC project was that of Bechtal et al. (1972). This research demonstrates the fluidity and "complexity of behavior during the time the television set is on." From video tapes taken of a sample of families actually viewing television in their own homes over a five-day period, this study revealed a behavior pattern far different than that conjured up by most survey research: "The data point to an inseparable mixture of watching and nonwatching as a general style of television viewing behavior." It is "complex and various." It "does not occur in a vacuum; it is always to some degree background to a complex behavior pattern in the home" (1972: 298-299).

As provocative as this research was, its design violated so many of the normal science requirements for acceptable survey research that it had little impact on the major directions taken by the overall advisory committee program. Indeed this study was permitted only as a way of testing the validity of survey questionnaires. The somewhat radical theoretical implications of its findings were largely overlooked at all levels of review in the project — by the advisory committee, by Lyle in his overview, and by the investigators themselves.

More conventional research in Volume IV suggests that among teenagers television is not even the primary form of entertainment, that music listening, through the radio and records, plays a much greater role in the "everyday life space" of tenth graders (Lyle, 1972: 23). Further, it turns out that what most concerns many of those populations studied about the television they see is not the violence nor any other aspect of news or general content. "Across all age groups commercials were the major focus of complaints and negative attitudes toward television" (Lyle, 1972: 20).

Given the make-up of the advisory committee it is perhaps not surprising that the latter data went totally unreported in the summary volume. As the Paisley (1972) paper indicates, the mechanics of the summary report writing process and the insistence on providing a unanimous report allowed the industry defenders on the advisory committee to prevent just this sort of information from filtering through. In view of Senator Pastore's broader political purposes for the project, there were implicit understandings that would permit concessions to the industry.

As for the concessions by the industry, for the most part they were secured even before the advisory committee began work.

> The NIMH staff, under the direction of Eli Rubinstein, had already made a number of decisions about the research project prior to the first convening of the committee. "Overall, the twelve committee members had almost nothing to say about conceptualizing the research to be funded by 'their' million dollars, about soliciting research contracts, or about any detail either theoretical or methodological" [Paisley, 1972: 24].

Thus there was a certain stress on experimental work and field study correlation efforts that the advisory committee would have to confront and that would sweep it and the industry out of the relatively placid eddies of descriptive studies into the more dangerous currents of causal linkages.

As we have seen, much of the early research on the effects of film and television violence was experimental, conducted under carefully controlled laboratory conditions and growing out of the ongoing behavioral studies in learning and the psychology of aggression. It was this work, capable of demonstrating direct causal linkages between, on the one hand, information presentation and modeled conduct and, on the other, subsequent acquisition and imitative behavior. that did much to heighten the anxiety about television's putative power. As was clearly expected, it was the group of psychologists best known for their work in this area who were blackballed by the broadcast industry. Bandura, Berkowitz, and Tannenbaum, among others, were barred from serving as advisory committee members, and no research by them was sponsored under the committee's program. Nonetheless, the work of such researchers was hardly ignored in the overview reports to the technical volumes, and closely related experiments were conducted by others of similar methodological and theoretical persuasion.

The impact of this work is perhaps most clearly observable in Liebert's paper introducing Volume II. It is here and, though more indirectly, in Chaffee's introduction to Volume III, that the research is reviewed and presented in such a way as to make the strongest negative effects argument (Liebert, 1972; Chaffee, 1972). It is to these overviews particularly that the critics of the advisory committee are referring when they suggest that the technical volumes provide firmer, clearer evidence than does the summary report.

Liebert's approach is through the traditional channels of behaviorism. His perception of the television experience is adopted from the models of learning theory: "The scientific issue most fundamentally related to the particular question of the effects of television revolves around the nature of *observational learning*, i.e., the way in which the behavior of children (and adults) changes as a function of exposure to the behavior of others" (Liebert, 1972: 2). To explain the context for the research report in Volume II, he posits a framework of modeling, observational learning, acquisition, and acceptance that constitutes an assumptive base of experimental psychology and the first generation of media effects research, and that exhibits little or no interest in the communicative workings within the mind.

In part this is a celebration of the scientific method: Because "the investigator can conclude that the differences in the independent variable (or treatment) caused or produced differences in the dependent variable(s) . . . experimental research is widely considered to be the most powerful research tool in the social sciences" (Liebert, 1972: 7-8). But it is also a specific argument for direct effects as based on the experimental work of Bandura and others: "Regardless of their particular theoretical affiliations, investigators interested in socialization have virtually all acknowledged that a child's values, knowledge, and behavior may be developed and molded, at least in part, by observational learning" (1972: 2).

Such short term, directly imitative results are invested with great theoretical and policymaking significance, and a summary of the research from various aspects of the entire advisory committee project makes a neat scenario. Liebert begins by reviewing the descriptive findings from Volumes I and IV:

> Clearly, the first stage of the observational learning of aggression from television, *exposure*, does occur. At this writing, there appears to be no question that violent television fare is available in overwhelming abundance and that children do watch these programs both frequently and regularly [1972: 9].

He then summarizes the case for acquisition:

> The data reviewed in this section suggest that children are likely to acquire, with the level of repeated exposure which takes place, a good deal of the aggressive repertoire that they see in televised violence. In fact, by virtue of their ability to evoke emotional responses, programs containing violence appear particularly likely to be learned and retained from televised observational experience [1972: 12].

However, because the question of external validity is acknowledged as problematic, there is an attempt to link the findings of such research with the tendencies perceived in the correlational field studies. Since the research reported in Volume II was all experimental, Liebert has to rely on material from other volumes to build the field study case, particularly several of the studies in Volume III (Dominick and Greenberg; McLeod, Atkin, and Chaffee; Lefkowitz et al.). The efforts there were to link various measures of aggression to levels of exposure to violent content. In certain respects these results appeared to be successful. Liebert quotes from the McLeod et al. study that "among both boys and girls at two grade levels [junior high and senior high] the more the child watches violent television fare, the more aggressive he is likely to be. . . . Adolescents viewing high levels of violent content on television tend to have high levels of aggressive behavior, regardless of television viewing time, socioeconomic status, or school performance" (Liebert, 1972: 17).

Similarly he calls on the longitudinal study of aggression by Lefkowitz et al. arguing with them that "on the basis of the cross-lagged correlations . . . a substantial component of aggression at all three grade levels . . . can be predicted better by the amount of television violence which the child watched in the third grade than by any other causal variable measured, [reinforcing] the contention that there is a cause and effect relation between the violence content of television and overt aggressive behavior (Liebert, 1972: 18-19).

The Lefkowitz et al. paper (1972) occupies a strategic place in the advisory committee collection. While it is only one of several correlation studies, its particular features set it apart from most of the others, leading both Liebert and Chaffee to give it special emphasis in their respective overviews and forcing the advisory committee to expend a relatively large amount of energy to attempt to minimize its importance.

Besides lacking the fine controls of the laboratory experiment, the field study of violence effects is also vulnerable to scientific criticism on a number of other counts. For instance, in the interest of economy such research usually relies on self-report techniques such as diaries or recall questionnaires when measuring viewing patterns. However, as much methodological research suggests, including some in the surgeon general's project itself (e.g., Bechtel et al.), such measures are often at great variance with more direct observational evidence.

Similar weaknesses appear in the indices of aggression. Understandably reluctant to establish experimental conditions that might actually lead subjects into violent acts, the field researchers are constrained to rely also on peer or self-report measures of aggressive tendencies. Thus McLeod and his colleagues (1972) adapt several aggression indices from self-report scales developed for previous studies by other researchers. While such measures are carefully designed to be internally reliable, the researcher can never be certain they have external validity — that they adequately manifest aggressive behavior.

Another dimension of concern about such research is its tendency to focus on short-term effects. Field studies usually have to rely on the results of measures taken shortly after or in conjunction with viewing pattern measures. Effects research had been hampered by the recency of television's introduction and the difficulty of trying to sort out from the myriad complexities of a rapidly changing contemporary era those aspects of American life that could be attributed to television. By the time of the surgeon general's project, only two decades after the introduction of television, few research projects could be said to be developing any attributes of longevity. Some, such as Lyle and Hoffman (1972), did attempt to update earlier work, but at best most were rooted in data derived no earlier than the mid-1960s.

Because it relies on peer reports of aggression, the Lefkowitz study (1972) presents much of the same sort of methodological difficulties posed by the other correlational studies. But, because of its longitudinal nature and its cross-lagged correlational design, it appears to represent a unique, more powerful insight into the effects question. As Liebert enthusiastically reports in his overview to Volume II, by tracking viewing behavior and aggression ratings of members of the same sample at three different time periods over a ten-year span (third, eighth, and thirteenth grades), the Lefkowitz group and their predecessors offered reason to believe that they had "stronger evidence for a causal relationship than is usually available from correlational studies (Liebert, 1972: 18).

As is pointed out in a number of ways and in various places throughout the technical reports and in the advisory committee summary volume, correlational studies must be recognized for what they are — and are not — and they therefore must be interpreted with considerable care: "It is an axiom of science that correlation does not demonstrate causation. Covariation of two variables may occur for a great variety of causal and noncausal reasons, or for no discernible reason at all. Correlation is a necessary but not sufficient condition for causal inference" (Scientific Advisory Committee, 1972: 143). Again, in light of the constituency of the advisory committee and the high probability of its opposition to a clear-cut negative effects conclusion, it is not surprising to find such cautions, including an entire appendix (E) that serves as a lecture on the dangers of misinterpretation surrounding the use of correlation coefficients.

The Lefkowitz study thus seems to be especially significant. It attempts to advance the effects argument in a manner that appears to counter major weaknesses of field research; and because of its surface-level appeal — its longitudinal design, its differential, directional correlative findings, and its facility with the language of causality — the study proves to be attractive to the lay and political observer. For instance, Cater and Strickland highlight this study in their discussion of the surgeon general's field research. They give a brief nod to the "rival hypothesis" claim, noting that social scientists "caution . . . that such statistical correlations do not prove that one variable is the cause of the other. It might simply be that the children who were more inclined to be aggressive toward others were also more likely to enjoy watching aggressive actions on television" (Cater and Strickland, 1975: 49). But they quickly go on to emphasize the strongest conclusions of the study and to ignore other serious weaknesses in the research. To anticipate the consequences of such attractions the advisory committee report is obliged to expend considerable energy and space probing its faults and downplaying its significance:

> Lefkowitz reports a correlation of .31 between a measure of exposure to television violence among Grade 3 boys and peer ratings of aggression among the same boys ten years later. This finding, in and of itself, is supportive of the interpretation that relatively high early exposure to television produces, in some boys, aggressive tendencies which are manifested in behavior years later. However, other findings of the same study, together with certain unresolved problems regarding the measures employed, leave the dynamic not nearly as clear as the .31 correlation coefficient suggests, and are also supportive of an interpretation which would ascribe a considerable causal role to early (Grade 3 or earlier) aggressive tendencies, however these may have been engendered.
>
> But the instrument used at Grade 13 was phrased in the past tense (e.g., "Who started fights over nothing?" "Who used to say mean things?"), and the temporal reference of the replies is thus ambiguous; the Grade 13 youth may have been referring to the behavior of their prior classmates at different times across the ten-year span.
>
> [Thus] we can conclude only that the data cited are consonant with the interpretation that violence viewing leads to later aggression, but are not conclusive [Scientific Advisory Committee, 1972: 153, 154, 157].

In his overview to Volume III Chaffee is also careful in handling the Lefkowitz research and in discussing the general difficulty of making causal inferences from correlation studies. He recites the various problems of validity and meaning associated with the differences between parental and self-report measures of programming preferences, with the differing experiences for young people viewing television at ten-year intervals, and with the differing perceptions during that same growth period of the indices used to measure aggression.

> Now that a skilled research team has persevered long enough to complete such a study, it can be seen that this research model held out a false promise. The tools for causal inference from nonexperimental data require assumptions that will be met for few, if any, of the variables that interest us in developmental research [Chaffee, 1972: 29].

Chaffee's interpretative stance reflects the acute discomfort of so many social scientists involved in the surgeon general's project. The weaknesses of the negative effects position are that it is built on the foundation of purely experimental behavioral research. It therefore offers an opportunity for the proponents of imaginative field research. But even that form of research has drawbacks, and Chaffee and others know that they must be cautious enough to acknowledge them. Yet in so doing they find themselves in the somewhat embarassing position of appearing to provide a cornerstone of the broadcast industry apologia. Caught in this dilemma, Chaffee's strategy is characteristic of much of the advisory committee's response. He never strays far from discussion of the weaknesses in the field research, but whenever possible he advances cautious assertions in favor of the negative effects argument:

> Although a simple causal viewing aggressiveness function cannot reasonably be considered proven, neither can it be easily rejected. Of the various possible explantions for the finding, it has parsimony on its side, and it is probably the most commonly held "folk hypothesis" about television violence. At this stage in research on television violence, the present longitudinal finding (in the context of a wide variety of supportive experimental and field studies) appears to stand as the strongest evidence on behalf of the main causal hypotheses [1972: 29].

Then, having argued that the case, if not solid, is more compelling than heretofore, he is quick to grant the possibility of an explanatory "third variable, whose effect on television preferences occurs in childhood but which does not manifest itself in social aggressiveness until well into adolescence" (1972: 29).

This sort of vacillation continues to the end:

> If one were limited to a choice between the two possible two-variable causal hypotheses, there is decidedly more support here for the viewing-induces-aggressiveness interpretation than for the reverse. The data supporting that conclusion have survived a number of statistical controls for likely "third variables," but of course there is a potentially infinite list of such additional factors that might account for the correlations that have been found.
>
> What, in the light of these new studies, can be said of the scientific standing of the proposition that viewing of violent television programs induces tendencies toward aggressive behavior in adolescents? In several ways, that rather hazy hypothesis has been enhanced, in comparison with competing theories about the relationship between these variables.
>
> Meanwhile, the present studies have also demonstrated that adolescent aggressiveness is associated with a number of other factors that have nothing to do with television. . . . These studies rather conclusively eliminate the hypothesis that television is the sole, or principal, cause of aggressive behavior by adolescents. In all, it appears to make a relatively minor contribution. And the findings here cannot conclusively eliminate the possibility that this apparent contribution is an artifact of other causal processes that have yet to be discovered [Chaffee, 1972: 30, 32-33].

The advisory committee report itself also adopts a cautious stance. While the conclusions appear to tilt in favor of a negative effects argument, every statement is heavily qualified:

> As we have noted, the data, while not wholly consistent or conclusive, do indicate that a modest relationship exists between the viewing of violence and aggressive behavior.
>
> Several findings of survey studies can be cited to sustain the hypothesis that viewing of violent television has a causal relation to aggressive behavior, though neither individually nor collectively are the findings conclusive.
>
> The experimental studies . . . contain indications that, under certain limited conditions, television viewing may lead to an increase in aggressive behavior. The evidence is clearest in highly controlled laboratory studies and considerably weaker in studies conducted under more natural conditions.
>
> Thus, the two sets of findings converge in three respects: a preliminary and tentative indication of a causal relation between viewing violence on television and aggressive behavior; an indication that

> any such causal relation operates only on some children (who are predisposed to be aggressive); and an indication that it operates only in some environmental contexts [Scientific Advisory Committee, 1972: 16, 18-19].

It is readily apparent from this material that, if taken out of context, different elements of it could be adduced to either side of the effects debate. The report is a masterpiece of evasiveness, and as its conflicting conclusions began to be disseminated the report created substantial press and academic controversy.

THE 1971 HEARINGS

Even before the advisory committee's report was released, some of its research came under public scrutiny. Lyle and Hoffman, Greenberg and Gordon, McLeod and Chaffee, and Liebert and Baron all gave papers at a symposium during the American Psychological Association convention in Washington, D.C., in September 1971. Using many of the data gathered under their contracts from NIMH for the surgeon general's research, they provided an early glimpse of some of the contents of Volumes II, III, and IV in the forthcoming technical reports.

Though not large in volume, the brief flurry of publicity generated by these reports appears to have given Senator Pastore an opportunity to convene, two weeks later, a public meeting of his subcommittee to hear a "progress report" from Surgeon General Steinfeld. The breadth of this purpose was revealed during his opening remarks:

> Certain impressions have gotten abroad to the effect that they [the researchers at the convention] were speaking officially as to the final report of your committee. Those of us on this committee who have been following this know that this is not quite the fact. But frankly if you had not been a member of this committee and you were just a private citizen who was interested in what progress was being made, you would have gotten the wrong impression. . . . I thought that one of the chief reasons of bringing you here today is so that we could get this straightened out as to exactly what the situation is, whether or not these panel discussions were the opinion of your Advisory Committee, and naturally, of course, when a final report would be forthcoming.
>
> I think the public is entitled to know at this juncture just about where we stand, and when we can have something definitive so that action can be taken.
>
> For that reason, I want to serve notice on the FCC and the FTC and the networks and the broadcasters that this committee also expects

> them to follow the progress of the Surgeon General's committee closely so that when its final report is issued all parties will be in a position quickly to take whatever action, if any, that is necessary in their respective areas of responsibility. After all, the issue is too critical, and the stakes too high, to procrastinate if something must be done [Senate, Commerce Comm., Communications Subcomm., 1971: 2-3].

While at one level it appears that the senator was worried that the working papers given at the APA convention were being taken as official pronouncements of the advisory committee, it is apparent that he had much more on his mind and that he knew how to turn this opportunity to the service of such additional purposes. There is here an explicit exercise of pressure on the surgeon general, reminding him that the final report is expected as soon as possible. Further, there is the equally open "serving of notice" on the interested industry and government parties, couched in the rhetoric of the expectation that "whatever action necessary" will be taken.

Overall the senator appears to have been building a structure of publicity for the eventual release and subsequent debate about the report. Thus, while the 1971 hearings may have been designed in part to stem the leakage that might soften the impact of the later report release, they also served to enhance the image of a subcommittee closely involved in a matter of substantial public import and earnestly preparing to pursue significant "necessary action."

At the very least Chairman Pastore was reminding the advisory committee, presumably just then thoroughly engaged in writing its final report, of his original charge to provide a report substantial enough to use in the continuing communications policy debate: "I would hope that the Surgeon General in due time will come before this committee, not with a lot of ifs and buts but will tell us in simple language, whether or not the broadcasters ought to be put on notice and be very very careful in this area, because it might have an effect on certain people" (1971: 8).

It is difficult to believe that after all the research reported up through the period of the Eisenhower Commission and after the evidence available from the early working papers in the surgeon general's project that the senator could still, if he ever had, expect a definitive report. A more likely explanation was the continuing political need to appear to be seriously examining the problem, to be threatening action while yet hoping that changes might yet take place that would obviate the need for direct legislative remedy.

Senator Pastore was not the only one with a complex agenda within which this day of hearings neatly fit. Senator Baker had noticed in a Sunday newspaper an interview with Scott Ward about aspects o his research for the project and the finding that "by the time children reach the fourth grade they express contempt for TV commercials and many find them to be in bad taste, stupid, or false" (1971: 11). Senator Baker may have also noticed that the preliminary Lyle and Hoffman report delivered at the APA convention included similar findings: "Among our mothers the most frequent focus of complaints was, not violence, but commercials. Nine out of ten of the students at both sixth and tenth grade levels felt there were too many commercials. The majority gave commercials a low vote on credibility (1971: 44).[3]

Without explaining why, Senator Baker makes an effort to play down the significance of these insights. "I do not mean this question to be facetious, but being the father of children that have now safely negotiated that difficult period, being in the fourth, fifth and sixth grade, I recall that at the time they thought their parents were stupid and dumb and the like" (1971: 11). He then goes on both to broaden the focus of his inquiry and to sharpen his warning to the advisory committee. The following selections from his exchanges with Dr. Rubinstein tell us much about how political considerations impinged on the final drafting process of the advisory committee report:

> *Senator Baker:* . . . Those who advocate that we wait until we can do a perfect job of anything are in effect advocating inaction, and I disapprove of that. But it seems to me in this study that substantial account must be taken of all the significant environmental factors. I do not want to see us go off on a witch-hunt against television. . . . Would it be inappropriate for me to ask the representative of NIMH if he cares to give me any further views on this subject?
>
> *Dr. Rubinstein:* I think you are absolutely right, Senator. The issue of looking at television in this study inevitably makes it seem as if we are focusing on it somewhat inappropriately but in fact, as you well know, this is difficult enough in and of itself to do without getting involved in all the other aspects that you are referring to. I think the committee that is working on this is well aware of the problem that you are raising, that it may well seem by the time they get done that we have overemphasized the issue of television, and I am sure they will make some response to that possibility. . . .
>
> *Senator Baker:* . . . In view of the range and the scope of these hearings, carefully pointed out by the chairman to be an examination of the techniques used in gathering this information rather than a review of the information itself, I would hope that your report presents both sides of the situation so we can engage in what the Congress does so well; that is, carry on an adversary proceeding. . . . If we are to arrive at an intelligent legislative judgment on what ought to be done, we should understand all the environmental factors, not just the influence of television [1971: 12-13].

Senator Baker's role must be seen in light of the Nixon administration policies toward the broadcasting and print media. Perhaps the key element of that policy was a carefully modulated process of criticism and offers of cooperation. Whereas the stick of public attack was wielded by Vice President Agnew and others on the White House staff, the carrots of such things as S.2004 (the license renewal bill) and a softened surgeon general's report were offered through the liaison effected between Clay Whitehead's Office of Telecommunications Policy and the congressional communications subcommittees. As the ranking Republican member on the Senate committee, Senator Baker's role must not be ignored.[4]

Matilda Paisley reports on the internal politics of the report writing process. Working from selected press reports and her own personal contact with staff coordinator Comstock and others, she depicts a scenario in which one faction of a seriously divided advisory committee is worn down by the diligent, patient work of Klapper and others among the "network five." For example,

> The *Adolescent Aggressiveness and Television* subcommittee, chaired by Ira Cisin, wrote Chapter 7. Others on the group were Ithiel Pool, Joseph Klapper, Andrew S. Watson, and Thomas E. Coffin. The first draft was written by George Comstock. At the first meeting of this group only Klapper and Cisin were present to meet with Comstock. Pool and Watson were unable to attend. Klapper objected to almost everything in the 32-page draft. He objected to the style, the form, and the interpretation of findings. He brought in pages of specific objections. Cisin supported Klapper. Comstock agreed to rewrite the draft. He again followed the outline of Chaffee's overview paper, but added more documentation. This version ran 65 pages. Cisin and Klapper were still unhappy with the draft and rewrote it. Cisin remodeled the first half. He took the third variable issue and in general downgraded the evidence. Instead of saying what results had been found in studies that included third variables, he implied that the third variables that had been investigated were only a drop in the bucket (which may be true in some ultimate, policy-irrelevant sense). The Klapper and Cisin draft left much of the text the same. However, they recast the findings and conclusions. Pool helped to tone down the Klapper-Cisin draft, eliminating some of the overkill [Paisley, 1972: 31].

Another research coordinator, John Murray, reports on the tone of the advisory committee meetings: "There was a big move to get a consensus report. There was a lot of anger, the meetings were extremely tense with the warring factions sitting at either end of the table, glaring at each other, particularly toward the end" (Paisley, 1972: 28).

In an interview for the Cater and Strickland book Dr. Klapper portrays the differences among the committee members in a different light:

> There were twelve people there representing several different disciplines and, as is always the case in these situations, some of them had a point of view on the matter and some of them didn't, and the points of view differed. . . . I found it to be an exceptionally smooth running Committee. I saw no factions. . . . I never saw any major fight. . . . I would say that the differences that existed were differences in emphasis in research orientation. That is, there is a hell of a long way between an Irving Janis, who is an experimentalist and a goddamn good one, and a Charles Pinderhuges, who is a psychoanalyst and a goddamn good one. . . . So naturally there were differences in the degree of weight which different individuals would give to any individual piece of evidence [Cater and Strickland, 1975: 74].

He goes on to say that he saw "no glaring across the table," and that the most serious friction was between the committee and the staff.

Whichever of these versions is the more accurate, it is important to note that the problems in the advisory committee's work are characterized as internal ones, derived largely from the problems of industry influence, differential academic and professional backgrounds, or the tendency of committee staff to be more aggressive than the committee members themselves. These several analyses never seek to trace the struggles back to the external political process out of which the surgeon general's project emerged. One needs constantly to keep in mind the total context of communications policymaking considerations motivating the Congress, such as those reflected in the S.2004 debate. The issue of violence on television serves as a convenient middle ground for struggle among government, various publics, and the broadcast industry over certain surface-level matters, allowing them to engage in ritual forms of combat while yet avoiding the more serious implications of confrontation with fundamental structural and policy issues such as ownership, control, and purpose.

It is helpful as well to recall the discussion above of the special motives guiding the few published analyses of the project. Frustrated by the repetitiveness and limitations of the issues investigated in the project, many analysts have begun increasingly to conceive of the questions about television primarily as problems of improved policymaking mechanisms. Reflecting the strengths and weaknesses of similar recent trends in the study of so many other social issues, this approach has not been any more successful in communications. Instead of providing insights into the nature of the social and cultural issues associated with communications, much of the research in this field has come to be dedicated to enhancing the legitimation of communications policymaking research per se. Although they may offer important information about the details of episodes such as the surgeon general's project, these reviews seem to be unaware of the implications of their respective celebrations of the communications policy research enterprise. None seem to realize how, in view of the larger political context, they too are crucial elements in sustaining the mutual accommodations among government, the broadcasting industry, the academy, and even reformers.

It should thus be clear that in addition to not being independent of direct industry pressure, the advisory committee was not working independently of the various — and often contradictory — governmental influences either. From the very outset it had been directed by the surgeon general not to make any policy recommendations (Cater and Strickland, 1975: 24). As its work progressed, the committee could not fail to take heed of Senator Pastore's impatience, of Senator Baker's warnings, or of the potential role its report might be forced to play in the overall patterns of White House initiatives against the mass media that had taken shape precisely during the life of the committee. For its part, and in spite of all its reported aggressiveness, the NIMH staff group serving the committee could not have operated without cognizance of NIMH's previous history and future funding prospects. The staff's seconding to the surgeon general must have been seen as the temporary assignment it was, requiring care in providing what Congress and the White House seemed to want. In short, it had cautiously to coordinate the project's various elements so as to thread a safe path through the minefield of conflicting political pressures. Thus the various research summaries and histories of the study are remarkable for failing to see that the issues surrounding the project were something more than those of industrial vetoes, inappropriate research questions, inadequate methodologies, and mistaken press reports.

In light of this broader political context it is perhaps easier to make sense of the events occurring in the wake of the informal transmittal of the advisory committee's report to the surgeon general on December 31, 1971. Primarily through the hearings held by the Senate communications subcommittee during March 1972, Chairman Pastore managed to alter substantially the impression left by the contents of the report and the initial press accounts of it.

Several of the histories and critiques make much of the alleged misinterpretations that appeared to create a widespread initial impression that the report found no significant causal links between television viewing and aggressive behavior in children. Apparently having been leaked more than one copy of the report prior to its scheduled release by Steinfeld, Jack Gould of the *New York Times* wrote the first story under a headline that read, "TV Violence Held Unharmful to Youth." Gould's key summary was that "the office of the United States Surgeon General has found that violence in television programming does not have an adverse effect on the majority of the nation's youth but may influence small groups of youngsters predisposed by many factors to aggressive behavior" (Cater and Strickland, 1975: 79). Charges of "whitewash" by Congressman John M. Murphy (D-N.Y.), strong denials in a press conference by Steinfeld, public reaction by a few of the participants in the research program, and a variety of conflicting newspaper and magazine stories combined to create a range of confusing impressions about the conclusions and significance of the report.

But, as we have seen above, the report *is* tentative and equivocal. The critics may be correct that the influence of the industry within the advisory committee did much to set this tone. But the claim that the technical reports make the causal linkages case so much more strongly is equally the product of selective reading. A determination to make the data fit prior convictions was not a sin committed exclusively by the pro-industry representatives among the researchers and committee members.

Thus the public confusion during the early weeks of 1972 is an understandable and, in retrospect, appropriate response. It may not, however, have been the reaction anticipated by Senator Pastore. In spite of his public requests for an unequivocal report, there was always some question about the definitiveness of the results he expected. The cautious, highly qualified conclusions of the report were probably the most politically useful results desired. But now there was danger that the appearance of inconclusiveness was being carried too far. Should the report appear to conclude that the content of American television programming was largely harmless, it would cut across the grain of a great deal of liberal, reformist public opinion, weakening the ability of the subcommittee to sustain the political leverage necessary to mediate that critical public opinion and to maintain the image of close scrutiny of television that had motivated the original decision to establish the surgeon general's project.

NOTES

1. For a sharply critical analysis of the Aspen Program, see Schrag (1975).

2. To buttress its case for the necessity of reservations, the ad hoc Joint Council on Educational Television sponsored a series of studies of the programming on the commercial television stations in five major cities during 1951 (see National Association of Educational Broadcasters, 1951). While these studies were crucial in the FCC decision to set aside channels for noncommercial television, the policy parallels with 1969-1974 must not be overdrawn. During the "freeze" of 1948-1952, there was still room for making changes in the allocation of spectrum space. Two decades, later, with the television industry well established physically and economically, any scientific determinations of shortcomings in commercial television were not likely to have a dramatic potential impact on federal policies.

3. A reprint in the hearings appendix of an unpublished paper by Jack Lyle and Hiedi R. Hoffman, "Television in the Daily Lives of Children," presented at the APA convention, September 4, 1971.

4. Senator Baker's role in congressional communications policymaking has often been difficult to follow. Usually well versed in the issue at hand during the periodic subcommittee hearings, his defense of certain industry goals and Republican administration policies was always subtly hidden in his careful, sharp articulation of "all sides." His service in this sort of capacity was perhaps more publicly apparent during the Senate Watergate Committee hearings (1974), when he also served as the ranking minority member. In January 1981, following the Republican victories in the elections of the previous November, Senator Baker became Senate majority leader.

Chapter 7

THE IMMEDIATE AFTERMATH OF THE SURGEON GENERAL'S REPORT

The Hearings and Public Debate (1972)

THE PASTORE SUBCOMMITTEE (1972)

In order to continue to manage the terms of debate and interpretation of the Scientific Advisory Committee's report, it would be necessary to extend the process of public review. Accordingly, Chairman Pastore held four days of hearings on the report in March 1972, and he used them in an attempt to create the appearance of what he and several of his witnesses came to call a "new consensus." Having issued an unanimous report, the advisory committee members now found themselves haled before Senator Pastore's subcommittee on the first day, along with Surgeon General Steinfeld and Dr. Rubinstein, to rearticulate their conclusions. On the second day four members of the FCC were heard, and then the critical experimental researchers had their opportunity to present their charges against the advisory committee's constituency and its conclusions. On the third day the network and NAB chiefs were forced to confront the "consensus" engineered during the first day, and on the fourth a variety of public and other interest group representatives were allowed to recapitulate the criticisms of the report, the committee, and the industry's responses.

On the first day, during his initial remarks about the report, Senator Pastore says:

> To everyone who has read it — laymen as well as scientists — it is apparent the report is couched in conservative, cautious terms. After all this is a highly complex subject. Nevertheless certain basic conclusions have emerged. During the course of these hearings the committee will hear from the Surgeon General, members of his

> committee, and many of the experts who did original research for the report. Among other things, I would hope these distinguished men and women will spell out as simply as possible for the benefit of us all what these conclusions are; and what steps the Surgeon General, the scientific community, the agencies of Government, and the broadcast industry and [sic] should take in view of them [Senate, Commerce Comm., Communications Subcomm., 1972: 4-5].

It would not have escaped the attention of these witnesses that Senator Pastore was insisting that the report contained "certain basic conclusions." Nor would they have missed the significance of their being invited to testify first and then having that testimony and the report subjected to critical review by other researchers, included among whom were to be some of the more militant of the contract researchers and several of the blackballed advisory committee candidates. As Senator Pastore went on to say: "There are many who contend that the research and studies underlying the report support much stronger and more positive conclusions than the Surgeon General's committee unanimously made. We should have the benefit of these views. It is only prudent to do so" (1972: 5).

It would have been difficult for the surgeon general and his committee to ignore the opportunity being given them to forestall the scorching criticism that was likely to occur under these circumstances. The publicity surrounding this set of hearings was bound to be substantial, and scientific reputations were going to be made or broken. Having labored long and hard to reach just such a pinnacle of status and influence, few communication researchers in so vulnerable a position were going to expose themselves unnecessarily to controversy, criticism, or ridicule. The record of the 1972 hearings shows that they did not.

Having observed the volatility of the industry veto issue, Senator Pastore moves quickly to defuse it. In recounting something of the history of the project in his opening remarks, he takes immediate note of the blackball episode and implies that he knew nothing about it until "more than one year after creation of the Surgeon General's Committee" (1972: 2). He enters into the record the pertinent correspondence among himself, Dr. Steinfeld, Dr. James J. Jenkins, then chairman of the Board of Scientific Affairs, American Psychological Association, and Dr. Edwin B. Parker, the communication researcher at Stanford who apparently first exposed the affair by making inquiries about the advisory committee selection process.

The immediate digression into this history permits Senator Pastore to do several things. By bringing it up himself, he blunts the impact of references to it that were sure to be made by subsequent witnesses. He creates the impression, virtually unchallenged since, that he himself was innocent of any involvement in that original policy decision to permit the veto. He creates an opportunity for himself and Dr. Steinfeld to express reservations about that decision, thereby placing the blame on the former surgeon general, William Stewart, and finally he is able to use the event in positive support of the impression about the report that he seeks to create:

> I believe that the offer of veto even though it involved only seven of the 40 names compiled by the Surgeon General was most unfortunate. However, I am reassured by the advisory committee's discussion of this issue and their recommendations. However, we do have a report which in the words of the Surgeon General "represent substantially more knowledge than we had two years ago" [1972: 4].

That is, in spite of the veto, and, by implication, in spite of the presence of the industry representatives on the advisory committee, we have here a report that is stronger than anything issued officially heretofore. The very vulnerability represented by the veto issue is thus transformed into a strength, creating a subtle but effective argument for Senator Pastore's consensus. Throughout the hearings one is constantly reminded of the thought that, if so biased a panel as this produced a report containing elements that appeared to lean toward a causal linkage interpretation, though tentatively stated, how much stronger might have been the report of a more balanced committee?

In his own opening remarks Senator Baker again demonstrates the light footwork of someone determined to prevent the report from becoming anything more than a well-padded cudgel, lightly administered.

> It is obvious that the task of the advisory committee was not easy. Social behavior and mental health are not subject to precise analysis. And where specific conclusions are possible, it is often difficult to translate these conclusions into public policy.
>
> But as tentative as the conclusions of this report may be, they must not be used as an excuse to postpone their serious consideration by parents, educators, government, and the broadcasting industry. As others will inevitably do, I find some questions contained in the report more interesting than others. I will be particularly interested in the effect of the child's environment on his behavior and how the various factors in that environment affect his reaction to television and televised violence [1972: 7].

But such reassurances to the industry are tucked in briefly and unobtrusively. The balance of the introductory process is given over to the more critical posture reflected in the complaints of the blackballed experimentalists. Careful not to associate himself too closely with these views, Chairman Pastore allows them to be introduced through the testimony of Congressman John Murphy, whose presentation faithfully recites the dissident critique. He enters into the hearings record examples of the correspondence solicited by him from such critics as Garry, Bandura, Stein and Friedrich, Huesmann, Berkowitz, and Eisenberg. Murphy's testimony and these letters touch on all the sore spots: the continuing discrepancies between network statements of intention and the subsequent levels of violence in various types of programs, the veto issue, the earlier experience of the JCRTC (see Chapter 5), and the rationale for a stronger, less qualified conclusion. He then goes on to urge the Senate committee "to take whatever steps are necessary to force the highest officials in the television industry to act responsibly" (1972: 11-12). One notes, however, that, apart from the chairman's warm expression of appreciation to the congressman for his appearance, Murphy's call for "steps" goes undebated and otherwise ignored. The question of the subcommittee's power has always been more problematic than television's critics have been willing to admit.

The Advisory Committee

The first public evidence that the subcommittee was about to get the kind of clarification of the research findings that it sought came at the outset of Surgeon General Steinfeld's testimony:

> After review of the committee's report and the five volumes of original research undertaken at your request, as well as a review of the previous literature on the subject, my professional response today is that the broadcasters should be put on notice. The overwhelming consensus and the unanimous Scientific Advisory Committee's report indicates that televised violence, indeed, does have an adverse effect on certain members of our society.
>
> While the committee report is carefully phrased and qualified in language acceptable to social scientists, it is clear to me that the causal relationship between televised violence and antisocial behavior is sufficient to warrant appropriate and immediate remedial action. The data on social phenomena such as television and violence and/or aggressive behavior will never be clear enough for all social scientists to agree on the formulation of a succinct statement of causality. But there comes a time when the data are sufficient to justify action. That time has come.
>
> I would also emphasize that no action in this social area is a form of action: it is an acquiescence in the continuation of the present level of televised violence entering American homes [1972: 26].

Presented with this opening Pastore drives his point home, setting up the subsequent testimony:

Senator Pastore: Doctor, of course there have been various interpretations of this report by the news media. I have read headlines that stated unequivocably that there is a causal effect between violence on television and the aggressive behavior of young children. Then, I have read other headlines that said the Advisory Committee submitted a whitewash on the subject. Now, in very simple language, will you tell me if this report by the Advisory Committee contains enough evidence and states there is a causal effect?

Dr. Steinfeld: Yes, sir, Mr. Chairman, I think the Committee report contains sufficient data to justify action and I believe that many of the people who have been writing about the report, not being social scientists, have misinterpreted what the members of the committee intended. And, I believe this will become apparent when you hear testimony from the members of the committee. . . . The evidence is strong enough that it requires some action on the part of responsible authorities, the TV industry, the Government, the citizens [1972: 27-28].

Not surprising in light of the Pastore statements in 1969, it is nonetheless important to note here the extent to which the problem of violence on television has been reduced to the terms of legal case making and how unquestionably social science has been seized on as an efficacious evidentiary tool. Both aspects have become so thoroughly ingrained in the public debate that there is no self-consciousness or dissent from these forms of expression by any of the major actors in the drama.

But having created the image of television being on trial and having presumably "proven" the case, the matter of "sentencing" becomes more troublesome. At different points in his testimony Dr. Steinfeld is questioned about appropriate remedies. Here is how he responds, first to Senator Pastore:

There are a number of alternatives, Mr. Chairman, in this extremely complex field. It seems to me that whatever we do, we must keep in mind the First Amendment and the problems that might accrue from any attempt at censorship. Yet, there is a wide spectrum of actions which could be taken, all of the way from the writing and producing and editing of television programs, through the use of the code we have, or a modified code, through the scheduling of TV programming on the air, and the actual viewing in the home [1972: 29].

Shortly thereafter there is this exchange with Senator Baker:

Senator Baker: . . . can you recommend any particular action on the part of the Congress, the administrative agencies, or the networks, by way of law or regulation?

Dr. Steinfeld: Well, Senator, I would be getting out of my field if I moved into any specific recommendations. I think once the scien-

> tific community establishes a relationship and gets as specific as it can about some of the phenomena that occur, then it seems to me we turn to regulatory bodies, perhaps those who write broadcasters and other groups. So I don't, I would not feel competent to make specific recommendations other than those broad guidelines I indicated earlier.
>
> *Senator Baker:* I agree with you, Doctor, . . . but I hope you will forgive me for wondering if this distinguished scientist who appears before us could venture an estimate of any particular action that should be undertaken, other than, as I understand it, watching television with your children which might be classified as unconstitutional, cruel, and inhuman conduct.
>
> *Dr. Steinfeld:* Well, there were a broad range of suggestions which include setting up a foundation to monitor and publish the violence ratings and other ratings on TV and much more aggressive interpretation or utilization of the code, timing, looking at independent stations, consideration by those who purchase time, the advertisers, looking at TV specifically to see if violence is used as punctuation or to get people back after the commercials, rather than being needed for a particular story. There are a lot of things, I think [1972: 34-35].

The number of "things" is in fact not very large, and as juxtaposed to the serious language of "putting the broadcast industry on notice" and "taking whatever action is necessary," these recommendations are remarkably hesitant and unconvincing. Further, for the most part they ignore evidence, some of it even from studies in the surgeon general's own project, of their past failures. Having been prodded to provide the senators with evidence of the danger to society in violent television content, the witnesses now find themselves being used indirectly to provide the rationale for political avoidance.

Nonetheless, as Dr. Steinfeld is followed by Eli Rubenstein and several members of the advisory committee, the process of consensus building on the meaning of the research gathers steam:

> *Dr. Rubinstein:* In an area as complex as this one on television and social behavior, there can be honest differences of opinion about the data. I should add that considering the total body of data, the general conclusions of the committee and the various researchers do not differ as much as some of the recent publicity about the committee report may seem to suggest. . . .
>
> *Senator Pastore:* Let me ask you a question, Dr. Rubinstein. You have heard the testimony of the Surgeon General and the conclusion

he reached as an individual, and as a doctor. Do you agree with that conclusion?

Dr. Rubinstein: I do, sir.

Senator Pastore: Does anyone on the Advisory Committee disagree with it? If you do, please identify yourself and say so.

(No response)

Dr. Pool: Twelve scientists of widely different views unanimously agreed that scientific evidence indicates that the viewing of television violence by young people causes them to behave more aggressively. That, in a one-sentence lead, is the significance of the Surgeon General's report. There are qualifications about amount, circumstances, and the certainty of that, as of any scientific conclusion. But news stories which focused on the qualifications rather than on the main conclusion have turned the report on its head [1972: 45-47].

Joseph Klapper had perhaps the most difficult role to portray. He seems to be admitting something of the case for causal relationships, but his strategy remains one of admission thoroughly laced with qualifications:

There are certainly indications of a causal relationship. . . .

We have three types of evidence before us, really. We have evidence that in laboratory situations children, given the opportunity to do so, will mimic aggressive behavior. We have evidence that, in laboratory conditions, given the opportunity to do so, some children are being held by television, or at least after seeing some aggressive television, will engage in certain types of aggressive behavior.

Now, these pieces of aggressive behavior are relatively limited. They are essentially play behavior. . . .

Then we come to studies which go into correlations of these, what people do in real life and there we find the relationship. We are talking now about really serious antisocial aggression. There we find the relationship more uncertain, although again there are indications.

So, what I want to say is, there certainly are indications. And I think that it is because of these three different types of evidence that the preliminary and tentative surrounded that terminology and should have surrounded the terminology. . . .

But just what are you going to do. I would point out, for example, that the report indicates that a modest reduction in violence, what would be the effect of this? Nobody knows. For one thing people . . . probably would go and seek out violence elsewhere. The total elimination of violence has never been seriously considered as a viable alternative by any reputable group or body or whatever.

Another point that is made in the report is that the sheer amount of violence may not be as important as the way in which it is portrayed. But, as the report says in those words that Dr. Rubinstein mentioned, nobody knows how it should be portrayed, which makes it very difficult [1972: 57].

Correctly sensing the need to offer something more than this line of argument, Klapper launches into a discussion of his own "thoughts" about "what to do." Both of the ideas he raises here serve neatly to turn attention away from network programming purposes and processes. One of them, using community-level forums to encourage greater parent-child discussion of the evils of violence and antisocial behavior, even allows him to inject his usual argument concerning findings that parental attitudes about aggression are at least as important as television in forming juvenile attitudes. The other, while dealing with programming, introduces the politically attractive notion of "prosocial" programming.

Having given Dr. Klapper sufficient time to show his hand, Senator Pastore interrupts him to try to secure the more explicit admission he needs. He positions Klapper to face the sort of climactic and what, for a network research executive, is a most uncomfortable question — one that represents the final installment on the bill owed Senator Pastore for permitting the networks to be so closely involved in the surgeon general's project.

Senator Pastore: May I interrupt you Doctor? You talk about the responsibility of the parents, and I agree with you. You talk about the maximization of professional [prosocial] programs, I agree with you. But, why don't we talk about the minimizing of excessive violence? Why isn't that a part of the question? . . .

You are a scientist with the broadcasting industry, CBS. It is one of the three networks. Don't you think there has been much violence on television that is unnecessary?

Dr. Klapper: Yes.

Senator Pastore: Now, why don't we cut that out? That is what I am talking about. That is what we should do, where we should start. . . . If it can be helped, I say for goodness gracious, let's do it [1972: 59].

At this point Senator Baker quickly intervenes and is almost successful in pulling Klapper off the ropes. By initiating a discussion of the catharsis theory and by picking up on an earlier Klapper comment about the thought that "if violence is dropped from television, there may be a shift to some other form of violence," the senator creates a diversion that reduces the impact of Pastore's line of questioning. Nonetheless, the chairman returns to his pursuit, and before Klapper is released he is made to walk with the chairman through the following lecture:

> *Senator Pastore:* On page 79 of your report, I think you make a very significant statement. "Although many among network personnel express interest in reducing violence in their programming, they feel constrained by the economic realities of broadcasting. In order to induce advertisers to finance programming, networks must draw large audiences with demographic characteristics attractive to advertisers."
>
> That is essentially what we are interested in, in these hearings. This idea that the profit controls the amount of violence, I think, is not only inimicable to the criteria for granting a broadcast license, but it is harmful. We all know there is a certain amount of violence in life. But what we are talking about here is violence for the sake of violence, excessive violence. Where you talk about the human restraints on the part of the individual, there is no one in the top echelon of CBS that doesn't know the difference between right and wrong and when something is being overdone. If it is being done to get more advertising and more viewers, I say it is all wrong, and that is what we are talking about. We are talking about restraints here.
>
> *Dr. Klapper:* I am not one to disagree with that statement, sir.
>
> *Senator Pastore:* I am glad you agree. Can we hear from the others? [1972: 62]

Among the others, of course, was Thomas Coffin of NBC. He too was encouraged to participate in the process of building the impression that the evidence was sufficient to justify "action."

> *Senator Pastore:* Do you agree with this idea that there should be some action taken?
>
> *Dr. Coffin:* I think that, yes, I would agree with that. I think that we have at NBC, at any rate, been trying progressively, as the seasons have gone by, to really do two things, one, to minimize the sort of violence which we felt would be harmful in the character, and, two, to put progressively more and more programs in our schedule which would have a professional [prosocial] effect [1972: 77].

One by one, all of the rest of the advisory committee members present this day (Cisin, Mendelsohn, Pinderhughes, Pool, and Siegel) are called on to justify the committee's conclusions and to join in the consensus that the causal link, though still tentative, might be more positively stated than in the report and that it is sufficiently clear to dictate action.

But the issue of what would constitute appropriate remedies remained unresolved. From the outset the committee had been banned from making formal recommendations (other than as related to research), and there were thus no broadcasting policy suggestions in the report to which the witnesses might refer. Nevertheless, during the hearings several of the committee members were prepared to offer policy advice. While there were several variations on these suggestions, and other ideas as well, those by Alberta Siegel perhaps best encompass those of her colleagues:

> I have several suggestions of alternatives to self-regulation. The first one I want to make is . . . we need an independent monitoring agency to provide regular reports on the level of violence in television entertainment. . . . I think these reports should be broadcast over television and should appear in newspapers and magazines, these smog reports on violence pollution. They should indicate how much violence is occurring, which networks and stations are broadcasting it, the times it is being broadcast, and how many child viewers are estimated to be watching at those times. . . .
>
> Second, I suggest that consumers convey their disapproval of violence vendors in two ways. We may refuse to purchase their products. And we may refuse to buy stock in their firms. . . .
>
> A third suggestion derives from my observation that TV producers are mimics. . . . When successful new formats of non-violent entertainment are devised, they will be copied. I recommend increased support for public television because I believe that the craftsmen in public television are likely to turn their energies and talents to creating constructive programs for children. . . .
>
> It is the imitative capabilities of TV producers that prompt my fourth suggestion as well. . . . I recommend that travel fellowships be offered to the writers and producers of children's television programs so that they may observe firsthand how our neighboring nations . . . have succeeded in attracting child audiences without saturating them with violence.
>
> Fifth, I believe the Federal Communications Commission could be more effective in obtaining fair treatment for children and adolescents. I suggest that a child advocate be appointed to the staff of the FCC. This individual should have frequent and direct communications with the Commissioners, advising them on questions bearing on the welfare of children. He or she should be well acquainted with social scientific research and also in close communication with the professions serving children [1972: 66-67; also in Cater and Strickland, 1975: 90-91].

As Cater and Strickland point out, none of these suggestions went far toward government involvement. Nor did any of those by others on the committee or by the more critical contract researchers. Virtually all recommendations by the academics associated with the project, while occasionally couched in language highly critical of the industry, were chary of proposing the sort of direct congressional or regulatory agency action toward programming that would flirt with First Amendment confrontations.

The Federal Communications Commissioners

The subcommittee hearings went on for three more days, and the cast of characters remained noteworthy. At one level the testimony of three of the FCC members on the second day seemed to be directed toward the obvious question of what responsibility the commission might have in the wake of the advisory committee findings. Thus Chairman Burch claims that

> we at the FCC are engaged in an intensive self-education effort. Dr. Steinfeld has already met with us for one backgrounder, and we have his standing offer to put at our disposal the expertise of the National Institute of Mental Health for additional guidance. Our Children's Unit has already begun to take him up on that offer. We regard these hearings as the next essential step. That is why we will study the full record developed here with the greatest interest. Commission staff has been engaged for months on analysis of the economics of the television industry. They are also studying the legal and Constitutional implications of possible rule makings. And, as you know, we have received voluminous comments in two proceedings that bear closely on the concerns before us today.
>
> For my own part, I have held informal meetings in recent days with executives of the three national networks — partly to pick their brains and partly, to be perfectly candid, as a continuation of my effort to keep their feet to the fire. (Among other things, and whatever our ultimate decisions as to [what] appropriate FCC actions might be, I want them to know that we're looking over their shoulders with intense interest.) [1972: 104].

Burch goes on to discuss plans for panel discussions and oral arguments before the commission on matters pertaining to children's television. He then lists two lines of response the commission believed appropriate for the broadcasting industry:

> First: the reduction to near-zero of all gratuitous and needless violence in the programming that is specifically directed to children or that children tend to watch in large numbers; and
>
> Second: the creation of substantial amounts of new and diversified programming, not just the usual diet of cartoons, designed to open the eyes and expand the minds of young viewers [1972: 105].

For the most part Commissioners Lee and Wiley aligned themselves with their chairman during their testimony, and in discussion with them, Senator Pastore is able to articulate the broadcast regulatory dilemma and to signal his preferences for how the commission, as an arm of Congress, ought to proceed:

> Under the law the Commission has no authority, that is I am speaking now of the Communications Act of 1934, to censor programs, and that law would have to be changed if you were to be able to censor. Then you run against the First Amendment of the Constitution which forbids it.
>
> There are certain limitations upon what actions the government can take. But after all, these people do come up for licenses, they do have a public responsibility, they are answerable to the Commission for the renewal of those licenses.
>
> And there I think you see the way to bring about a true understanding. Through cooperation some remedies can come forth. I would hope that we are just not here exercising eloquence, rhetoric, and listening to scientific people and getting individual views and then ending up with nothing [1972: 125].

Commissioner Johnson's approach was less cautious of broadcaster sensibilities and perceived constitutional limitations. Reminding the subcommittee of the long history of congressional investigation and broken network promises, he goes on to equate the children's programming policies of the networks with the criminal behavior of child molesters and to cast the ills of children's programs in the broader context of what he sees as distorted economic and moral values in the larger commercial environment.

> The networks are benefiting from a common failure of our society. We condemn particular instances of what we ignore — or even reward — in the mass.
>
> A man who kills one other man will be tried for murder. But a President who has presided over the death of 422,000 persons in Southeast Asia — according to his own count — can seriously undertake a campaign for reelection as a man of peace.
>
> A Presidential assistant was dismissed by President Eisenhower because he had accepted a vicuna coat from a businessman dealing with the government. But when ITT is charged with giving $400,000 to President Nixon's campaign, the men who were involved in permitting the conglomerate corporation to get antitrust approval to acquire another billion-dollar corporation end up as an Attorney General designate, the President's campaign manager, a U.S. District Court Judge, and a Presidential assistant. . . .

> And so it is with child molesters. If you do it during the week, on the school playground, to one child, you are driven off to prison in a police car. But if you do it Saturday morning, in the living room, to millions of young children, you are just driven home, by a chauffeur, in a long black limousine [1972: 116-117].

To a large extent rooted in certain aspects of the anxieties and frustrations permeating American life during the period of the Vietnam War, the surgeon general's chapter in the television violence inquiry nonetheless had managed to proceed virtually without reference to that larger context. Johnson's testimony during the 1972 hearings was one of the few instances in which the harsher external reality was permitted to intrude.

In part because it was so obviously partisan and nearly slanderous, Johnson's statement could not go unchallenged. But the rejoinders may have also arisen in reaction to the feeling that these remarks violated the tacit understanding among most of the principal actors that there would be no attempt to cast the communication policy questions in light of the broader domestic and international issues. Thus some members of the subcommittee and all three of the other FCC commissioners present take exception to Johnson's remarks. Senator Baker responds with the most heat, calling the Johnson testimony "one of the most violent statements that I have heard before any committee at any time since I have served in the Congress of the United States" (1972: 123). However true, Baker goes on to reveal the anger felt by those operating within the framework of normal politics at the style and substance of then current political dissent:

> I feel an outrage, Mr. Johnson, that you have brought to this hearing a trauma of emotionalism that will positively impede our progress in trying to arrive at a sensible solution to a real problem, and that is how to improve the quality of children's television. You have drug a red herring across the trail, you have made innuendos, charges of guilt of the greatest sort against people who have the responsibility for doing what ought to be done, to improve the quality of television.
>
> Your statement is replete with innuendos and I think that is violence to this society, at this time, at this place in history, that has come to be just as destructive in terms of the psyche of adults as well as children, as that portrayed on television, which you are charged with trying to regulate [1972: 124].

A further cause of the strong response may be found in another aspect of what Johnson had to say. The commissioner offered a number of recommendations that cut much more closely to the heart of the underlying economic issues than any other policy advice advanced during the hearings:

(1) Fund the Public Broadcasting Corporation at no less than $500 million a year. . . .
(2) Require that the three commercial networks provide one-third of all prime time on a nonsponsored basis for entertainment, dramas, cultural, and public affairs programming. . . .
(3) Require counteradvertising, as the Federal Trade Commission has courageously proposed to a reluctant Federal Communications Commission. . . .
(4) As for violence, simply require that two commercial minutes be removed from every half hour containing violence, and be made available at no cost to responsible professionals to program information to children (and adults) about the adverse consequence of violence, the alternative approaches to resolving human conflict, or other balancing information thought by the professionals to be appropriate.
(5) I will add at this point another proposal which I mentioned to the Violence Commission in 1968, and that is that tort actions ought to be seriously considered by parents and by the victims of violent actions, naming the networks as defendants. . . .
(6) Reduce the permissible number of commercial minutes (a standard now set by the industry, not the FCC) to one-half of current levels.
(7) Require all commercials to be bunched on the hour and half-hour.
(8) Forbid networks to own programs, program production facilities, or stations. . . .
(9) Finally, fund the long-overdue across-the-board continuing review of the impact of television upon all aspects of our society — before we face yet another national crisis, and Presidential Commission or Congressional committee inquiry [1972: 118-119].

The last recommendation, of course, had become a standard item well before the surgeon general's project. It was now taken as given that the political inquiry into violence on television would be continuous and that it could be maintained only if built on the foundation of similarly continuous social science investigation.

But it is also clear from Chairman Burch's reactions that many of Johnson's recommendations are simply too threatening to the accommodations worked out among the industry, Congress, and commission:

> I would say the question of funding the public broadcasting corporation is obviously not a Commission responsibility. . . .
>
> I don't think, frankly, the Commission has the authority to take one-third of all prime time and make it non-commercial, absent some direction from this Congress.

> . . . Counter-advertising is before us now in a rule-making proceeding. It was filed, we will have hearings on it commencing next week. I don't know what the reluctant FCC is that Commissioner Johnson refers to. . . .
>
> The question, number four, is simply an extension of three, reduce the permissible number of commercial minutes. If you will recall, back when the FCC seriously suggested this, the Congress stepped in and that was the end of that. Require all commercials to be bunched on the hour and half-hour. I don't know what that has to do with children's violence, but it is an arguable thing, I suppose.
>
> It might be more desirable, I think, if it were economically desirable that the networks might come around to it. It is done in certain societies. The question of forbidding the networks to own anything . . . is something that presumably either the Justice Department or the FCC could do, if it felt that were the appropriate course of action.
>
> I don't know what this long overdue across-the-board review of the impact is. I presume that is something that either the Commission or the Congress could do [1972: 121].

Chairman Burch wielded an effective fire-extinguisher, casting doubt on the commission's authority to deal unilaterally with most of these matters and thereby dousing this flare-up by a single, rebellious colleague. Burch's testimony amounts to a clear warning about the major policy implications involved — about the substantial requisite shifts in executive, legislative, and regulatory agency policies toward broadcasting. That warning was sufficient to forestall any further discussion during these hearings of any remotely radical structural or economic changes.

The only item on Johnson's list that Chairman Burch accepts as possibly a commission responsibility is the matter of the FTC proposal for counteradvertising. But, while the commission did indeed hold the promised hearings on the issue, it turns out that Johnson's point about commission reluctance was well founded. After two years of consideration, the FCC rejected the FTC proposal, in large part because of concerns about the economic impact on the industry (FCC, 1974b: 26382-26383).

The Critical Experimentalists

Later, during the day of the testimony by the FCC members, some of the critical experimental researchers were given their hearing. Liebert, Berkowitz, and Lefkowitz testified, generally advancing the thesis that the advisory committee report was too cautious. During discussions with these witnesses the cleverness reflected in Senator

Pastore's handling of the veto issue and in eliciting the stronger sense of consensus from the surgeon general and the advisory committee members on the first day of hearings is repeatedly revealed. Whenever the critique becomes heated enough to undermine confidence in the advisory committee report — and therefore in the entire drama Senator Pastore has written — the senator is able to recall the previous day's accomplishments:

> *Senator Pastore:* Were you here yesterday?
>
> *Dr. Liebert:* No, I was not.
>
> *Senator Pastore:* I wish you had been. Because I was very much pleased with the testimony of the Advisory Committee. I more or less had the same doubts as you had, from reading the newspapers, and the headlines. Some said it was a whitewash, others said there was a causal relationship between violence on television and aggressiveness in children. It was rather confusing.
>
> As you read the report, of course, it was conservative and cautious. The members of the Committee all admitted that yesterday for the simple reason that they were trying to achieve a unanimous report. Otherwise they would have come out with 12 different views, and that would have been even more confusing. . . . But if you listened to each of them, and the position each took, I don't think they were very far from what you said here today.
>
> *Dr. Liebert:* I am certainly glad to hear you [1972: 136-137].

There were similar exchanges with Berkowitz and Lefkowitz:

> *Dr. Berkowitz:* I think a new consensus seems to be evolving at perhaps a stronger level than had initially existed, under the influence of hearings and statements made by Dr. Liebert and others . . . [1972: 139].
>
> *Senator Pastore:* So, frankly, the point I am making here is that as I listened to those who felt the report didn't go far enough — I am speaking now of the scientists who were involved and those who felt what the report did say was the best way a consensus could be reached. I find the space between them is not really a chasm. They seem to be getting closer and closer together.
>
> I thought I should make that observation to you.
>
> *Dr. Lefkowitz:* Yes, sir. I am in the unfortunate position of having the gap closed in on me, so to speak, while I was away. From the time I wrote until yesterday, it was the general opinion, particularly if one looked at the news media, that there was a lot of hedging on the report and it was hardly as unanimous as now seems to be the case [1972: 146-147].

The Industry Spokesmen

Thus, by the third day of the 1972 hearings, when the network representatives were to testify, Senator Pastore feels it possible to project an image of great impending achievement: "I want to say, as an introductory remark, that in the past 2 days, I think we have reached the banks of the Rubicon. I hope with the testimony that is adduced here today, we will be able to cross it and achieve success" (1972: 177). That crossing is not made without some difficulty, however. The network representatives are well practiced at avoiding pitched battles, and in many ways it again appears that Senator Pastore is also content to engage only in relatively minor raids and skirmishes.

As in former hearings the networks carefully insert into the record references to the popularity of their services and recitations of the merits of various aspects of their programming. But this time, knowing that the hearings have been designed to foster the image of a research consensus around the causal linkage argument, the networks are also careful not to challenge this assumption too directly. Rather the attempt is one of aligning themselves with the recognition of the potential seriousness of the situation and agreeing that, while the case may not yet be conclusive, the networks have a certain responsibility to take those possibilities into account in programming decisions. This is how Julian Goodman, president of NBC, develops his position:

> I believe . . . it is proper to recognize that one of the main conclusions of the report states that the "accumulated evidence does not . . . warrant the conclusion that televised violence has a uniformly adverse effect nor the conclusion that it has an adverse effect on the majority of children."
>
> The report goes on to say that televised violence may, however, stimulate aggressive behavior by some children, under some circumstances.
>
> We accept that fact, and it places a responsibility on us. Although the extent of the causal relationship, the circumstances under which it operates, the number and kinds of children that may be affected are not yet understood, we recognize that pointing to these gaps in knowledge is not the proper way of fulfilling our responsibility [1972: 178].

John Schneider, then president of CBS/Broadcast Group, adopts a similar posture, pledging not to eliminate all violence, but to be guided by the advisory committee report in program development and scheduling and to emphasize more "prosocial material" (1972: 194).

In both cases Senator Pastore gently chides them, using a combination of his empathy with the imperatives of the competitive economics in network operations and, nonetheless, the networks' long history of broken promises as a backdrop against which to project an image of his own patient, but increasingly less content, tolerance. He is careful not to go too far here. The industry is not being threatened — yet. But some sign of compliance with the political concern is in order:

> I want it clearly understood that no one wants to put the television industry out of business. . . . All we are talking about here is a little bit of restraint, undoing the abuse and undoing the overkill, that is about the size of it all.
>
> . . . I think the report is clear. I mean you can dance around it any way you want, but essentially the central point of the report is that there is a causal effect.
>
> . . . We started this, as Mr. Goodman knows, a long, long time ago. I think we have made progress. I don't think we have reached the end of the line, however.
>
> I think, myself, if we try harder we can do a much better job. That is all we are trying to do [1972: 189-190].

Throughout the hearings Senator Pastore repeatedly returns to the issue of constitutional restrictions, and in responding to Schneider he places the issue in the context of reasonable, responsible self-regulation.

> I would hope that Dean Burch will pursue his plan and I would hope that you would cooperate with him because I think in the final analysis there has got to be self-restraint in the industry. Like you pointed out, we are shackled by the first amendment in a sense that we cannot interfere or impinge upon free speech and nobody wants to do it.
>
> And the Commission is limited under the Communications Act of 1934 so that it cannot dictate programming and we don't propose to do that. All we are asking for here is a reasonable attitude toward this very important subject by men who are considered to be mature men, reasonable men, family men who have a tremendous responsibility in this particular area. And I put you in that class, sir [1972: 197-198].

The president of ABC, Elton Rule, proves himself much more tractable, thereby earning himself even gentler treatment at the hands of the chairman. Other than some brief inquiries from senators Pastore and Baker about the broadcasting and film code review processes, Rule's statement that ABC program planning will have to be managed in accordance with the knowledge imparted by the advisory committee report and his explanation of ABC's children's programming initiatives and research plans are accepted with praise and little debate.

The president of the NAB, Vincent Wasilewski, also finds himself confessing that he agrees with Senator Pastore's contention that the time has come "when the data are sufficient to justify action" (1972: 230). But at this point the claim that the industry can and should adequately regulate itself is not enough. Conscious of the NAB's role in representing the individual station licensees, Pastore uses this opportunity to deliver what is perhaps the most explicit set of warnings, even threats, to emanate from the hearings:

> I will tell you frankly you represent the group that in the final analysis has the most to lose; you represent those who are granted a license; and you know what the development has been lately since the WHDH case. I am telling you frankly unless the industry takes hold of this and does what needs to be done the only possible result is going to be an aroused citizenry. . . .
>
> What I am trying to say to you, Mr. Wasilewski, is this. We did not invent this. The reason why this Committee requested this Study in the first place, and the reason why we have held hearings right along is because of the complaints that have been made to us. Made to us by mothers in many, many instances, and by people who are aroused and concerned about what has been going on.
>
> . . . Broadcasters are in the most lucrative business in the world. They are given a license that can only be given to a few. With the exception of a few small stations anyone who gets a license to operate a television station puts his hands on the pot of gold [1972: 230-231].

At any time few station owners would fail to take note of such a line of admonishment. But they would be particularly sensitive to it now, in light of increased citizen group challenges to broadcast licences, the then recent Nixon administration complaints about network news coverage, and the related White House and congressional overtures about extended, more secure, license renewals.

The Policy and Citizens' Interest Groups

By the fourth day Senator Pastore felt the drama was continuing to progress sufficiently well for him to announce at least one element of the follow-up action anticipated earlier in the hearings:

> When the Surgeon General appeared to tender the Report of his Committee on televised violence and its impact on children, I said our journey was just beginning. In my judgment, what has taken place in the past few days is nothing less than the scientific and cultural breakthrough. For we now know there is a causal relation between televised violence and antisocial behavior which is sufficient to warrant immediate remedial action. . . .
>
> I am, therefore, requesting the Secretary of Health, Education and Welfare, the Surgeon General, and the FCC to establish a method of measuring the amount of televised violence entering American homes — a violence index — so that the Secretary may report to this committee annually the results of his study. This is only part of what we expect to be done [1972: 243].

For the most part this final day of testimony was given over to those who as individuals or as representatives of public interest or policy study organizations sought to reinforce the impression of consensus around the research findings and to advance the call for action.

Douglass Cater had been a White House staff member during the Johnson administration. As such he had been closely involved in fostering the first Carnegie Commission on public broadcasting and he had served as the administration's liaison with Congress during the subsequent legislative effort that led to passage of the Public Broadcasting Act of 1967. Those efforts had brought him into close contact with Senator Pastore and his subcommittee. More recently, as the director of the then new Aspen Institute Program on Communications and Society, he had coordinated the first formal symposium on the surgeon general's project. That conference, held just a month before Pastore's hearings, had led to a report coauthored by Cater and Stephen Strickland and later, of course, to their book. One of the arguments in that earlier report is that there was substantial agreement among the conferees on a number of recommendations, one of which was for "a cooperative effort to create an institution outside government capable of continuing attention to television's effects. As a beginning, it might develop techniques for monitoring the quantity and nature of televised violence in order to provide a trustworthy pollution index for the public airwaves" (Cater and Strickland, 1972, in Senate, Commerce Comm., Communications Subcomm., 1972: 166).

As might have been expected, Cater's testimony during the Pastore hearings reiterated that recommendation. Further, Cater used the occasion to publicize a letter to Dr. Steinfeld from Aspen supporter Lloyd Morrisett, president of the Markle Foundation, declaring interest on the part of Markle and the Russell Sage Foundation in helping promote "discussions of ways of producing continuing social indicators of violence on television" (1972: 259). As expressed in the earlier conference report and during Cater's testimony, the idea of having a nongovernmental agency conduct or supervise this monitoring would have fit neatly into the self-prescribed agenda of the new Aspen communications program.

Action for Children's Television (ACT) had also already made itself felt in certain corridors of television policymaking. The then current FCC rule-making proceeding on the proposal to ban all commercials in children's television had been initiated as a result of an ACT petition. In their testimony before the subcommittee, Peggy Charren and Evelyn Sarson were also able to publicize an agenda for their organization:

> (1) That the FCC declare children's television a public service area and eliminate all commercials from children's programs.
> (2) That the FCC require every station to provide a minimum number of hours of children's programming.
> (3) That if the FCC fails to act, that the Senate Commerce Committee introduce legislation to secure this protection for our children [1972: 263].

Another witness this day was Leo Bogart, and he also urged specific action — in this case that in exchange for suspension of the recently imposed prime time access rule the television industry engage in an experiment to increase the quality of early hour prime-time programming. But of more interest for our analysis here is the apparent conflict between his perceptive observations about some of the difficulties associated with the surgeon general's project and his expectation that social science research nonetheless remains an undervalued tool in public policymaking. This was to be the difficulty discussed in Chapter 6 in reference to Bogart's *Public Opinion Quarterly* (1972-1973) paper published some months later.

On the one hand Bogart sees how the common-sense impressions about television's impact and the tendencies of public officials to think in legal terms led to the investment in social science as the means for determining whether, and which, measures should be taken against television programming practices. This discussion reveals an astute awareness of the complexity of the effects issue and of the political motivations underlying the television violence inquiry:

> The studies understandably focused on the effects of violence on the displays of aggression. But some of TV's most significant influences may be felt in areas of behavior and belief which are difficult or impossible to measure.
>
> The "invisible" effects of individual incidents of TV violence may add up to patterns that would leave their traces upon the culture

> even when individual episodes could not be related to specific effects [1972: 245].
>
> With due respect for the wisdom and zeal of your subcommittee, and with an understanding of its limited province, why has the subject of TV violence received such a high research priority? Are there not other far more pressing items on the national agenda that demand the same large-scale funding, the same sense of urgency, the same collaborative effort and variety of research techniques? [1972: 250].

Yet in the end even Bogart's insights, in many ways some of the most careful and disinterested of the entire set of hearings, cannot abandon the social-scientific siren. While conscious of a number of mistakes involved in the surgeon general's project, his approach here and in his later paper nevertheless remains one of promoting the advance of social science in public policymaking in communications.

> The million dollars might have been more wisely spent on a continuing research program than on one designed and executed on a crash basis, but I don't believe it would have been more productively spent. Large and continuing problems do require continuing research, but the task force concept embodied in by this project has proven its value as a way of mobilizing an exceptional outpouring of talent and energy [1972: 250].
>
> I hope that it adds to government's awareness of the contribution that social science can make to broader fields of national policy [1972: 252].

Therein, of course, lay much of the significance of the surgeon general's effort. The government had indeed been made increasingly aware of the contributions of social science to communications policymaking, though perhaps not quite in ways that Bogart and other well-intentioned researchers and critics had expected.

THE INITIAL POSTREPORT STATUS OF VIOLENCE EFFECTS RESEARCH

By the time it had run its course, the Surgeon General's Television and Social Behavior Program had served a number of closely related constituencies and purposes. For example, as evidenced during the final day of the 1972 hearings, those individuals and organizations seeking to broaden the base of public policymaking in communications found in the advisory committee report and the five technical volumes considerable support for their claims that television largely exploits children and that further close study of television industry practices and impact would be necessary to pursue measures that might mitigate that state of affairs. Primarily through license renewal challenges and other regulatory avenues, the public interest or citizens' action and the policy study groups had already begun to find footholds for establishment of an increasingly significant role in the public debate over television — a role, ironically, that put them in league with some aspects of the Nixon administration initiatives against the mass media. But the violence research issue proved to be a particularly effective means for dramatizing their critiques of the broadcasting industry. It helped considerably as these groups formulated and proposed their various programs of action before the foundations, the FCC, and Congress. In the end it became clear that the general communications reform effort had only a limited impact, and in certain important ways, was severely compromised (see Rowland, 1982a). For the moment, its efforts seemed to be making considerable headway, and for aspects of that work, the communication research enterprise seemed to be most useful.

For its part the broadcasting industry, while seemingly chastened and "put on notice," found that it still had the ability to exercise considerable influence over the form and consequences of the effects research campaign. This influence was obvious in its ability to secure representation on the advisory committee and to exercise the right of veto in the selection of the remaining members. However, as this narrative would suggest, the veto issue was merely the surface-level manifestation and an extension of a much longer, more subtle effort. Through careful cultivation of appropriate academic and political interests over the course of a generation, the industry had succeeded in using its social research activities to define the popular questions about television and its significance within a certain matrix of scientific tradition. Not without its perils to the long-range interests of the industry, this effort did subject television to increasingly sharp slaps on the wrist. Considerable sting was administered during the public debate and congressional hearings on the surgeon general's report. However, such reprimands and the subsequent, relatively minor programming adjustments were the extent of injury suffered. Even during this period, when governmental initiatives against all media were particularly strong, the industry's long-term strategy for influencing the research debate helped commercial broadcasting to avoid any major changes in its structure, operations, and profitability.

The dilemma for federal legislators had changed little over the half century of broadcasting history, though with the growth of television it had intensified. The government remained committed to certain constitutional provisions and associated economic assumptions that severely constrained the range of action open to it in defining public policy toward broadcasting. But in many ways the public experience with television remained troubled. The extent and rapidity of changes taking place across the face of American society provoked serious anxieties and uncertainties. As both mirror and contributing element, as both habit and symbolic content, television became inextricably interwined and identified with this mood. It was widely felt that some explanatory, problem-solving framework had to be found. Thus, as in so many spheres of contemporary public debate, when the traditional, guiding assumptions began to appear increasingly inadequate, the popular promise of scientific resolution became proportionately more attractive.

In specific form and timing, the surgeon general's project was largely the work of Senator Pastore and the federal mental health bureacracy. But in light of the broader social and cultural anxieties, the project may properly be seen as part of a collective political response. Not only was it widely supported throughout the formal structures of the legislative and executive branches of government; it was also concurred with across a wide gamut of formal and informal social institutions. The press, religion, medicine, education, and a variety of other interest groups all endorsed and closely followed the search for a scientific answer.

To most it must have appeared that little would be lost in this stratagem, and much might be gained. Should the results of the surgeon general's research prove definitive, the government would have the evidentiary base, and the intense, even emotionally aroused, public support necessary to take steps that would otherwise be impossible. If the results were inconclusive, a rationale would exist for doing little or nothing.

In the end the results were largely inconclusive. Every summary statement of causal linkage between viewing of television violence and antisocial behavior was carefully qualified. But many dismissed these results as merely misrepresentations generated by inappropriate industry influence. To a considerable degree, therefore, the pressure on the government to appear to be doing something did not slacken. Indeed, in the public outcry welling up in the wake of the leak of the advisory committee's report, Senator Pastore read an urgent need to satisfy the critics that something definitive had been learned. The 1972 hearings of his subcommittee were thus devoted, in large part, to creating the impression of a "new consensus" and to assuring the critics that the foundation for action now existed. Nonetheless, the underlying constraints and the actual inconclusiveness of the research were allowed to surface periodically and with sufficient impact to blunt any radical legislative initiatives.

The communication research community found in the surgeon general's project an unprecedented opportunity. Increasingly significant in previous rounds of legislative investigation into television violence, the social science tool now became the central, indispensible element in the new inquiry. Although federal money had been available before, and many of the surgeon general's contracts were merely extensions or reincarnations of previous grants, the federal funds were now offered through the NIMH staff and the advisory committee at an unprecedented level over a relatively short period of time. The previously diffuse financial relationship between the government and the communication research community had implied a certain distance in other respects. Now, as a result of the decision to have the government directly underwrite a large-scale program of violence effects research, the distance between the two was dramatically, and perhaps forever, shortened.

There was rapid confirmation that the new relationship was something more than a temporary affair, to be ended with the publication of the surgeon general's report. As he had announced in the March 1972 hearings, Senator Pastore asked HEW and the FCC to cooperate in developing a violence index for annual monitoring of television performance. In June, in response to that request, staff members from NIMH and the FCC held a workshop with a group of social and behavioral scientists to consider how to develop such a measure and to plan other follow-up efforts (Withey and Abeles, 1980: viii, 308). Among the suggestions made at that meeting was a recommendation that the Social Science Research Council might now become involved. In December the SSRC responded by appointing a ten-person Committee on Television and Social Behavior, which in turn submitted to NIMH a proposal for a three-year program of research. That project was funded in September 1973, and the new committee proceeded to meet regularly for the next two years to make recommendations about the television profile and other plans for research on television and social behavior. In other words, communication effects research had been admitted into the federal social science research establishment.

The impact of the 1969 and 1973 bonanzas was substantial. In many respects, still on the margins of academic power and influence at the outset of the surgeon general's project, members of departments of communication and associated fields who took the television violence and effects issues as their own could now demonstrate the sort of outside support on which other social and behavioral science empires had been built. More graduate students could be supported, new courses added, old programs expanded, and new ones initiated. Applications for faculty promotions and the attractiveness to other schools of the contract researchers and their students would be greatly enhanced. In general, new dimensions of status and prestige would accrue to those in communication research who became affiliated with the project and its subsequent activities.

Not totally unaware of important contemporary debates in the philosophy of science, symbolic theory, and political economy that raised serious questions about the significance of their work, the television violence research group had no more reason than the rest of their fellows in the social sciences to be notably self-reflective. The issues of social health seemed highly important, and the public and government seemed to need answers immediately. Academic politics and the liberal sense of social responsibility thus combined to dictate widespread, energetic compliance with the demands of the project.

For some there were private, and even occasionally public, misgivings about the program. But for the most part these were procedural concerns, and they seldom interfered with the determination to proceed. The project offered a welcome opportunity to continue much work that had already been begun. Its theoretical and methodological boundaries were well established, the attendant findings and conclusions well known and rehearsed. The exercise thus offered much of the security and comfort associated with the pursuit of normal science in other fields.

In other ways naive to the broader political purposes of the project, many of the contract researchers and advisory committee members were content not to enlighten themselves and thereby threaten a set of relationships with government and the broadcasting industry that, at least in the short run, seemed only to be enhancing their professional well-being. Those outside the project found themselves generally watching and applauding in respectful deference. The few scattered complaints and reservations could be dismissed as jealous essentially frivolous, grumbling. That there might be any broader questions about the implications of trying to resolve fundamental cultural, moral, and political issues through the scientific prism went generally unacknowledged by participants and observers alike.

Part III

THE EXHAUSTION OF VIOLENCE EFFECTS

Chapter 8

THE EMERGING POLICY DILEMMAS (1972-1974)

THE HOUSE APPROPRIATIONS COMMITTEE (1970-1974)

Although the Pastore hearings in 1971 and 1972 dominated the political use of the television violence issue in the immediate wake of the surgeon general's report, other congressional players proved anxious to become involved and to play a larger role. For instance, in the aftermath of the Eisenhower Commission report and during the work of the Scientific Advisory Committee, the House appropriations committee began to inject itself into the debate. In 1970 and during each of the following four years, the Housing and Urban Development Subcommittee of the full appropriations committee, under chairmen Joe Evins (D-Tenn.) and Edward Boland (D-Mass.), took the opportunity during its annual review of FCC budget requests to query the commission about its activities in the areas of televised violence, obscenity, and children's programs. As Senator Pastore and the advisory committee members worked out their terms for the public interpretations of the research findings in the 1971 and 1972 Senate communications subcommittee hearings — as the stronger causal linkages argument became ever more widely accepted — the House appropriations subcommittee became increasingly emboldened and began to demand more response from the FCC about the steps it might take to resolve the public and political anxieties about programming issues. The House committee was taking its cue from the results of the Pastore subcommittee work, but unlike the previous Pastore approach of dealing directly with the networks and generally avoiding the regulatory mechanism, the House committee was trying to effect changes through the FCC.

The questioning of FCC Chairman Dean Burch in the 1970 hearings set the pattern for the subsequent years. In it the subcommittee began to press Mr. Burch and his colleagues about the commission's apparent failure to pursue the violence issue more aggressively.

> *Mr. Wyman:* We hear a lot about the term "jawboning." Has there been any attempt or is it considered to be possible to get these large networks together, their representatives, and at least implore them or ask them or suggest to them that in some manner they seek to reduce the percentage of poison and murder and mayhem and so forth that appear on television under their sponsorship? . . .
>
> *Mr. Burch:* I don't believe that there has been any effort by the FCC in that respect. . . .
>
> *Mr. Cox:* Senator Pastore held some hearings last year on this subject where he had the three network presidents in. I think in our program investigations of the early sixties, this was raised with the networks.
>
> I think they are very conscious of it and make some efforts to comply but under the thrust of competition it always seems to come back . . . [House, Appropriations Comm., HUD Subcomm., 1970: 1141-1142].
>
> *Mr. McDade:* Isn't there some way we can begin to try to get the FCC, which is supposed to regulate this national asset, to sit down and ask some large questions? If you have to, we would be glad to build a wall around you for a year and say, "How do we fight the problem of violence and how does it affect the people of our Nation? What does it do to them? On news programming; on children's programming; can't we attack that some way?"
>
> *Mr. Burch:* At the moment we haven't facilities to attack it on any kind of meaningful basis.
>
> *Mr. McDade:* Facilities translates itself into money though, doesn't it?
>
> *Mr. Burch:* Yes.
>
> *Mr. McDade:* Can't we get the talent in the Nation . . . isn't there some way we could begin to try to get at least some consensus in our Nation with all its talent, wealth and technology on what violence on TV does to the people of this country?
>
> *Mr. Jonas:* I agree, I concur in your comments and views. I think it is the responsibility of the Commission to display some leadership in this field.
>
> *Mr. McDade:* How do we put the spectrum, a public asset, or resource, to the optimum use.
>
> *Mr. Jonas:* That is right; and what I would like to see the Commission do is start attacking this problem and show us some leadership and if it takes some legislation, why we will help you get it [1970: 1147-1148].

During this discussion, Commissioner Cox had taken note of a recent rule-making request by Action for Children's Television seeking what he termed "fairly drastic action" directed at the commercial base of children's programming. The ACT petition had been just recently filed (February 5, 1970), and it had indeed been relatively drastic, calling for the elimination of commercials in all children's programming, the banning of performer use and mention of products or services on such programs, and the imposition of a minimum quota of children's programming (14 hours weekly) for all stations. In response to that petition, the commission did finally institute an inquiry into children's programming and advertising practices (January 1971), though in so doing it was careful to draw the inquiry narrowly enough to avoid violence and obscenity issues (FCC, 1971). But, as indicated as early as the 1970 hearings, pressure was building to have all these matters considered together.

Yet all the brave words from Representative Mc Dade (R-Penn.) and Jonas (R-N.C.) notwithstanding, Mr. Burch must have sensed the difficulties facing him and his colleagues should the commission proceed too far down the road being shown them here. Lacking clearer, formal legislative direction, it was doubtful that the sort of programming and even commercial review being urged on the FCC would, in fact, have much widespread, lasting congressional support. In any case, as a former Republican national committee chairman and as a protege of Senator Barry Goldwater (R-Ariz.), Burch was of a generally conservative mind about regulatory activity and First Amendment issues. While doubtless genuinely concerned about the content of much television and its possibly less-than-ideal impact on young people, Burch was unlikely to be willing to lead the commission into any practice of intense program review. Accordingly, his strategy for this year and the next was to note the lack of resources available to the commission for the sort of in-depth studies being requested and to buy time by pointing to the Pastore and surgeon general's project, suggesting thereby the need to wait on its results — to defer to the research process going on elsewhere.

This effort was to prove to be only marginally successful. As became apparent in the 1971 hearings, Mr. Mc Dade and other appropriations subcommittee members were intent on pursuing the violence and program content issues:

Mr. McDade: Let's go to violence. Who do you have assigned to this?

Mr. Burch: Very candidly, the Surgeon General is.

Mr. McDade: The FCC is not?

Mr. Burch: The FCC is awaiting, frankly, the Surgeon General's report. We do not have any facilities of the sort that are necessary to get into that kind of field. You are talking psychologists and psychiatrists?

Mr. McDade: We had quite a hearing last year, you will recall, about the possible impact of violence, particularly on children and whether or not the television really was, in that sense, having an unknown but untoward effect on children. This language was inserted by the committee [in its appropriations report] to direct the FCC to start moving on a problem like violence and to decide whether or not there were parameters within which we could begin to discuss the problem. You could have discussed it with the television stations across the Nation.

Mr. Burch: I will be very candid, Congressman. I am happy to take heat on this.

Mr. McDade: I don't want you to take the heat. I want to know where you are going.

Mr. Burch: Our job would start at such a point that the Surgeon General gave us some tools with which to work. I would be very candid that if I were told by this committee to "take what money you need and go out and solve the violence problem," you would have to have a bag with a hole in it because I would be back for a lot. I don't think we could do it with our type of staff. . . .

Mr. McDade: You will just rely on whatever the Surgeon General says?

Mr. Burch: I can only speak for myself in this thing, but I think I would be inclined to at least take a lead from the Surgeon General's report . . . [House, Appropriations Comm., HUD-Space-Science Subcomm., 1971: 575-577].

Mr. McDade: . . . I'd like to be assured that you are not just closing your eyes to the question of whether or not it might be a negative impact on children. I am not a psychiatrist or sociologist either, but I would think the FCC ought to be concerned about this problem.

I thought we established in the hearing last year that the FCC was concerned. That is why I quoted you the language of our report to try to find out what was being done. We had a colloquy on this subject on the floor of the House. There are an awful lot of people in the Congress who are interested in knowing answers to these questions. . . .

We will be looking forward to some action.

Mr. Burch: There has been some action in the children's field, but not in the field of violence specifically because I do think that is a medical problem that we need a little information on. The policy questions that will be raised, assuming the Surgeon General says

> there is a relationship, are tremendous, as you can imagine. We will address those, I can assure you [1971: 581].

In fact, because of fundamental reservations by the chairman and most of his commissioners about the extent of their programming review authority under the Communications Act and the Constitution, the FCC did as little as possible to address the policy questions raised when the surgeon general's report did appear. The action "in the children's field" to which Chairman Burch referred was the creation in his office of a special children's television study project. This effort, staffed by an economist with a communication research degree and other social scientists, was designed to help the commission deal with the ACT petition and to demonstrate a certain degree of FCC involvement in reviewing children's television policy without, however, committing the commission to a major research activity beyond its practical budgetary and political means. The project resulted in a staff report in 1973 that, while offering some radical recommendations, such as prohibiting commercials directed at preschool children, and insisting on formal FCC rules rather than exhortations for improved industry self-regulation, nonetheless on the whole "recommended rather mild changes" (Cole and Oettinger, 1978: 273; see pp. 248-288, for a fuller treatment of the FCC's children's inquiry through 1977). The commission effectively buried the report and took only limited action in response to it. Thus the ultimate impact of the project was largely symbolic, giving a seemingly higher place to social science in the working of the FCC, encouraging certain minor industry self-regulatory reforms, but leading to no real policy changes on the part of the commission.

As for the violence question, the FCC continued to back away from any formal activity, attempting to leave this matter to Congress, and particularly to Senator Pastore. In the spring of 1972, in his prepared statement to the House appropriations subcommittee during the hearings on the 1973 budget, Chairman Burch demonstrates his intent to focus on the work of his children's television study group and on the self-regulatory measures emerging in the industry. He also makes a stab at pointing out the inconclusiveness of the surgeon general's report and then diverting the discussion into the matter of the children's inquiry and the implicit efforts by the commission through its children's Television Unit to head off the more radical aspects of the ACT petition by seeking certain industry self-regulatory changes:

> In the broadcast area, we are devoting increasing effort — and whatever resources it may take — to the critical problems of chil-

> dren's television, and, more broadly, the impact of television generally on young viewers. . . .
>
> There have also been important recent developments within the broadcast industry itself. . . . The NAB's Television Board voted in January [1972] to reduce the amount of commercial time on programming designed mainly for children [on weekend mornings] from the present limit of 16 minutes to 12 minutes per hour. The number of program interruptions will be cut in half, and program hosts and cartoon characters will not be utilized to deliver commercials either within or adjacent to the programs on which they appear. All these code changes will become effective January 1, 1973 [House, Appropriations Comm., HUD-Space-Science Subcomm., 1972: 276-277].

In this statement Chairman Burch goes on to note a few additional children's programming and advertising practice changes being undertaken individually by the networks.

During his actual testimony the chairman reiterates most of these points, and on the whole the violence matter is not pursued too much further by the subcommittee. Representative Giaimo (D-Conn.) reminds Burch of the subcommittee's concern during the previous years, and Representative Giaimo also lets Mr. Burch know that the commission's evasiveness had not gone unnoticed. But in both these instances the questioning is allowed to diverge into other matters and no direct reply is ever exacted during the remainder of the 1972 hearings.

This pattern is repeated in the following year's hearings. Again in his prepared oral testimony, the chairman outlines the commission's continuing process of inquiry about children's programming and of related industry self-regulatory measures:

> In early October [1972] we held three days of public panel discussions. We heard from broadcasters, advertisers, educators, child psychologists, and citizen group representatives on a wide range of issues — program diversification, age-specific programming, responsive scheduling of children's program, advertising practices directed toward children, alternative methods of financing children's programs and the strengths and weaknesses of self-regulation. In January [1973] we held three days of oral argument on the ACT petition (Docket No. 19142). In addition to these proceedings, we are considering the special needs of children in connection with license renewals and ascertainment requirements, and in our review of the prime-time access rule [House, Appropriations Comm., HUD-Space-Science Subcomm., 1973: 152-153].

Mr. Burch then goes on to reiterate the NAB code changes with regard to limits on host selling, commercial minutes, and other matters. His remarks also include a mixture of praise for and warning to the industry:

> These are marks of progress. The industry expresses concerns that parallel our own — which I believe are made in good faith — and promises that its efforts to upgrade and diversify children's programming will be a continuing one.
>
> But that does not relieve the Commission of its own obligations. We are considering whether rule making or policy statements or some combination of both is required. . . . The staff has been directed to prepare option papers, and our decisions should be forthcoming by late spring [1973: 153].

The colloquy with the subcommittee goes into the matter of the surgeon general's report, but Chairman Burch is permitted to try to develop the inconclusiveness theme and to point out the difficulties of applying the report findings in any firm regulatory proceeding:

> The only tangible proposal that [the surgeon general's] group made was that a regulatory agency, such as ourselves, ought to investigate the possibility of a violence index, a thing comparable to what the movies now have. . . . We have been working with the National Institute of Mental Health, seeking their advice as to what kind of indicators you would use, and how this sort of an index would, (a) be structured and then, (b) who would be responsible for making the decision on it. . . . We have not come up with any conclusions yet [1973: 224-225].[1]

Thus in the immediate wake of the surgeon general's report and the 1972 Senate hearings, the commission was laying low. Throughout this period of sparring over the violence issue, the only real activity on the House side had come from the appropriations committee. The House communications subcommittee, under Chairman Torbert Macdonald (D-Mass.), had proven to be little interested in the topic, not pursuing the matter much in its own FCC oversight hearings and leaving the field largely to its Senate counterpart.[2] This lack of interest no doubt contributed to the appropriations committee frustration, and it served as a justification for the use of the budget review process to raise the programming content issues with the commission. But the lack of House consensus on just how far to push these matters did permit the commission to avoid undertaking any serious review of the violence matter, at least for a while.

By the spring of 1974, however, the appropriations committee redoubled its efforts and made a concerted effort to force some sort of action out of the commission. The budget hearings for fiscal year 1975 coincided with a change of leadership at the commission. Under heavy siege as the Watergate crisis worsened, the White House had for some time been asking Dean Burch to join its staff as counselor to the president in hopes of helping hold the Nixon administration together. Finally acceding to that request, Burch left the commission in early March 1974, and on March 8 Richard Wiley, who had been a commissioner since 1971 and the FCC general counsel for a year before that, was elevated to chairman. Wiley was from Illinois, where he had established solid business and Republican party credentials, and in his few years in Washington he had earned a reputation as a clear-headed, efficient bureaucrat, impressing many in Congress and the administration as a likable, safe, moderate conservative. His views on private enterprise, regulation, and First Amendment matters were seen to be similar to those of his predecessor, and they were likewise unlikely to guide him toward much formal commission program review activity.

As it happened, Mr. Wiley's first working day was the date that had been previously scheduled for the Commission's hearings before the Senate appropriations subcommittee, chaired by William Proxmire (D-Wisc.). The new commission chairman was asked to make a perfunctory presentation at that hearing, and although some of the inquiry had to do with children's television programming and advertising and with the work of the Children's Television Unit, those questions came at the very end of the two-hour hearing, and they were relatively light and cordial (Senate, Appropriations Comm., 1974: 219-282). In part this gentle treatment was in deference to the circumstances surrounding Mr. Wiley's sudden appearance as the new chairman. However, the appropriations subcommittee, of which Senator Pastore was also a member, knew that the communications subcommittee chairman was preparing for a much more extensive set of hearings on violence and related matters a month later. There was little need here to pursue the matter.

That was not to be the attitude of the House appropriations subcommittee the following week, when on his third working day as chairman Mr. Wiley was to appear on the other side of Capitol Hill (House, Appropriations Comm., HUD-Space-Science Sucbcomm., 1974: 1-244). There he ran into the buzzsaw of anger and frustration that had been building since at least 1970. Most of the prinicipal inquisitors from previous years were in attendance — particularly Chairman Boland and Representatives Giaimo, McDade, and Tiernan — and, as it soon became clear, if the House communications subcommittee was going to fail to pursue intense FCC oversight proceedings, this subcommittee was not. Further, the members indicated that they were no longer willing to defer to the Senate and Chairman Pastore. These congressmen held a substantial portion of the Commission's purse strings, and they intended to pull them.

Therefore, virtually all aspects of the commission's activities were reviewed and criticized, frequently harshly, over the course of a long day and a half of hearings. While the program content issues were to come in for particularly intense scrutiny, that attack must be seen in light of a whole range of complaints the subcommittee expressed on such matters as the commission's licensing and paperwork backlog, its shifting, confused set of cable television regulations, and various other major unresolved common carrier telecommunications issues. The congressmen were plainly upset with the commission across the board, and neither Wiley's newness as chairman nor the lack of clarity in Congress's own signals on many of these matters over the years afforded him any protection.

As for the violence, obscenity, and children's programming questions, the lines were quickly drawn when Representative Tiernan inquired whether Wiley was concerned about a recent newspaper story on television violence. Wiley replied that "the Commission has had the question of violence on TV presented to it before. We have had testimony before Senator Pastore. Naturally, this of concern to every American, and it is of concern to the FCC." But he quickly went on to note the restrictions he believed were placed on the Commission: "I would also counsel you that we have certain limitations from the statutory standpoint, and also, to some extent, from the constitutional standpoint, as to how much we can inject our own personal views in the programming of American television" (1974: 60).

Representative McDade, who had consistently been the most critical member of the subcommittee, joins the discussion, and it then heats up considerably:

> *Mr. McDade:* . . . I am delighted to hear you make reference in your agenda to the importance of programming as it affects children. You do read the committee's reports, do you not? . . .
>
> *Mr. Wiley* Yes, sir. I know you have discussed it before with us.
>
> *Mr. McDade:* Yes. Last year half of the language in the committee's report that was devoted to the FCC had to do with violence in programming and its effects on children. I could take you back to a report this committee issued with similar language back in the 91st

Congress, in which we directed the attention of the FCC to this same kind of problem. I do not see much happening. . . .

We, in this committee, have been trying for a heck of a long time now to get the FCC to take this responsibility. How much of your budget is devoted to this problem this year? How many people can you specifically identify for the committee who are delegated to work on this problem?

Mr. Solan: I do not think there are any totally identified with this.

Mr. Wiley: There were some. The Children's Television Unit —

Mr. McDade: Is the answer "none"?

Mr. Wiley: The answer may be "none" at this stage.

Mr. McDade: Not "may be." What is it? What is the answer? How many are there? How much of the budget is directed toward this problem?

Mr. Wiley: From my knowledge going back over 3 days as Chairman of the Commission, I would have to say I am not aware of any people specifically assigned in this area . . . [1974: 62-63].

Mr. McDade: . . . I want you to understand, and the Commission to understand, that this 4 years of apparently fruitless effort to bring the matter forcibly to your attention still weighs very heavily on the mind of the committee. It involves the issue of obscenity. It involves the issue of the quality of television as it affects children, and whether or not it might have an impact related to violence It involves the question of so-called spontaneous talk shows and their delving into obscenity and other matters. . . .

Mr. Chairman I realize you are new, but if I do not let you know how strongly I feel about it, and I think members of this committee pretty generally feel the same about this, we are just going to have a plain shootout. . . .

We can sit around here for the next 7 years and hear about the slippery slope we are on. I think it is time we brought some of these issues to a head. . . .

I think the time has come for us to seize the issue and for the Commission to get some definitive rulings, if necessary, from the Supreme Court. If we need legislative changes, let's hear about them. . . .

Mr. Wiley: While I share all of the concerns you state and I think they are entirely appropriate, I implore you also to consider the legal issues and, indeed, the constitutional issues involved in this matter.

Mr. McDade: You are a fine lawyer. How do you resolve a constitutional issue? . . . You make a case. . . .

Mr. Wiley: I put it to you. There is a variety, I suppose a whole scale of gradations of violence that may occur on television. Exactly what kind of rule would you see as appropriate? I think if you were to attempt to answer that as we have, you would find —

Mr. McDade: Where have you attempted to answer it?

Mr. Wiley: I think we have considered the issue. We have looked at it in the past.

Mr. McDade: When you were general counsel?

Mr. Wiley: Yes.

Mr. McDade: What kind of recommendations or conclusions did you come up with?

Mr. Wiley: I had not heard, until I heard about the violence index thing, of a promising new idea in this area that might have some credibility. I think there are continuing studies as to whether it has viability or not. Again, the Commission is not made up of people who can judge the effects of violence on children. We do not have social scientists. We do not have that kind of expertise. We are an engineering, legal and processing agency. I hope we can expand our scope so we can consider some of the sociological aspects of television.

Mr. McDade: If that is your hope, how much money have you requested for that in this budget?

Mr. Wiley: I have to say again to you that I think the Commission has done some studies of children's television.

Mr. McDade: Everybody has done studies on children's television. . . . [1974: 66-69].

Mr. McDade: I hope somebody might appologize for the fact that we, the Congress of the United States, have been telling the FCC for 4 years to get going, and we are still waiting. We are still hearing that we cannot be imprudent, that we have to be judicious about it. . . . If we are going to see the whole thing come apart every time a new Commissioner comes in, we will be doing this ad infinitum. Maybe we ought not to appropriate any money and tell the Commission we will set up some kind of new organization. . . . [1974: 74].

If the subcommittee irritation was not clear enough to Chairman Wiley by the end of this drubbing, it became patently so not long after when on June 21 the appropriations committee issued its report and "threatened to take 'punitive action' if the FCC didn't supply it with a report of its own by December 31, 1974, 'outlining specific positive actions taken or planned by the Commission to protect children from excessive programming of violence and obscenity'" (Cowan, 1979: 88). From the substance of the March hearings it was evident that the committee was encouraging commission action that would take violence, obscenity, and children's programming practices into account in license renewals and that might set up a court challenge on the respective meanings and likely conflicts between the "public interest" standard of the Communications Act and Section 326, its anticensorship provision. They were urging the commission to "make a case," and in effect, seek federal appellate court, and possibly Supreme Court, review of the extent of the commission's authority under the Act.

The 1974 House hearings thus represent something of a watershed. A new set of congressional interests had added its voice to the groundswell of support for the interpretation of the research and program content findings worked out by the end of the 1972 Pastore hearings. But rather than merely attempting to "jawbone" the industry as had been the senator's practice, the House appropriations subcommittee had decided that the case against much of television's program content was strong enough to try to force the issue by, this time, using the regulatory tool. In this scenario the violence matter was to be pursued by pushing the FCC into more direct review of station and network program content. The efforts of Chairman Burch and others to point to the inconclusiveness of the surgeon general's report were to be brushed aside and some of the more serious policy implications of the entire violence investigation history were to be tested.

Again it was not at all clear how wide was the extent of the support for that pattern of action throughout the rest of the House or even in the Senate, and such support would have had to exist if the sort of judicial and legislative changes Representatives Mc Dade and Giaimo were apparently contemplating were to be undertaken. However, the tactic here was one that might force the hand of a reluctant Congress. For if Chairman Wiley were pressured into pursuing a line of regulatory activity that led to court review, Congress might be placed in the position of having to revise the Act and resolve the program oversight ambiguities implicit in it.

To be sure, this was a gamble that, from the critics' standpoint, might well flounder on a strict court interpretation of the First Amendment. But the appropriations subcommittee, more than any congressional group previously, was willing to take that chance, and even if the effort failed in a legal sense, the political consequences might be quite acceptable. As so often before, attacks on the morality and presumed deleterious impact of a medium of communication could afford the elected official considerable publicity, except that this time the nobility of the cause was much enhanced by the existence of the seemingly significant research findings. Yet, also as before, any ultimate policy changes were probably still safely circumscribed by the constitutional provisions and the general unwillingness of Congress to deal directly with broadcasting industry purpose and structure, at least for the moment.

THE FINAL PASTORE HEARINGS (1974)

If there were doubts in the House about where the authority for review of the television violence and program content issues lay, this was not the case in the Senate. From time to time the Senate appropriations committee would raise questions about them in its own FCC budget reviews. But with Senator Magnuson as the chairman of the full appropriations committee and with Senator Pastore as a senior member of the appropriations subcommittee that dealt with FCC matters, there was little likelihood that the prerogatives of Pastore's communications subcommittee in the commerce committee would be violated by other Senate groups.

On the whole Pastore might well have been pleased to leave the violence issue at the seemingly successful point he had reached in 1972. There he had managed to create the impression of widespread consensus on the research findings, he appeared to have exacted concessions on that basis from the industry, and through it all he had managed to avoid undertaking any drastic policy changes toward commercial broadcasting. But two years later conditions dictated that he reenter the lists.

For one thing, as the House appropriations subcommittee activities progressed during the early 1970s, it became clear that several of its members were serious about pursuing the violence issue. The genie that Pastore had let out of the bottle in 1971-1972 was still very much at large. If anything, the consensus that had been established about the surgeon general's report was too complete, too successful. The impression of an erring industry — and the need for appropriate congressional response — had been spreading so readily that questions were beginning to be raised about when the political leader in this matter was in fact going to do something about the results his own work had presumably revealed. The demands for action were bolstered by the continuance of various of the surgeon general's research projects, particularly the annual violence measures, which continued to suggest that after 1972, in spite of all the research findings and the FCC's protests to the contrary, not much had been happening in the industry and that what had occurred owed more to the sort of inquiries being raised by the House appropriations subcommittee than to any efforts on the Senate side.

Thus by the time of the 1974 hearings it seemed ever more certain that a challenge had been mounted for control of the debate about violence on television. Not only were the House members willing to pick up the issue and take it further than Pastore had ever permitted it to go; they had proven themselves prepared to broaden it into the realms of obscenity and of children's programming and advertising. Further, the House subcommittee seemed bent of provoking a fundamental constitutional test, the end result of which could not be guaranteed. The senator simply had to take cognizance of this activity in the House, lest the pattern of understandings and accommodations worked out in 1972 and during all the years before be undermined.

Finally there were matters of a personal nature. By early 1974 it was increasingly likely that Pastore would retire in 1976, at the end of his term. In the wake of such episodes as the S.2004 affair and against the general sort of reformist criticism that was increasingly willing to attack the terms of compromise with the industry that had marked his chairmanship of the communications subcommittee, the senator had reason to want to keep the record focused on his public interest accomplishments as they were reflected in the popular interpretations of the violence debate. At one level and as always before, he doubtless did want to see some changes in what he genuinely considered offensive and inappropriate programming content. At other levels he also likely did not wish to see his own image as the public's arbiter and responsible diplomat be swept aside. The end of this public career could afford a better closing picture than that which might emerge if the House group and others were allowed too much say in redefining the issues and the consequent policy agenda. Therefore, in April, Senator Pastore held another three-day round of hearings as "a continuation of the committee's ongoing concern that the Department of Health, Education and Welfare, the Federal Communication Commission, the scientific community, and the broadcast industry implement and build upon the Surgeon General's report" (Senate, Commerce Comm., Communications Subcomm., 1974a: 1).

He had held general oversight hearings for the FCC only a week before (Senate, Commerce Comm., Communications Subcomm., 1974b). But in order to concentrate attention strictly on the violence issue, to refocus the inquiry along the lines of his prior pattern, and to swing it away from the recent House appropations committee emphasis on the regulatory option, he scheduled these hearings as a special event, quite apart from the regular oversight proceedings. The senator used these hearings to document the series of research and industry activities that had taken place since the 1972 hearings. Citing correspondence with the secretary of HEW and the chairman of the FCC, and using the testimony of NIMH officials and a few academics conducting research for these agencies and for the Social Science Research Council, Pastore continued to build the image of being able to employ the research tool for the process of presumably intense federal scrutiny of television programming.

However, a close reading of the 1974 hearings suggests that the pattern of federal control over the violence effects research enterprise was shifting. The utility and support for such research was not necessarily diminishing, but it was clear that the relatively firm authority that had been exercised by Congress through Senator Pastore and the mental health bureaucracy during the period of the Scientific Advisory Committee investigation and its immediate aftermath was now dissipating. Among the other considerations the 1974 hearings may be seen as an attempt by Senator Pastore to call congressional attention to that slippage and to try to stop it.

On the surface it might have appeared that the full-scale program of research under the original senatorial mandate was to continue. Dr. Bertram Brown, director of NIMH's Drug Abuse and Mental Health Administration, testifies that a dozen research projects were receiving support totaling about $500,000 a year, roughly the rate during the surgeon general's period. But this testimony suggests that most of these studies were only continuations of work begun under the surgeon general's program, and that no new research was being supported under the former pattern of an organized project coordinated by NIMH. Further, there was evidence that NIMH research funds not only would not be increased, but were also beginning to be reduced (1974a: 5). It had begun to appear that the large program of research proposed to NIMH by the Social Science Research Council the previous year might not be fully funded after all.

Correspondence with the subcommittee by the secretary of HEW demonstrates that the department was intending to interpret the implicit instructions from the 1972 hearings to pursue the study of effects only in the context of a "more constructive profile of TV violence . . . made up of indices of a number of significant dimensions — level, frequency, characteristics of those involved, their motivations, whether the violence is explained or not, audience perception of the violence, and its short and long-term effects on various kinds of viewers" (1974a: 2).

Brown's testimony reveals that NIMH was interpreting the recommendations of its 1972 research planning workshop as calling for establishment of only the continuing violence profile. He acknowledges that NIMH had made a grant to the Social Science Research Council in 1973-1974, but he claims that the charge to the SSRC was only for "planning and stimulating research into television and social behavior that will have significant social policy relevance — and especially research leading to development of a violence profile"

(1974a: 4). The appositive phrase is important, because it suggests that, although "significant policy relevance" is the goal, the SSRC had in fact a mandate to proceed down only the relatively narrower path of counting violent acts. The account by Withey and Abeles (1980: viii-ix) suggests that that mandate had originally been much broader. As for the profile, one also notes that it never developed along the lines of the movie-rating index system suggested by the Eisenhower Commission and later discussed by NIMH and the FCC.

Having used Brown at the outset of the hearings to introduce the problem of declining NIMH research funds, Senator Pastore calls on Eli Rubinstein, who had since left NIMH for an academic post at the State University of New York at Stony Brook, to dramatize the situation more explicitly:

> Unlike the case in the Surgeon General's program, the National Institute of Mental Health was not given a special allocation of money or additional staff to fulfill your request to develop a violence index. Omission of special priority undoubtedly hampered efforts toward effective action, especially in view of the marked reduction in recent years in overall Federal funding for research and training programs in the mental health field. . . . The reduction in the NIMH research program is having and will continue to have a direct negative impact on extending our knowledge about how we cope with the various influences on our behavior, including the pervasive impact of television [1974a: 16-17].

Rubinstein had, of course, been a loyal soldier for Pastore. As staff director of the surgeon general's project, he had overseen preparation of a report that was imbued with a subtle mixture of conflicting conclusions, yet in 1972 he had testified that on the whole its findings were clear. His testimony during the 1974 hearings and in other forums after 1972 tended to continue this pattern. In one breath he takes cognizance of the lack of conclusiveness; in the next he endorses the impression of negative findings and then goes on to repeat the plea for appropriate action:

> While the research of the Surgeon General's program may not have been definitive, it has, I believe, answered the basic question about the relationship to later aggressive behavior. . . . While some of the research now underway will, hopefully, lead toward a better understanding of how television influences social behavior, we still are not close to the kind of policy changes which seem implicit from the conclusion of the hearings 2 years ago [1974a: 20-21].

To keep up the pressure Rubinstein argues that the government ought to fund some form of independent, "long-term instrumentality" for research:

> The major areas of activity might be: (a) A continuing research program to study ways of enhancing the value of television to the child viewer and to explore the impact of new technology on child development; (b) A clearing house and distribution center for periodic progress reports; (c) A public advocate role to provide testimony on matters relating to children and television. Certainly an annual violence index or a violence profile could be a part of such an effort [1974a: 22].

This is a reiteration of one of those proprosals made during the 1972 hearings by the surgeon general's contract researchers and by others during many of the earlier investigations. Its implementation would, of course, represent attainment by the effects research community of status as permanent brokers in public policymaking for broadcasting.

As one of the framers of the surgeon general's report, Rubinstein did not overlook the possibility of exploiting one of its recommendations for further research. He notes that he had begun to undertake research of his own to demonstrate "how prosocial content on regular children's programming can produce prosocial behavior" (1974a: 20), and then he goes on to make the continued support of such research one of his three recommendations for an on-going program of effects study. Members of the advisory committee, Rubinstein, and others had argued that if negative effects could be discerned, then perhaps the same research tools could be turned to the analysis of those factors contributing to ameliorative television. This proposal had become a staple in television effects planning conferences during the immediate post-1972 period.

However, the prosocial approach depended on the very theoretical models and methodologies employed in the violence effects campaign, and, of course, the assertion of proved results notwithstanding, that research structure had not in fact demonstrated its validity. Further, the very question of who determines and what constitutes "prosocial" response remains troublesome and resistent to resolution. As a result, the initial enthusiasm for the prosocial line of inquiry may be waning in some quarters. While much research has been conducted in this area, much of it remains unpublished, at least in those communication and social science journals governed by peer review. Its primary forums of activity may be in the applied, formative, and summative behavioral research programs of those agencies producing instructional television and in the commercial broadcasting networks, as part of their continuing efforts to build up reserves of research demonstrating the positive social value of their programming.

Another principal area of research proposed for continuing support after the surgeon general's report was, of course, the annual analysis of network programming content. During the 1974 hearings, George Gerbner is called on to explain and promote this project. He reviews the history of the study, noting its origins in the reserach for the Eisenhower Commission (NCCPV) and its continuance for the advisory committee and later under NIMH alone. He reports as well that the 1972 conference of NIMH research consultants (which had included himself) had discussed the problem of measuring televised violence and had recommended continuance of the research, but with a broadened scope. The former "violence index" was now to become a "violence profile, . . . that 'would take account of the social relationships portrayed by the violence . . . and the correlation of known viewing patterns of target audiences . . .' with the content presented on television" (1974a: 40). Gerbner argues that beyond merely counting acts of violence the project intends "to trace the nature and role of televised violence, both on the screen and in the lives and minds of our viewers." The profile is presented as "an objective, reliable and multidimensional indicator of violence on television and of some conceptions of reality that heavy viewing of television appears to cultivate" (1974a: 41).

In his prepared testimony Gerbner attempts to justify the project on the basis of intellectual considerations that may not have direct policy impact. As such the profile is seen as part of a "project called Cultural Indicators [that] is designed to trace broad trends in television content and in audience conceptions about a variety of significant issues" (1974a: 57). But such concerns are not the motivating force behind Senator Pastore's interest in the project. He will permit the name change from "index" to "profile," but as chairman of the communications subcommittee, he wants hard data he can use to chart the performance of the networks. To continue to sell the project Gerbner finds that he must comply:

> *Senator Pastore:* . . . In the final analysis you see, the responsibility of this committee would be to persuade the networks and broadcasting industry to do something about it. To make a study without accomplishing any results is a study in vacuum, you will agree with that, won't you?
>
> I mean, we have to prove to the American people that we are putting our money in this study in order to reach some conclusions that

> would indicate to the American public that we are improving the situation. Otherwise we're wasting the money.
>
> *Dr. Gerbner:* That's right.
>
> *Senator Pastore:* We end up with something that is very academic. But insofar as the viewer is concerned and the result upon our children and people who view these programs and what violence will do to them, we have wasted our time unless we can show some improvement.
>
> I would like to approach the representatives of the networks when they come here after you have testified to say to them, look, the situation is better than it was. Now, keep going and make it a little better. And if it's worse, I would like to say to them, where have you been all these 2 years? Do I make myself clear on this?
>
> *Dr. Gerbner:* Yes, indeed.
>
> *Senator Pastore:* All right, now, give me the answer in simple English.
>
> *Dr. Gerbner:* Well, I hope I can make myself equally clear in saying that if your advice to the networks wishes to be credible, it depends on what continuing measures we have available.
>
> Now this is not an academic study. It's a concrete study of policy. It reflects policy. It has no greater theoretical or academic value. It is done in the interest of public interest and the needs of policy determination. It's like the weather report. It is made up of different elements and different currents and crosscurrents [1974a: 48-49].

The quid pro quo for continuing federal support for communication research could not be more clear.

The question of Senator Pastore's willingness, or ability, to continue to stimulate such support was, however, somewhat less clear. As is apparent from his use of certain witnesses during these hearings, there is little doubt about his interest in furthering at least some aspects of the research developed during or recommended by the surgeon general's project. But one remains uncertain about just how adamant he was.

Part of the difficulty in assessing his intent derives from recognition of the political realities in the administration of the federal government in 1974. After six years of planning and implementation, the budget policies of the Republican administration had begun to take their toll among a wide variety of programs that had been carried over from the "Great Society" projects of the mid-1960s. The congressional leadership, although still Democratic, could no longer hold out uniformly against the administration's program of cuts. Whatever else it may have begun to effect, the developing Watergate affair did not alter the current trends in federal budget realignments. Therefore, to the degree that the research program on television and social behavior was tied to a mental health research budget in NIMH that had been designated for reduction, Senator Pastore may no longer have retained much control over his program. There may have been no practical opportunity to do more than wind up a number of projects from the surgeon general's program, initiate a few prosocial inquiries, continue the most elementary aspects of the violence profile, and seek funding for new projects in other federal programs.

However, from another perspective that situation may not have been entirely unfortunate for the chairman. For as the "findings" of the surgeon general's project had become popularly accepted during and after the 1972 hearings, the communications subcommittee had begun to find the pressure building for clearer, more certain action commensurate with the impression of deleterious effects. The House appropriations committee activities noted above were only one manifestation of that pressure. As well, a variety of public interest groups had seized increasingly on the research findings and had begun to form alliances with those among the social science community who had concluded that their research had been sufficiently definitive to justify action. Faced with various demands for far more explicit legislative or regulatory measures than he had ever contemplated taking, it may not have dismayed Chairman Pastore to see the research fever cooled by someone else's policy of fiscal austerity.

Seen in this light, the significance of the violence profile as the most visible major continuing project from the surgeon general's program is more readily apparent. In spite of the regular criticism it encountered from the broadcasters, the profile remained of little threat by itself. As long as it was at heart a monitoring project, accounting primarily for trends in network program violence, the profile provided no basis for causal inference. Politicians could continue to request its funding and broadcasters could critique its methodology, but this research would present neither party with the sorts of data that would tend to "prove" negative effects. The content analysis could continue to help build the presumptive case against television, but it would never supply the firm evidence of direct causality necessary for substantially revised federal policy toward broadcasting operation and regulation.

By the time of the 1974 hearings Frank Stanton had retired from CBS, and with him went the industry's chief proponent of diversionary social research. But in his absence the industry had not neglected the value to it of maintaining a regular effects research presence, nor had it forgotten the recommendation of the Eisenhower Commission and its own promises in the 1972 hearings to pay more attention to such research in program development. All three of the network presidents or chairmen testifying during these hearings point to research projects they have been sponsoring, and they attempt to demonstrate how such research is presumably affecting program choices and production. On the whole, however, nothing reported by these executives proved to be any more illuminating about effects or any more damaging to the industry than the earlier CBS, NBC, and JCTRC projects had been.

Indeed, testimony by John Schneider, then president of the CBS Broadcast Group, suggests that the former pattern of diversion was as strong as ever. The only research by the CBS Office of Social Research that Schneider reports was a violence analysis of CBS programming that was clearly designed for no other purpose than to refute the results of the Gerbner profile (which had shown an increase in violent incidence in network programming) and to try to demonstrate that, on the contrary, "between the 1971-1972 season and the current broadcast season, the number of acts of violence has declined by about 25 percent" (1974a: 119).

Walter Schwartz, president of ABC-TV, and Alfred Schneider, vice-president, begin their testimony by recalling the five-point policy statement to which ABC had committed itself during the 1972 hearings:

> ABC is taking the following actions, some of which are extensions of earlier policy determinations:
>
> (1) By the fall of 1972 cartoon series which depend solely on "action" and are devoid of comedy will have been eliminated from the network's children's schedule.
>
> (2) We are placing additional emphasis on resolving conflict in children's programs through non-violent means.
>
> (3) The overall balance of the different types of programs in our schedule will be considered even more carefully in the future.
>
> (4) When selecting the time periods in which new series will be scheduled, in the future, greater emphasis will be focused on the possible adverse impact which the program's content might have on young viewers.
>
> (5) ABC has budgeted $1,000,000 over the next four years for an intensified program of original research in this area [1974a: 129-130].

Most of their testimony is devoted to elaboration of Schwartz's statement that "I can report to you now that those actions have been implemented and will continue to be an integral part of ABC's overall programming policy" (1974a: 130).

In light of ABC's previous lack of interest in supporting the industry's social research image, its commitment after 1972 is remarkable. By industry standards for this sort of work its financial commitment was substantial, and, like the CBS projects of a decade or more before, it attempts to build in the appearance of academic validity and a wide-ranging focus:

> Since February, 1970, Drs. Heller and Polsky and Dr. Seymour Lieberman have been engaged as independent outside consultants to conduct specific research programs. . . .
>
> The Heller-Polsky study was initially conducted as three separate projects extending over a 2-year period to explore "Responses of Emotionally Vulnerable Children to Televised Violence," to compare "Cartoon and Human-Portrayed Violence in Emotionally Vulnerable Children," and to conduct "Television Studies With Young Adult Offenders."
>
> This 2-year phase of ongoing research concentrated on the immediate and long-range effects of televised violence on certain test groups of children, and young adults.
>
> The third year of investigation went beyond the study of televised violence and it involved antisocial effects to explore, in addition, the prosocial effects of television on children [1974a: 139-140].

This research was firmly cast as having practical value, thereby appealing to the popular expectations for applicability:

> *Senator Pastore:* Now, you have mentioned three very distinguished scientists who are your counselors in this matter. Are they very much involved in these programs? Do they view them, too?
>
> *Mr. Schwartz:* Yes, sir.
>
> *Senator Pastore:* And pass judgment upon them?
>
> *Mr. Schwartz:* Yes, sir. . . .
>
> *Mr. Schneider:* . . . Drs. Heller and Post [Polsky?] visited with our editors on the west coast and conducted what we are calling inservice training workships, the purpose of which is to take various programs, including children's programs, review the script, review them on the screen and review with the editors what is or is not appropriate in terms of what the children ought to be seeing [1974a: 133].

In using research evidence the networks can be said, again, to be acting responsibly, and such a consideration may have become increasingly important to ABC during the mid-1970s and may help explain its new interest in social research. Perenially the lowest-ranked network, ABC had begun to overcome its various competitive disadvantages (particularly the UHF handicap), and by the mid-1970s had begun a series of programming changes that were to reverse its fortunes. As it saw its ratings rise (and those of CBS fall) during these years, its increased visibility and the criticism of the programming responsibile for its improved position may have led ABC to feel a need for a more public show of "social responsibility" than had previously been required of it. If the appearance of an active, serious research program had provided such evidence for the other networks when they were the leading targets, there was every reason to suppose it would work for the new leader too.

As was the pattern for years before, the ABC research can be seen as an attempt to confound critical academic research. Further, of course and also as before, the research is never debated and published in normal academic forums. Instead it remains in reserve with competing measures of violence and assessments of impact, lest the political critique begin to make too much of the surgeon general's report and to lead toward dangerous new policy conclusions.

Julian Goodman, then chairman of NBC, testifies that NBC was continuing a longitudinal study of "television's influence on children's behavior in real-life situations over a period of years." Further he claims that

> our social research people keep abreast of the studies on the impact of television programming. They try to go beyond the abstract research data and raw statistics, to refine and analyze the information in ways we can apply to our programming. . . .
>
> We differentiate between violence that might be harmful to viewers and violence that is unlikely to lead to antisocial behavior. This is the heart of the problem, and it cannot be reached by any simple formula or by removing all forms of violence from television. It places on us the task of judgment — the responsibility to assure that any violence in entertainment programs is in a context that does not condone it or does not present it as a desirable solution to human problems [1974a: 159-160].

But, of course, in trying to show that NBC is conducting effects research and paying attention to it, Goodman's testimony is designed to reassure the subcommittee of the appropriateness of continuing to allow it autonomy in making the content decisions

Throughout the hearings the network chiefs attempt to show evidence of programming changes that take account of the surgeon general's report, claiming that they have minimized the incidence of the gratuitous appearance of violence generally and its appearance in children's programs and early-evening programming specifically. Pastore allows each network representative in turn to present his version of this claim of improvement, but always, just before the witness is finished and might have appeared to have made his case, the senator interjects a note of doubt and caution, acknowledging their "encouraging pledges" of responsible action, yet securing their agreement that "this is a matter that has to be constantly watched" (1974a: 122-123).

In all three cases the impact is the same. For whether or not the reality of the changes was ever as dramatic as the claims (on the last day of the hearings Senator Pastore permits one witness, a law student, to testify that it is not), the networks were each shown to have received the message of the 1972 hearings and to have bowed to the congressional will for at least some token of change in program practice. They have given the chairman of the Senate communications subcommittee the appearance of a major public victory.

It would appear, then, that in spite of the challenges posed by the House appropriations subcommittee the exercise that Senator Pastore had initiated in 1969 had succeeded rather well. Just before closing the 1974 hearings, the senator was able to say to Julian Goodman, "and as I told the president of ABC and the president of CBS, this committee is going to keep your feet to the fire, and I am hopeful that when you come before us next year we can still say that we have improved on last year" (1974a: 164). But as it happened, the senator never again felt compelled to hold further major hearings on television violence.

The matter did come up the following year during the House and Senate communications subcommittees' respective oversight hearings for the FCC. In both instances Chairman Wiley took the opportunity to outline the general findings of the recent FCC report on violence and obscenity that the House appropriations committee had demanded the previous year, in which the commission's continuing preference for industry self-regulation is made quite clear (FCC, 1975). Wiley then goes on to note the recent developments surrounding the emergence of the industry's new "family viewing hour" (see Chapter 9). In the House hearing, perhaps smarting under the appropriations committee's challenges in 1974, Chairman Macdonald demonstrates a good bit more interest in the violence issue than he had for sometime (House, Interstate and Foreign Commerce Comm., Communications Subcomm., 1975a: 18, 41-42, 46-49). In fact, toward the end of the morning-long hearing he launches into a long, one-sided colloquy with Wiley, lashing out at the industry for what he contends is continuing poor programming performance and at the commission for undue faith in the industry's oft-broken promises:

> I would like to get back to what I think, perhaps, is my underlying discontent with the report which you filed on television violence and that mainly I would think, deals with your otimism concerning the industry's willingness for self-regulation. I, perhaps, don't go quite as far as Mr. Carney did in his questioning, but I must say that the

> industry . . . and I have many good friends in the industry, and secretly . . . they have one motivation and that is the bottom line. They don't care what they put on that screen as long as the ratings show that it is attracting a vast majority of Americans to watch it. I know you have been with the Commission since 1970, so you can't be naive about what motivates the broadcasting industry as a whole, and therefore, when you say that this whole thing is going to depend on their reasonableness and their good faith, that is, in my judgement, like writing a letter to Santa Claus [1975a: 46].

As is clear from an earlier exchange with Wiley, much of Chairman Macdonald's ire this day derived from a recent episode in which the commission had taken an important AT&T rate-making decision without first informing the subcommittee of its intentions (1975a: 31-35). Therefore, one must be careful not to read more into the congressman's concern about violence and obscenity than might be there. In the middle of the colloquy Wiley suggests that the new "family viewing hour" plan is about "as far as the Commission can go under the current law," and he invites clearer congressional legislative direction on the content issue problem (1975a: 47). Suffice it to note that other than the points about ascertainment and the license renewal process, Chairman Macdonald declines the invitation and slides away from the matter of congressional responsibility for setting policy in all this.

The review of the violence question in the Senate subcommittee's oversight hearing a month later is also relatively brief, though considerably less acrimonious (Senate, Commerce Comm., Communications Subcomm., 1975: 4-5, 37-38). The hearing is noteworthy only as yet another reflection of how the issue had come to be seen as settled by Senator Pastore and as a record of his final treatment of the issue in a formal subcommittee proceeding. The subcommittee permits Wiley to make his presentation of the FCC report and the family viewing hour plan, and the majority of the members seem content to leave the matter at that.

That statement sets the stage for a vintage Pastore recapitulation of his position. In what appears to have been his last public committee speech on television violence, he once again snuffs out any hint of rebellion and leaves little doubt about how he wants the issue, and his role in it, to rest:

> Of course tremendous progress has been made in this area. There was a time when television was virtually saturated with violence. It just went on ad infinitum. I think recently there have been a lot of attempts by the networks to improve the situation. I think in the children's hours that we're talking about, where a large part of the audience is young people not in school, or in first or second grade, there's been an immense improvement. . . .

> They're not going to eliminate all violence and no one is suggesting that, but you have to eliminate violence for the sake of violence. We have had a very scientific study made and the Surgeon General came before this committee as he did on the question of cigarette smoking and said there is a causal connection between violence on television and the behavior of children. That was established.
>
> We must admit not every child responds the same way or every adult, for that matter. People are susceptible to emotional reactions in different ways. But, all of us know that just as television can sell soap or cereal, it can sell an idea, good or bad. The fact is that restraints on excessive televised violence should come from the broadcasting industry.
>
> None of us can define this kind of violence but it's there. To borrow from Justice Stewart's dictum on pornography, I can't describe it, but I know it when I see it [1975: 34].

The ritual had changed little over the years. Once more the senator invokes both common sense and the authority of science, reinforcing the impression that the problem is real, building up the image of conclusiveness, carefully introducing a few caveats, praising progress by the industry, reiterating the importance of self-regulation, and through it all taking credit both for stimulating progress and for doing nothing dangerous.

Thus for his purposes Senator Pastore never had to hold any further television violence hearings. By the end of the 1974 inquiry, he had already achieved the goal toward which he had been working for at least five years and which had been the objective of many others for a much longer period. Violence effects research had served its political purpose, and the actual subsequent performance of the networks was of little importance. What mattered was that, in spite of the real limitations on its power (and perhaps even its willingness) to exercise much control over network television programming policy, Congress had successfully created an image of being able to do so. To cast this significance more generally, it could be said that the 1974 hearings capped a quarter century of effort by politicians and regulators, broadcasting critics, academics, and a wide variety of public groups to secure legitimacy for the application of social science research methods and findings to the process of public policymaking for broadcasting, while yet ignoring questions about whether such research would ever be likely to lead to substantive change in that policy.

However, within this accomplishment there also lay the outline of a major dilemma that would persist beyond Senator Pastore's tenure. As indicated by the response of the House appropriations committee, the emerging political consensus about the research had begun to dislodge the balance of forces in the debate over televised violence.

The policymakers, and particularly those in Congress, were faced with critics and reformers of all varieties who now seemed to have in hand just the sort of evidence that the politicians had previously been able to say was inconclusive. The demands for "action" were no longer so readily dismissed. But those members of Congress acceding to such demands soon found themselves encountering the principal economic and political assumptions wrapped up in the Communications Act and, behind it, the Constitution. Under the legislation, there were severe constraints on the regulatory action permissible for the FCC. Various commission chairmen could be badgered and bullied, and even pushed to new lengths in encouraging industry self-regulation, but the further such activities went, the more likely they would be to impinge on broadcasting content decisions in such a way as to be construed as contravening the law and the First Amendment.

For years Congress had been successful in raising its eyebrows, in "jawboning" the industry, and in appearing to be seriously reviewing policy for broadcasting without in fact having to make any substantive changes in the underlying terms of its operation. Now, however, Congress was finding itself being edged closer and closer to having to consider taking what might actually become major policy decisions in this area. If the rhetoric of deleterious impact continued to spread so successfully, Congress would eventually have to accept the long-deferred burden of revising the legislation. But that option would, of course, force it to confront the basic broadcasting control assumptions as well as all the contending interests that had previously been kept at bay or in balance with one another. More and more the criticisms of broadcasting performance were centering on its economic basis and its fundamental purposes, and beyond that lay unthinkable questions about the adequacy of the entire system of private, free enterprise communications.

NOTES

1. Of course, under the terms of its mandate from Senator Pastore and the secretary of HEW, the surgeon general's committee had made no such specific recommendations or any policy recommendations whatsoever. Chairman Burch is probably confusing the surgeon general's report with the earlier Eisenhower Commission report, which included among its recommendations the suggestion that the movie rating system be considered (see Chapter 5).

2. For instance, see U.S. House, Committee on Interstate and Foreign Commerce (1969: 40-44), where there is some discussion of the matter, and (1971), where there is none.

Chapter 9

THE CONTINUING RESEARCH AND POLICY DEBATES (1975-1981)

THE PERSISTENT CAMPAIGN TO RATIFY THE FINDINGS

During the mid- and late 1970s, the federal and private roles in violence effects research continued to undergo adjustment. In spite of the exhortations by Senator Pastore and others in 1974, NIMH continued to experience slippage in political support for the research program it had worked out through the SSRC. Then in 1976, the chief patron of communication research retired. As a result of his departure and a number of other significant leadership changes in the Senate during the following session, it was unclear whether the communications subcommittee would maintain its formerly intense interest in the television violence issue. As for NIMH, these political uncertainties in combination with the previous years of decline in its budget led it to reconsider even its support for what was left of the original television and social behavior program, namely, the violence profile. Indeed, in 1977 it indicated that it was unlikely to continue funding the program as long as it remained primarily a monitoring project, even though that was precisely the restricted role the SSRC committee on television and social behavior had determined for it in 1975 (see Withey and Abeles, 1980: 307-324, App. II). This situation raised questions about how much longer public funding of the index and the entire effects research enterprise could be sustained, and it required the interested research community to keep the effects issue alive, to dramatize the value of what had been accomplished.

Such efforts paid off for the violence index when it became apparent that some private sources, such as the American Medical Association and the national Parent-Teachers Association, might be willing to help take up the slack. As part of his effort to broaden the base of support, Professor Gerbner announced plans for expansion of the project "to create a resource center for anyone wanting data on TV trends and patterns" (Broadcasting, June 6, 1977: 45-46; August 29, 1977: 43). Beyond monitoring violence, the project would develop profiles in such areas "as medicine, business, the military, energy and transportation, politics and foreign cultures." Gerbner is reported to have said "It'll work like a public opinion polling agency," and that it could even be of use to the networks to "answer unjustified criticism" of television.

Meanwhile, there was other evidence that, although specific projects might have fallen from political favor, the general effects research enterprise would continue to garner significant support under the aegis of other federal and closely related private funding programs. For instance, even before the mental health program began to decline as the primary source of federal support for communication effects research, a variety of public and private agencies, particularly those interested in providing research for telecommunications policy planning, had begun to play a significant role in such funding. The Telecommunications Policy Research Program, administered through the Research Applied to National Needs (RANN) office of the National Science Foundation, began in 1972. It represented the collective determination of communication research funding needs among the FCC, the Office of Telecommunications Policy, the Department of HEW, the Office of Telecommunications in the Department of Commerce, the Office of Management and Budget, and other agencies (National Science Foundation, 1975: 1-2). Related support for conferences and research projects was provided during the early and mid-1970s by the Ford Foundation, the Markle Foundation, and others. Much of this research and research planning dealt with policy concerns in the areas of technological capability, economic implications, and regulatory issues, but in nearly every conference and general research program time and funds were set aside for continuing research under such rubrics as "television and children" or the "social impact of television." Many of the conference participants and funded investigators in these areas were, of course, principals from the surgeon general's project and the preceding efforts to establish the effects research enterprise, and much of their effort was devoted to consolidating the gains they had secured for the field by 1972.

One of those principals was George Comstock. A Schramm advisee from Stanford, he had served as Eli Rubinstein's senior research coordinator during the surgeon general's project, and like Rubinstein, he continued during the ensuing years to help make the public case for the definitiveness of the report, for the legitimacy of the general approaches reflected in it, and for the need for further funding of related research. After 1972 Comstock had moved on to a post at the

Rand Corporation, a leader among those private firms whose primary support comes from research grants and consultancy contracts with foundations and the federal government, principally the defense department. In 1974, supported by an Edna McConnell Clark Foundation grant to Rand, Comstock directed the preparation of a series of further summaries, bibliographies, and evaluations of priorities for social and behavioral research on television's impact (Comstock and Fisher, 1975; Comstock, 1975; Comstock and Lindsey, 1975). Whenever these compilations touch on the issue of violence effects they tend to support the image of conclusiveness or at least to suggest that the impression of disagreement among the various studies and reviews can be resolved by focusing the debate on other topics. Thus, Comstock summarizes the surgeon general's report and the 1972 hearings as saying:

> The [Scientific Advisory] Committee concluded that the sum of data was "a preliminary and tentative indication" that violence viewing increased aggressiveness. The Surgeon General (Dr. Jesse Steinfeld) testified that the evidence indicated a causal relationship. Industry spokesmen acknowledged that violence probably should be restrained [1975: 236].

Elsewhere in the same volume, he argues that

> the true locus of conflict is not the nature of the findings, but two other broad areas representing the nature of the questions put to the findings. They are:
>
> - The criteria invoked for alarm about effects.
> - The structure employed to lay out evidence for evaluation.
>
> Another way of putting it is to say that the real issues are the *degree of seriousness of effect which must be demonstrated before one is ready to agree that possible remedies should be reviewed, and the concepts and general schema which are most useful for making such a determination from the available empirical evidence* [1975: 38].

In certain respects this reorientation of the debate has merit, but, of course, it assumes the reality of deleterious effects and entertains no doubts about the validity of the effects research exercise.

The central object of the third report in this series, *The Research Horizon,* is "a description and analysis of the scientific community's state of mind concerning television and human behavior. Our focus is on the implications of that state of mind for future research" (Comstock and Lindsey, 1975: 5).

The report is based on two stages of research: first, the "interviewing in depth [of] a sample of persons currently active in television research which represented a wide spectrum of views and interests," and, second, after preparation of a draft report of the results of that survey, its submission "to a panel of social scientists . . . to test our hypothesis that we had constructed a fairly accurate portrait of the thinking of the scientific community" (Comstock and Lindsey, 1975: 5).

Unfortunately, no list of those sampled is included in the report, nor is there any description of just how they were chosen. Appendix B of the report does contain a long list of members of the communication research community, but it appears that these were queried for the section of the report on research then in progress. There is no suggestion that this is the group interviewed for the section on priorities. It is therefore difficult to evaluate the claim of width for the interests of those interviewed in the first stage of this research.

It is clear that the review panel at the second stage reflected virtually no breadth. All five (Chaffee, Katzman, McCombs, Roberts, and Rubinstein) are behavioral scientists whose training in the normative-empirical tradition suggests that their individual impressions of significant research questions and appropriate methodologies would be far more notable for their similarities than for their differences. As with Comstock, four of the five had taken their Ph. D.s at Stanford under Schramm during the previous decade — the period coinciding with the rise to preeminent status of communication behavioral research — and, due to their participation in the surgeon general's project, all five had considerable professional stake in the continued identification of communication effects research in the terms of that effort.

Not surprisingly, then, the chief priority found by this study is for research on "television and the socialization of young persons," and within that topic the emphasis is on such standard effects questions as: contingent conditions for antisocial and prosocial behavior; processes of belief, value, and attitude acquisition; and factors influencing cognitive learning. The tradition of effects research and the definition of appropriate social science in communication had become so tightly focused, inbred, and self-sustaining that this report on research priorities could cast itself only in the narrowest terms of behavioral impact. By way of contrast, one notes that the report has almost no sense of importance for the study of television in the context of broad social and cultural questions about, say, meaning, history, and community. To the degree that it even appears to recognize the legitimacy of such issues (and it is arguable that it does), the report seems to see them as secondary, as derivative of positivistic, empirical studies of behavior.

This general argument and its restricted paradigmatic focus were to be sustained in the formal publication of a textbook synthesis of the

Clark Foundation-Rand reports carrying the same *Television and Human Behavior* title (Comstock et al., 1978). There, under Comstock's general management, the Rand review panel recapitulated the entire corpus of behavioral effects research findings as it perceived them to have emerged during and after the surgeon general's project. Following the pattern of previous reports, this volume discusses the content of television, the characteristics of its audiences, and their viewing habits — with particular emphases on children and political and advertising effects. At the theoretical level the book seeks to articulate a general psychological model of effects that of course, turns out to resemble closely the behavioral models that had been the guiding images for the empirical effects tradition during most of the preceding generation (1978: 400). The implications for communication theory are therefore little advanced: "Television probably should be considered a major agent of socialization, although its influence is often indirect and contingent on interpersonal relations and other factors" (1978: 14).

At the applied level the objective of the volume was to reassert the policy relevance of this sort of research, celebrating its prior contributions to the surgeon general's effort and renewing the calls for such things as better-focused programs of organized research, new and better structures for research information dissemination, and more use of social and behavioral science research in broadcast regulation and policymaking (1978: 491-510). As with the earlier Rand volume, this book tries to broaden the effects research focus and move beyond matters largely of antisocial behavior. Nonetheless, it remains circumscribed by the behavioral impact tradition, and it relies heavily on the reiteration of the putatively conclusive findings of the violence research efforts as presumedly reflected in the Scientific Advisory Committee's report. Here, as there, the argument is not careless; many of the caveats are recorded:

> science cannot tell us conclusively whether television violence contributes to serious crime because its methods are too imperfect [1978: 2-3].
>
> The viewing of television violence appears to increase the likelihood of subsequent aggressiveness. This conclusion derives from the pattern of results of dozens of laboratory experiments, field experiments, and surveys. It also hides many complexities. The relationship of television violence to aggression and antisocial behavior is a topic that reveals the strengths and weaknesses of social and behavioral science, and illustrates many of the problems in drawing generalizations applicable to future events from the limited circumstances of specific studies [1978: 13].

The carefully modulated rhythms of conclusiveness and caution are played and replayed. A major general finding is put forward, it is carefully modified, and then it is subtly reinstated again:

> The evidence is that television may increase aggression by teaching viewers previously unfamiliar hostile acts, by generally encouraging in various ways the use of aggression and by triggering aggressive behavior both imitative in kind from what has been viewed. Effects are never certain because real-life agression is strongly influenced by situational factors, and this strong role for situational factors means that the absence of an immediate effect does not rule out a delayed impact when the behavior in question may be more propitious [1978: 13-14].

Over and over again, the weight of the collective evidence is invoked and then cautiously softened: "The quantity of studies with consistent results provide considerable confidence about the relationship between television violence and subsequent aggression, but the studies do not provide direct evidence on whether television contributes widely or generally to serious antisocial behavior" (1978: 14).

Yet through it all there is a consistent attempt to advance the argument that the "no-effects" and catharsis conclusions are incorrect (1978: 390-391) and that as reflected in the surgeon general's and subsequent work a substantial body of scientific evidence has been building up to at least make more probable the deleterious impact conclusion. The authors permit even the earlier caveats to evaporate, and they return to the persistent refrain, "that the best interpretation of the full array of evidence is that television viewing of violence increases the likelihood of aggressiveness on the part of young viewers" (1978: 495).

To the extent doubts about the conclusiveness of the violence effects issue might remain, they are dismissed at the outset as emanating from the mistakes of the doubter: "The wrong question is being asked" (1978: 3). Again a safe retreat is prepared—do not ask science to do what it cannot. Yet the communication research science of which this book is a major summary volume grew for years precisely on the promise of being able to answer such questions, and the policy-useful relevance of such research is a major theme of the book and most of the post-surgeon general's recapitulations. The problem of asking too much of science is reitereated in the closing passages, where an analogy is drawn to the presumed similar strengths and weaknesses of the law. Yet the significance there lies not so much in the relative merits of the analogy, but in the very compulsion to use it, to reassert the claim for social science of its long hoped-for new level of policy status. There are indeed other questions to be asked, but they are never posed in this volume, nor in many of the normative post-surgeon general's discussions.

Shortly after the Rand reports were published in 1975, both Comstock and Rubinstein became closely involved in helping organize and guide a conference at Reston, Virginia, cosponsored by NSF and the Ford and Markle foundations, to determine priorities for research on television and children. The final report on the conference cites the Rand reports, particularly the *Horizons* volume, as influencing the decision to hold the meeting, and it reprints Comstock's remarks, "Setting the Stage for a Research Agenda," as one of the two opening session presentations (Ford Foundation, 1976: 4-5, 6-10).

The participants in the Reston conference included a mixture of representatives from the communication research community, the broadcasting industry, public interest groups, the foundations, and government research and regulatory agencies. While there were some relatively new faces in this group, among the communication researchers there were several who had been closely associated with the violence effects enterprise at various stages of its history. In addition to Comstock and Rubinstein they included Bogart, Chaffee, Gerbner, Himmelweit, Liebert, Lyle, Pool, Schramm, Siegel, and Tannenbaum. In light of the Rand reports' influence on the conference agenda and the inclusion of this particular cast of characters, it is hardly surprising to find that the discussions of appropriate research questions and the expectations of them were part of the traditional pattern and that the eventual 1978 book should follow along so faithfully. Virtually all the recommendations appearing in the final Reston report were part of that familiar list of proposals that had been accumulating during the preceding two decades of congressional hearings. These were, of course, the calls for more behavioral and methodological research, greater attention to policy relevance, more centralized organization, and, as always, more funding.

Going beyond the terms of the conference recommendations, one notes that the very existence of the gathering is of as much, if not more, significance. The widening base of established private and public institutions represented in its funding organizations, the processes by which it was conceived and organized, and the status of its participants all signal the ever-increasing legitimacy of the social science research approach to communication policymaking. The enterprise would appear to have taken on a certain life of its own that could sustain it through fluctuations in congressional mandate.

Meanwhile, the Social Science Research Council's committee on television and social behavior had not been idle, even though the limitations on NIMH funding and the emergence of the Rand and NSF/RANN projects had led to a narrowing of the SSRC agenda. The committee worked first on the limited aspects of the violence profile questions and then turned its attention to various theoretical and methodological issues in television effects that were intended to go beyond the violence and children considerations. That effort involved two workshops in 1975, one on the entertainment functions of television and the other on television and its portrayal of ethnicity, especially blacks. The workshops and the research and other meetings associated with them led to the publication of two SSRC volumes in 1980, *Television and Social Behavior: Beyond Violence and Children* and *The Entertainment Functions of Television*. The former was edited by Stephen Withey (Institute of Social Research, University of Michigan) and Ronald Abeles (National Institute on Aging and formerly an SSRC staff member); the latter by Percy Tannenbaum, one of those blackballed from the surgeon general's Scientific Advisory Committee.

Among the ten members of the SSRC committee and the other participants in the two workshops were several familiar figures from the effects research community, many of whom had been involved in the surgeon general's project or other aspects of the violence inquiries — Seymore Feshback, Eleanor Maccoby, Harold Mendelsohn, Leo Bogart, Hilde Himmelweit, Jack McLeod, Aimee Dorr Liefer, Irving Janis, and Joseph Klapper, plus various research representatives from the commercial broadcasting industry. Several of the academics, of course, overlapped with the NSF/Reston project, and as might be expected, this composition led to a relatively conventional, normal science interpretation of the effects questions (Withey and Abeles, 1980: 6-8). Indeed, the direction of the entertainment functions work was clearly set in the choice of the participants for that part of the project:

> We opted for a relatively small group made up primarily of social psychologists who had demonstrated an interest in and/or had conducted research on some aspect of entertainment in the media. We had earlier discussed the desirability of a more broadly based collection of scholars who would address the issue of entertainment from the perspectives of a wider variety of disciplines. However, the judgment was that a more narrowly focused collectivity of psychologists and sociologists — reflecting the composition of the SSRC Committee and, in fact, substantially overlapping with it — was more appropriate for such an initial undertaking [Tannenbaum, 1980: 3].

The approaches represented by this group were by no means homogenous, and the Tannenbaum introduction goes on to take account of the variations:

> There are basically three dimensions that distinguish the conceptual space defined by the "television and entertainment" rubric, when considered in terms of the motives of the investigator. One emphasizes the television medium and is thus more independent-

> variable oriented. A second is preoccupied with entertainment as a behavioral phenomenon and can be considered to be more dependent-variable oriented. The third focuses on some other social psychological phenomenon (e.g., fantasy), which has some relationship to both TV and entertainment [1980: 5].

One notes, of course, that the varience of theory and method reflected here becomes less apparent the farther one steps back from the project and the more one tries to evaluate it in the context of the entire range of contemporary social science philosphy. As it developed, there are aspects of the ultimate *Entertainment* volume that seem to acknowledge elements of that wider context and that spill over into areas hardly acknowledged by previous effects science compendia (e.g., the Comstock collections). For instance, the Mendelsohn and Spetnagel chapter ("Entertainment as a Sociological Enterprise") on the development of entertainment in Western societies provides a richness of historical background usually missing in television effects literature, and the Bogart chapter ("Television News as Entertainment") reflects important features of developing insight by communication research into such matters as the process of electronic journalism, the nature of image perception and distortion, and the problems of entertainment-information dichotomies (Tannenbaum, 1980).

Similarly, there are portions of the Withey and Abeles *Social Behavior* volume that reach out beyond the normal bounds of empirical television research. The Gans chapter ("The Audience for Television — and in Television Research") attempts to locate that discussion within the framework of various industrial, socioeconomic, and television research conditions. Particularly with regard to the issue of the role of the research community, Gans raises questions about the political uses of the violence research effort — questions not unlike many of those appearing throughout this book. The Hirsch chapter ("An Organizational Perspective on Television") on organizational and economic matters tries to broaden the frame of reference for considering the nature of the television process. These two chapters, plus Withey's ("An Ecological, Cultural, and Scripting View of Television and Social Behavior") attempt to bring to bear in the empirical context important questions about the meaning, role, and consequence of television that had seldom before been reflected in the central, effects-oriented summaries of the content of communication research (Withey and Abeles, 1980).

In noting these attributes of the SSRC volumes, one hastens to observe the constraints reflected in them as well. By and large these excursions into new paradigmatic realms are rather limited. With a few exceptions the bibliographic references of the various chapters reflect only a minimal grounding in the full range of work in communication research in such areas as cultural, critical, institutional, qualitative, and policy studies. In light of some of the clues offered by Gans and Hirsch, the Withey chapter (the one that by title would seem the most logical place to explore the other dimensions) turns out to be particularly elementary and uninformed.

Part of the explanation for these limitations relates to the disciplinary backgrounds of the majority of those involved in the SSRC committee projects. For many of the participants, the behavioral, psychological, and normal sociological questions remain the more interesting and readily asked—the broadly cultural, institutional, and epistemological are simply too little understood or deemed irrelevant. Additionally, it would appear that the purposes of the SSRC work were never clearly articulared — doubtless due in part to the uncertain funding situation and the competition posed by the Rand and NSF/RANN projects. Consequently, the volumes are only loosely edited; many of their chapters tend to be unrelated collections of informal, personal reflections and hunches.

Finally, there is as well that old nagging problem of political chariness. For instance, in trying to explain why the SSRC project did not deal in more detail with the matters of the industry's institutional structure and internal organization, in spite of much committee discussion of their importance, Withey offers the following:

> Despite great interest in this topic, it proved extremely difficult to organize a sustained, productive activity focusing on the television industry. A few informal and exploratory contacts were made between the committee and television industry personnel, including a productive discussion as part of the Study Group on Television and Ethnicity. . . . However, it became evident that the investigation of such a sensitive topic as program decision-making would require the development, over a long period of time, of a sense of trust in the research community by the members of the television industry. This is probably best accomplished through the establishment of individual relationships between researchers and television personnel. Unless members of the committee were either willing themselves to undertake a research program or could identify others who were, it seemed counterproductive to pursue the initial overtures. That is, if the committee appeared to have been "investigating" the television industry, this might have aroused the suspicions and fears of individuals in that industry and made access by other researchers more difficult [Withey and Abeles, 1980: 5].

Providing no formal conference or study focus on this topic, the committee arranged merely a presentation by Elihu Katz and Paul Hirsch on their research on organizational aspects of television, and the attendance by Hirsch "at an informal discussion with two television executives." Once again, the established, federally sponsored social science research community dealing with television matters had felt it necessary to seek prior accommodations with, and to restrict its inquiry into, the subject industry.

This constraint on the SSRC work, exacerbated by the continuing questions about its funding prospects during the mid-1970s, reintroduces the issue of policy relevance of the effects research efforts. Occasionally there is recognition among members of the communication research community of the policy limitations of their work. For instance, when it discusses research on the social impact of television, the 1975 NSF summary of its "Telecommunications Policy Research Program" notes that "policy making in this area will always involve a substantial measure of value judgment, and can never be based entirely on scientifically derived information." Yet this report goes right on to hope otherwise: "In such areas as the effects of advertising directed to children, or the relations between television viewing and violent behavior, however, research may provide a factual base for policy making" (National Science Foundation, 1975: 4).

The chapter by McLeod and Reeves ("On the Nature of Mass Media Effects") in the Withey and Abeles volume provides a similar contradiction. It offers a large number of insights into the difficulties associated with achieving policy relevance in empirical research, yet it consistantly seeks ways to "make a deliberate effort to correlate policy goals and research perspectives" (Withey and Abeles, 1980: 46). In his chapter ("After the Surgeon General's Report: Another Look Backward"), Bogart extends the argument of his previous congressional testimony and papers on the topic, seeking to account for the influence of the report on the policies of the government and the broadcast industry throughout the 1970s. Again he celebrates the impact of the report, arguing "that the events in its wake" demonstrated that social research can influence social policy, even in the face of rather heavy odds" (Withey and Abeles, 1980: 131). As before, he holds out the hope that the social science enterprise as applied to communications can transcend the political constraints on it and have objectively ameliorative public policy impact.

Some arbiters in the determination of federal and foundation research priorities are more aware than others of the implications of the different perspectives dividing those involved in communication research and its application to policy matters. In his introduction to the report on the 1975 Airlie House telecommunication policy research conference (sponsored by OTP and Aspen) Bruce Owen notes that

> few academics are content to take the regulator's set of policy options and mechanically grind out a set of consequences in dimensions determined by the regulator to be relevant. And the regulator or policymaker is seldom content to pay for anything else. So that kind of "research" is done, on the whole, by organizations which the academic is inclined to view with disdain or even alarm, and it tends to produce those answers the policymaker wanted to hear. . . . More important, virtually no one on either side asks really deep philosophical questions about policy choices, or tries to address such questions in a disciplined way.

Further:

> Social scientists and engineers, who dominate research in telecommunications, are apt to be impatient and even contemptuous of so-called "humanistic" approaches to policy issues. This is so because humanists are regarded as inexact and fuzzy in their approach to such problems. I do not think that this is always true, and I think that it does not ever *need* to be true. A concern with humanistic issues is absolutely central to the formation of policy in the area of media regulation, and probably has at least some proper role even in common carrier regulation. Social scientists and engineers act as if they assumed that the human and ethical issues were resolved, and go about designing their "systems" without concerning themselves with the difficult questions of political and ethical philosophy. On the other hand it is true that humanists are sometimes unnecessarily fuzzy and inexact and inconsistent. The two groups have much to learn from each other [Owen, 1975: 5-6].

In the euphoria of the continuing expansion of economic research approaches in communications policymaking, joined now by the ascension of empirical social and behavioral research, the Owen cry is a voice in the wilderness. It can be little heeded, particularly since it is uttered in a forum for which the goal is bureaucratic accommodation — the effort to find a rational modus operandi to get on with the policymaking enterprise. From such a task-oriented perspective it is difficult to do much more than take cognizance of the difficulty, let alone recognize that the humanistic perspective in fact takes this argument one devasting step further by questioning the very foundations of the concept of policymaking. The pragmatic demands of policy research severely constrain the opportunity for reflection about the assumptions behind that process, and the research recommendations emanating from the various conferences in this area consistently ignore such questions.

Thus, among the outcomes of the Reston and Airlie House conferences was an NSF-RANN solicitation for "policy related research on the social effects of broadcast television" — a project for which

NSF was to provide $1,500,000. Three-fourths of this money was to go to behavioral research, the chief topics of which were to be:

> a. Original behavioral research on the effects of television. . . .
>
> b. Studies of the impact of television advertising on children. . . .
>
> c. Studies which describe viewing behavior. . . .
>
> Behavioral research on any effect of television should concentrate on one or more of the following subtopics: improving the conceptualization and measurement of effects; specification of the causal mechanisms through which effects occur; specification of the psychological and social conditions under which an effect is likely to occur; specification of the aggregate extent or pervasiveness and the social significance of an effect [National Science Foundation, 1976: 1-2].

The remaining funds were to go to summative and evaluative research, which was defined as:

> a. Research which evaluates the effects of research methods, concepts, and designs on the findings and conclusions of prior research on the effects of television.
>
> b. Research which summarizes, integrates and interprets previous behavioral research in order to facilitate public understanding of the research results.

However, "understanding" was not to be too broadly defined. There was an important caveat built into the general purpose of this project: "Research supported under this Program Solicitation is intended to provide information about policy issues; it is not intended to include specific recommendations concerning public policy, industry practice, or public action." Given this restriction it is not surprising to find that there was no attention in this solicitation to questions such as those raised by Owen about the implications of the policy research process and of the predominant approaches reflected in it. In this light the limitations on the various SSRC projects are also better understood.

The explicit no-recommendation restriction in the NSF solicitation repeats the similar ban placed on the surgeon general's project, and it recalls the general long-term pattern of policy applicability limitations inherent in the effects research efforts. Throughout the history of television violence research there have been instances when the constraints have worked more subtly and have been tied to a less conscious process of accommodation. But whatever the correct characterization of the federal support process at any given moment, the results have consistently been the same, namely that, while the research effort earns a bit more official endorsement, the industry's needs are duly noted and the subsequent policy changes remain minimal.

THE FAILURE OF THE FAMILY HOUR AND THE WITHDRAWAL OF THE FCC

To be sure, the critics were tossed a few bones during the post-surgeon general's period. For instance, in October 1974, largely due to the pressure being applied by the House appropriations committee, the FCC concluded a major portion of the ACT-petition inquiry it had begun in 1971. In this action the commission issued a "Policy Statement," establishing guidelines for children's programming and advertising (FCC, 1974a). The statement called on stations "to make a meaningful effort" to provide programming for children, including "a reasonable amount . . . designed to educate and inform," material for "preschool and school aged children," and more diversified scheduling. It also called for reductions in the levels of advertising during children's programming, for clear separations between program material and commercials, and elimination of host-selling and other objectionable commercial practices. To implement these guidelines the commission said it would amend the television license renewal form to obtain more detailed information about the amount of commercial time broadcast by stations, and it claimed that it would expect compliance with the guidelines by January 1, 1976.

Since assuming the chairmanship earlier that year, Richard Wiley had been continuing the practice of his predecessor of holding meetings with industry leaders to discuss these sorts of issues and to encourage changes in industry behavior without formal FCC rules. As a result, many of the guidelines in the Policy Statement had already been adopted by the NAB code authority, and, as suggested in the various 1974 and 1975 congressional hearings, the industry appeared to be making some adjustments in Saturday morning children's programming content and commercial practices. To continue to try to blunt some of the congressional criticism of his agency, Chairman Wiley initiated a new series of meetings with network officials that led them and the NAB to agree in 1975 to adopt the "family viewing hour" plan for prime-time program rescheduling.

But all such regulatory activities and changes in industry practices were minor or of limited durability. The guidelines in the commission's Policy Statement were nothing more than that. They were never made into requirements, and therefore they were never enforced. Sensing that this would be the outcome, ACT and others asked the commission to reconsider and strengthen the statement. Simultaneously, ACT took the issue to court, arguing that by failing to adopt formal rules in the statement, the commission had abused its discretion. Eventually, the commission denied all the petitions for reconsideration and the court sustained the commission's position that "it did not act arbitrarily or otherwise abuse its broad discretion in declining to adopt ACT's proposed rules as its own, or, for that matter, in declining to adopt any rules whatsoever for the time being" (see Cole and Oettinger, 1978: 280-288).[1] Meanwhile the industry's adjustments in children's programming continued to fall far short of ACT's principal goal of eliminating all commercials from such programming, and the family hour soon ran into serious legal and economic difficulties.

Many aspects of the family viewing hour tale have been told elsewhere. Especially useful is Cowan's (1979) account of many of the immediate details surrounding its origins and implementation in the 1974-1976 period. However, for our purposes it is important to underscore the roots of the plan in the longer history of popular anxiety about the impact of television and mass communication and in the many compromises among industrial and political forces throughout the entire history of broadcasting. Those were the essential conditions that had set the stage for each phase of congressional investigation of television violence, including the entrance of the House appropriations subcommittee and its increasing pressure on the FCC during the early 1970s for some sort of regulatory response.

The proximate causes of the family hour rested in the demand by the Boland subcommittee during the spring of 1974 that the FCC submit a report on its plans to deal with the violence and obscenity problems. Under the threat of "punitive action" Wiley, then new in the chairman's seat, determined that he had to take steps that would demonstrate effective commission attention to the matter, but that would somehow avoid the sort of direct regulatory involvement in program content to which he was personally opposed as a matter of principle and which he believed to be a violation both of the Communications Act and of the First Amendment. The question was, what steps might lead to industry action — self-regulation — without direct FCC guidance? A strong clue to a useful procedure had been offered in March by Senator Pastore when, during the course of the Senate communications subcommittee's oversight hearings for the commission and shortly before the Senator's last hearings on television violence, he had pointed to his own practice:

> I realize the inhibitions upon you on the grounds of censorship. I think you, back as far as 1934, were forbidden to censor or dictate what a program should be. But on the other hand, it strikes me that from time to time you could sit down informally with the heads of these networks to review this whole matter as to their responsibility.

> Now, certainly the networks are not under the jurisdiction of the FCC excepting of course in the ownership of the licenses they have. We have done that in my office. I have had the presidents come in. . . . I wonder if from time to time your Commission cannot sit down with these people and make them recognize they are participants, and they are citizens. Make them recognize what their obligations are. . . .
>
> Without twisting anyone's arm these people would be called from time to time to discuss the responsibility, and if you do not want to do it, I will do it [Senate, Commerce Comm., Communications Subcomm., 1974b: 92-93].

Wiley responded by noting that he had already begun to meet "with the three Washington vice presidents of the networks and also their code personnel," presumably on matters having to do with the children's programming inquiry. Now with this mandate from Senator Pastore in hand, he apparently became increasingly convinced that this sort of activity was not only appropriate, but also perhaps an effective way to get industry concessions. Accordingly, during subsequent months additional meetings were held with industry leaders, and by early 1975 the networks and NAB had worked out and adopted in the industry code statement the terms of the family viewing hour proposal, the key provision of which was that "entertainment programming inappropriate for viewing by a general family audience should not be broadcast during the first hour of network entertainment programming in prime time and in the immediately preceding hour" (National Association of Broadcasters, 1976). Meanwhile, in February, 1975, Wiley also delivered the requested report, and the sort of self-regulation associated with the family hour served as the basis of the commission's recommendations therein (House, Appropriations Comm., State, Justice, Commerce Subcomm., 1975: 355-356).

As enthusiastically reported by Comstock, Bogart, and others, the family hour seemed to be a sign of the policy relevance of the surgeon general's project and of the entire social and behavioral science effects research tradition (Comstock et al., 1978: 473; Withey and Abeles, 1980: 130-131). Here, it appeared, was proof that a change in regulatory attitude and industry practice could be traced to the findings of an applied research effort. Unfortunately for this interpretation, the episode actually serves to demonstrate the limitation of the scientific and general reform efforts in changing basic policy. For it is clear in retrospect that, having been barely launched, the family viewing hour quickly ran aground on the shoals of questionable constitutionality and internal industry competitive pressures.

Because of its implications for the content of programming during the effective hours, the policy struck many in the Hollywood "creative community" — the program producers, writers, actors, and directors, including Norman Lear — as representing undue censorship. Several production companies, guilds, and individuals filed two suits against the networks, the NAB, and the commission, contending that, in view of Chairman Wiley's actions in meeting privately with the networks and in operating outside of the properly open, public FCC rule-making process, the industry had been coerced into adopting the family hour plan and that therefore the policy violated the First Amendment rights of the producers.

In the first court test of the case, Judge Warren J. Ferguson of the U.S. District Court in Los Angeles found for the plaintiffs, arguing that the family hour adoption was indeed "an impermissible product of government action." The Ferguson judgment did not enjoin enforcement of the policy, but in finding the process by which it had been established to be unconstitutional it determined that the private defendants (broadcasters) were liable for damages, and it threw into question the legality of the entire NAB code procedure. As a result of these conclusions the networks variously found it necessary to challenge the decision. Usually, of course, the broadcasters are at odds with the FCC in litigation on program matters, and under other circumstances they would have been delighted with Ferguson's views about programming freedom. Indeed, it light of its satisfaction with the opinion's prohibition on governmental interference on programming, NBC decided to file only a limited appeal. Nonetheless, the broadcasters did find themselves in the unusual position of joining the commission in appealing the Ferguson decision to the U.S. Court of Appeals in San Francisco.

Their cause was successful when in 1979 the Ferguson ruling was overturned, and then in 1980 the Supreme Court denied a petition for review, thereby upholding the reversal. But the appellate court decision rested more on matters of improper judicial authority in the Ferguson decision than on the constitutionality of the policy, and the case was remanded to the commission for further review (Broadcasting, October 13, 1980: 66). Meanwhile, the continuing struggle for ratings support superiority among the networks during the late 1970s had led to program scheduling practices that suggested that the industry was effectively abandoning the key provision of the policy anyway. The language of the entire policy remained in the Code through the early 1980s, but broadcasters were no longer abiding by the scheduling provisions of the plan. Furthermore, as a result first of the Ferguson decision and then a 1979 Justice Department antitrust suit against various advertising provisions in the Code, the NAB began to suspend elements of its Code enforcement process in both broadcast standards and advertising, and in 1982, following a federal district court ruling on portions of the advertising provisions, it began dismantling its Code authority office (Broadcasting, July 5, 1982: 31).

Thus while the family hour did rise at least in part out of the research findings associated with the surgeon general's program and the growing public and political pressures for limitations on violent content, it turns out to have been a transient, severely limited success. Much of the significance of the suits against the policy lay in the struggle between producers and networks from the commission's review of the family viewing plan, it is unlikely to have any impact on the deep-seated aspects of public policy for broadcasting. For regardless of whether the commission was even to try to get the industry to reinstate the policy, the process of industrial-political accommodation would be sustained, and the basic forms of broadcasting content and purpose would remain. With or without a family hour the general structure of private commercial ownership and large, profit-oriented corporate organization of television was not to be at all threatened.

Meanwhile, throughout the late 1970s, during the period in which the family hour was being debated and was working its way through the courts, the communication research efforts to promote the deleterious impact conclusions proceeded apace. In addition to the major Rand reports and subsequent books written by Comstock and his colleagues, the surgeon general's principals continued to disseminate their interpretation of the results by regularly publishing papers and chapters in various journals and books and by giving addresses before numerious academic and other groups (see, for example, the chapters by Rubinstein and by Comstock in Palmer and Dorr, 1980). And, at least as measured by the quantity of activity, empirical behavioral and social effects research seemed to have begun to reach the levels of status and impact envisioned for them a generation before. The various government, foundation, and broadcast industry grant programs fostered a continuing expansion of the effects research projects with the result that in the period between 1971 and 1980 the amount of commonly cited literature in the field appeared to have increased tenfold (see Murray, 1980: 11).

Such a collection of continuing efforts had been crucial in encouraging the coalescence of forces that had pressured the FCC into initiating the steps that led to the family viewing plan. But, whatever the difficulties associated with that project, the regulatory process did not leave the matter there. Though there were periodic adjustments in the exact administrative structure of the commission's staff work in children's television, such efforts as those initiated by Chairman Burch continued in some form or another throughout the 1970s.

In 1978, under Chairman Charles Ferris, a Democratic appointee of President Carter, those efforts led to the establishment of a Children's Television Task Force, which issued a report in 1979 (FCC, 1979b). That report relied heavily on a good deal of recent and even specially commissioned empirical research. Among other things the report concluded that the broadcasters, while making some improvements in advertising practices, had "not complied with the programming policies" called for in the Commission's 1974 Policy Statement (FCC, 1979b: 2). "Almost five years of experience with industry self-regulation under the Policy Statement indicates that it has produced no changes in the programming practices of broadcasters and has falsely raised the expectations of interested members of the public" (1979b: 74). Based on such conclusions the report recommended that the commission establish for the short term a series of rules governing amounts, types, and scheduling of children's programming. However, sensing the increasing hostility within even Chairman Ferris's commission to the use of programming rules of any kind, the task force staff called for the commission to implement "longer-term structural solutions that involve more broadcast outlets and options for parents to pay directly for programming services" (FCC, 1979b: 80). There were additional recommendations as to support for children's programming on public broadcasting and certain other federally funded children's program projects, but the key element of the policy recommendation lay in the "structural solutions." Echoing a theme of economic theory becoming more prevalent in congressional and White House policy debates, the report strongly recommended that "over time, regulatory efforts should be directed to making it possible to rely on the incentives of the private market to stimulate quality children's programming, as only then will the efforts of the broadcaster be harnessed toward achieving the public good" (FCC, 1979b: 81). The shorter-term programming rules were less desirable to the task force, but the experience of industry self-regulation had been so disappointing that this option could not be easily dismissed. Further, they could be implemented and held as hostages to encourage industry movement toward a presumably more diverse open programming and delivery "marketplace." The industry reaction to the report was predictably negative and, although the commission proceeded to accept one of the report's recommendations, to initiate a notice of proposed rule making in which it outlined the possibility of requiring specific kinds and quantities of children's programming, it was not at all clear that the commission would be willing to develop such rules (FCC, 1979a; Broadcasting June, 23, 1980: 52).

Meanwhile, the Federal Trade Commission had been proceeding with its own inquiry into the relationship between children's television and advertising. President Carter had appointed as chairman a highly active, "consumerist," Michael Pertschuk, under whose leadership the FTC began to develop a wide range of stronger product standard and commercial practice rules. In 1978 the FTC issued a staff report on television advertising aimed at children (FTC, 1978b), and shortly thereafter, it initiated a rule making to consider certain restrictions on such advertisements (FTC, 1978a). As an extension of these efforts the FTC even became a party to the FCC proceeding, joining the reform groups in calls for stricter regulation of licensing insofar as children's programming was concerned.

The simultaneous existence of these two separate regulatory agency investigations into such closely related aspects of essentially the same topic reflects something of the increased pressure on and from Congress for more evidence of government attention to the matter of television's suitability, at least for youngsters. Not surprisingly, the communication research community played an important role in guiding the research thinking in the inquiries. Yet, equally to be expected, the investigations led to no new basic policy changes. In fact the activity of the FTC in supporting tougher regulations led to such a firestorm of industry reaction that during the process of congressional review of the agency's funding requests for fiscal year 1981, the FTC suffered severe budget cuts and was threatened with an explicit ban on proceeding with the children's television inquiry. In the end the ban was not imposed, but Congress did severely narrow the commission's authority in that rule making. In 1981, after Ronald Reagan's election as president the preceeding November and his appointment of a new FTC chairman, the commission staff recommended dropping the entire proceeding (see Broadcasting, February 11, April 28, 1980; March 2, April 6, 1981).

The irony here was that the actions of the FTC were in many ways engendered by the congressional review of the effects research and related complaints about television up through the mid-1970s, yet that liberal political sentiment had now begun to run into a rising tide of general business and conservative opposition to many facets of federal regulation. Such opposition had, of course, been developing for sometime, in large measure as a reaction to the apparent success of the reformist expansion of regulatory activity throughout the federal government in the wake of the Kennedy-Johnson period of Great Society programs. Congress had been a major fostering force in that expansion, but particularly since the elections of 1976 and 1978, it had begun to sense a new wind blowing. Its actions toward the FTC and such other agencies as the Occupational and Health Safety Administration (OSHA) were harbingers of the much broader assault on regulation to come following Reagan's election.

The FCC never experienced the same degree of public villification and budget cutting by the FTC, but there were few doubts about the practical limitations facing it too. As with the FTC, the new president moved quickly to change the membership of the FCC, within several months of his inauguration appointing a new chairman, Mark Fowler, and three other commissioners. In light of these changes it soon became evident that the FCC's children's proceeding would also lead nowhere. The deregulation efforts in a number of broadcasting and common carrier areas that had actually begun under Chairman Ferris were now to be hastened and made more widespread. Any commission proceeding that contained elements of both content and financial restrictions on the industry could expect little sympathy in the new administration.

THE EXACERBATED CONFLICT OVER CONTENT

The matter of television violence was, of course, closely related to the children's television issue, for even though the concerns about violence were raised relative to all groups in society, they were particularly directed at the question of its impact on the young. The ebb and flow of the policy debate about television violence during the late 1970s therefore tended to parallel the pattern of policy development for children's television and advertising.

By the mid-1970s it had become apparent that in spite of all the research warnings, congressional jawboning, and industry promises there was little change in the actual programming practices of the networks and stations. The annual violence index suggested that after a period of steady if slight decline in the overall prevalence, rate, and characterization of violence between 1967 and 1973, the figures had begun to rise thereafter. The Gerbner team reported that between 1975 and 1976, "Television violence increased sharply in all dramatic categories including 'family viewing' and children's programs on all three networks," and that "increase resulted in the highest Violence Index on record" (Gerbner et al., 1977: 171). After initially arguing that their research showed a different, declining pattern, CBS had to acknowledge that even its own research showed an increase in violence during prime-time programming in the 1976-1977 season (letter from Gerbner and Larry Gross to Lionel Van Deerlin in House, Interstate and Foreign Commerce Comm., Communications Subcomm., 1977a: 471).

As outlined by Cowan and as touched on by a variety of other sources, this seeming intransigence by the industry led to renewed efforts by many of the critics and reformers. The continuing reiteration of the putative findings of the surgeon general's report by members of the communication research community and the pressures by ACT and others on the FCC and FTC are clearly part of that reaction. The most dramatic efforts however were those revolving around the formation of a coalition of forces including the American Medical Association, the National Congress of the Parent-Teachers Association, the National Citizen's Committee for Broadcasting, and a variety of other groups.[2] The primary strategy of this coalition was to aim at the commercial base of the industry, by casting publicity on those advertisers supporting program series containing the highest incidence of violence. Meeting in Dallas in July 1976, the House of Delegates of the American Medical Association adopted a resolution declaring that televised violence "is a risk factor threatening the health and welfare of young Americans, indeed our future society," and encouraging "all physicians, their families and their patients actively to oppose TV programs containing violence, as well as products and/or services sponsoring such programs" (included in House, Interstate and Foreign Commerce Comm., Communications Subcomm., 1976c: 121). There had been some debate at the convention about the exact wording of the resolution, resulting in a substitution of the language "actively to oppose" for the original "to boycott." In light of this change the AMA officially denied that the resolution constituted a call for a boycott of advertisers sponsoring violent programs. Nonetheless, even with the change it was clear that the general intent remained at least to raise the spectre of nationwide product and service boycotts should major advertisers continue to support those programs deemed too violent.

The principal issue at this stage was to settle on an adequate, mutually acceptable violence rating system. Initially the NCCB used the Gerbner index. However, because of the breadth of material swept up by its definition of violence, the critics found themselves in the position of seeming to condemn some kinds of programs that many parents even television critics would not find objectionable. That is, given a rigorous application of the Gerbner scheme, many programs of a rather light and comedic nature, with their high proportions of slapstick violence, and many programs that were dramatizations of fairy tales and other classical children's stories, could easily receive high ratings on the violence index. Such a situation was making the violence indexing process appear ridiculous, leaving it vulnerable to criticism by industry apologists, especially the CBS social research office, and by common-sense appraisals of the issue. As Sandman (1978: 36) observes:

> CBS was clearly on to something. People do have trouble getting exercised over earthquakes and custard pies. Roger Wagner [a

> Washington advertising executive] puts the point succinctly: "You can't get a network, or an ad agency, or even a local police chief, to take a definition seriously when it makes *I Dream of Jeannie* or *Shields and Yarnell* the most violent show on TV. They laugh at you."

As a result, Cowan notes, some advertisers such as General Foods could be "labeled among the 'most violent' although it avoided all hard-action police shows" (Cowan, 1979: 253). Further, the use of such a measure infuriated many of the reformers' friends in the independent production, anti-family hour, Hollywood community who viewed the indexing process as a "potentially dangerous exercise incapable of differentiating between junk and art." There was concern by many that the indexing effort could readily lead to ratings and censorship efforts along all sorts of other dimensions.

To deal with such matters the NCCB secured a grant from the AMA and engaged Roger Wagner to develop a second ranking system, his " 'murder and mayhem' index" (Sandman, 1978: 36), "computed according to a narrower list of selected acts of 'agressive personal violence' " (Cowan, 1979: 256). In the fall of 1977 Wagner and the NCCB used the two systems simultaneously, an experiment that led to dramatically different results. The Wagner use of Gerbner's scheme seemed to show a large (more than fifty percent) increase in television violence, with the Wagner/NCCB system showing a decline of nine percent. However, another tally by the Gerbner team itself, now also supported by the AMA, likewise showed a decrease between 1976 and 1977, with the latter figure coming "close to the record low of the 1973 season" (Gerbner et al., 1978: 181).

For a period of time, then, the reformers appeared to have achieved a certain degree of success. The NCCB effort had been aimed at developing rankings of individual sponsors by the amount of violence their advertising supported, and as a result of the use of the Wagner scheme, the NCCB claimed that between 1976 and 1977 there had been changes in sponsorship patterns among a number of leading advertisers. However, during subsequent years the figures appear to have continued to fluctuate, and the judgment of the Gerbner team remains that "the frequency of violence and the patterns of victimization in the world of dramatic television are remarkably stable from year to year" (Gerbner et al., 1980: 12). Therefore, in view of the overall picture, the sponsor-to-sponsor changes and even the year-to-year total industry fluctuations were insignificant. In the end the levels of violence would not stay down, and the reformers and the communication research critics of television kept finding that their agenda of permanently decreased violence would not be met.

Furthermore, it would appear that in those instances in which the industry would downplay violence, it would fill the vacuum with other programming material that many critics would find equally objectionable. During the late 1970s the networks began to introduce a large number of programs that, rather than appealing to tastes for action and violence, pandered more to licentious interests. In a number of comedic and dramatic forms there appeared a noticable increase in programs that were variously described as "steamy," "smirky sex," "T 'n A," "soft porn," "jiggly," and "eye candy." Audience tolerance for sexually looser themes had been tested and expanded to a great extent during the early part of the decade with the emergence of the "socially relevant" situation comedies of Norman Lear and other independent television producers. In those cases the intent had been to deal with the serious, difficult matters of prejudice, morality, and contemporary social and political values, albeit within a humorous context. The new programs of the late 1970s traded in many of the "liberated" sexual themes, but typically they were devoid of the more difficult sociopolitical issues.

This shift reflected the continuing frustrations of the reform expectations. Behind the complaints about violence there had always lain a concern about the overall quality of television, that progressive instinct to see mass media content serve a generally more educative role, encouraging a higher standard of popular taste in entertainment and journalism. Now it was evident once again that attacks on violence alone would not necessarily guarantee television industry attention to that broader goal.

Moreover, the reform tradition could no longer be certain that it controlled the terms of criticism of the industry. Those liberal, progressive, urban, secular, scientific, middle- and upper-middle-class interests, whose various forms of applied research and policymaking activity had constituted the backbone of the assault on television violence during the previous two or three decades, were now finding that other interests, including some reflecting decidely different political perspectives, were also beginning to claim authority for injecting themselves into the public debate over television content. The liberal reform groups, those such as ACT, NCCB, the older National Association for Better Broadcasts (NABB), and the newer National Coalition on Television Violence (NCTV), represented the communication spinoffs of the civil rights, antiwar, consumer, and environmental protest movements of the 1960s and 1970s. They had long been allied with the pragmatic traditions in the academy, especially among the behavioral and social science research communities, and in time they had also secured support from the liberal wings of the medical, education, and social professions, particularly from the national PTA and among the psychiatric, pediatric, and family practitioner groups within the AMA. Their primary targets had been violence and children's programming and commercials, and while among various of their constituencies, for example, the feminist groups, there was concern about pornography, on the whole they were less worried about the liberalized treatment of sexual themes in television. Matters of obscenity and looser moral conduct did not upset them in the same way as did acts of agression and what they considered to be antisocial behavior.

Yet it was precisely the emergence of the various newer forms of sexually permissive programming, both the socially "progressive" and less redeeming types, that helped spark the emergence of the new critical interests. These groups, represented most noticeably by the Coalition for Better Television (CBTV), were the spinoffs of the Moral Majority, the National Federation for Decency, and other generally conservative, populist, rural, religious, working- and middle-class interests, whose concerns in communications, while hardly indifferent to the liberal anxieties about violence, were rooted in a somewhat different tradition of ideas about morality, family structure, and community standards.[3] Of course, such interests were not new; they had been manifest from the earliest days of organized debate about the role and impact of the mass media, sharing with the liberal reform groups roots in the various religious, educational, secular, and other organizations initially involved in the struggle over the content of the popular press and film. But the rise of television and the public debate about it had coincided with the growth of a form and range of social and political protest dominated by the liberal tradition. During that period the cultural and taste concerns of the more conservative interests had not been as widely or as effectively articulated.

But by the late 1970s that situation had begun to change. The conservative publisher and political commentator, William Rusher, articulates much of the spirit of the shift:

> The liberals — and I don't mean that term more than ordinarily pejorative, just the people who have felt permissive about this entire situation in the last 20 years — have had things pretty much their own way. Twenty years ago, like it or not, divorce was a felony just about everywhere in this country. There were lots of abortions, but it was a felony. Pornography was available if you knew which counters to seek it under, and anybody who wanted it did. But it didn't leer at us from theater marquees and storefronts in all the major cities in the country. There were plenty of homosexuals 20 years ago, but we did not have the parades we now have in New York every June or in San Francisco, with the police chief usually in the first car. And drunks were only a small part of the national scene.

They certainly hadn't bitten as deeply into the high schools and even below the high-school levels as they have today.

All this has happened in the last 20 years. It all happened with little or no opposition. It all rolled forward so fast, I think people who didn't approve of it were not organized to resist it, didn't know how to resist it. All the placards that were being shoved in people's hands were placards of those who were changing the situation. It wasn't Jerry Falwell. He wasn't trying in these last 20 years to impose his views on anybody. The aggression was all coming from the other direction.

Now, suddenly — or it seemed suddenly; it really has been over a period of time — the opposition has organized itself. Did we think that nobody was noticing that these things were happening to America? Did we think nobody was ever going to do anything about it or try to? If so, we were very naive. The opposition is now organized, it is numerous, and it has its political and social aims, and what it is doing is addressing itself to that question of where we draw the line [Margulies, 1981: A-5].[4]

In the general political forum, beginning as early as the late 1960s, disenchantment with the social and economic programs of the Great Society led to a series of conservative electoral victories at all levels of government, including greater pressures for deregulation and reductions in public spending, all culminating in Reagan's election of 1980. In the cultural arena these sentiments were reflected in the various fundamentalist critiques of the moral turpitude of the mass media generally, and, through the CBTV, of television particularly. Although not so singlemindly concerned with violence, the conservative interests were encouraged by the apparent findings of the liberal tradition's research efforts, and they went on to borrow other aspects of its tactics. First, they established monitoring projects, the standard procedure of recording and analyzing television program material, now, however, in order to keep tabs, not on acts of violence, but on the levels and forms of moral content. Then the CBTV and others began to threaten to use the major economic weapon — the boycott of sponsors of offending programs. Whether this boycott campaign would be anymore successful than those of the liberal groups remained to be seen.[5] But the irony of the situation was certainly clear. Having had only limited success in its efforts at television reform, the liberal tradition was now finding its thunder and its methods being expropriated by interests whose own agenda for content change was quite different and even, in the liberal eyes, highly objectionable.

The battle over television violence had thus now spread to include a wider range of parties and issues, adding yet another layer of complexity to the public debate about the content and impact of the electronic media, and revealing more explicitly and more strongly than ever before the social and cultural terms of the struggle over television. Many aspects of the conflict had previously been economic and institutional, reflecting status and power struggles among key industrial, professional, and political interests. Now, however, it was possible to observe woven into those conflicts a series of other tensions rooted in long-standing differences along religious, sectional, ethnic, and class lines. Furthermore, there were even serious conflicts among some of the newly articulate and powerful voices. For instance, although generally part of the broader drift of conservative political sentiment reflected in the calls for less regulation and for a wider reliance on free enterprise dynamics, the new fundamentalist critics also demonstrated characteristics of religious dogmatism and content pressure that alarmed other conservative interests historically tied to normative First Amendment views about media control and censorship. The fervancy of the CBTV critiques and its invocation of boycott solutions had therefore begun to exacerbate the policy dilemmas already long associated with the more liberal attacks on television. The more recent developments would add weight to the pressure on other key institutional parties in the debate, particularly the industry and the government policymakers, to seek legislative and regulatory release from the constitutional and economic conflicts that had been continuing to build.

NOTES

1. See also various FCC "Memoranda Reports and Orders," 55 FCC 2d 691 (1975), 58 FCC 2d 1169 (1975), 62 FCC 2d 465 (1976), and 63 FCC 2d 26 (1977); and Action for Children's Television v. Federal Communications Commission, 564 F. 2d 458 (D.C. Cir. 1977).

2. Much of this analysis of the experience of the coalition and of the debate over the violence rating schemes is drawn from Cowan (1979: 242-270) and from Sandman (1978: 35-40).

3. For information about the emergence and activities of such groups and the reactions of the advertisers and industry, see a series of articles included in *American Film* (October 1981: 57-64, 81).

4. William Rusher, remarks to a conference called jointly by the Academy of Television Arts and Sciences and the Caucus of Producers, Writers and Directors in Ojai, California, May 1981.

5. CBTV's plans seemed somewhat ambivalent. It called for a boycott in the fall of 1981, postponed those plans, issued yet another threat for the winter of 1982, let that deadline pass, then set another. For the details of this uncertain peregrination, see *Broadcasting* (February 9, June 22, 29, July 6, November 23, 1981; February 1, 15, 1982).

Chapter 10

THE CONGRESSIONAL SEARCH FOR AN ESCAPE

The New Technologies and Deregulation

THE VAN DEERLIN SUBCOMMITTEE (1976-1977)

After Senator Pastore's retirement in 1976, his communications subcommittee demonstrated little continuing interest in the violence issue. His successor as chairman, Ernest F. Hollings (D-S.C.), appears not to have been much concerned about the matter, and to the extent the public outcry continued, he resisted mounting further violence inquiries and hearings.

Meanwhile, changes in leadership were also occurring on the House side, although here the patterns of communications subcommittee activity had been developing along somewhat different lines. Under Chairman Torbert Macdonald, the subcommittee had tended not to share its sister subcommittee's enthusiasm for the violence issue. Throughout the period of the surgeon general's project it had deferred to the Senate, and its relative lack of interest had been a major reason for the entry into the issue by the House appropriations subcommittee during the early 1970s. The indifference of the communications subcommittee lasted until the 1974 budget hearings when, through its heavy attack on the FCC, the appropriations subcommittee threatened to wrest away control of the issue. But even then, in spite of his harsh words during the 1975 oversight hearings about the industry and the failures of self-regulation, it was unclear just how far Chairman Macdonald really wished to go in pursuing the television content matters. That situation seemed to have changed little by mid-1976 when, in May, Macdonald died.

However, this is not to suggest that in the year or so before his death, Chairman Macdonald's committee had simply been idle. To the contrary, beginning at least as early as mid-1975, the communications subcommittee had undertaken a series of inquiries that cut across the full range of communications policy questions, and it soon became apparent that these investigations were to take the subcommittee far beyond the matters of television violence. Eventually, in 1976-1977, the subcommittee was to look into the violence question, but by then its work in other areas had proceeded to such an extent that the environment for considering television violence and content issues had changed sufficiently to establish the possibility of a significant new emphasis in the related policy debate.

There were at work here at least two important conditions that would frame the somewhat different context. One of these had to do with the membership of the subcommittee itself. Reflecting the rapid turnover occurring throughout the House all during the 1970s, many of the communications subcommittee members were relatively new to Congress and were therefore committed neither to the long-term prior sets of understandings about the original communications legislation nor to the accommodations that had been worked out among the various interested parties during the subsequent decades. As a group the committee members were generally more disposed at least to entertain questions about the policy assumptions at work in American communications.

The second important condition was the increasing awareness among the members of the extent to which during recent years technological change had been proceeding throughout communications and how such developments were beginning to place serious strains on the very terms of the Communications Act and the regulatory perspectives that had grown up under it. The executive branch had been much quicker than Congress to recognize the extent of changes taking place in cable, satellites, computers, and a host of basic technologies. Between 1968 and 1975, there had been a half-dozen major presidential and high-level official and private task force or commission reports and myriad special federally sponsored studies on such developments, and the formation of the Office of Telecommunication Policy in the White House in 1969 was, among other things, indicative of how seriously various presidents were taking these matters (Carnegie Commission, 1967; President's Task Force, 1969; Sloan Commission, 1971; the Conference Board, 1972; Cabinet Committee on Cable, 1974; Committee for Economic Development, 1975; plus numerous Rand and Aspen titles).

During the early 1970s neither the House nor the Senate communications subcommittees had paid much attention to the breadth and far-reaching implications of these developments, but when by the mid-1970s Congress began to take cognizance of them, it was the

House subcommittee that initiated the process. The scrutiny began at least as early as the spring of 1975, when Chairman Macdonald announced a reorganization of the subcommittee, in which its oversight responsibilities in the area of power and energy would be divested and its staff would be enlarged for increased attention to FCC and communications matters (House, Foreign and Interstate Commerce Comm., Communications Subcomm., 1975a: 1). The changed emphasis was reflected first when in July 1975 the subcommittee held hearings on the extent of telecommunications research and policy development activities in the federal government (House, Communications Subcomm., 1975b). Those hearings were followed almost immediately by a detailed subcommittee staff study of cable and of the related regulatory and policy problems (House, Communications Subcomm., 1976a). That report, released in January 1976, set the stage for what was to become several years of intense review of all aspects of communications policy and major effort to revise the Communications Act. In the spring of 1976 the subcommittee held an exhaustive series of hearings on cable and the associated regulatory issues raised by the staff report (House, Communications Subcomm., 1976b). A year later, in May 1977, the staff published a much wider-ranging series of studies, the *Options Papers*, reviewing the policy issues facing Congress in broadcasting, cable, and common carrier telecommunications (House, Communications Subcomm., 1977b). For several years thereafter, from 1978 to at least 1982, every session of Congress was marked by serious attempts to rewrite major sections of the Act.[1] By the summer of 1981 those debates had led to passage of a revised portion of the broadcasting provisions, extending the length of radio and television license periods (to five and seven years, respectively), and offering strong indications that even further, more sweeping provisions for most areas of telecommunications would be forthcoming in subsequent years. During the summer of 1982, a similar maneuver involving the use of budget legislation led to the enactment of a provision reducing the size of the FCC from seven to five members.[2]

Together, then, the changes in its membership and the broad range of policy issues posed by the new technologies made it increasingly likely that the House subcommittee would be more willing to reconsider perennial television content problems outside of the old framework of specific institutional and political arrangements. Concerns about violence, obscenity, and their impact on youth were not suddenly to disappear, but as they continued to be reviewed and as such traditional issues as censorship and industry self-regulation were confronted again, it began to appear that there might now exist opportunities for the policymakers and the industry to seek new paths out of the old dilemmas.

The Denver Hearing

The passing of Mr. Macdonald led to the appointment as chairman of Lionel Van Deerlin (D-Cal.), a former broadcast and newspaper journalist and a member of Congress since 1963. With a long-time interest in broadcasting and communications policy matters, the new chairman was anxious to make a mark in this field, and he quickly moved to reinforce the expansion of activities that the subcommittee had begun under his predecessor. His aspirations were shared by several newer members of the subcommittee and by the young, ambitious, and still growing staff he had inherited. There was a growing feeling within the subcommittee that for the first time since 1934, a major legislative initiative was necessary and even possible.

While the focus of policy review had been broadening, particularly to account for cable and the new technologies, the subcommittee nonetheless still had to deal with the violence, obscenity, and general children's television issues. This was particularly true after October 1975, when the various Hollywood production community interests had filed their family viewing hour suits. It had become obvious that the plaintiffs were taking their case quite seriously. They had organized themselves well, they were prepared to expend considerable resources on the battle, and now it was apparent that they were going to continue to be important players in the television content policy debate. This situation, of course, reflected one of the significant changes in the internal workings of the industry during the preceding decade, in which several independent producers had managed to achieve a number of prime-time program successes and had thereby become increasingly important suppliers to the networks and competitors to the major film studios. The family hour suit represented a growing sense of power by the independents and by a large number of writers, directors, actors, technicians, and others. It was their expression that they were now an economic force with which to be reckoned and that they clearly were no longer willing to permit the network and NAB code authority offices to retain the former degree of program content standards control. Many of the independents had developed successful programming vehicles precisely by bucking industry standards, which they considered to be too stuffy, outdated, fearful of controversy, and politically sensitive. In their view, if the family viewing plan was not fought, it might undermine many of the gains they had made during recent years.

For the various interests in Congress, this dispute turned out to represent something more than a side show. For industry defenders and some critics alike, the suit represented a challenge to the traditional process of congressional and FCC-inspired self-regulation. For the harsher critics and for many reformers, the suit highlighted the inadequacy of that process and the need for even stronger regulatory or legislative measures. For yet others, the suit reflected the futility and even serious constitutional dangers of the regulatory and political review efforts in this area, indicating the need for wholesale rethinking of the entire range of public policy options.

Additionally, and particularly for several members of the House communications subcommittee, the emergence of the independent production interests also represented an important political consideration. As an increasingly self-conscious professional community in communications, with considerable skill at publicity and mass media image making, the independents were beginning to have an important impact on the political process. Having finally recovered from the attacks suffered during the McCarthyite period of the early 1950s, the Hollywood community was now beginning to reinject itself into a wide range of national political issues, many of them going well beyond communications policy matters. The implications of such activities were not lost on at least two of the subcommittee members, including the new chairman, who represented districts in southern California. Although Van Deerlin was from San Diego and was therefore not directly a representative of the Los Angeles-area production community, his district was close enough and the local reach of Los Angeles media was sufficient for him to be conscious of how his record would play among that group. His Democratic colleague, Henry Waxman, had to be even more directly concerned. Representative Waxman's district, the twenty-fourth, included portions of Hollywood and West Hollywood, the center of the television and film industry, and many of the plaintiffs in the family viewing hour suit were his constituents.

As the new chairman of the House subcommittee, Van Deerlin thus had a number of important considerations to accommodate. His own legitimacy had as yet to be established. He had a relatively young, inexperienced group of subcommittee members, with a variety of interests and needs and among whom consensus on television matters was not necessarily apparent. Unlike Senator Pastore's position at the outset of the surgeon general's project, Van Deerlin had no longevity as chairman, his authority was untested, and he had a more fluid, uncertain senior leadership structure in his house. Moreover, the technological, economic, and social issues were now becoming increasingly complex. As the subcommittee had begun to encounter the broad range of changes implied in those matters, and as it had begun to observe the extent to which they were exacerbating many aspects of the otherwise difficult enough federal policy and regulatory dilemmas, it became evident that such an intricate set of conflicting interests was emerging that it would be difficult to achieve satisfactory, lasting policy compromises.

One way of dealing with these sorts of pressures was for the new chairman to try first to accommodate the immediate needs of key members of his own subcommittee. Thus the timing and locations of the initial rounds of hearings in the 1976-1977 House inquiry into televised violence and obscenity are significant. The first day of testimony, July 6, 1976, was held in Denver, Colorado, at the home of subcommittee member Timothy Wirth, and the second and third days, August 17-18, were held in Los Angeles, in the backyards of both Waxman and Van Deerlin. It would hurt none of these congressmen, especially Wirth and Waxman, who were first-term congressmen, to have such hearings and the attendent media coverage in or so near their districts just a few months before the general elections in November of that year.

Of course, the motives here were more complex than simple reelection needs. As so often before, the political values of being able to seize on and to try to guide the public debate about television content turns out to be intermixed with apparently genuine personal concerns about social, cultural, and educational health of American society.[3]

By and large the day spent in Denver is devoted to hearing from various Colorado area broadcasting, academic, religious, and citizens' group representatives. Chairman Van Deerlin, reflecting the recent debate about the family viewing plan and charges of censorship associated with it, opens the hearing by trying to defuse the issue:

> Today we are going to hear from 14 people expressing a wide variety of views on the issue of televised violence and obscenity.
>
> This is, of course, a highly controversial issue and an appropriate one for discussion in a forum such as this one. Later today, when we hear from broadcasters, some of them are likely to raise the spectre of Government control and censorship. Today's hearing, let me assure them and everyone, marks no step in that direction on the part of the Congress. . . . That determination is well-spelled out in the Communications Act itself, under which we operate. I make this point not as a Member of Congress, but as a former newspaperman and broadcast reporter.
>
> . . . But we should all reflect from time to time that our freedom brings with it great responsibility. Today's hearing is designed to

inform and educate us on what is an extensive and serious issue. [House, Interstate and Foreign Commerce Comm., Communications Subcomm., 1976c: 1].

In taking up this issue the chairman thereby finds himself in the position of his several congressional predecessors over the previous generation, of trying to establish an image of concerned inquiry while yet trying to reassure the industry of the limits implicit therein.

To give his colleagues the appropriate visibility, the chairman turns to Wirth for a lengthier introduction, the bulk of which constitutes an outline of the history of congressional interest in the violence and obscenity issues. Before closing those remarks, Representative Wirth cites the violence index research, suggesting that the levels of violence had not dropped in the first season of the family viewing plan. But then he notes the difficulty of the issue:

Quite frankly, this is a very thorny problem. On one hand, I believe that self-regulation — so far — has failed to work effectively, but on the other I am loath to advocate governmental regulation [1976c: 4].

The testimony of one of the first witnesses, a psychiatrist from the University of Colorado Medical School, is used as the ritualistic opening device to establish the presumed seriousness of the issue, but the most intriguing testimony is to come from another early witness, Professor Harold Mendelsohn. Chairman of the Department of Mass Communications at the University of Denver, Mendelsohn had been a member of the Surgeon General's Scientific Advisory Committee, he was also a participant in the SSRC project, and he was in general no stranger to this sort of hearing. With such a background the Mendelsohn testimony would be significant enough. But it is particularly notable for the strength of its attack on the accepted view of the advisory committee conclusions and therefore on the calls for stronger federal measures toward the industry. Professor Mendelsohn's approach is to provide a critique of the strict behavioristic mass communication research interpretations, charging them with an oversimplified view of the communication process, resting too heavily in laboratory experimental and stimulus-response models of behavior. He suggests that such research leads to censorship and a line of policy thinking that reflects "the needs of elitists who seek to impose [external standards] on individuals, communities, and society for various self-serving personal, ideological and political reasons" (1976c: 14).

In many respects the Mendelsohn testimony reprises the functionalist arguments of the industry representatives and gentler critics from the advisory committee. It also of course reflects a combination of his own training at the somewhat unorthodox New

School of Social Research, a period of professional survey research, and aspects of academic work over the years that regularly involved contract research with the broadcasting industry. From his perspective professor Mendelsohn contends that the research evidence is in fact not all that conclusive, and he worries that, under First Amendment considerations, there is little government can or should do about the matter.

But perhaps the most interesting observation by this seasoned veteran of the violence research battles comes in the context of his discussion of the censorship issue, where he delivers a previously little heard critique of the role of social science in the policy debate:

> To avoid any possible misunderstanding, I am not denying that the media presently are subjected to all kinds of censorship at the hands of producers, editors, advertisers, publishers, trade codes, boards of censors, and the like. Neither am I proposing that criticism of the media is unwarranted or that it should be stopped. To the contrary, I endorse lively normative criticism of the media on philosophical, aesthetic, moral and any other humanistic grounds. What concerns me is the increasing trend toward the utilization of social science research as a rationale for criticisms of the media, giving such criticisms and the policy recommendations accompanying them an aura of scientific validity and legitimacy they never before had [1976c: 11].

Representative Wirth observes how this testimony seems to run against the grain of the popular interpretations of the conclusiveness of the surgeon general's report, and he reminds Professor Mendelsohn of the latter's participation as a member of the advisory committee. Dr. Mendelsohn replies by noting the emphasis in the key surgeon general's conclusion on the caveat of "some viewers," and by recalling the weaknesses of the correlational data in the Liebert study. He also suggests that the surgeon general's call for "action" was based on a misreading of the scientific evidence and was essentially a "political conclusion" (1976c: 18). Representative Wirth is unsuccessful in shaking Mendelsohn from his view that television is only one of several important socialization vehicles for the young and that, while there may be some risk in televised violence, the problem is not worth all the research and political review effort put into it.

A number of Colorado broadcasters testify during the afternoon session of the Denver hearing, and Representative Wirth uses that occasion to return to the theme that "there is some correlation between violence on television and violent behavior or attitudes." He suggests that "there would appear to be a lot of evidence that there is this causal relationship" (1976c: 67). In reiterating the case for increasing conclusiveness, Representative Wirth wonders whether if "we get to the point where maybe the evidence becomes more formidable, we are going to have to start thinking about who has that responsibility, whether we leave that in the marketplace or make the assumption that the airwaves are a terribly important public product" (1976c: 68). Here, of course, he notes the essential dilemma that had been implicit for decades, but which had been emerging more explicitly since at least 1974, namely, the extent to which the public interest standard of the legislation should be interpreted as offering grounds for strict program content review in license proceedings, particularly if the scientific evidence should prove to be as strong as many obviously were contending it was. The question about leaving the spectrum to the marketplace suggests something of the debate developing elsewhere in the subcommittee's reassessments of federal policies on cable and the new technologies and in its criticisms of the various trends in FCC regulatory behavior. In the search for a way of breaking through the increasingly complex policy problems, it would perhaps not be long before there was convergence on the economic metaphor.

The Los Angeles Hearings

The hearings in Southern California afforded Van Deerlin and Waxman the opportunity to lend sympathetic ears to the independent television producer interests. During the two days of testimony, a number of the leading Hollywood lights testify, among them Norman Lear, Grant Tinker, Gene Rodenberry, and Larry Gelbart, and the terms of their collective opposition to the family viewing hour and the reasons for their suits against it are well aired.

Both Waxman and Van Deerlin reiterate the standard approach, that they have no intention of sanctioning censorship, yet that they also wonder (Van Deerlin) how "a medium that claims it can sell adults anything from detergents to automobiles, on the one hand, to candies and toys to children, on the other, can then turn around and argue that violence has no selling effect whatever" (1976c: 71). Waxman contends that "there must be an understanding of the responsibility incumbent upon those who use the public's airwaves to meet legitimate public concerns" (1976c: 73).

Again the marketplace notion begins to loom larger and larger in the minds of the subcommittee members as they continue to wrestle with the tricky policy issues being raised by the critics of television programming. Representative Waxman draws from Grant Tinker (then president of MTM Enterprises) an important admission about the nature of the producer-network relationship:

> *Mr. Waxman:* Is there really a free marketplace, in terms of what the viewers have an opportunity to see, if the three networks have the

decision-making power to decide what is and is not appropriate for the American people to watch?

Mr. Tinker: Well, answering that question commercially, there is not a free marketplace as it exists in other businesses in television. . . . We don't just bring our wares here to your three networks and put them on this table for you to feel and touch and evaluate and buy at some price. It is a very one-to-one relationship from the very beginning of the development of a program idea.

I am working only with you, NBC, and chances are if you and I fail together in the development of this idea, it is dead forever, and I won't get it over to ABC or CBS [1976c: 94-95].

Becoming schooled by economic evidence brought to them by their staff and consultants, some members of the subcommittee were beginning to recognize the relatively small, restricted, competitive nature of the existing television production market and, perhaps most significantly, they were becoming willing to discuss those conditions publicly. As reflected in the *Options Papers*, the debates within the subcommittee were coming increasingly to center on questions about appropriate means for opening up the program market, and, as the debate continued, such means would seem increasingly to rest in the multiple-channel capacity of cable television and other new technologies. Somewhat later in the hearings, during the testimony of Gene Roddenberry, the producer of *Star Trek*, the lure of the new technologies is demonstrated even more strongly:

Mr. Roddenberry: I think some of the problem is going to be solved for us, unless Congress is unwise and keeps these things from happening, solved for us by cable television. There are those in cable television now who know it pretty well; who predict that we will probably be a complete cable nation well within a dozen years.

We have now very close to a capacity of direct satellite television to the home. We are very close to that. Disco-vision [videodiscs], and many other things, are coming around which may give us an ultimate possibility of sort of a demand television, where you can sit in your home and really order what you want, rather than sitting there and having to take what someone else decides to give you at a given time.

Mr. Van Deerlin: So you say the expanding technology itself might encourage diversity — widening, rather than limiting choices to the viewer?

Mr. Roddenberry: Yes, yes. Unless that technology is halted or restricted by Federal law [1976c: 273-274].

Representative Waxman tries to focus on the problems posed by the economics of the business:

> *Mr. Waxman:* Well, let's change the system for a minute and say that it is not to sell the advertised product, but it is just to get the most viewers, because the most viewers for an author of a book means more money for those people who are purchasing the book for a television program, or it would be more people watching the show itself.
>
> . . . The product is being produced for as large an audience as possible, and . . . the kinds of things that might well appeal to as large an audience as possible is a factor to be taken into consideration, either by the writer, even without the middlemen, so to speak, or by the other people who are talking about the more immediate profit.
>
> *Mr. Roddenberry:* If I understand your question, in order for a book, though, or other things to be viable, you do not have to have that kind of mass audience. You can very comfortably sell a couple of million copies of a book and become a famous author.
>
> What we must do on television, though, because of this system, we must, on prime time, attract and hold each week a minimum audience of something like 18 million people [1976c: 279].

The terms of the Roddenberry response become important pieces of the subcommittee's thinking as it goes on to embrace the cable marketplace notions. As reflected in their questions, Representatives Van Deerlin and Waxman wonder initially whether, in spite of all the promise of expanding channel capacity, there will remain in commercial telecommunications a relentless drive for ever larger audiences. Eventually, however, that instinctual concern is overcome.

For the moment, at least in these hearings, the new policy option is not fully explored, and the pattern of testimony comes back to the issues of violence and obscenity and the nature of the producers' complaints about the family viewing plan. At one level the objections are clearly rooted in the traditional concerns of the artist — about interference and censorship.

> *Mr. Van Deerlin:* . . . I gather, from what you have said, that your input from the networks is more in the direction of their trying to restrain you than trying to encourage you to more sex and violence.
>
> *Mr. Gerber:* Yes; they are worried, because of the Government. They have licenses, as you know, of their own and the affiliates, and I feel the threat, or the implied threat, of censorship from the

> Government has made them very cautious and somewhat rigid in some of their approaches to programming standards where drama is concerned [1976c: 77].

Mr. Gerber (producer of *Police Story*) goes on to claim that "it is our dramatic integrity . . . a freedom that we are looking for" (1976c: 82). Grant Tinker echoes the impression of censorship and reiterates a point made by Gerber and others that prior to the family plan the relationships with the program standards people at the networks and the NAB had been far more preferable: "The network system, the censorship system, the standards and practices, and the way that they performed those jobs prior to family viewing, was, with some occasional exceptions, more of an innocent variety, I think it was a good system" (1976c: 89).

Among the interesting aspects of this line of testimony is that the producers reflect the traditional libertarian fears of government constraints, but they are not nearly so concerned by such restrictions as a product of commercial enterprise:

> *Mr. Waxman:* If you have a bureaucrat who is on the public payroll, as opposed to a bureaucrat who is on the network payroll, who decides that he thinks something might offend someone and therefore wants to modify it and change the creativity that the people who make the programs wish to put into it, that does not bother you, but how do you distinguish? . . .
>
> *Mr. Burns:* Because I think the network bureaucrat, if you characterize him that way, has some experience in the business. I would hope that he has been working in the business for part, or if not all of his adult life, and might have come creative ideas of his own. I think governmental bureaucrats are too often influenced by outside pressures [1976c: 95-96].

This attitude, of course, reflects the closeness of the relationship among the producers and the networks, a bond that, while full of important tensions, is also mutually supportive. Aspects of that relationship have been regularly demonstrated by the movement of people between the two institutions, as, for example, Mr. Tinker's own career.[4] The struggle between the two sides has always been for relative influence, status, and access to profits within the given television system, not for any real change in its basic purposes and terms.

In his testimony, Norman Lear (president of Tandem Productions) proves more willing to attack the networks and NAB directly. He recognizes the pressure of the FCC behind them, but he is not as conciliatory as his colleagues.

> The family hour is nothing more than a smokescreen and a public relations ploy. If the networks and the National Association of

> Broadcasters had been sincere about their desire to clean up the airwaves, why didn't they call a meeting with the creative community to discuss the problem? . . . The reason they never did so is really quite simple. Each network has two departments which deal with the creative community. The programming department is responsible for ratings, and ratings are responsible for network income; dollars.
>
> The program practices department is responsible for the content of television on the network. Because violent shows paid off in previous years, the programming department coaxed more action, a euphemism for violence, out of the producers, while the program practices department told the producers to hold the violence down.
>
> It is because of this schizophrenia at each of the networks, the opposing signals from the two departments, which result in a subtle and unacknowledged conflict, that the subject of gratuitous sex and/or violence on television could never be discussed in an open meeting in an honest and sincere manner.
>
> And so, to throw a bone to a concerned public, and the Congress, the networks acceded to the intrusive suggestions of the FCC in defiance of the first amendment. . . . Has family hour resulted in additional censorship? Yes it has [1976c: 261].

David Gerber was one independent who did not object to the provisions of the family hour. He did not feel choked by it. What he did share with Lear and the others was anger at the manner in which the plan had come into being: "What we are saying is, it is wrong to be legislated. It was wrong to be told. It is wrong not to be consulted. It is wrong not to seek our input. It is wrong to say, here it is, do it" (1976c: 83).

Among the other aspects of the producers' testimonies that are of interest here is the extent to which they agree with the complaints about the amount of violence on television, but feel that the anti-obscentity charges are unfair:

> *Mr. Burns:* . . . I think it is interesting that you gentlemen have to differentiate it between sex and violence, because I think they are two totally different things. I think there is too much violence on television. I think there is, on the other hand, almost no sex; certainly no explicit sex on television, and I am glad that you have made that distinction. . . . [1976c: 88].
>
> *Mr. Waxman:* I gather one of your objections to the family hour is that they lump the notions of sex and violence together and try to deal with them in a certain time frame; is that correct?
>
> *Mr. Tinker:* Well, they tarred us with that same brush, exactly.
>
> *Mr. Waxman:* Do you feel there is too much violence on television programming today?

Mr. Tinker: I do . . . yes, I think my answer to that, just as a private citizen or a viewer, would be I think there is too much, and a great deal of it is gratuitous . . . [1976c: 93-94].

Ms. Nolan: . . . And as for the sex part of the sex violence, I think it is absurd to link the two. . . . In my opinion, there is not enough sex on television. But let me clarify. Sex has come to mean a one-dimensional, stereotyped concept which most surely needs correcting. The whole area of sexuality needs to be examined. Sexuality takes place between people. It is embedded in their roles and their relationships . . . [1976c: 129].

Mr. Gelbart: . . . It is very important, at the outset, to separate one [sex and violence] from the other. There is explicit violence on TV. There is not explicit sex. We are all at least somewhat clear about what we mean by violence. But by sex on TV, we mean so much, and the least of it seems to [be] the sex act itself. Sex on television means, to a large extent, talk. Talk about homosexuality, talk about abortion, talk about birth control and prostitution and premarital or postmarital relationships. It means jokes and discussions. It means essentially a whole vast area of important human concern [1976c: 140].

The underlying thrust of these observations — the suggestion that much of the critique of television is misguided in that is is directed against the more liberal treatment of adult or mature themes — reflects a crucial development in the expanding debate about American communications. While anxious to pursue such themes, and increasingly successful at it, the independent producers are more troubled by violent content. They more readily see societal danger in excessive portrayals of one form of content than of another. They reflect that strain of social and political thought that had previously dominated the debate about television programming. In broad terms they have been the social and cultural allies of the reformers, social scientists, and policymakers who have been at the forefront of the violence critique.

What is becoming apparent during these hearings in the mid-late 1970s is a gradual unveiling of the social and cultural differences among those groups concerned about television. As discussed in Chapter 9, those differences were there from the earliest days, during the struggles over the content of the popular press and film, yet they were overlooked during most of the history of the television violence debate. As the image of conclusiveness in the research findings developed, it encouraged participation in the critique of television by more and more parties. The liberal, progressive, secular, and research-oriented reform interests, whose primary area of concern about television had been its violence, were now being joined by the more conservative, populist, and religious-based interests whose concerns were directed more toward matters of pornography and morality. The testimony by the independent producers reveals something of the emerging sorts of social, cultural, and political differences that would soon make the struggle over television even more complex than it had been. The producers' insistence on drawing the distinctions among types of programming about which to be concerned points to the different perspectives about "reform" that would confuse the critique of the industry and make any alliance between liberal and conservative groups shaky and ultimately untenable, with the likely result of confounding all parties' expectations for change in television content.

The Washington Hearing

The Van Deerlin subcommittee held its last hearings on sex and violence on March 2, 1977, over six months after the initial round and well after the 1976 elections and the inauguration of a new Congress and president. Van Deerlin's legitimacy as chairman and his interests in the status and authority of the subcommittee were given renewed support by the House leadership in the new Congress. The core of the membership from the previous Congress remained, but the size of the subcommittee was doubled. Likewise, the recent build-up in its budget and staff continued.[5]

As for the matter of jurisdiction within the House over questions relating to television content, the communications subcommittee's interests here were also sustained. When the divisions of responsibility for federal agency oversight had been made within the appropriations committee at the outset of the 94th Congress, the FCC had been shifted from the subcommittee on housing and urban development to the subcommittee on the departments of state, justice, and commerce, under the chairmanship of John Slack (D-W. Va.). This adjustment removed the commission from the pressures brought on it during recent years by Congressman Boland and his colleagues, and beginning with the budget review process for fiscal year 1976, the state and commerce subcommittee was much gentler on the commission about matters of television programming and its impact on children. This arrangement continued during both sessions of the 94th Congress and into the 95th, with the appropriations subcommittee making little demand on the commission to go much beyond the relatively passive, marking-time approach it had historically adopted and leaving the field clear for the communications subcommittee to reestablish primary responsibility for the content and children's questions if it so wished (see, for example, House, Appropriations Comm., State, Justice, Commerce Subcomm., 1976: 1261-1325).

In its own March 1977 hearing, the Van Deerlin subcommittee called the types of witnesses and followed the pattern of discussion that were structurally similar to those in most previous congressional inquiries, especially those of the Pastore era. As in Los Angeles the new group of players, the independent producers, were represented, but for the most part the subcommittee now reverted to the traditional process of entertaining testimony from the major contending parties — the network and industry leaders, the communication research community, and the citizens' interest groups.

Again the chairman opens with the obligatory bow to the First Amendment and Section 326 of the Communications Act, and yet, as is now also part of the standard gambit, he cites the "duty" of the committee to review the matter in order "to consider options open and available to us" (House, Interstate and Foreign Commerce Comm., Communications Subcomm., 1977a: 1). The scientific tool is quickly invoked: "We can also discuss the latest research, and see if more needs to be done in this area," and the networks are invited to make their ritualistic explanation of "what they intend to do, if anything, about the levels of violence in their programming" (1977a: 1).

Congressman Murphy, a new member of the subcommittee, but one of the few House members who had injected themselves into the issue during the Senate's earlier period of managing the matter, reiterated the thrust of his 1972 testimony before the Pastore subcommittee, citing the strong causal relationship interpretation of the findings of the surgeon general's report plus the more recent AMA pronouncements and the related psychiatric research presumably all supporting that position. He uses this opportunity to introduce a bill that would place limits on the amount of programming stations could take from individual networks and that would limit station ownership to one per license (1977a: 1-7).

Among those other subcommittee members making opening remarks, Representatives Wirth and Waxman were prominent, and the thrusts of their comments suggest that their interests in the television content matters went deeper than might have been apparent when the earlier hearings presented them with those preelection opportunities to exploit a newsworthy topic. To be sure, Wirth replays the standard research conclusiveness argument and makes the typical calls for better action on the part of the networks, the FCC and parents. But unlike previous congressional patterns of rhetoric along these lines, Representative Wirth, in discussing the family viewing case, also takes note of an important feature of these investigations: "I don't think it is fair for those of us in Congress to absolve ourselves entirely of blame for the way Mr. Wiley handled that matter. . . . I would like to say that, if the Government has violated the Constitution, then those of us who have exhorted the FCC to do something about TV violence should not let the FCC alone incur Judge Ferguson's wrath" (1977a: 8).

While directed at a particular case, this observation is indicative of a certain degree of new appreciation among some members of Congress about the role they play in the general process of broadcasting policy review. It hardly signals a major change in behavior, but it does suggest that the ritualistic pattern of congressional inquiry in the program content area might be becoming more widely understood, if not more difficult to sustain.

Most of Representative Waxman's remarks are designed to identify his position with that of his Hollywood constituents, and his review of the family hour case is a summary of the plaintiffs' briefs and an endorsement of Judge Ferguson's decision. Waxman continues to entertain some consideration of basic economic and structural matters (1977a: 11), but his concerns are directed at the "network monopoly," and he gives no indication of any willingness to press too far into the fundamental issues of the general patterns of private enterprise purposes and content in telecommunications, from which, of course, his constituency greatly profits.

In spite of the funding difficulties associated with the violence profile project, the annual studies of television content had been continuing at the Annenberg School, and the subcommittee had asked Professor Gerbner to appear and to bring the figures up to date. As so often before, the content analysis presentation serves as a major focal point for the hearing. It provides evidence that, in spite of the family viewing plan and all the promises by the industry, the amount of violent content on television has continued to rise:

> Television violence increased sharply in all categories [between 1975 and 1976], including family viewing and children's program time, on all three networks. The increase resulted in the highest violence index on record. The only score that comes close to the current record of 203.6 was the score of 198.7 in 1967, the year of turmoil that led to the establishment of the Eisenhower Violence Commission and our "TV Violence Index" [1977a: 13].

The presentation also permits Professor Gerbner to continue to try to promote the less mechanical aspects of the project. Persisting in the attempts rebuffed by Senator Pastore in previous years, Dr. Gerbner discusses the various social and power relationship findings of the project. He is trying here to demonstrate the importance of what he was coming to call "cultivation analysis" in relating the study of television content to something other than mere counts of violence, to develop the terms of a hypothesis that television contributes to the public perceptions of its existence in a "mean" or "scary world" (1977a: 13). This effort, of course, seeks to broaden the base of interest in the project and to secure greater academic legitimacy for it — a particularly necessary approach as long as the funding picture remained tenous, but one defensible too on intellectual grounds.

Because of the intrinsic interest by most parties in the violence statistics and trends, the scheduling of the Gerbner testimony early in the hearing is apparently accepted as appropriate and uncontroversial. That location does, however, offer him the advantages of being able to anticipate the new wave of criticism of the study that the industry had recently begun to mount. Thus he is quick to assert that the project is based on "the most exacting and reliable methodology in any social science research of this type" (1977a: 16).

The industry threat turns out to be more than a criticism of methods. Professor Gerbner reveals that there are now efforts underway to secure access to his data base, doubtless to conduct a reanalysis and to try to undercut the validity of those violence index findings that continued to be so unfavorable. The Gerbner introduction and handling of this matter is noteworthy for its sophisticated sense of how to anticipate a critique and to take the initiative by offering a political compromise:

> We propose that we pool our research data and those gathered or commissioned by network researchers pertaining to the analysis of network television program content for the purpose of comparative examination by qualified researchers on both sides. . . .
>
> With your permission, Mr. Chairman, and with the consent of network representatives who will soon testify there, we shall proceed to contact the Librarian of Congress, Dr. Daniel Boorstin, to make the necessary arrangements for establishing such a television data archive in the national interest [1977a: 16-17].

Whatever ambush the network leaders may have been preparing for later in this hearing day, it is effectively stymied by this proposal. As for the methodological criticism, any member of Congress or industry representative seeking to develop such an issue finds it difficult to overcome Dr. Gerbner's diplomatic and seemingly reasonable prior rebuttal. For example, when Congressman Gore presses him on the methodological and definition questions, Gerbner's well-rehearsed, assured response readily repells the attack. In reply to every quibble and hypothetical exception, he patiently and clearly reviews the coding and analytic procedures of the project (1977a: 132-133).

Throughout the colloquy Gerbner successfully maintains the demeanor of the careful, disinterested scientist, as for example when the ranking minority member, Louis Frey (R-Fla.), asks him for advice as to how Congress should deal with the conflict between the First Amendment and the concerns about the violent content:

> *Mr. Frey:* . . . How do we limit? Do we as a Government limit it? I don't think we can, personally. What is your response?
>
> *Mr. Gerbner:* Mr. Frey, sitting on this side of the issue, rather than on yours, I have no legislative proposals.
>
> *Mr. Frey:* I am on no side of the issue, I am just trying to figure out what to do.
>
> *Mr. Gerbner:* Our approach and our contribution to this is taking seriously the assumption that an informed electorate is a wise electorate, which is the assumption that the first amendment is designed to protect [1977a: 131].

Sensing an opportunity here to promote his vision for communication research, Gerbner reiterates and expands his idea for the data archive:

> What we believe is needed — and perhaps my suggestion about a national data archive can be carried one step further — is a national information source like the economic statistics produced every year, like the social indicators. That is why we have tried to contribute a set of cultural indicators dealing with violence and other issues. These indicators show [not] only the state of affairs at a particular time, but also follow up year after year the consequences of policies, the reality or unreality of policy changes or promises about policy changes. They can follow up and show the American people and the parents and the legislators, but most particularly the industry, the consequences of some of their actions [1977a: 132].

In the process of this response he manages not only to avoid answering the intractable question originally posed by Representative Frey, but also to continue to build up the pragmatic image of communication research — to indentify its potential with the highest level of applied public policy uses of economics and the social sciences.

When Congressman Luken (D-Ohio) tries to get him to agree with the conclusions about the relationship between increases in television violence and increases in juvenile crime, Gerbner is cautious not to draw extensive, unwarranted conclusions from the violence profile research:

> I would prefer to stay with the data that I know and I can trust. There are many remarkable correlations in this world that may be coincidental or not. . . . At the present time, I just cannot say that we have any evidence to suggest that [the causal relationship] is so. I think that there is reason to speculate that it might be, but we have no evidence to really warrant that assertion [1977a: 141].

Similarly, when Representative Waxman pursues the behavioral research analogy between advertising influence on purchasing decisions and televised violence on antisocial behavior, Gerbner responds with a thoughtful, polished discourse on the relative differences between the two sorts of measures and the difficulties of drawing the explicit analogy (1977a: 142-143).

On the other hand, as his closing remarks suggest, Gerbner does see his research as part of the general pattern of evidence rooted in social learning theory. While he is careful to disclaim too many direct causal implications being drawn from the cultivation analysis research, he leaves little doubt about his impression of deleterious impact:

> We believe that the pattern of responses that we get are the results of long-range cumulative conditioning and that they are of a long-range nature in which no easy or quickly produced changes will be perceived.
>
> So . . . the answer is "yes." I think these are lasting imprints, if you will, that most people who are born into a television dominated culture will carry with them in one form or another throughout their lives [1977a: 146].

At one level this view offers little comfort to the direct effects school, but overall it lends considerable weight to the empirical research community's insistence on the existence of certain significant effects, albeit perhaps indirect and difficult to measure. Other evidence that the social learning perspective still dominated congressional policy thinking is offered later in the hearing. Bradley Greenberg and Charles Atkin, whose work on television violence stretched back at least to the research of the Eisenhower Commission and the surgeon general's project, testify toward the end of the day, reporting on their findings from a U.S. Office of Child Development study. That effort, which combined content analysis and an assessment of impact on children, had been designed to examine the television portrayal of a wide range of antisocial behavior beyond physical violence (verbal aggression, deceit, cheating, nonviolent crime), the balance between antisocial and prosocial acts and their intensities. But overall the results of this study were typical of the normative post-surgeon general's projects.

> In sum, the television networks broadcast an extensive amount of violent content — about 15 acts of physical aggression each hour. Our survey investigation supports previous research demonstrating that TV violence produces aggressive behavior. The content is as violent and the effects are as strong in 1976 as 5 years ago when the Surgeon General reported on the problem. Parents can help combat

negative impact by viewing with their children. However, reduction of the quantity and intensity of violent content presented to child audiences remains the most effective option to solve the problem [1977a: 440].

Here as in so much of the work being reported elsewhere by Comstock, Rubinstein and other surgeon general principals, the causal connections are taken as proven and as no longer debatable. The appropriate research questions "are no longer really asking whether there is a relationship." Rather they are "trying to specify the conditions under which the relationship is strongest or the conditions under which we can weaken that relationship" (1977a: 445). Thus the violence profile, the cultivation efforts, and the standard forms of social effects research remain crucial pieces of the effort in the wake of the surgeon general's report to reinforce the impression of adverse societal effects of American television.

Clearly the violence profile was not entirely free of criticism. As reported later in the hearing, the National Citizen's Committee on Broadcasting (NCCB) was beginning its own violence ranking system as part of the effort to narrow the definition of countable violent acts to the "common-sense" notions of antisocial behavior and to begin on the basis of such a presumably more defensible index to bring pressure to bear on the advertisers (see Chapter 9). But by and large, at least for the purposes of this hearing, Professor Gerbner had done a masterful job of anticipating and dealing with the industry attacks.

A substantial irony of this achievement is that, within a relatively short time, the violence profile was to begin encountering a series of academic objections that would be potentially much more threatening on deep-seated theoretical and methodological grounds. The following year Horace Newcomb was to publish a paper that was closely related to the growing general body of concern within various pockets of communication research that the empirical research traditions and their continuing focus on effects issues were in substantial need of reevaluation and that various other approaches — interpretative, cultural, humanistic, political economic, cultural, critical — were beginning to offer possibly more important insights into the nature and significance of mass communication (Newcomb, 1978). A subsequent critique by Paul Hirsch was rooted much more directly in the empirical tradition itself, deriving its power from an exhaustive reanalysis of the "scary world" hypothesis that the cultivation approach had been developing since the mid-1970s.[6]

Whatever their eventual impact might be, neither of these attacks had been published by the time of the 1976-1977 hearings, and they were therefore unavailable for use by the industry or other interests. Further, although they raised questions about the approach represented in cultivation analysis, neither of them really argued with the details of the violence index findings — that portion of the analysis that continued to have the most use in the process of political oversight.

After dealing with the Gerbner material — having carried on the tradition of giving a prominent position to this major representative of the communication research community — and knowing that the deleterious effects conclusions would be reiterated by Greenberg and Atkin later, the subcommittee turns to the Washington policymaking interests, taking testimony from, first, Henry Geller, former general counsel to the FCC and, second, Richard Wiley, then still FCC chairman. Unacknowledged in these colloquies but certainly well known by the subcommittee were the expectations that, under the new presidency of Jimmy Carter, the Republican and Nixon-appointed Wiley would soon be stepping down and the Democrat and reform-minded Geller would be appointed assistant secretary of commerce and director of the new National Telecommunications and Information Administration, becoming thereby the president's principal adviser on communications policy matters. This portion of the hearings was thus set in the context of federal policy in transition, and it was rife with uncertainties about the television content review interests of the new administration.

On the surface the two men differ dramatically on the matter of the family viewing hour court case, with Geller essentially agreeing with Judge Ferguson's decision, at least with the FCC-related portions of it, and with Wiley obviously opposed. But their differences turn out to be more over the question of the relative accuracy of the interpretation of the FCC's role in the case, i.e., whether or not the commission was a coercive force. Apart from that issue both men appear anxious to move beyond the family hour matter to explore other means for dealing with violence and obscenity. For Geller the issue is fundamentally constitutional, and he argues against government content regulation even if the research evidence were stronger, suggesting that eventually the problem would boil down to defining "hardcore violence," thereby recreating "the same mess that the courts are in today with obscenity" (1977a: 147-148).

This view clearly puts him at odds with those reformers and researchers who had come to see the scientific evidence as worthy of dictating policy. But Geller does not abandon hope for some sort of government inspired action:

> I think that the Government should try to create a climate to permit broadcasters to act effectively. The Government, the FCC, the Antitrust Division, and Congress, if necessary, should make clear that broadcasters can act together to reduce or eliminate gratuitous

violence — with no enforcement, however, by the FCC or any industry agreement.

> Another action that would be positive and would, I think assist the public interest here is for the Commission to finally conclude docket 19154 [and] . . . adopt percentage guidelines in the area of informational and educational programming to children.
>
> If this turns out to be feasible, affiliates could then substitute other programming when they thought the network program was too violent. And the Government, in line with what Dr. Gerbner said here, could sponsor further research on the effects of violent programming on children [1977a: 150-151].

In the first example Geller has in mind proposals made as early as 1962 by then FCC Chairman Newton Minow and by several others since that the Justice Department grant antitrust waivers to the networks so that they might collaborate in program scheduling to permit a rotating presentation of worthwhile children's programs. In the second example he is recommending putting specificity into the vague "reasonable amounts of time" standard of the commission's 1974 guidelines. But the members of the subcommittee are variously troubled by these suggestions and by the continuing dilemma facing the commission in an arena bounded on the one side by the First Amendment and on the other by the public interest standard of the legislation. Mr. Geller is fully aware of the conflicts here, and he tries to clarify his views on what government action is permissible:

> What I am saying is that the Government cannot intervene to get rid of gratuitous violence. All the Government can do is to create a climate, and the climate I am talking about is the ability of broadcasters to take joint action — to agree that use of violence is getting out of hand and that we the networks, we the broadcasters, will eliminate gratuitous violence [1977a: 156-157].

Yet in the end it becomes clear that Geller is, like many others, beginning to think about a way of creating a new set of conditions that would make moot the conflicts bedeviling him and the congressmen:

> We all talk about the present system. The best thing that could happen is to create a climate where you get more diversity through breaking this television of scarcity and getting to a television of abundance. . . . New technological devices, pay, pay cable, satellite; all those things are of greater importance, I think, than trying to strain the present system to do something [1977a: 163].

In light of the family viewing case, Chairman Wiley cannot escape defending his role in it, and he spends several moments at the outset doing so. However, here and elsewhere during the colloquy whenever the issue surfaces, he finds himself being gently handled and warmly applauded by the subcommittee, even by those strongly opposed to his actions. When the hearing returns to the more general issue of the appropriate government policy in violence and obscenity matters, Chairman Wiley's persistent antiregulation stance remains firm. During his statement and the subsequent discussion he rejects nearly every one of the Geller proposals as involving too much government interference. Where he does agree with Mr. Geller is on the potential for the marketplace model (1977a: 172).

In the end, though, he takes a pragmatic view of the given situation, imagining the possibility of new legislative standards, but assuming that for the near future, the 1934 law would remain intact:

> This committee is looking at the whole Communications Act. Perhaps you can come up with a better system, but suffice it to say that in 1934 the framers of the current act decided not to opt for an all-Government system or to auction off the frequencies in an all-private system, but to create this hybrid, taking a public resource and licensing it into private hands and having a Government agency regulate in the public interest, but not censor.
>
> Now, I suggest to you that this system has inherent rubbing points and conflicts, and we are always going to be faced with this problem of private against public responsibilities.
>
> Hopefully, there are countervailing protections, and one of them is public involvement in the process. That is one of the most important aspects of localism in broadcasting, and I would hate to see that broken down [1977a: 182].

The testimony by the various industry representatives in this hearing, as in so many before it, is rife with similar appeals to the myths of localism, public involvement, and the prevalence of socially responsible motives among broadcast licensees. In the familiar pattern NAB spokespersons, station leaders, and network executives all variously reassert their concern about television violence and their conscientious efforts to deal with the question. Thus, for instance, Vincent Wasilewski, president of the NAB, claims that "when a problem does exist, such as violence on television, we know it will be up to us to deal with it through self-regulation and self-discipline," that "family viewing was a conscientious attempt by this industry to take a positive step to contain violence on television, and it was an indication that we acknowledge the problem and assume our share of the burden of finding some type of solution," and that in spite of the Ferguson decision "we are still committed to doing something about excessive violence in television programming," including a NAB board decision "to attempt to draft program guidelines that we believe will reduce the problem (1977a: 183-184).

Various of the subcommittee members poke at these contentions by Wasilewski and other industry representatives. Chairman Van Deerlin, for instance, proves willing to pursue questions about the inadequacy of station influence on network decisions and the weak sanctions in the NAB Code review process (1977a: 187-192), and Representative Waxman carries the process a bit farther by raising questions about the adequacy of "public input" into broadcaster decisions about program content (1977a: 198). Such lines of inquiry are yet further evidence that some members of this generation of congressional communications subcommittee members are more willing to discuss publicly the weaknesses of the various positions historically taken by the industry. These matters are not pressed, however, and the parade of industry witnesses continues without significant diversion.

As to be expected the spokespersons for the networks launch a multifaceted attack on the charges about their continuing failure to respond to the concerns about televised violence. John Schneider, president of the CBS Broadcast Group, picks up almost where he had left off during the final Pastore hearings in 1974 by baldly claiming not only that CBS remains concerned about the problem, but also that it has done something about it. In support of the latter he argues that since the late 1960s significant changes had taken place in Saturday morning children's programming, with a greater emphasis on "prosocial and informative" content and a reduction in the number and character of "incidents of violence" (1977a: 199). Robert Howard of NBC and Frederick Pierce of ABC join in by noting the problems associated with defining acts of violence, determining inappropriate levels, pointing to the new nonviolent program plans of their respective networks, and claiming continuing adherence to the family viewing policy in spite of the Ferguson decision.

Adopting the technique perfected by industry representatives years before, the three network executives invoke the efforts of their separate research offices and cite evidence from a series of special projects commissioned by them. To demonstrate the purported seriousness of the CBS intentions in the prosocial area, Schneider submits a booklet that outlines the network's use of research in program development. He also reviews the violence-counting research being conducted by the CBS Office, implying that its method is similar to that of "various social scientists," arguing that it entails a better week-sampling procedure, and claiming that it "clearly demonstrates a decline in the number of incidents of violence in CBS prime time dramatic programming" between 1975 and 1976 (1977a: 200-205).

For his part Howard reminds the subcommittee that "NBC also has a social research department which maintains contacts with the social science community" and that it too has used "a panel of distinguished social scientists to consider issues pertaining to [Saturday morning] children's programs; . . . to work closely with both our program and broadcast standards departments and attempt to apply social science information and analysis to programming questions" (1977a: 232). As evidence of his network's continuing concern Pierce recalls ABC's $1 million support of the two five-year (1971-1976) Heller, Polsky, and Lieberman projects that he had referred to in the 1974 hearings (Heller and Polsky, 1976).

What is not made clear, but what of course should have been apparent to the subcommittee, was that various aspects of these several projects were part of the continuing efforts by the networks to debunk the methodology and findings of the Gerbner studies. The reprint in the hearings record of a speech by Heller makes that intention of the research abundantly clear. One brief paragraph from the middle of the speech provides a good example:

> Although some may see a scientific basis in this Gerbner — now PTA — definition of violence and counting system, I find that it not only strains logic, but ignores the reality of children's experiences, and any concern about context or the emotional impact of a given scene upon the viewer. In my view, the Gerbner count, pursued with computerized accuracy, is insensitive to the circumstances in which the violence is portrayed [1977a: 327-328].

This had been a persistent refrain by the networks since the earliest editions of the violence index, and it had been one of the reasons, as discussed in Chapter 9, that the NCCB had recently decided to develop its own counting system. It was also an argument Professor Gerbner had patiently tried to anticipate earlier that morning.

Pierce's testimony notes that ABC had made "five new research grants, specially chosen from among 327 applicants from major colleges and universities" (1977a: 241). Among the researchers involved, one was also simultaneously participating in the SSRC project — that federally funded effort that had encountered serious industry-sensitive restraints — and another was soon to be hired by ABC as the manager of its own Office of Development and Social Research. At least one of those involved in the CBS research projects was also part of the SSRC effort.

Pierce closes his testimony with the following observation:

> Now, I have recently suggested that various interested parties within and without the television industry join a comprehensive scientific analysis of the relationship of programming to viewer behavior that will enable us to continue to define and pursue objective guidelines for both broadcasters and parents in both the prepa-

> ration and viewing of television entertainment. In the long run, this would seem to me to be the most productive and responsible approach to the problem [1977a: 241].

In other words, ABC, now a ratings leader and a new power among the networks, is proposing that the broadcast industry recapture control of the scientific agenda in communication effects research. Whether conscious of the parallel or not, Pierce is advocating the reestablishment of the mechanism and process that had been developed by Frank Stanton and CBS nearly two decades earlier, particularly as reflected in the experience of the Joint Committee for Research on Television and Children. There is no indication in the 1977 hearing that the subcommittee or anyone else testifying is aware of that parallel and of the discredited nature of the JCRTC history.

In spite of all the efforts by the surgeon general's researchers to promote the image of conclusive antisocial effects evidence in the existing communication research, the networks are proving themselves once again to be capable of confounding the issue and slipping out of the reform-oriented net. Professor Gerbner had anticipated the attacks on his own project and had therefore been able to deflect much of this industry sniping. Yet the network representatives were still able to retake some aspects of the initiative and, as always before, to articulate the problem in such a way as to make serious legislative measures difficult. The bemusement of the new generation of congressional investigators is made painfully evident in a subsequent colloquy between the network executives and Representative Wirth:

> *Mr. Wirth:* . . . You are saying that ABC officially believes there is still a question as to whether there is a correlation of violence in the behavior of kids, is that right?
>
> I thought we have gone beyond that and that is why you were drawing off all of this violence, and that is why the advertisers are concerned, and we are, as I say, beyond that watershed for the first time. I was about to breathe a sigh of relief and go on from there, but maybe we have not come to that point.
>
> *Mr. Pierce:* I think we have changed our program to reflect this concern. Just speaking scientifically, though, I do not know if that has been definitely proven, yet. . . .
>
> *Mr. Wirth:* So for artistic reasons or economic reasons you are taking violence off, not because there is any sense that maybe it is having a severe impact on kids. Is that correct?
>
> *Mr. Howard:* I am saying that there are no scientific findings that show that.
>
> *Mr. Wirth:* Mr. Schneider?

> *Mr. Schneider:* We do not accept any direct causality with what is on television, but we have reduced violence substantially; as long as there may be an assumption or presumption of causality, we think the responsible course of action is to reduce.
>
> *Mr. Wirth:* All right. All three networks at this point are saying that you still think the jury is out and that there is not evidence so far? This kind of reminds me, in a way, of the tobacco industry 20 years ago; there is no relationship between smoking and health [1977a: 339-340].

The testimony of the network representatives continues for a while longer, with various of the subcommittee members trying to draw them into the sorts of admissions about the existence of a television violence problem that they had been willing to make during the 1972 and 1974 Senate hearings. At one point Representative Waxman even becomes palpably angry:

> The question of violence on television and the impact that is has on society had been of concern for 20 years, and quite frankly . . . I think it is insulting to come before Members of Congress and to come before the American people and say you are doing something about the problem.
>
> I just think this whole thing is a smokescreen. If we end up with more violence on television than we had before family viewing, then, what is family viewing doing other than trying to give you a gimmick for public relations to fool the American people into thinking that maybe there is some way out and that maybe the networks ought to be able to continue along the lines that they have been so successful in following [1977a: 387-388].

But the industry responses here, as in the earlier colloquy with Representative Wirth, are cool, calm, and utterly self-confident about the lack both of a serious research case against them and of any sincere willingness by Congress to pursue beyond the heat of rhetoric the matters of broadcasting profitability and commercial purpose. In the end the network executives project an image that has recovered from that of the contrite industry bowing under the lash of Senator Pastore in previous years. Having weathered the storm of the immediate post-surgeon general's period, the industry had managed to continue to peck away at the conclusiveness myth, and once again it had demonstrated its ability to play a divided, pragmatic social science off against itself and to keep the legislative oversight process from going much beyond the process of inquiry.

The rest of the day's hearing is taken up by the testimony from representatives of the public interest groups, the writers guild, the academy, and the psychiatric community. However, due to the length of the earlier colloquies the time available for these final witnesses is rather brief, and while they are all permitted to make their formal presentations, the discussions with them are not extensive. As a result, although the exchanges here touch on a few of the important dilemmas facing the subcommittee, the final hour or so of testimony has an air about it of anticlimax and perfunctoriness. The atmosphere is perfectly cordial, particularly when Peggy Charren of ACT and Ted Carpenter of the NCCB testify, but there is an impression that for all the cordiality, there is no new ground to break here and that the old problems and constraints remain.

Charren reiterates the longstanding ACT concern about the failures of commercial broadcasting to provide adequate and responsible program service for children. She places the problem of violence in the context of the lack of sufficient hours of all forms of children's programs and the persistence of unsuitable advertising in what programming there is. She calls on the FCC to make stronger use of its license renewal authority to provide for stricter terms of station accountability and to encourage a wider diversity of children's programming. Carpenter outlines the beginnings of the NCCB violence indexing project and of its effort to bring pressure to bear on the advertiser. He notes that the NCCB had observed that, in spite of all the studies, there had been little change in broadcaster behavior and that the appeals to government action were regularly constrained by the First Amendment issues.

The differences between the approaches of the two reform groups are instructive. For the most part the original ACT agenda remains the same — to have children's television needs treated separately and to eliminate advertising from such programs. Clearly ACT also knows where the power to effect change resides: "ACT believes that Congress, either as part of the rewrite of the Communications Act, or within a specific license renewal bill must redefine the licensee's responsibilities to children" (1977a: 396). In general, though, this means sticking with the old pattern of seeking reform through regulation, trying to get the FCC to adopt the reformer's notion of the meaning of the public interest standard and to take a stronger hand with the broadcasters through the threat of license denial.

While ACT obviously is aware of the economics of television and how such factors limit the possibilities for change, it is reluctant to use the economic weapons itself. Ms. Charren even notes that ACT, as a national organization, has not actively sought license renewal denials. The NCCB approach is much less reticent. Noting the failures of previous reform efforts, the NCCB determined "that we ought to try a marketplace notion about influencing what is happening in the industry" (1977a: 422). Yet even here in what was probably the most vociferous and most aggressive of the liberal reforms groups, reflecting the outspokenness of its chairman and driving force, Nicholas Johnson, the NCCB was careful not to go too far (1977a: 433). The reformers could point fingers by developing "most violent sponsor" rankings, and they could even argue that they were having some impact as a result of that effort. Yet in the end even the least bashful of citizens groups would, like its AMA sponsor, shy away from the language of boycott, mass action, and any strong direct assault on the economics of the television industry. There were always implicit understandings of the rules of the game.

The Report

Unlike any of the Pastore hearings after the surgeon general's report, the 1976-1977 Van Deerlin inquiry was followed by a formal published subcommittee report (House, Interstate and Foreign Commerce Comm., Communications Subcomm., 1977c). Presumably designed both to reflect the seriousness of the House subcommittee's concern about television violence and to demonstrate the extent and unified determination of its then current wide-ranging examination of the communications legislation, the report ends up revealing all the constraints at work in the process of congressional review of communications policy and the enduring dilemmas of the television content disputes.

Among the principal features of the report is the lack of consensus within the subcommittee about its very terms. Reflecting the original reformist zeal of some among the new, young subcommittee staff, the initial draft of the report was apparently quite critical of the networks (see Broadcasting, May 23, July 25, August 1, 1977). Unsatisfactory to a majority of the subcommittee, this draft was put through at least five revisions in an effort to get the staff to soften the charges. The disagreements over the several drafts delayed the report's publication from May or June 1977 to late September. By then the rifts within the subcommittee were painfully and publicly evident, and the less critical forces among the staff and members had prevailed, if only barely. In order to get acceptance of a report, Chairman Van Deerlin had to accede to a greatly watered-down draft that was adopted by a mere 8-7 margin and that was so disappointing to the critical members that they insisted on and were granted the right to include three dissenting statements in the official published version. The irony of the vote lay in the fact that all seven of those opposed to the report were Democrats, the majority party in the House and subcommittee, and all four of the Republicans on the subcommittee sided with the chairman and three other Democrats to give Mr. Van Deerlin his one-vote victory.

This sort of compromising was a harbinger of the difficulties soon to come as the chairman attempted to effect some sort of consensus on the terms of his "top-to-bottom rewrite" of the Communications Act. His efforts there were to be even less successful than those here, though it would take another two or three years for that evidence to become clear.

The final report is not long, and a reading of its major findings and recommendations quickly demonstrates why the critical minority was upset. In its introduction the report briefly reviews the history of the hearings and the recent activity of Congress and the FCC in this area (incorrectly suggesting that the House appropriations committee had become involved in the issue only in 1974), the controversy over the family viewing hour, and the major conflict between the calls for government action and the provisions of the First Amendment and Section 315 of the Communications Act. Then the report presents five conclusions:

(1) The level of violence on television continues to be a cause for serious concern. Although it may be impossible at this time to "prove" a precise cause and effect relationship between televised violence and aggressive behavior, excessive viewing of violence may have harmful effects [1977c: 4]
(2) Responsibility for the present level of violence on television rests largely with the television networks, which exercise substantial control over the programming that they purchase and make available to their affiliates and, to a lesser degree, with broadcast licensees, program producers, advertisers, and the viewing public [1977c: 7].
(3) Parental supervision is probably the most effective way to curb negative effects of excessive viewing of televised violence by children [1977c: 10].
(4) Industry self-regulation is a potentially effective way to limit the level of televised violence, and, indeed, to adjust broadcast content of any kind to the tastes and concerns of the general public, or segments of that public. The subcommittee, however, is concerned with the results to date of the industry's efforts to regulate itself [1977c: 11].
(5) There are avenues through which the subcommittee, the Federal Communications Commission, and the public can address the problem of televised violence consistent with the First Amendment [1977c: 13].

There are one to four pages of discussion accompanying each conclusion, with a liberal use of testimony and other evidence from the hearings to try to explain the reasoning in each case. But all in all the majority report is cautious and unwilling to pursue either strong criticism or radical measures. Instead, as had been hinted throughout the hearings, the key to the subcommittee's thinking on new policy approaches came to lie in the promise of technology:

> To the extent that current problems are a function of the limited number of communications outlets now available, it is likely that the growth of new technologies will bring about a more long-term solution. If legislative and regulatory barriers to the introduction of new telecommunications technologies can be eliminated, the public will be able to enjoy the benefits of a broader range of program options. In an environment of programming abundance, we may find that violent content represents only a small fraction of the total material available and its impact may diminish accordingly. It is with this hope in mind that the subcommittee will continue its efforts to review the applicability of existing statutes and regulations to the development of telecommunications technologies [1977c: 14].

What is perhaps most significant about this passage is that it reflects only one side of the discussions about the new technologies and the marketplace that took place during the hearings. Here we see only the expression of hope and faith. The more skeptical thoughts on these matters that were raised by several subcommittee members, including Chairman Van Deerlin, are all ignored.

In light of the terms of the majority report it is not entirely surprising that the critical minority insisted on having an opportunity to take exception to the majority report. Representatives Waxman, Wirth, Mikulski, Murphy, Markey, and Gore concur in a blistering dissent, the essential particulars of which are laid out in a first-page introduction:

> The subcommittee's report . . . is, in our judgment, a disservice to those who will read it in the hope of finding firm and sound guidance from this subcommittee on this very serious and complex issue. We believe the report is seriously deficient in several critical respects.
>
> It is too hesitant in its conclusions regarding the adverse effects of viewing television violence.
>
> The report spreads the blame for violence on television away from the networks to such an extent that it reaches the meaningless conclusion that we are all (viewers, licensees, advertisers, producers) to blame for the excessive levels of violence on television — thereby implicitly stating that no one is really to be held accountable.
>
> The report pointedly ignores what may be a crucial link between the structure of an industry dominated by three major networks and the level of violence on television. The report shuns asking any further questions about this relationship.

> The report refuses to recognize that there are other, affirmative regulatory actions which may be undertaken, consistent with the first amendment, to limit the amount of violence on television by enhancing the opportunity for the presentation of greater amounts of children's and public affairs programming.
>
> The report takes a favorable view of industry self-regulation which we believe is unwarranted.
>
> By stating that parents "must" assume greater responsibility for their children's viewing habits, the report fails to recognize that it is difficult if not impossible for millions of parents to continually or effectively supervise their children in this regard.
>
> In so doing, the report implicitly tells the American people that with respect to the issue of violence on television, there is no need to worry, everything is under control, the networks know how best to handle the situation, and there is little else that needs to be done.
>
> We reject these conclusions. We believe the subcommittee report is a calculated distortion of the hearing record on these questions, and that it deliberately evades a more conscientious examination of them. We believe this report is biased in favor of the networks.
>
> We therefore respectfully dissent from the subcommittee's views as expressed in this report [1977c: 17].

The key position of the dissenters is that the majority understates the nature of the research evidence. The minority associates itself with the stronger causal relationship school that had been so actively promoting the conclusiveness of the surgeon general's report (1977c: 18-19). As articulated in the dissent this position is careful not to overstate the case. There is no expression of absolute certainty; the vagaries of trying to determine any firm "realities" about human behavior are readily conceded. But at the foundation of the minority position lies a firm conviction that the social and behaviorial research evidence on the matter of television violence is reasonably clear. In this respect the minority position is not unlike that of the Pastore subcommittee some years before. What is different is that the House subcommittee dissenters are somewhat more willing than any prior congressional group to go the next step and to discuss the economic factors at work in the production and distribution of American commercial television programming. Further, the iconoclasm of the minority stretches even to the point of questioning the guarantees of diversity in a restructuring of the industry, and therein rested the seed of a potentially serious challenge to the conventional policymaking process. For while not pursued any further in their dissent, the minority's tendency to question even the new policy orthodoxy was adding more fuel to the anxieties of the broadcasting and telecommunications industries about the directions that might emerge from the House subcommittee's sweeping legislative review. After all, the minority had very nearly been the majority, and there was no certainty that the narrow margin in the final vote on the violence report might not be reversed on more substantial matters of economic and structural policy.

In an additional dissent Representatives Murphy, Mikulski, and Wirth expand on the larger minority's critique of the majority's unwillingness to debate the structural matters. Again there is a strong reiteration of the negative effects research evidence, and the additional dissent goes on to repropose the legislation that Murphy had introduced during the hearings, which would restrict the amount of programming affiliates could accept from networks and limit network ownership of stations. In light of such provisions it is hardly surprising that this bill was never seriously considered even as part of the subcommittee's various subsequent effort's to draft revisions of the Communications Act, but its proposal was indicative of the sorts of dangers the industry was beginning to perceive in the "rewrite." Such awareness was to lead to a major lobbying effort to discourage any serious legislative threats to fundamental industry interests.[7]

For the moment, however, the situation may have appeared to the industry to be somewhat fluid and therefore dangerous. For instance, the additional minority dissent returns to and concludes on the most telling aspect of the larger minority's critique:

> The majority report . . . decrees that the subcommittee may not even begin to examine the institutional structure of American television, at least not in the context of the violence problem. The effect of the subcommittee's action is to reject out of hand the option of restructuring the television industry as a way of solving the problem of televised violence. We find this rejection both incomprehensible and shocking. It strips the subcommittee of considerable power and limits it to the proposal of relatively minor remedies. And it forces the viewing public to rely on network self-regulation. If past is prologue, that is not a happy fate [1977c: 32].

This persistent point in the minority reports cuts directly to the heart of the congressional strategy over the preceding decades. The entire process had become a well-rehearsed ritual — one of study, inquiry, review, research, debate, and reports — but no congressional subcommittee had ever seriously contemplated major structural change in American broadcasting. In this light the dissenters in the 1977 House subcommittee should not really have been shocked. They must have understood the underlying realities that could not permit any substantial disturbance of the ritual. Moreover, it is unclear from either the hearing records or these minority statements just how radical might be the dissenters' ideas about industry restructuring. It was apparent from the hearings and the subcommittee report that the rhetoric of the new technologies and of the return to the marketplace were increasingly central to the federal policy approach to matters of television industry performance. Yet, although the dissenters had occasionally provided insight into the weaknesses of the new orthodoxy during the hearings, those notions were never well developed, and they barely resurfaced even in the dissents to the report.

As was soon to become evident in the subcommittee's rewrite activity during the 1977-1980 period, attempts to introduce major changes in the legislation do not necessarily lead to fundamental adjustments in the basic purposes and terms of control of broadcasting and telecommunications. The efforts to deal with the complexities of the new technologies and with the traditional opposing concerns about the quality of programming and government interference were to take federal policy down the libertarian paths of expanded delivery capacity and a putatively free and open marketplace, without, however, there ever being any real certainty that such conditions could or would emerge. So for all the seeming victories of the effects research community during the 1970s, for all its ability to create an impression of a case proved and to play thereby a leading role in the congressional review process, the traditional paradoxes and inherent limitations in that process were to persist, substantially clouding the moment of glory and weakening the actual impact of the social and behavioral sciences in federal communications policymaking.

THE NEW NIMH REPORT (1982)

This consequence was revealed when the television violence issue reasserted itself once again in the early 1980s. In response to the ever-growing amount of research on television and social behavior a number of social scientists working in the field asked the surgeon general to arrange for a review and assessment of the literature that had developed since the 1972 report. In 1979 the Behavioral Science Research Branch of the NIMH undertook that review and in mid-1982 published a summary report as the first of two volumes intended to synthesize and evaluate the current state of the research (National Institute of Mental Health, 1982 [Vols. 1 and 2]; see "Symposium," 1981, for an initial discussion of the report).

The report had been expected at least a year earlier, but was delayed when it became embroiled in the process of budget reductions and government program reviews associated with the arrival of the

Reagan administration. In part to draw attention to the report and to prevent it from being dropped or buried, Congressmen Ronald Mottl (D-Ohio), under the auspices of Chairman Wirth's telecommunications subcommittee, held another round of television violence hearings in October 1981 (House, Committee on Energy and Commerce, 1981). By May 1982 the NIMH staff had secured administration clearance and the summary report was published with an accompanying fanfare of popular and trade press coverage.

Based on the first volume it would appear that the NIMH review did attempt to broaden the focus of attention in the realm of empirical television research, moving away from the 1972 report's nearly exclusive interest in television and aggression.[8] Reflecting certain important developments within the behavioral and social sciences, "The new report addresses such issues as cognitive and emotional aspects of television viewing; television as it relates to socialization and viewers' conceptions of social reality; television's influences on physical and mental health; and television as an American institution" (1982: I: iii). The report admits, though without explanation, that it did not include matters having to do with news, public affairs, or advertising. In view of the political and industrial sensitivities associated with such issues, the reasons they were deemed "inappropriate" for the report are not difficult to surmise.

As for that part of the review dealing with violence and aggression, it carries forward the ever-increasing confidence of the Rand, SSRC, and other reports published during the mid-1970s, contending that "after 10 more years of research, the consensus among most of the research community is that violence on television does lead to aggressive behavior by children and teenagers who watch the programs" (1982: I: 6). The disclaimers are there: "Not all children become aggressive, of course, but the correlations between violence and aggression are positive," and the report acknowledges countervailing industry research findings. But overall it is unshaken in its conviction that "a causal link between televised violence and aggressive behavior now seems obvious" and that the "research question has moved from asking whether or not there is an effect to seeking explanations for the effect."

Yet for all the impression of social scientific conclusiveness and the unmistakable intent of the NIMH staff and consulting research community that their conclusions lead to policy action, the results have so far been no more telling than in any of the previous cycles of government reports on television violence. The Mottl hearings in 1981 attracted only minimal attention and did not become incorporated into the rewrite efforts in any direct manner. Similarly, after the brief flurry of publicity accompanying the new NIMH report, the issue appeared to fade away once more. The House subcommittee had promised hearings on the report, but in the spring of 1982, amid all the other confusion then associated with the various streams of rewrite activity and all the pressures attendant on the imminent fall elections, the hearings were cancelled (NCTV News, 1982). The interested clinical and social science research communities and reform groups gnashed their teeth, but it appeared that little would come of their efforts. The more stridently the putative research findings were put, the more they seemed to be ignored in the climate of deregulation and marketplace appeals.[9]

NOTES

1. During the first two years of rewrite activity the principal pieces of proposed legislation in the House communications subcommittee were: "Communications Act of 1978," H.R. 13015 (95,2), June 7, 1978; "Communications Act of 1979," H.R. 3333 (96, 1), March 29, 1979; "Telecommunications Act of 1979," H.R. 6121 (96, 1), December 13, 1979 (reintroduced in January 1980 as the "Telecommunications Act of 1980"). They were followed in 1981 and 1982 by H.R. 1297, H.R. 1298, H.R. 3239, H.R. 4726, H.R. 4780, H.R. 4781, H.R. 5158, and H.R. 5242. In the Senate subcommittee during the initial period the principal bills were: "Communications Act Amendments of 1979," S. 611 (96, 1), March 12, 1979; and "Telecommunications Competition and Deregulation Act of 1979," S. 622 (96, 1), March 12, 1979. They were followed in 1980, 1981, and 1982 by S. 2827, S. 1629, S. 1791, S. 2172, and S. 898, the latter of which was actually passed in the Senate (though not in the House) in October 1981.

2. The increased license periods were included as part of the Omnibus Budget Reconciliation Act of 1981, P.L. 97-35, August 13, 1981, the FCC reduction measure as part of the Omnibus Budget Reconciliation Act of 1982, P.L. 97-253. For a more thorough treatment of the communications policy developments, see Rowland (1982b).

3. Wirth's situation is particularly interesting, for as a Ph. D. in education, the Denver congressman represents a unique blend of the political and academic communities. Moreover, his role in the policy debates was to assume even more importance when in 1981, following Representative Van Deerlin's 1980 electoral defeat, he became chairman of the subcommittee. At that time the luxury of the subcommittee's exclusive focus on communications as arranged by Chairman Macdonald in 1975 was to be eliminated, and its mandate reexpanded to include consumer and other economic issues. This change was reflected in a change of name to the Subcommittee on Telecommunications, Consumer Protection, and Finance.

4. As president of MTM enterprises, Tinker had developed his then wife's highly successful *The Mary Tyler Moore Show,* plus several other prime-time situation comedy and dramatic successes. Previously he had been a program producer for two

large advertising agencies (1954-1961), a programming vice-president of NBC (1961-1967), and a vice-president for two major film studios (1968-1969); later (1981) he was to return to NBC as its chief executive officer, replacing Fred Silverman.

5. For the rewrite and related efforts, Chairman Van Deerlin received a fiscal year 1977 appropriation of nearly $500,000 and authority to employ ten staff members and consultants (see Broadcasting, September 7, 1981: 91).

6. The Hirsch papers evoked a strong rebuttal from the Gerbner camp and a series of further counterrebuttals from both sides. See Hirsch (1980, 1981a, 1981b; Gerbner et al., 1981a, 1981b).

7. The industry concerns about the Murphy bill were subsequently eased when a few years later whatever influence he may have wielded for a time within the subcommittee evaporated as a result of his trial and conviction on charges stemming from the FBI's ABSCAM investigation of kickbacks and influence peddling in Congress.

8. The second volume became available only after this manuscript had gone to press.

9. Also after this book had gone to press, the author was advised that a manuscript reprinting various of the television violence reports was in preparation; George Gerbner (ed.) Untitled (Longman, forthcoming).

Chapter 11

THE SYMBOLIC AND POLITICAL USES OF VIOLENCE EFFECTS

The rise of violence effects research must be seen in the joint light of the conditions governing the development of American science generally and of the continuing public anxiety about television — indeed, about all new technologies and modes of communication. The emergence during the past century of successive waves of seemingly ever more powerful communications media, coupled with other dramtic changes in American social, economic, and political experience, not surprisingly has fostered periodic phases of public debate about the significance of the new communications forms and their relationship to the shifting conditions of modern life.

Those debates took place in various settings, including the popular and academic press. But over time one of the most consistent, revealing forums has been in Congress. There, as part of its general obligation to examine and debate major issues of apparent public importance and as part of its specific need to review the terms and operation of existing communications law and regulation, Congress has had ample opportunity to place the modern communications media, especially television, under the spotlight of public inquiry. As a result, there have been hearings and related legislative debate on some aspect of American television in nearly every session of Congress since the medium's inception. Television violence has been a persistent theme of such hearings, frequently serving as a topic for special, exclusive investigation. The extensive records of such hearings and all the related industrial, academic, and other supporting research and commentary have created a rich archive for examining the terms of the public debate about television and the agendas and perceptions of the principally interested parties. Although the cast of characters has varied occasionally over the years, their relative importance has periodically waxed and waned, and many of the specific leading actors have come and gone, the chief institutional parties have remained remarkably central to the continuing drama. The university research community, the broadcasting industry, the various governmental agencies, and the several branches of public or "citizens interest" groups have jointly commanded the lion's share of the lines, thereby controlling the major themes of the plot and expressing the central meaning of the play. The extensive review of the various stages or acts of the drama presented here permits a few summary observations about the contribution of each institutional character and its relationship to the continuing ritual of public freting and struggle over television.

THE PARTIES AT INTEREST

The Academy

The effects research tradition was born of industrial need and nurtured in political ambivalence, but its central rhetoric has remained the argot of the behavioral and social sciences. Its promises of predictability, generalizability, and conclusiveness created the impression that public anxiety about television could be resolved through scientific analysis. That the performance of effects research has not usually lived up to these promises has generally gone unacknowledged. The political value of the enterprise has been of such great mutual advantage to the interested institutions that it has been useful to ignore the inconsistencies. Because the general climate of opinion in contemporary American life tends to venerate science and to presume its positive social utility, there has been little popular pressure for close examination of the terms and consequences of its application to questions about television's impact.

American intellectual and scientific activity was cultivated from the start with demands that it serve the needs of an expanding economy and government. Science and the pursuit of new knowledge had to be applied to the solution of practical physical, economic, social, and educational problems. As the society grew around a given set of assumptions about political and economic order, a series of accommodating relationships developed among institutions of government, industry, academy, and reform. Those relationships helped ensure that the emerging sciences of society and behavior also conformed to the pragmatic tradition. As the media of communication expanded in technical capacity and apparent impact, and as the scientific enterprise began to focus attention on them, the new field of communications inherited the imperatives of applicability and practical accommodation to the needs of conflicting interests.

The received history of communication effects research has tended to accept the work of its leading figures at face value. In its discussion of successive models of communication and effects, it has tended to emphasize matters of relatively narrow theoretical and methodological commitments for the most part ignoring the institutional affiliations of the science used and the scientist using it. Effects science rejects traditional forms of authority — religion, education, and politics — as value laden and invalid, tending to assume that it is itself value free and neutral. Under the impression of its objectivity and validity, effects science has held out the promise of independent, trustworthy analysis of, and salutory recommendations for, the impact of television. Unfortunately, that impression has masked the problem of ideological and institutional relevance. Generally unconscious of its pragmatist origins — and therefore unaware of the history of accommodations and confusion in the progressivist tradition — the effects research enterprise has grown on a false hope. It has aligned itself with the mainstream of liberal reform in American social and economic thought, never comprehending that that affiliation implied commitment to certain forms of conceptualization and action that serve the very structure of political and industrial control that prompt the reform impulse in the first place. Altogether, then, inadequate attention has been paid to the relationship between the development of communication research and the social and political histories of the American experience generally and of the communications media and experience specifically.

A review of the history of violence effects research in light of such concerns demonstrates that the lines of inquiry developed under its rubric came to reflect above all else the mutual interests of the broadcasting industry and the government. For differing political reasons the industry and the federal government both helped underwrite extensive programs of public opinion and radio research, much of which began with questions of media impact. The broadcasting industry found such science useful in fending off criticism of its practices and forms of control. The government found such work useful in managing domestic and foreign propaganda campaigns. The research supported by these clients led, among many other things, to a regular series of brief, biannual, and more detailed decennial reports on the apparently positive public attitudes toward broadcasting. It led to a number of elaborate information and influence flow studies that served to provide impressions of public satisfaction with and the existence of only limited, nondeleterious societal effects of mass communication, thereby disarming criticism of commercial broadcasting. The corpus of sponsored research served as the basis for a series of textbook anthologies and academic journal publications that dominated the theoretical and methodological agenda of communication research for a generation.

For the operational and political support given industry and government through these efforts, the emerging communication research enterprise received in return substantial financial and institutional support. The academic reward structure had come to place increasing importance on visible involvement in matters of central public import. As the issues in communication gained in public significance, the communication research community proved to be no more resistant than aspects of the social and behavioral sciences before it to the temptation of large federal, foundation, and industrial grants. Effects research proved to be the first vehicle for communication science to begin the movement up the ladder of modern academic prestige. The contracts it undertook gave it the ability to organize itself into applied research units that under the banner of science and involvement in matters of apparent policy importance permitted it the respectability to gain entry to the academy. The publication program, both directly and indirectly sponsored, helped secure the initial entry and then support a long-term residence. It could now be said of communication research what a few critics were observing about the academy at large, that "the man of knowledge had gone off to Washington to do good — and wound up doing very well, indeed."

The accommodations during the process of legitimizing mass communication research meant that short-term practical research matters such as audience attendance levels, commercial and political persuasiveness, and reliable, readily administered methodologies came to displace longer-term, more complex issues of societal and cultural impact and significance. The service of those interests militated against any comprehensive, intellectually grounded discussion of the role and meaning of mass communications in society and culture. Along with the industrial and political communities, most communication researchers came to see the issues of television content as largely administrative problems and therefore as reducible to scientific analysis. As a result they tended to ignore the dissenting arguments of many, summarized well by James Q. Wilson:

> In the case of violence and obscenity, it is unlikely that social science can either show harmful effects or prove there are no harmful effects. It is unlikely, in short, that considerations of utility or disutility can be governing. These are moral issues and ultimately all

judgments about the acceptability of restrictions on various media will have to rest on political and philosophical considerations [1971: 61].

The Industry

The broadcasting industry has generally understood the futility of the popular expectations for effects research, and it has manipulated the related political and academic confusion to notable advantage. Broadcasting effects research originally developed as part of two closely related needs bearing on the financial and political health of the industry. First, as the newest and potentially most potent advertising medium, broadcasting required circulation data (ratings) to demonstrate its commercial value, especially over the print media. Such research was essential also as the tool for managing broadcasting's own internal competition. Second, as a regulated industry, broadcasting required evidence (or at least the semblance of it) to demonstrate that its performance obtained in the public interest. The industry always worked to tie the definition of that interest to the most simplistic notion of democratic process — majority rule — and, as measure of popularity of "cultural democracy," ratings served as a continual demonstration of apparent adherence to the fiduciary standard.

For these two purposes the broadcasting industry's leading institutions, the networks, each came to divide their research activities between two separate, internal departments. For their immediate administrative needs the networks established offices of program research, closely coordinated with, if not actually subdivisions of, their programming departments. Those offices gave day-to-day support to the tactical tasks associated with the essential business purposes of the enterprise — to determine which programs to chose, retain, or drop, and how best to schedule them in order to maximize the network share of the desired audience to be sold to the advertiser. For a set of more strategic and political purposes the networks established offices of social research, usually quite divorced from the operational programming matters. The objective here was to have available as necessary a source of seemingly respectable academic-type research on the behavioral and social impact of broadcasting. Whenever public and congressional concerns about possible deleterious effects, especially in the area of violence, reached critical levels, the work of the social research offices could be trotted out. As a result, the industry could make claims about maintaining a serious commitment to basic communication research, reassuring the public by trafficking in the popular, authoritative systems of the scientific age and thereby diffusing that part of the criticism holding that it neither cared about nor investigated its impact. Further such research could be readily designed to undermine the other major part of the criticism of the industry, namely the evidence of "conclusive findings" periodically produced by various independent representatives of academic research. Finally, of course, this entire effort could proceed without disturbing the essential operational research in the program departments.

To help establish both of these patterns of activity during the early years, the industry sought assistance from the marketing research branch of the social sciences and it did so by working with the academy to create nearly autonomous, contract-supported, applied research units of the university. For communication research this collaboration helped stimulate improvements in sociological methods of sampling, data gathering, and statistical analysis, and it helped legitimize the new science in the eyes of the academy. For the networks' operational needs the collaboration led to development of a series of mechanical ratings research procedures and devices such as audimeters and program analyzers. Of course, such methods and tools tended to reinforce industry conceptualizations of audiences and publics as salable markets and of mass communication media as essentially vehicles for commercial and political persuasion. Such views increasingly dominated the internal industry discussions with advertisers. For external consumption, however, the industry emphasized instead the notion of "ratings as democracy" and invoked its use of research as part of its adherence to the public interest standard.

More sophisticated criticism of broadcasting tended to reject such rationalizations, noting the industry's other arguments about persuasability and pressing home questions about social impact. To respond to such concerns, the social research offices of the industry fostered in the university-based research bureaus an academic program of inquiry into broadcasting effects. In such a setting the effects research program was associated with the traditional faith in the reality of academic freedom and the newer belief in the validity of the social sciences. Under this mantle of scientific independence and neutrality, the university effects research program added to the industry's appearance of supporting good faith, critical self-examination. Yet, due to that very industry influence in establishing its original terms of reference, the effects program had the consequence throughout most of its history of augmenting the industry's own internal program of social research by providing much of the detailed research base on which was being built the evidence of inconclusive findings. With this pattern of industry relationships it was also not surprising to find that the effects research enterprise was doing much to reaffirm the impression of the forms of private, commercial control and content of American broadcasting as being, on the whole, the least undesirable means of protecting the public interest in such media. The industry's support for a heavy commitment to the empirical effects research debate by the new communication research community had the consequence of helping constrain the research agenda, by encouraging the academy to ignore other emerging lines of inquiry that could deal seriously with matters of alternative purposes, control, and support of American broadcasting.

The Government

The political leadership responsible for federal policymaking for broadcasting has been caught in a constitutional and administrative dilemma. It has been bound between, on the one hand, its basic commitment to a free enterprise system of control and the associated constitutional demands for minimal public regulation and, on the other, the practical problems posed by broadcasting of administering communication media that depend on the use of the spectrum, generally taken to be a scarce public resource with limited access to its use. That latter consideration led to formulation of a policy for broadcast licensing and regulation on the basis of the fiduciary public interest principal.

Furthermore, political approaches to the regulation of broadcasting have been tempered by practical considerations of self-protection. Whether responding to legitimate concerns about the quality of public communication or to the diversionary need for a scapegoat among the institutions of such communication, and even without the matter of constitutional constraints on government oversight of broadcasting, the fact of dependence by elected officials on the forum provided by broadcasting and its seemingly crucial link with the voters remains. As a matter of public responsibility, members of Congress must periodically review the workings and impact of broadcasting, and evidence of such regular, serious investigation much exist. Yet those implicit limitations persist.

It was within the fabric of these dilemmas that the political value of effects research was discovered. The science of effects proved to be just sophisticated enough to lend credibility to the political claims of serious scrutiny, while yet proving to be sufficiently inconclusive to prevent any draconian measures. Throughout most of the period of governmental licensing of broadcasting on the basis of the public interest standard, the violence effects research efforts permitted little more than a marshaling of a presumptive case against the industry and avoidance of any radical readjustment of public policy toward broadcasting ownership and control.

From time to time the extent of public concern about violence and social disorder at large would increase to the point at which heightened pressure for stricter political investigation of television would emerge. At such times the demand for authoritative research evidence on the question of television's deleterious impact would become intense enough to force the academy to provide at least cautious confirmation of the politically necessary response. Under such conditions the balance of accommodations between government and industry could come dangerously close to being pushed out of equilibrium. Still committed to a basic private enterprise system of commercial communications and a limited form of regulation of it, Congress might nonethless find various of its subcommittees drawing the sorts of conclusions from effects research that would suggest a need for more vigorous regulatory attention to program content. Beyond that there would appear to lurk the spectre of formal legislative action and authorization for less-forgiving license renewal policies.

If handled carefully and if drawn out sufficiently over time, such pressures could be expected to set in motion forces of industry reaction and countermeasures — temporary or otherwise token program content adjustments, alternative research, lobbying for First Amendment protections, and strong proindustry regulatory and legislative proposals. The forces of compromise would then typically reassert the status quo conditions and reestablish the longstanding conditions of accommodation. The danger for the joint political and industrial interest lay in the possibility of the equilibrium being so far disturbed that effective countermeasures might not be possible. At that point it would become necessary to reevaluate the existing terms of the drama and to consider writing a whole new play.

Such a point was reached during the early and mid-1970s, and, proving to be more than mere tinkering with the rules of the regulatory process, the subsequent reassessment implied a wholesale shift in basic policy assumptions and legislation. From the standpoint of the old pattern of industrial and political accommodation, such a shift was fraught with dangers, and various interests within the industry and government initially resisted the process of legislative review. However, as the disequilibrium of prior arrangements become serious enough to be realistically threatening to effect a new balance of power and to raise ever persistent questions about the essential policy of government commitment to private industry needs, that resistence was overcome. To affect the outcome of the policy review, it would be necessary to participate in a manner that would seem more positive, less selfishly reluctant. In searching for ways to play such an active role, the industry and its congressional supporters nonetheless still sought means for influencing the results so that fundamental industry interests would be unharmed. They began to find that means in what for the broadcasters was an unlikely source. The increasingly rapid emergence of cable television and other communication technologies, initially seen as a threat by broadcasters, carried with them the promise of an end to spectrum scarcity. Serving as a new basis for communication policy, the doctrine of channel abundance began to undermine the most basic premise for federal regulation, offering industry and government officials an escape from the traditional policy dilemma. Public anxieties about television continued to support demands for some form of political oversight, but in an era of new technologies and strong deregulatory pressure, the fiduciary principle was tending to give way to the rhetoric of increased competition and marketplace solutions.

The Reformers

Among the distinguishing features of the American political experience is its dominance by a large central tradition of progressive liberalism. Varied in exact social and political prescriptions over time, and periodically more or less influential in the details of public policy, this movement has nonetheless had an enduring presence and strength. The source of its power has lain in several characteristics — a good-natured appeal to the better, more socially conscious instincts of large segments of the American people, tolerance of social and cultural diversity, avoidance of doctrinaire political positions, a commitment to improved social welfare without any serious challenge to private enterprise economics, and a reliance on practical compromise. Its optimism embodies a strong belief in the ability to improve the quality of the human mind and community. Essential means to those ends are enhanced opportunity and quality of education, science, and communication. As part of its pragmatic outlook, progressivism has tended to see the ills and dilemmas of American society as a series of problems that can be solved. In its view, therefore, the values of the search for knowledge are directly related to the extent of the applicability of its results.

As the modern media of mass communication became available, the progessive tradition held out considerable hope for their potential contribution to social and political improvement. However, as with other institutions in industrial America of the early and mid-twentieth century, it seemed evident that absent some degree of public oversight the promised benefits might never emerge. Therefore, while formal regulation proved to be impossible for such media as print and film, the liberal tradition tended to encourage some process of organized, if unofficial, review of media performance by groups of private individuals operating under some banner or another of public or citizen's interest. Due to the initial technological limitations, formal regulation was necessary for broadcasting, satisfying a substantial portion of the progressive desire for public accountability. Then as television emerged, as it seemed to become a pervasively powerful medium, and as the nature of the industrial-regulatory relationships became increasingly clear, the liberal pressure for reform of both the industry and the regulatory process began to increase.

However, always implicit in the background of the broadcast reform movement were the old, unresolved dilemmas of progressivism. The continuing pattern of paradox between the ideals of reform and the changing practical conditions under which it had had to work remained. It yearned for return to a form of community and experience that may never have actually existed in the first place and that in any case was now prevented by many of the fundamental conditions of modern life that progressivism itself had found necessary to accept. The hopes for a renewed democracy had been regularly compromised during the emergence of the large corporate/large government American economic and political structure, and the basis for a ritualistic process of government-industry interaction was reiterated with the emergence of each federal regulatory agency. Such paradoxes would bedevil progressivism as a whole through all of its successive phases, including its offshoots into broadcasting reform.

Indeed, during the early years of broadcasting the reform groups tended to work closely with and even be sponsored by the industry. The progressive faith in self-regulation and reform from within was then strong and uncynical. In time, and especially after the emergence of television, the communication reformers began to take a more militant posture. Reflecting the mainstreams of reform activism that were demonstrating increasing strength in such areas as the civil rights, antiwar, and consumer movements, the broadcast reform groups began to make more effective use of existing legislative and regulatory machinery, especially the courts, eventually coming to threaten the essential pattern of industrial and government accommodation.

The broadcast reform program ranged across a number of overlapping issues — program standards and quality, network powers over affiliates, license renewal procedures, acertainment, public access, cross-ownership and concentration, children's advertising, and the levels and impact of violence. Imbued with the liberal faith in a pragmatic science, the reformers eventually came to endorse its use in such areas as the violence and children's advertising inquiries. The empirical findings of persistently high levels of violence and of deleterious impact were taken as confirmations of the progressive lament about the failures of the industry. The scientific reports were added to the other body of evidence being accumulated in an attempt to force stronger measures of industry and government regulation. Involved in an essentially legal process of reform, the citizens' groups tended to look to communication research for its evidentiary value in FCC and court proceedings. Communication science was to be encouraged for its aid in making the case; its practioners valued for their ability to serve as expert witnesses. If there were other attributes of communication science and the study of television, they were seldom considered by the reform mind. At best they were relegated to some secondary status of interesting but essentially useless academic fuzziness.

Of course, much of the research agenda had been structured by the late 1960s when the reform groups became a more organized part of the policy debate. As a result, there was much in the way of research-industry-government accommodations that the reform movement could not disrupt. The terms of limited effects models and inconsistent findings had already become deeply embedded in the literature. During the post-surgeon general's period the reformers were able to work with the critical liberal forces within government to help enhance the impression of the emergence of ever more conclusive deleterious effects findings, and for awhile the entire broadcast reform effort seemed to be achieving an unprecedented and far-reaching degree of success. In a few cases television station license renewals were being denied and many others made contingent on negotiated agreements with reform groups, new regulatory initiatives appeared to be opening up broadcasting and the regulatory process itself for more public involvement, and there seemed to be a generally higher set of expectations for broadcaster performance in the courts, Congress, and the FCC.

Yet by the end of the 1970s it was becoming increasingly obvious that many of the reform achievements, including the violence effects case, were being undermined or being made moot by a sea change in the basic policy approach to broadcasting legislation and regulation. Indeed, largely as a result of the recent successes of the reform movement, the new developments in cable and other technologies were being seized on even more rapidly by the industry in an effort to secure new terms of deregulation and marketplace standards for broadcasting and telecommunications performance. The more successful the reform movement appeared to be, the more quickly it seemed to be encouraging the forces of reaction, hastening the conditions for removal of the public interest standard and the very basis for reform participation in the regulatory and policymaking process.

In the end the old uncertainty about ultimate progressive goals remained. The broadacst reform movement had come regularly to decry the programming consequences of commercial imperatives, and it had even begun to note the complicit role of the regulatory process. Nonetheless, its agenda for change had tended to deal with essentially surface-level, technical, regulatory, and legal adjustments — encouraging more entry into the industry by minorities and women, limiting the amount of advertising in children's programming, securing more support for public broadcasting. Although it had begun to make increasingly sophisticated analyses of the causes of the ills it perceived in American broadcasting, the reform movement could never bring itself to challenge the essential structure and purposes of the enterprise.

The limitations implicit in the reform movement approach had also come to be revealed in its ambivalence about proposals for initating economic sanctions against the industry. From time to time, as the violence effects case would seem to be strengthening, the more militant reformers would propose consumer boycotts of those advertisers sponsoring the more violent programming. However, many reformers found the possibility of such campaigns coming too close to a frontal assault on the fundamental economics of the industry, and they tended to resist them. Alternatively, they would adopt well-publicized monitoring projects in which the more violent programs would be determined, their sponsors identified, and the possibility of boycotts discussed, though never formally endorsed.

Meanwhile, the rise of the more conservative, "moral majority" influences in the television debate compounded the complexity of the traditional reform positions. Here were critics seemingly willing not only to accept the research evidence and to testify about the deleterious impact of television, but also to adopt the more militant tactics of the liberal campaign, especially in the area of boycotts. Yet such a populist movement, based in fundamentalist Protestantism and closely associated with the late-1970s resurgence of elements of American conservatism, appeared to embody a long-term set of goals for television content and other aspects of cultural expression that made the liberal, largely secular and urban, progressivist reformers uneasy. Having long sought program content adjustments the liberals were now fearful of "censorship," with its existence and relative seriousness apparently being associated with the political and religious affiliations of the particular critic.

Altogether, then, by the early 1980s the old ritualistic process of debate about violence continued to play a crucial role in the continuing struggle for control over television. But just as the "evidence" seemed to be reaching new levels of conclusiveness and just as the liberal reformers seemed to be achieving a certain new status in the debate and exercising a stronger degree of influence upon it, they found themselves faced with new conditions and challenges that, combined with the traditional paradoxes, severely constrained their range of action. As so often before, able only to react to the rapidly changing technological and policy conditions, the reformers were once again in danger of being elbowed aside. Along with many of the liberal research critics with whom they had become affiliated, the media reformers had still not come to recognize the symbolic nature of the violence effects debate and the ways in which it might actually have come to be working against the very changes they had hoped it would foster.

THE CONTINUING CHALLENGE TO COMMUNICATION SCIENCE

The violence effects research debate and the pattern of interaction among research, industry, government, and reform interests that sustained it for so long can now be seen in a revealing new light. Violence effects research has served both as a symbolic medium for public debate about the meaning of television in American society and as a means for accommodation among the interests of the principal parties to the policy debate. The communication effects research enterprise reflects one of the latest stages of the struggles among professional interest groups for authority in the public arguments about communications policy. Policymaking in communications had long been divided between the law and engineering. As social science gained in credibility and prestige, it began to claim certain territory as its own, particularly in economic matters. The rise of the psychological and sociological studies of communication increased the competitive position of the social sciences, and in the increasing governmental support for the effects research enterprise during the 1960s and 1970s, one sees the extension of their claim. Therefore, much of the dispute over the role of social science in communications policymaking is merely a spat over the redistribution of power and influence among those who are already enfranchised within the technocracy.

As a case study of the arrival of social science in general to a place of significance both in public and private administration and in popular imagination, the emergence of violence effects research thus serves as a manifestation of an important aspect of contemporary American culture. The history of this research debate demonstrates how the methods and forms of expression of social science have become widely accepted as legitimate means for conceiving of, and attempting to deal with, all manner of social, economic, and political problems. As such it is at least in part the story of the growth in status of a central form of imagination and definition of reality. Among the political, industrial, academic, and reform communities, the violence effects tradition proved to be the most mutually beneficial aspect of the emerging communications sciences. In its ascension are seen the processes of political avoidance, industrial rationalization, and intellectual and reform compromise that are attendant on the arrival of much of the social and behavioral sciences to a place of influence and authority in contemporary American public affairs.

But whatever the previous failings of the debate, one must be careful not to presume too quickly its demise. The history of violence effects research demonstrates that the issue is remarkably resiliant. Its symbolic and political value has always been such that it regularly reappears as a major topic for debate in congressional and academic forums and there are no signs, at least yet, that the issues will wither away entirely. The likelihood that communication science will continue to be tempted to participate in the debate thus remains.

In this respect it is useful to reflect on the general trends in much contemporary communication research thinking. The field has been marked increasingly by the development of schools of thought organized loosely around such rubrics as cultural, symbolic, interpretive, qualitative, institutional, and critical studies that had begun, though often in quite different ways, to suggest important new approaches for dealing with the nature, process, and significance of mass communications and television. Hardly new in the academy or even in American scholarship, the interpretive and critical lines of work had roots in various continental, British, and American schools of social, cultural, linguistic, and political-economic thought. These roots were diverse and powerful. Some were to be found in the neo-idealism of Ernst Cassirer (1973) and his student Susanne Langer (1951) with their particular stress on man's symbol-making nature. Others emanated from the "Chicago School" of symbolic interactionist social psychology and philosophical pragmatism as reflected in George Herbert Mead (1972) and John Dewey (1927), with their emphases on the process of social exchange through which meaning, and therefore reality, is constructed. Additional sources were the cultural studies tradition represented by Raymond Williams (1958, 1961) and that school of critical symbolic analysis associated with Kenneth Burke (1965), whose quite separate influences converged on the effort to articulate the "structure of feeling" embodied in the modern communications experience and to extract the meaning of such ritualistic and dramatistic forms of expression as public communication and science. The emphasis on the cultural and political determinants of science was indebted to the histories and discussion of philosophy of science by such diverse observers as Thomas Kuhn (1973) and Jurgen Habermas (1971).

But as applied to mass communication these approaches had been rather dispersed, and up through the period of the surgeon general's project, they had as yet had only limited impact in the field. By the late 1970s that situation was changing, and scholars working in the several different manifestations of these perspectives were beginning to find one another, their literature was emerging at an increasing rate, and in several of the graduate programs in communication they were fostering a whole new generation of faculty members for the field. To be sure, these newly self-aware approaches were often disparate and mutually contentious, but jointly they had begun to raise the serious questions about the validity, purposes, and consequences of much American empirical communication research, and they tended to share a common iconoclasm toward the traditional, received schools of effects. In this respect they had come to observe with Raymond Williams that:

> A particular version of empiricism — not the general reliance on experience and evidence, but a particular reliance on evidence within the terms of these assumed functions (socialisation, social function, mass communication) — has largely taken over the practice of social and cultural inquiry, and within the terms of its distortion of cultural science claims the abstract authority of 'social science' and 'scientific method' as against all other modes of experience and analysis [1974: 122].

Variously these critiques had adopted the injunction of C. Wright Mills against "grand theory" and "abstracted empiricism," noting that "as practices, they may be understood as insuring that we do not learn too much about men and society — the first by formal and cloudy obscurantism, the second by formal and empty ingenuity" (1959: 75). There finally was an increasing tendency to endorse Mill's view that the pragmatic, technically obsessed forms of modern American social science had lost touch with their classical tradition and to recognize the consequences of their decision long before to refuse any longer to root themselves in "problems of biography, of history and of their intersections within social structures" (Mills, 1959: 143).

Simultaneously, within the empirical universe itself the atmosphere was no less turbulent. Reflecting the theoretical shifts that had also been going on for sometime in the parent disciplines, particularly in psychology and sociology, many of those continuing to be concerned about television's impact on individuals and society were joining the attack on traditional behaviorist and functionalist perspectives. As with such adjustments in any academic field, the breaks and changes were not occuring altogether or in any absolutely clear fashion. The shifts were coming in bits and pieces, and they demonstrated themselves in various ways. Whereas much of the work on violence and antisocial behavior remained locked into the traditional behavioristic patterns common to the field during the previous generation, other work on television's impact, while also grounded in psychology, was showing important different orientations, as in the basic theoretical reformulations associated with the rise of cognitive and information processing theories. Similarly, other research in the normal sociological and economic traditions was showing evidence of humanistic, critical, and interpretative perspective intrusions, suggesting that the various multistep, functionalist, and uses and gratifications models were soon to go the way of their behavioral counterparts. The several empirical disciplines were finding new means of approaching and understanding communication.

A principal consequence of all this paradigmatic shifting has been to foster a better understanding in communication about the terms of its own origins and the dangers of its too ready acquiescence in the applied terms of the policy debate. Whatever their different perspectives, the disagreements among lawyers, engineers, and normative social scientists are not nearly as great as those between those groups as a whole and the emerging interpretive and critical schools of communication scholarship. In this sense the differences among world views, and therefore among definitions of significant issues, operate at a much deeper level. As predominantly organized in contemporary American intellectual life, those aspects of the social sciences addressed to communication share with law and engineering a fundamentally applied, practical purpose, whereas interpretive and critical approaches to communications study entail a basic concern with matters of epistemology and ideology that not only calls attention to the implications of the theoretical and methodological commitments of the contending professional communities, but also calls into question the assumptions of the very concept of policymaking itself.

The empirical schools are hardly dead, and they will continue to play an important role in the struggle over television. But they will no longer be able to operate in a naive world of political innocence, under scientific mantles of value freeness and institutional neutrality. Henceforth every debate about the impact of television that casts itself in the language and data of positivism will have to demonstrate a greater degree of self-reflection, manifesting a much more direct sense of its beginnings and presuppositions. The science of effects will also have to take greater cognizance of the meaning and consequences of the process in which it is engaged. To do any less would be to continue to accept political and industrial control of the field, to avoid the most important intellectual challenges facing contemporary social science, and to guarantee theoretical and methodological stagnation for much of communication research.

REFERENCES

General

Adorno, Theodor W. "Scientific Experience of a European Scholar in America," in D. Fleming and B. Bailyn, eds. *The Intellectual Migration:* Europe and America, 1930-1960. Cambridge, MA: Harvard University Press, 1969.

Bainton, Roland H. *The Reformation of the Sixteenth Century.* Boston: Beacon, 1959.

Barnouw, Erik. *A Tower in Babel.* New York: Oxford University Press, 1966.

——— *The Golden Web.* New York: Oxford University Press, 1968.

——— *Tube of Plenty.* New York: Oxford University Press, 1975.

Beard, Charles. *The Reformation of the Sixteenth Century in its Relation to Modern Thought and Knowledge.* London: Willows & Norgate, 1907.

Berelson, Bernard. *Content Analysis in Communication Research.* Glencoe, IL: Free Press, 1952.

Berelson, Bernard and Morris Janowitz, eds. *Reader in Public Opinion and Communication.* Glencoe, IL: Free Press, 1950.

Blakely, Robert J. *To Serve the Public Interest: Educational Broadcasting in the United States.* Syracuse, NY: Syracuse University Press, 1979.

Blumer, Herbert. *Movies and Conduct.* New York: Macmillan, 1933.

——— *Symbolic Interactionism.* Englewood Cliffs, NJ: Prentice-Hall, 1969.

Blumer, Herbert and Philip M. Hauser. *Movies, Delinquency and Crime.* New York: Macmillan, 1933.

Blumler, Jay G. and Elihu Katz, eds. *The Uses of Mass Communications: Current Perspectives in Gratifications Research.* Beverly Hills, CA: Sage, 1974.

Bogart, Leo. *The Age of Television.* 3rd ed. New York: Frederick Ungar, 1972 (first published 1954).

Boorstin, Daniel J. *The Americans: The Democratic Experience.* New York: Vintage, 1974.

Bower, Raymond T. *Television and the Public.* New York: Holt, Rinehart & Winston, 1973.

Bryson, Lyman, ed. *The Communication of Ideas.* New York: Institute for Religious and Social Studies, Harper, 1948.

Burke, Kenneth, *Permanence and Change.* 2nd ed. Indianapolis: Bobbs-Merrill, 1965.

Carnegie Commission on Educational Television. *Public Television: A Program for Action.* New York: Harper & Row, 1967.

Cassirer, Ernst. *An Essay on Man.* New Haven, CT: Yale University Press, 1973.

Cater, Douglass and Stephen Strickland. *TV Violence and the Child: The Evolution and Fate of the Surgeon General's Report.* New York: Russell Sage Foundation, 1975.

Chandler, Alfred D., Jr. "The Origins of Progressive Leadership," in Elting E. Morison et al., eds. *The Letters of Theodore Roosevelt*. Vol. 8. Cambridge, MA: Harvard University Press, 1954.

Chaney, David. *The Processes of Mass Communication*. London: Macmillan, 1972.

Charters, W.W. *Motion Pictures and Youth: A Summary*. New York: Macmillan, 1933.

Cole, Barry and Mal Oettinger. *Reluctant Regulators: The FCC and the Broadcast Audience*. Reading, MA: Addison-Wesley, 1978.

Committee for Economic Development. Subcommittee on the Economic and Social Impact of the New Broadcast Media. *Broadcasting and Cable Television: Policies for Diversity and Change*. New York: Committee for Economic Development, 1975.

Comstock, Anthony. *Traps for the Young*. Edited by Robert Bremner. Cambridge, MA: Harvard University Press, 1967. (Reproduction of the original 1883 document).

Comstock, George A. *Television and Human Behavior: The Key Studies*. R-1747-CF. Santa Monica, CA: Rand, 1975.

Comstock, George, Steven Chaffee, Natan Katzman, Maxwell McCombs, and Donald Roberts. *Television and Human Behavior*. New York: Columbia University Press, 1978.

Comstock, George A. and Marilyn Fisher. *Television and Human Behavior: A Guide to the Pertinent Scientific Literature*. R-1746-CF. Santa Monica, CA: Rand, 1975.

Comstock, George A. and Georg Lindsey. *Television and Human Behavior: The Research Horizon, Future and Present*. R-1748-CF. Santa Monica, CA: Rand, 1975.

Conference Board. *Information Technology: Some Critical Implications for Decision Makers*. Report No. 537. New York: Conference Board, 1972.

Cowan, Geoffrey. *See No Evil: The Backstage Battle Over Sex and Violence on Television*. New York: Simon & Schuster, 1979.

DeFleur, Melvin L. and Sandra Ball-Rokeach. *Theories of Mass Communication*. 3rd ed. New York: David McKay, 1975.

Dewey, John. *The Public and Its Problems*. New York: Henry Holt, 1927.

Dowling, Jack, Lelia Doolin, and Bob Quinn. *Sit Down and Be Counted*. Dublin, Ireland: Wellington, 1969.

Dreher, Carl. *Sarnoff: An American Success*. New York: Quadrangle, 1977.

Duncan, Hugh Daziel. *Communication and Social Order*. New York: Oxford University Press, 1970.

Edelman, Murray. *The Symbolic Uses of Politics*. Urbana: University of Illinois Press, 1964.

Emery, Walter. *Broadcasting and Government*. East Lansing: Michigan State University Press, 1971.

Fleming, Donald and Bernard Bailyn, eds. *The Intellectual Migration: Europe and America, 1930-1960*. Cambridge, MA: Harvard University Press, 1969.

Ford Foundation. *Television and Children: Priorities for Research*. New York: Ford, 1976.

Galbraith, John Kenneth. *The Age of Uncertainty*. Boston: Houghton Mifflin, 1977.

Graham, Hugh Davis and Ted Robert Gurr. *Violence in America*. New York: New American Library, 1969.

Grundfest, Joseph A. *Citizen Participation in Broadcast Licensing Before the FCC*. R-1896-MF. Santa Monica, CA: Rand, 1976.

Guimary, Donald L. *Citizens' Groups and Broadcasting*. New York: Praeger, 1975.

Habermas, Jürgen. *Knowledge and Human Interests*. Boston: Beacon, 1971.

Haight, Timothy R., ed. *Telecommunications Policy and the Citizen*. New York: Praeger, 1979.
Halloran, James D., ed. *Mass Media and Socialization*. Leicester, England: IAMCR/Unesco, 1976.
Head, Sydney W. *Broadcasting in America*. 3rd ed. (2nd ed., 1972) New York: Houghton Mifflin, 1976.
Heller, Melvin S. and Samuel Polsky. *Studies in Violence and Television*. New York: American Broadcasting Companies, 1976.
Hofstadter, Richard. *The Age of Reform*. New York: Alfred A. Knopf, 1954.
Horowitz, Irving Louis, ed. *The Use and Abuse of Social Science*. New Brunswick, NJ: Transaction, 1970.
Hovland, Carl Iver, Irving L. Janis, and Harold H. Kelley. *Communication and Persuasion: Psychological Studies of Opinion Change*. New Haven, CT: Yale University Press, 1953.
Jowett, Garth. *Film: The Democratic Art*. Boston: Little, Brown, 1976.
Kahn, Frank J., ed. *Documents of American Broadcasting*. 2nd ed. New York: Appleton-Century-Crofts, 1973.
Katz, Elihu. *Social Research in Broadcasting*. London: British Broadcasting Corporation, 1977.
Klapper, Joseph T. *The Effects of Mass Communication*. New York: Free Press, 1960.
Komarovsky, Mirra, ed. *Sociology and Public Policy: The Case of Presidential Commissions*. New York: Elsevier, 1975.
Krasnow, Erwin G., Lawrence D. Longley, and Herbert A. Terry. *The Politics of Broadcast Regulation*. 3rd ed. New York: St. Martin's, 1982.
Kuhn, Thomas. *The Structure of Scientific Revolutions*. 2nd ed. Chicago: University of Chicago Press, 1973.
Langer, Susanne K. *Philosophy in a New Key*. Cambridge, MA: Harvard University Press, 1951.
Lasswell, Harold. *Propaganda Technique in the War*. New York: A. A. Knopf, 1927.
Lazarsfeld, Paul F. *Radio and the Printed Page*. New York: Duell, Sloan & Pearce, 1940.
——— "An Episode in the History of Social Research: A Memoir," in D. Fleming and B. Bailyn, eds. *The Intellectual Migration: Europe and America, 1930-1960*. Cambridge, MA: Harvard University Press, 1969.
Lazarsfeld, Paul F., Bernard Berelson, and Hazel Gaudet. *The People's Choice*. New York: Duell, Sloan & Pearce, 1944.
Lazarsfeld, Paul F. and Harry Field. *The People Look at Radio*. Chapel Hill: University of North Carolina Press, 1946.
Lazarsfeld, Paul F. and Elihu Katz. *Personal Influence*. Glencoe, IL: Free Press, 1955.
Lazarsfeld, Paul F. and Patricia Kendall. *Radio Listening in America: The People Look at Radio – Again*. Englewood Cliffs, NJ: Prentice-Hall, 1948.
Lazarsfeld, Paul F. and Frank Stanton, eds. *Communications Research, 1948-1949*. New York: Harper & Brothers, 1949.
——— eds. *Radio Research, 1941*. New York: Duell, Sloan & Pearce, 1941.
——— eds. *Radio Research, 1942-1943*. New York: Duell, Sloan & Pearce, 1944.
Leigh, Robert D., ed. *A Free and Responsible Press*. Chicago: University of Chicago Press, 1947.
Lessing, Lawrence. *Man of High Fidelity*. Philadelphia: J. B. Lippincott, 1956.
Lynd, Robert S. and Helen M. Lynd. *Middletown: A Study in Contemporary American Culture*. New York: Harcourt, Brace & World, 1929.

Lyons, Gene M. *The Uneasy Partnership.* New York: Russell Sage Foundation, 1969.

Macdonald, Dwight. *Against the American Grain.* New York: Vintage, 1962.

Madge, John. *The Origins of Scientific Sociology.* New York: Free Press, 1962.

Mayer, Martin. *About Television.* New York: Harper & Row, 1972.

McQuail, Denis. *Towards A Sociology of Mass Communications.* London: Collier-Macmillan, 1969.

Mead, George Herbert. *Mind, Self, and Society.* Charles W. Morris, ed. Chicago: University of Chicago Press, 1972.

Merton, Robert K. "Social Knowledge and Public Policy: Sociological Perspectives on Four Presidential Commissions," in M. Komarovsky, ed. *Sociology and Public Policy: The Case of Presidential Commissions.* New York: Elserier, 1975.

Metz, Robert. *CBS: Reflections in a Bloodshot Eye.* New York: New American Library, 1975.

Mills, C. Wright. *The Sociological Imagination.* New York: Oxford University Press, 1959.

Murray, John P. *Television and Youth: 25 Years of Controversy.* Boys Town, Nebraska: The Boys Town Center for the Study of Youth Development, 1980.

National Association of Broadcasters. Code Authority. *Television Code.* 19th ed. (June 1976) in F.J. Kahn, ed. *Documents of American Broadcasting.* 2nd ed. New York: Appleton-Century-Crofts, 1973.

National Association of Educational Broadcasters. *Monitoring Studies.* Nos. 1-5. Urbana: NAEB, 1951.

Nisbet, Robert A. *The Degredation of the Academic Dogma: The University in America, 1945-1970.* New York: Basic Books, 1971.

——— *Tradition and Revolt.* New York: Random House, 1968.

——— *Twilight of Authority.* New York: Oxford University Press, 1975.

Noble, David W. *The Paradox of Progressive Thought.* Minneapolis: University of Minnesota Press, 1958.

Osborn, Frederick et al., eds. *Studies in Social Psychology in World War II.* Vols. I-IV. Princeton, NJ: Princeton University Press, 1949.

Owen, Bruce M., ed. *Telecommunications Policy Research: Report on the 1975 Conference Proceedings.* Palo Alto, CA: Aspen Institute, 1975.

Palmer, Edward L., and Aimee Dorr, eds. *Children and the Faces of Television.* New York: Academic, 1980.

Parsons, Talcott. *Essays in Sociological Theory.* Rev. ed. New York: Free Press, 1964.

Popper, Frank. *The President's Commissions.* New York: Twentieth Century Fund, 1970.

Porter, William E. *Assault on the Media: The Nixon Years.* Ann Arbor: University of Michigan Press, 1976.

President's Research Committee on Social Trends. *Recent Social Trends.* New York: McGraw-Hill, 1933.

Roper, Burns. *What People Think of Television and Other Mass Media, 1959-1972.* New York: Television Information Office, 1973.

Roper Organization. *Public Perceptions of Television and Other Mass Media: A Twenty-Year Review, 1959-1978.* New York: Television Information Office, 1979.

Salomon, Leon L., ed. *The Independent Regulatory Agencies.* New York: H.W. Wilson, 1959.

Schlesinger, Arthur M., Jr. *The Age of Roosevelt: The Crisis of the Old Order, 1919-1933.* Boston: Houghton Mifflin, 1957.

Schramm, Wilbur, ed. *Communications in Modern Society*. Urbana: University of Illinois Press, 1948.

——— ed. *Mass Communications*. Urbana: University of Illinois Press, 1949.

——— ed. *The Process and Effects of Mass Communication*. Urbana: University of Illinois, 1954.

Schramm, Wilbur, Jack Lyle, and Edwin Parker. *Television in the Lives of Our Children*. Stanford, CA: Stanford University Press, 1961.

Schwartz, Bernard, ed. *The Economic Regulation of Business and Industry*. Volume 1. New York: Chelsea House, 1973.

Seldes, Gilbert. *The 7 Lively Arts*. New York: Sagamore Press, 1952 (first published 1924).

——— *The Great Audience*. New York: Viking, 1951.

——— *The Public Arts*. New York: Simon & Schuster, 1956.

Short, James F., Jr. "The National Commission on the Causes and Prevention of Violence: Reflections on the Contributions of Sociology and Sociologists," in M. Komarovksy, ed. *Sociology and Public Policy: The Case of Presidential Commissions*. New York: Elsevier, 1975.

Skolnick, Jerome H. "The Violence Commission: Internal Politics and Public Policy," in I.L. Horowitz, ed. *The Use and Abuse of Social Science*. New Brunswick, NJ: Transaction, 1970.

Sloan Commission on Cable Communications. *On the Cable*. New York: McGraw-Hill, 1971.

Smith, Anthony. *The Shadow in the Cave*. Urbana: University of Illinois Press, 1973.

Steiner, Gary A. *The People Look at Television: A Study of Audience Attitudes*. New York: Alfred A. Knopf, 1963.

Tannenbaum, Percy H., ed. *The Entertainment Functions of Television*. Hillsdale, NJ: Lawrence Erlbaum, 1980.

Tunstall, Jeremy. *The Media Are American*. New York: Columbia University Press, 1977.

Weiss, Walter. "Effects of Mass Media of Communications," in Lindzay, Gardner, and Aronson, eds. *The Handbook of Social Psychology*. 2nd ed. Vol. V: Applied Social Psychology. Reading, MA: Addison-Wesley, 1969.

White, Llewellyn. *The American Radio*. Chicago: University of Chicago Press, 1947.

Wiebe, Robert. *The Search for Order, 1877-1920*. New York: Hill & Wang, 1967.

Wiley, Malcolm W. and Stuart A. Rice. "The Agencies of Communication," in President's Research Committee on Social Trends. *Recent Social Trends*. New York: McGraw-Hill, 1933.

Williams, Raymond. *Culture and Society, 1780-1950*. London: Chatto & Windus, 1958.

——— *The Long Revolution*. London: Chatto & Windus, 1961.

——— *Television: Technology and Cultural Form*. London: Fontana/Collins, 1974.

Withey, Stephen B. and Ronald P. Abeles, eds. *Television and Social Behavior: Beyond Violence and Children*. Hillsdale, NJ: Lawrence Erlbaum, 1980.

Wright, Charles. *Mass Communication: A Sociological Perspective*. New York: Random House, 1959.

Journal, Periodical, and Unpublished Materials

American Film. "Special Report: Pressure Groups and the Media." October 1981, pp. 57-64, 81.

Atkin, Charles K., John P. Murray, and Oguz B. Nayman. "The Surgeon General's Research Program on Television and Social Behavior: A Review of Empirical Findings." *Journal of Broadcasting*. Winter 1971-1972, 16(1): 21-35.

Bartos, Rene. Interview. "Frank Stanton: Our First CEO." *Journal of Advertising Research*. June 1977, 17(6): 26-29.

Berelson, Bernard. "The State of Communications Research." *Public Opinion Quarterly*. Spring 1959, 23(1): 1-6.

Bogart, Leo. "Warning: The Surgeon General Has Determined That TV Violence is Moderately Dangerous to Your Child's Mental Health." *Public Opinion Quarterly*. Winter 1972-1973, 36(4): 491-516.

Branscomb, Anne W. and Maria Savage. "The Broadcast Reform Movement: At the Crossroads." *Journal of Communication*. Autumn 1978, 28(4): 25-34.

Broadcasting. "Battling over TV violence." October 26, 1981, p. 38.

——— "Boycott threat is revived." November 23, 1981, p. 56.

——— "Butler speech sets off waves of dispute over television sex and violence." June 22, 1981, pp. 19-21.

——— "Cowed ad industry surrending to Wildmon?" June 29, 1981, pp. 28-29.

——— "Crusade sets out to clean up TV." February 9, 1981, pp. 27-29.

——— "Different tacks from Wildmon and Falwell." February 15, 1982, p. 44.

——— "Face-off at FCC children's TV." June 23, 1980, p. 52.

——— "Family viewing case easing out of the picture." October 13, 1980, p. 66.

——— "The fight that faces the losers in the decision on family viewing." December 6, 1976, pp. 36-39.

——— "The First Fifty Years of Broadcasting, 1977." September 7, 1981, p. 91.

——— "FTC staff waves white flag on children's ad standards." March 2, 1981, p. 66.

——— "FTC staff would pull the plug on kidvid inquiry." April 6, 1981, p. 39.

——— "Gerbner is told to get a new act." June 6, 1977, pp. 45-46.

——— "Gerbner plans to put more of TV on his couch." August 29, 1977, p. 43.

——— "House and Senate conferees agree on FTC legislation." April 28, 1980, p. 25.

——— "Industry still in disarray after decision on family viewing." November 15, 1976, pp. 38-53.

——— "Networks still the villains in Van Deerlin staff report on TV violence." July 25, 1977, pp. 19, 22-23.

——— "Pastore submits antistrike bill." May 5, 1969, p. 58.

——— "Senate puts the kibosh on FTC children's ad proceeding." February 11, 1980, p. 34.

——— "TV networks can expect less whip in upcoming Hill violence report." May 23, 1977, pp. 50-51.

——— "Van Deerlin takes firmer control of violence report." August 1, 1977, p. 23.

——— "Wildmon calls off boycott, declares he won the war." July 6, 1981, p. 28.

——— "Wildmon to make another stab at boycott." February 1, 1982, pp. 31-32.

——— "NAB, Justice Dept. closer to resolution of antitrust suit involving TV code." July 5, 1982, p. 31.

Cater, Douglass and Stephen Strickland. "A First Hard Look at the Surgeon General's Report on Television and Violence." Aspen Institute Program on Communications and Society. (Unpublished, March 1972.)

Chaffee, Steven H., ed. "Contributions of Wilbur Schramm to Mass Communication Research." *Journalism Monographs*. No. 36. October 1974.

Champaign-Urbana Courier. "Trustees Raise Schramm to Dean." February 16, 1950, p. 3.

Fuchs, Douglas A. "Television Violence Reinvestigated: The Million Dollar Misunderstanding." (Unpublished, 1972.)

Gerbner, George and Larry Gross. "Living with Television: The Violence Profile." *Journal of Communication*. Spring 1976, 26(2): 173-179.

Gerbner, George et al. "Cultural Indicators: Violence Profile No. 9." *Journal of Communication*. Summer 1978, 28(3): 176-207.

——— "A Curious Journey into the Scary World of Paul Hirsch." *Communication Research*. January 1981, 8(1): 39-72. (a)

——— "Final Reply to Hirsch." *Communication Research*. July 1981, 8(3): 259-280. (b)

——— "The 'Mainstreaming' of America: Violence Profile No. 11." *Journal of Communication*. Summer 1980, 30(3): 10-29.

——— "TV Violence Profile No. 8: The Highlights." *Journal of Communication*. Spring 1977, 27(2): 171-180.

Hirsch, Paul M. "The 'Scary World' of the Nonviewer and Other Anomalies: A Reanalysis of Gerbner et al.'s Findings on Cultivation Analysis, Part I." *Communication Research*. October 1980, 7(4): 403-456.

——— "On Not Learning from One's Mistakes: A Reanalysis of Gerbner et al.'s Findings on Cultivation Analysis, Part II." *Communication Research*. January 1981, 8(1): 3-37. (a)

——— "Distinguishing Good Speculation from Bad Theory: Rejoinder to Gerbner et al." *Communication Research*. January 1981, 8(1): 73-95. (b)

Lyle, Jack. "An Overview of Research Done for the Scientific Advisory Committee to the Surgeon General of the United States on the Problem of Television and Social Behavior." (Unpublished paper delivered to the International Congress of Psychologists, Tokyo, August 1972.)

Margulies, Lee, ed. "Symposium, 1981: Proliferation of Pressure Groups in Prime Time." *Emmy Magazine*, Summer 1981.

Meyer, Timothy B. and James A. Anderson. "Media Violence Research: Interpreting the Findings." *Journal of Broadcasting*. Fall 1973, 17(4): 447-458.

Morrison, David E. "The Beginnings of Modern Mass Communication Research." Centre for Mass Communication Research, University of Leicester, England. (Unpublished, 1977.)

——— "Paul Lazarsfeld 1901-1976: A Tribute." *Osterreichische Zeitshrift fur Soziologie* II/III. 1976, pp. 7-9.

NCTV News. "Congress Cancels Hearings. NCTV Calls for Advertiser Pressure." March-May 1982, 3(2-3): 1.

Newcomb, Horace. "Assessing the Violence Profile of Gerbner and Gross: A Humanistic Critique and Suggestion." *Communication Research*. July 1978, 5(3): 264-283.

Paisley, Matilda B. "Social Policy Research and the Realities of the System: Violence Done to TV Research." Stanford University, Institute for Communications Research. ERIC Reports, ED 062 764. (Unpublished, 1972).

Rowland, Willard D., Jr. "The Illusion of Fulfillment: The Broadcast Reform Movement. *Journalism Monographs*, December 1982. No. 79. (a)

——— "The Process of Reification: Recent Trends in Communications Legislation and Policy-Making." *Journal of Communication*. Autumn 1982, 32(3): 114-126. (b)

Rubinstein, Eli A. "Televised Violence: The Flow from the Fortieth View." (Unpublished paper delivered to a colloquium, Annenberg School of Communications, University of Pennsylvania, November 6, 1972.)

Sandman, Peter M. "The Fight over Television Violence Ratings." *MORE*. April 1978, pp. 35-40.

Schrag, Peter. "Douglass Cater's Secret Mission." *MORE*. June 1975, 5(6): 10.
Schramm, Wilbur, David Riesman, and Raymond A. Bauer. "Comments on 'The State of Communications Research.'" *Public Opinion Quarterly*. Spring 1959, 23(1): 6-17.
"Symposium." *Journal of Broadcasting*. Fall 1981, 25(4): iii-iv, 327-400.
"Violence Probe on the Firing Line." *Behavior Today*. July 20, 1970, 1(11): 1-2.
Whiteside, Thomas. "Annals of Television: Shaking the Tree." *The New Yorker*. March 17, 1975, pp. 41-91.
Wilson, James Q. "Violence, Pornography, and Social Science." *The Public Interest*. Winter 1971, 22: 45-61.

Government Documents and Legal Citations

General

Atkin, Charles K., John P. Murray, and Oguz B. Nayman, eds. *Television and Social Behavior: An Annotated Bibliography of Research Focusing on Television's Impact on Children*. Washington, DC: DHEW, 1971.
Baker, Robert K. and Sandra J. Ball. *Violence and the Media: Mass Media and Violence*. Vol. 9. Staff Report to the National Commission on the Causes and Prevention of Violence. Washington, DC: Government Printing Office, 1969.
Bechtel, Robert B., Clark Achelpohl, and Roger Akers. "Correlates Between Observed Behavior and Questionnaire Responses on Television Viewing," in E. A. Rubinstein et al., eds. *Television and Social Behavior*. Reports and Papers. Vol. IV: *Television in Day-to-Day Life: Patterns of Use*. Washington, DC: DHEW, 1972.
Briand, Paul L., Jr., ed. *Violence and the Media: Mass Media Hearings*. Vol. 9A. Staff Report to the National Commission on the Causes and Prevention of Violence. Washington, DC: Government Printing Office, 1969.
Cabinet Committee on Cable Communications. *Cable: Report to the President*. Washington, DC: Government Printing Office, 1974.
Citizens Communication Center et al. v. FCC. 477 F. 2d 1201, 1971.
Communications Act of 1934. P.L. 416. 73rd Congress. June 19, 1934.
Comstock, George A. "New Research on Media Content and Control (Overview)," in G. A. Comstock and E. A. Rubinstein, eds. *Television and Social Behavior*. Reports and Papers. Vol. I: Media *Content and Control*. Washington, DC: DHEW, 1972.
Comstock, George A. and Eli A. Rubinstein, eds. *Television and Social Behavior*. Reports and Papers. Vol. I: *Media Content and Control*. Washington, DC: DHEW, 1972. (a)
——— *Television and Social Behavior*. Reports and Papers. Vol. III: *Television and Adolescent Aggressiveness*. Washington, DC: DHEW, 1972. (b)
Comstock, George A., Eli A. Rubinstein, and John P. Murray, eds. *Television and Social Behavior*. Reports and Papers. Vol. V: *Television's Effects: Further Explorations*. Washington, DC: DHEW, 1972.
Cantor, Muriel G. "The Role of the Producer in Choosing Children's Television Content," in G. A. Comstock and E. A. Rubinstein, eds. *Television and Social Behavior*. Reports and Papers. Vol. I: *Media Content and Control*. Washington, DC: DHEW, 1972.
Chaffee, Steven H. "Television and Adolescent Aggressiveness (Overview)," in G. A. Comstock and E. A. Rubinstein, eds. *Television and Social Behavior*.

Reports and Papers. Vol. III: *Television and Adolescent Aggressiveness*. Washington, DC: DHEW, 1972.

Dominick, Joseph R. and Bradley S. Greenberg. "Attitudes Toward Violence: The Interation of Television Exposure, Family Attitudes, and Social Class," in G. A. Comstock and E. A. Rubinstein, eds., *Television and Social Behavior.* Reports and Papers. Vol. I: *Media Content and Control*. Washington, DC: DHEW, 1972.

Gerbner, George. "The Structure and Processes of Television Program Content Regulation in the United States," in G. A. Comstock and E. A. Rubinstein, eds. *Television and Social Behavior.* Reports and Papers. Vol. 1: *Media Content and Control*. Washington, DC: DHEW, 1972. (a)

——— "Violence in Television Drama: Trends and Symbolic Functions," in G. A. Comstock and E. A. Rubinstein, eds. *Television and Social Behavior.* Reports and Papers. Vol. 1: *Media Content and Control*. Washington, DC: DHEW, 1972. (b)

Lefkowitz, Monroe M., L. D. Eron, L. O. Walder, and L. R. Heusmann. "Television Violence and Child Aggression: A Follow-Up Study," in G. A. Comstock and E. A. Rubinstein, eds. *Television and Social Behavior.* Reports and Papers. Vol. III: *Television and Adolescent Aggressiveness*. Washington, DC: DHEW, 1972.

Liebert, Robert M. "Television and Social Learning: Some Relationships Between Viewing Violence and Behaving Aggressively (Overview)," in J. P. Murray et al., eds. *Television and Social Behavior. Reports and Papers*. Vol. II: *Television and Social Learning*. Washington, DC: DHEW, 1972.

Lyle, Jack. "Television in Daily Life: Pattterns of Use (Overview)," in E. A. Rubinstein et al., eds. *Television and Social Behavior.* Reports and Papers. Vol. IV: *Television in Day-to-Day Life*. Washington, DC: DHEW, 1972.

Lyle, Jack and H. R. Hoffman. "Children's Use of Television and Other Media," in E. A. Rubinstein et al., eds. *Television and Social Behavior.* Reports and Papers. Vol. IV: *Television in Day-to-Day Life: Patterns of Use*. Washington, DC: DHEW, 1972.

McLeod, Jack M., C.K. Atkin, and S. H. Chaffee. "Adolescents, Parents, and Television Use: Adolescent Self-Report Measures from Maryland and Wisconsin Samples," in G. A. Comstock and E. A. Rubinstein, eds. *Television and Social Behavior. Reports and Papers*. Vol. III: *Television and Adolescent Aggressiveness*. Washington, DC: DHEW, 1972.

Murray, John P., Eli A. Rubinstein, and George A. Comstock, eds. *Television and Social Behavior.* Reports and Papers. Vol. II: *Television and Social Learning*. Washington, DC: DHEW, 1972.

National Broadcasting Co., Inc. et al. v. United States et al. 319 U.S. 190. May 10, 1943.

National Commission on the Causes and Prevention of Violence. *To Establish Justice, To Insure Domestic Tranquility.* New York: Praeger, 1970.

National Institute of Mental Health. *Television and Behavior: Ten Years of Scientific Progress and Implications for the Eighties*. Vol. 1: *Summary Report*. Vol. 2. *Technical Reviews*. Washington, DC: DHHS, 1982.

National Science Foundation. "Program Solicitation: Policy Related Research on the Social Effects of Broadcast Television." Washington, DC: NSF 76-6, 1976.

——— *Telecommunications Policy Research Program: Summary of Activities and Description of Research Projects/Fiscal Years 1972-1975*. Washington, DC: NSF 75-36, 1975.

Office of War Information. Bureau of Intelligence. *Report from the Nation*. Washington, DC: OWI, 1942.

——— *OWI in the ETO: A Report on the Activities of the Office of War Information in the European Theater of Operations, January 1944 - January 1945*. Washington, DC: OWI, 1945.

Omnibus Budget Reconciliation Act of 1981. P.L. 35. 97th Congress. August 13, 1981.

President's Task Force on Communications Policy. *Final Report*. Washington, DC: Government Printing Office, 1969.

Red Lion Broadcasting Co., Inc., et al. v. FCC et al. 395 U.S. 367, June 9, 1969.

Rubinstein, Eli A., George A. Comstock, and John P. Murray, eds. *Television and Social Behavior.* Reports and Papers. Vol. IV: *Television in Day-to-Day Life: Patterns of Use*. Washington, DC: DHEW, 1972.

Surgeon General's Scientific Advisory Committee on Television and Social Behavior. *Television and Growing Up: The Impact of Televised Violence*. Washington, DC: Government Printing Office, 1972.

Regulatory Agencies

Federal Communications Commission. *Report on Chain Broadcasting*. Commission Order No. 37. May 2, 1941.

——— *Public Service Responsibility of Broadcast Licensees*. March 7, 1946.

——— *Annual Reports*. Nos. 25-28, 1958-1961.

——— *Policy Statement Concerning Comparative Hearings Involving Regular Renewal Applicants*. 22 FCC 2d 424, January 15, 1970.

——— "In the Matter of Petition of Action for Children's Television (ACT) for Rulemaking Looking Toward the Elimination of Sponsorship and Commercial Content in Children's Programming and the Establishment of a Weekly 14 Hour Quota of Chidren's Television Programs." *First Notice of Inquiry,* Docket No. 19142. 28 FCC 2d 368, January 26, 1971.

——— "Children's Television Report and Policy Statement." Docket No. 19142. 50 FCC 2d 1, October 31, 1974. (a)

——— "Fairness Doctrine and Public Interest Standards: Handling of Public Issues." 39 Fed. Reg. 26382, July 18, 1974 (b)

——— *Report on the Broadcast of Violent, Indecent and Obscene Material*. February 19, 1975.

——— "Memoranda Reports and Orders." 55 FCC 2d 691 (1975); 58 FCC 2d 1169 (1975); 62 FCC 2d 465 (1976); 63 FCC 2d 26 (1977).

——— *Action for Children's Television v. Federal Communications Commission*. 564 F. 2d 458, D.C. Cir. (1977).

——— "Children's Television Programming and Advertising Practices." Docket No. 19142. *Notice of Proposed Rule Making*. 45 Fed. Reg. 1976, December 28, 1979. (a)

——— Office of Plans and Policy. *Television Programming for Children: A Report of the Children's Television Task Force*. October, 1979. (b)

Federal Trade Commission. "Children's Advertising, Notice of Proposed Rulemaking." 43 Fed. Reg. 17967, April 27, 1978. (a)

——— *FTC Staff Report on Television Advertising to Children*. February, 1978. (b)

Congress

U.S. House. Committee on Appropriations. Subcommittee on the Departments of State, Justice, and Commerce, the Judiciary, and Related Agencies. *Depart-*

ments of State, Justice, and Commerce, the Judiciary, and Related Agencies Appropriations for 1976. Hearings, Part 6. (94,1), May 7, 1975.

——— *Departments of State, Justice and Commerce, the Judiciary, and Related Agencies Appropriations for 1977*. Hearings, Part 7. (94,2), March 16, 1976.

U.S. House. Committee on Appropriations. Subcommittee on HUD-Space-Science Appropriations. *HUD-Space-Science Appropriations for 1972*. Hearings, Part 3. (92,1), April, May, 1971.

——— *HUD-Space-Science Appropriations for 1973*. Hearings, Part 2. (92,2), March, 1972.

——— *HUD-Space-Science-Veterans Appropriations for 1974*. Hearings, Part 1. (93,1), February, March, 1973.

——— *HUD-Space-Science-Veterans Appropriations for 1975*. Hearings. (93,2), March, 1974.

U.S. House. Committee on Appropriations. Subcommittee on Independent Offices and Department of Housing and Urban Development. *Independent Offices and Department of Housing and Urban Development Appropriations for 1971*. Hearings, Part 1. (91,2), February, March, 1970.

U.S. House. Committee on Energy and Commerce. Subcommittee on Telecommunications, Consumer Protection, and Finance. *Social/Behavioral Effects of Violence on Television*. Hearing. (97,1), October, 21, 1981.

U.S. House. Committee on Interstate and Foreign Commerce. *Federal Motion Picture Commission*. Hearing. (73,2), March 19, 1934.

U.S. House. Committee on Interstate and Foreign Commerce. Subcommittee on Communications. *Federal Communications Commission Overview*. Hearings. (94,1), March 11, 1975. (a)

——— *Telecommunications Research and Policy Development Overview*. Hearings. (94,1), July 8-10, 1975. (b)

——— *Cable Television: Promise versus Regulatory Performance*. Staff Report. (94,2), January, 1976. (a)

——— *Cable Television Regulation Oversight*. Hearings, Parts 1-2, (94,2), May-September, 1976. (b)

——— *Sex and Violence on TV*. Hearings. (94,2), July 9, August 17-18, 1976. (c)

——— *Sex and Violence on TV*. Hearing. (95,1), March 2, 1977. (a)

——— *Options Papers*. Staff Report. (95,1), May 1977. (b)

——— *Violence on Television*, Report together with Additional, Dissenting, and Separate Views. (95,1), September 29, 1977. (c)

——— "Communications Act of 1978." H.R. 13015 (95,2), June 7, 1978.

——— "Communications Act of 1979." H.R. 3333 (96,1) March 29, 1979. (a)

——— "Telecommunications Act of 1979." H.R. 6121 (96,1), December 13, 1979. (b)

U.S. House. Committee on Interstate and Foreign Commerce. Subcommittee on Communications and Power. *Review of FCC Activities 1969*. Hearing. (91,1), March 6, 1969.

——— *Review of FCC Activities 1971*. Hearing. (92,1), April 29, 1971.

U.S. House. Committee on Interstate and Foreign Commerce. Federal Communications Commission Subcommittee. *Investigation of Radio and Television Programming*. Hearings. (82,2), June, September, December, 1952.

U.S. House. Subcommittee of the Committee on Interstate and Foreign Commerce. *Motion-Picture Films*. Hearings. (74,2), March 1936.

U.S. Senate. Committee on Appropriations. Subcommittee. *Departments of Housing and Urban Development, Space, Science, Veterans and Certain Other Independent Agencies Appropriations for Fiscal Year 1975*. Hearings. (93,2) January-April, 1974.

U.S. Senate. Committee on Commerce. Subcommittee on Communications. *Federal Communications Commission Policy Matters and Television Programming*. Hearings. Parts 1-2. (91,1), March 1969.

——— *Scientific Advisory Committee on TV and Social Behavior.* Hearings. (92,1), September 28, 1971.

——— *Surgeon General's Report by the Scientific Advisory Committee on Television and Social Behavior.* Hearings. (92,2), March 21-24, 1972.

——— *Violence on Television.* Hearings. (93,2), April 3-5, 1974. (a)

——— *Overview of the Federal Communications Commission.* Hearings. (93,2), March 26-27, 1974. (b)

——— *Oversight of the Federal Communications Commission.* Hearings. (94,1), April 21-22, 1975.

U.S. Senate. Committee on Interstate Commerce. *Radio Control.* Hearings. (69,1), January, February, March, 1926.

U.S. Senate. Committee on the Judiciary. Subcommittee to Investigate Juvenile Delinquency. *Juvenile Delinquency (Television Programs).* Hearings. (83,2), June, October, 1954.

——— *Comic Books and Juvenile Delinquency.* Interim Report. (84,1), 1955. (a)

——— *Television Programs.* Hearings. (84,1), April 1955. (b)

——— *Television and Juvenile Delinquency.* Interim Report. (84,1), 1955. (c)

——— *Investigation of Juvenile Delinquency in the United States. Part 10. Effects on Young People of Violence and Crime Portrayed on Television.* Hearings. (87: 1, 2), June, July, 1961; January, May, 1962.

——— *Television and Juvenile Delinquency.* Interim Report. (88,2), 1964.

U.S. Senate. Subcommittee of the Committee on Interstate Commerce. *Compulsory Block-Booking and Blind Selling in the Motion-Picture Industry.* Hearings. (74,2), February 27-28, 1936.

ABOUT THE AUTHOR

WILLARD D. ROWLAND, Jr., is Assistant Professor in the Institute of Communications Research at the University of Illinois, Urbana-Champaign, where he teaches courses in the history, regulations, and policy of American broadcasting and telecommunications, international and comparative broadcasting, the history of communications, and popular culture. During 1978-1979, he served as Director of the Long-Range Planning Project for the Public Broadcasting Service in Washington, D.C. Dr. Rowland has also served as consultant to the Carnegie Commission on the Future of Public Broadcasting, the Public Broadcasting Service, the National Association of Educational Broadcasters, and the Governor's Advisory Task Force on Public and Educational Television in Illinois. He is the author of numerous articles on mass communications, including broadcast reform, communications policy, and public broadcasting. He received his B.A. from Stanford University (1966), M.A. from the University of Pennsylvania (1971), and Ph.D. from the University of Illinois (1978).